Secession, State & Liberty

Secession, State & Liberty

Edited with an introduction by
David Gordon

Transaction Publishers
New Brunswick (U.S.A.) and London (U.K.)

Fourth paperback printing 2009

The publisher acknowledges the assistance of the Ludwig von Mises Institute, Auburn, Alabama 36849, in the preparation of this volume.

This book is printed on acid-free paper that meets the American National Standard for Permanence of Paper for Printed Library Materials.

Library of Congress Catalog Number: 97-46825
ISBN: 978-1-56000-362-5 (cloth); 978-0-7658-0943-8 (paper)
Printed in the United States of America

Library of Congress Cataloging-in-Publication Data

Secession, state and liberty / edited with an introduction by David Gordon.
        p. cm.
    Includes bibliographical references and index.
    ISBN 0-7658-0943-5 (alk. paper)
    1. Secession—History. 2. State, The. 3. Liberty. 4. Secession—Southern States. I. Gordon, David, 1948-.

JC311.S471   1998
302.54—dc21   97-46825
                                                              CIP

To the Memory of Those
Who Gave Their Lives That
Others Might Be Free

Acknowledgements

The idea of this book first took shape at a conference, sponsored by the Ludwig von Mises Institute, on the political economy of secession. The conference was held at Charleston, South Carolina, in April 1995. Many of the papers in this book were first delivered at that meeting. Pat Heckman, of the Institute, made sure the conference came up to scratch. I would like to thank the Institute for its sponsorship of this book, in particular its president, Llewellyn H. Rockwell, Jr., and its research director, Jeffrey Tucker. This book could not have appeared without the devoted work of publications director Judy Thommesen and typesetter Scott Kjar. I would also like to thank the many donors to the Mises Institute, whose generous contributions have made this book possible. —D.G.

TABLE OF CONTENTS

INTRODUCTION

Grant defeated Lee, the Confederacy crumbled, and the idea of secession disappeared forever, or at least that's what the conventional wisdom says. However, as readers of this work will soon discover, secession is of no historical irrelevance. Quite the contrary, the topic is integral to classical liberalism. Indeed, the right of secession follows at once from the basic rights defended by classical liberalism. As even Macaulay's schoolboy knows, classical liberalism begins with the principle of self-ownership: each person is the rightful owner of his or her own body. Together with this right, according to classical liberals from Locke to Rothbard, goes the right to appropriate unowned property.

In this view, government occupies a strictly ancillary role. It exists to protect the rights that individuals possess independently—it is not the source of these rights. As the Declaration of Independence puts it, "to secure these rights [life, liberty, and the pursuit of happiness], governments are instituted among men, deriving their just powers from consent of the governed."

But what has all this to do with secession? The connection, I suggest, is obvious: if government does not protect the rights of individuals, then individuals may end their allegiance to it. And one form this renunciation may take is secession—a group may renounce its allegiance to its government and form a new government. (It is not, of course, the only form. A group can overthrow its government altogether, rather than merely abjure its authority over them.)

The Declaration of Independence adopts just this position: whenever a government "becomes destructive of these ends, it is the right of the people to alter or abolish it." But the American colonists did not attempt to abolish the British government; rather, they "altered" it by withdrawal of the colonies from it's authority. In brief, they seceded from Britain. As such, the right of secession lies at the heart of our country's legitimacy. Deny it, and you must reject the American founding.

One might here interpose an objection. Regardless of one's opinion of Jefferson and the Continental Congress, is it not consistent to accept natural rights, as conceived of by classical liberals, but refuse to recognize a right of secession? On this position, individuals have natural rights, but once they choose a government they are stuck with it. In response to this objection, we must distinguish two cases.

First, the position might hold that even if the government violates the rights it was established to secure, its subjects may not depart from it. But this is a strange contention: government exists for certain purposes, but it may continue unabated even if it acts against these very aims.

To this, it might be replied that to protect individual rights, resort may be had to means other than secession. One must concede to this view that alternatives to secession do indeed diminish the force of the imperative in its favor. After all, if a state may interpose its authority to block an enactment of the federal government within its borders, why must it also be accorded the right to leave altogether?

This view, I think, is logically consistent, but it has little to recommend it. Why should people give up this very potent means of keeping their government in check? To do so leaves their natural rights, if recognized in theory, nugatory in practice. At the very least we may say this: those who deny the right of secession have the burden of advancing a rationale for their view. Why should supporters of natural rights reject the right of secession?

Opponents of secession may, however, take a less extreme position. They may concede that secession is to be allowed should the government violate individual rights, but not otherwise. A group may not renounce duly-constituted authority just because it would rather be governed by others. Does not the Declaration itself say that governments should not be changed for "light and transient causes"?

This position no doubt is stronger than the utter repudiation of secession, but we must once more inquire: what is its justification? *Prima facie*, it appears that to hold that a group may remove itself from a government's authority whenever it pleases is more in line with classical liberalism's purely functional view of government. To deny this insinuates that the state is something other than a tool to secure rights. Just as an individual need not retain the services of a business, but may change to another, why may not a group switch protective agencies?

Further, the Declaration of Independence need not be read to endorse only a limited right of secession. The passage that refers to light and transient causes forms part of a discussion of when change of government is prudent, but the issue that concerns us here is not prudence, but rights. Many exercises of one's rights are imprudent—I may have the "right" to walk into oncoming traffic, if the signal is in my favor—but I have these rights regardless. Thus, a group may secede imprudently, but act within its rights. Once more: if not, why not?

The argument may proceed one more step. Suppose a group wishing to secede is guilty of violating individual rights. Does it still have the right to secede? I do not see why not. Of course, it should not violate individual rights, but why should the fact that the group does so compel it to submit to a government it no longer wishes to obey?

Allen Buchanan, whose *Secession* is the most influential discussion of our topic in contemporary American philosophy, rejects the legitimacy of Southern secession in 1861 on the grounds just suggested.[1] Since slavery violated rights, no slaveholding state had the right to leave the Union. But why does this follow? (Incidentally, Buchanan holds that Southern secession, absent slavery, *would* have been justifiable.) Clearly, Buchanan's discussion of the Southern case would have gained from close attention to the contemporary arguments of the Southern secessionists.

We may distinguish an even more difficult case. Suppose that a group which violates individual rights secedes. May the government formerly in authority interfere only to the extent necessary to secure the rights of those put at risk by the secession?

Even here, we need to sound a note of caution. The attempt to resist secession may itself lead to rights violations, and the benefits of intervention need to be weighed carefully against its costs. Even if one agrees with Locke that there is a general *right* to enforce the law of nature, this generates no *duty* to do so.

Robert Barro, a distinguished economist associated with the "rational expectations" movement, has addressed this issue with insight. Of course, during the Civil War, Lincoln's government did not act only to secure the rights of the enslaved. But suppose that it had. Would it have been justified in using force to resist secession?

Not, Barro suggests, given the cost of doing so:

> The U.S. Civil War, by far the most costly conflict ever for the United States . . . caused over 600,000 military fatalities and an unknown number of civilian deaths, and it severely damaged the southern economy. Per capita income went from about 80 percent of the northern level before the war . . . to

[1]Allen Buchanan, *Secession: The Morality of Political Divorce from Fort Sumter to Lithuania and Quebec* (Boulder, Colo.: Westview, 1991).

about 40 percent after the war. . . . It took more than a century after the war's end in 1865 for southern per capita income to re-attain 80 percent of the northern level.[2]

But, it may be replied, this quotation from Barro does not address the point at issue. No one denies the costs of the Civil War, but our question concerns justification: does one have the *right* to interfere with a secessionist group that violates rights?

Yet, surely the point raised by Barro *is* relevant. The costs of an action cannot be dismissed as irrelevant to morality. This is all the more true if one takes account of another issue that Barro raises. The claim, once more, is that the Civil War illustrates (or rather, would illustrate, had it been conducted differently) the thesis that secession may be blocked to protect individual rights.

Barro here makes a typical economist's point. The goal of defending individual rights could likely have been secured through less costly means.

> Everyone would have been better off if the elimination of slavery had been accomplished by buying off the slave owners—as the British did with the West Indian slaves during the 1830s—instead of fighting the war.[3]

And what if this proposal is dismissed as unrealistic? What would have happened to slavery had the Southern states been allowed peacefully to secede? Barro suggests that slavery would soon have come to an end anyway. Here a more detailed discussion by historian Jeffrey Hummel lends support to Barro's view:

> No abolition was completely peaceful, but the United States and Haiti are just two among twenty-odd slave societies where violence predominated. The fact that emancipation overwhelmed such entrenched plantation economies as Cuba and Brazil suggests that slavery was politically moribund anyway. . . . Historical speculations about an independent Confederacy halting or reversing this overwhelming momentum are hard to credit.[4]

But have we not addressed our question on too narrow a front? However ill-advised Northern policy was during the Civil War, this does not suffice to show that *any* resistance to secession that aims to defend individual rights is without justification. Here,

[2]Robert J. Barro, *Getting It Right: Markets and Choices* (Cambridge, Mass.: MIT Press, 1996), pp. 26–27.

[3]Ibid., p. 28. Several of my remarks have been adapted from David Gordon, "In Defense of Secession," review of *Getting It Right: Markets and Choices*, by Robert J. Barro, *The Mises Review* 3, no. 1 (Spring 1997): 1–5.

[4]Jeffrey Rogers Hummel, *Emancipating Slaves, Enslaving Free Men* (Peru, Ill.: Open Court, 1996), p. 352.

for once, I grant the objection, but those who wish to restrict secession in cases of this kind need to show how *their* preferred interventions may avoid the costs that our example illustrates.

At one point, I fear, this analysis of secession lies open to misunderstanding. Secession arises from individual rights: I have not attempted to defend it as a group right unreducible to individual rights. Thus, it by no means follows that the majority of those living in a territory can compel these residents to secede who do not wish to do so. The question is not one of majorities or minorities but of individuals. As such, the argument offered here in no way depends on "democratic" assumptions.

The issue has been addressed with unsurpassed clarity by one of the foremost of all classical liberals, Ludwig von Mises.

> The right of self-determination . . . thus means: whenever the inhabitants of a particular territory, whether it be a single village, a whole district, or a series of adjacent districts, make it known, by a freely conducted plebiscite, they no longer wish to remain united to the state to which they belong at the time . . . their wishes are to be respected and complied with.[5]

Mises emphasizes that this right

> extends to the inhabitants of every territory large enough to form an independent administrative unit. If it were in any way possible to grant this right of self-determination to every individual person, it would have to be done.[6]

Once one has grasped Mises's point, the fallacy in an often-heard argument is apparent. Some have held that the Southern states acted "undemocratically" in refusing to accept the results of the election of 1860. Lincoln, after all, received a plurality of the country's popular vote.

To a Misesian, the answer is obvious: so what? A majority (much less a plurality) has no right to coerce dissenters. Further, the argument fails on its own terms. It was *not* undemocratic to secede. The Southern states did not deny that Lincoln was in fact the rightfully elected president. Rather, they wanted out just because he was. Democracy would oblige them only to acknowledge Lincoln's authority had they chosen to remain in the Union.

But a problem now arises. I have endeavored to defend secession from an individual-rights standpoint. Notoriously, Mises

---

[5]Ludwig von Mises, *Liberalism: In the Classical Tradition* (Irvington-on-Hudson, N.Y.: Foundation for Economic Education, 1985), p. 109.
[6]Ibid., pp. 109–10.

did not acknowledge natural rights. I fear that, like Jeremy Bentham, he regarded declarations of rights as "nonsense on stilts." Why, then, did Mises accept self-determination?

Mises's reasoning is characteristically incisive. If people are compelled to remain under a government they do not choose, then strife is the likely outcome. Recognition of the right to secede "is the only feasible and effective way of preventing revolutions and civil and international wars."[7] Mises's argument does not rest on natural rights, but it is of course consistent with the approach I have sketched out. Regardless of one's moral theory, it is surely a strong point in favor of a view that it has beneficial consequences.

I owe the reader an apology. I have so far presented my own analysis of secession, ignoring the contributors to this volume. By no means do they subscribe to every jot and tittle of the argument just presented.

Donald Livingston, for one, finds appeal to rights dangerous. Political theory, as he sees it, must shun the abstract individual and the rights that febrile theorists ascribe to him. Instead, the foundation of a free society lies in the settled practices of small communities. In his essay, "The Secession Tradition in America," he finds strong arguments for federalism and secession in the work of the great eighteenth-century Scottish philosopher David Hume. A firm supporter of the right of the American colonies to secede from Britain, Hume, Livingston says,

> put into words, for the first time, an ideology of "Americanism," the thought that there are political principles specifically American. What were those principles? They were the corporate liberty of a people to govern themselves and free trade.

Like Livingston, Steven Yates sympathizes with the southern case for secession, and looks to philosophy to justify his position. The thinker in whom he finds inspiration is the philosophical novelist Ayn Rand. In "When is Political Divorce Justified?" he shows the bearing of her thought on secession. As readers will discover, Yates finds the idiom of rights far more congenial than does Livingston.

Scott Boykin, in "The Ethics of Secession," defends the right to secession on the basis of an "agent-relative" theory of values. Boykin's principal target is Allen Buchanan, whose book I have earlier mentioned. Boykin forcefully contends that Buchanan unduly restricts the cases in which secession is legitimate.

---

[7]Ibid., p. 109.

Those acquainted with the work of Murray N. Rothbard will not be surprised to learn that he vigorously champions rights. Indeed, the position I sketched out above rests heavily on Rothbard's views. In "Nations By Consent: Decomposing the Nation-State," Rothbard asks a question typical of him: how can the conclusions of political philosophy be applied to the daily world of events? Rothbard comments on a large number of historical and contemporary cases, each analyzed in iron consistency with his principles.

Secession may have a strong basis in theory, but has it any relevance today? Even if individuals have the right to secede, it does not follow that secession in contemporary states is justified. In the United States, for instance, state governments do not obey Lockean precepts. Why then should classical liberals who endorse secession be interested in states' rights?

Clyde Wilson meets this challenge head on. In "Secession: The Last, Best Bulwark of Our Liberties," he remarks:

> I know there are many moral and social problems that are not solved by political arrangements and that the level of statesmanship in the states is not much higher, if at all, than with the federal government. But if we are to speak of curbing the central power, the states are what we have got. They exist. They are historical, political, cultural realities, the indestructible bottom line of the American system.

Not only is the argument for secession solidly based in theory, secessionist ideas rest on a firm basis in American history. In "Republicanism, Federalism, and Secessionism in the South, 1790 to 1865," Joseph R. Stromberg argues that Jefferson, during the early years of the Union, strongly endorsed states' rights and secession. Jefferson's radical position reflected a "monolithic republican consensus" in the South on the scope and limits of government.

And support for secession was by no means absent in New England. In "Yankee Confederates," Thomas DiLorenzo shows that opposition to the War of 1812 led many Federalists to hold a distinctly Jeffersonian position.

But whatever its philosophical backing, many have found secession abhorrent. Several contributors to this volume devote attention to the foremost enemy of secession in both theory and practice, Abraham Lincoln. They see in Lincoln an ardent centralizer with little regard for individual liberty. Livingston argues that the U.S. Constitution established a central government of strictly limited powers, but,

by an act of philosophical alchemy, the Lincoln tradition has
transmuted this essentially federative document, marking out
the authority of distinct political societies, into a consolidated nationalist regime having as its *telos* the instantiation of
an abstract metaphysical proposition about equality.

Those interested in a detailed account of Lincoln's disregard
for the Constitution, as understood by its framers, should consult
James Ostrowski's careful analysis "Was the Union Army's Invasion of the Confederate States a Lawful Act?" I add only one detail to supplement Ostrowski's discussion. So extreme was Lincoln's disregard for the Constitution that he wrote out papers for
the arrest of Chief Justice Taney, who had dared to hold Lincoln's suspension of *habeas corpus* unconstitutional.[8]

The argument for secession has been brilliantly restated and
applied to contemporary Europe by Hans-Hermann Hoppe in
"The Economic and Political Rationale for European Secessionism." Classical liberalism, Hoppe contends, fares best not within
large, centralized nations, but in small governmental units.

Pierre Desrochers and Eric Duhaime show the relevance of
the secessionist case to Canada, in an argument that fits in perfectly with Hoppe's analysis. The hope of a free society lies in
the secessionist movements that will dissolve those leviathan
states that threaten us worldwide.

The secessionst argument may be further extended. Many
have thought that administrative problems imposed practical
limits to secession: two or three people do not suffice for a state.
But ingenious methods of settling disputes privately often enable
small groups, or even single persons, to gain some of the same benefits secession provides. Bruce Benson describes the new developments in arbitration in "How to Secede in Business Without Really Leaving."

Secession, then, is not a matter of "battles long ago," of interest only to Civil War buffs. As readers of *Secession, State, and
Liberty* will I am confident agree, secession is a key issue of our
age.

David Gordon
Los Angeles, California
October, 1997

[8]Hummel, *Emancipating Slaves*, pp. 142, 154. The arrest warrant was not served.

1

THE SECESSION TRADITION IN AMERICA

Donald W. Livingston

The United Nations Charter asserts the self-determination of peoples as a fundamental human right. From this, there has developed a lively debate among international jurists about whether the right of self-determination includes a right of legitimate secession.[1] But while the concept of legitimate secession is being explored in the world at large, it forms no part of contemporary American political discourse. There was a time, however, when talk about secession was a part of American politics. Indeed, the very concept of secession and self-determination of peoples, in the form being discussed today, is largely an American invention. It is no exaggeration to say that the unique contribution of the eighteenth-century American Enlightenment to political thought is not federalism but the principle that a people, under certain conditions, have a moral right to secede from an established political authority and to govern themselves. In what follows I would like to sketch out this all-but-forgotten American political tradition.

The English verb "to secede" comes from the Latin "secedere," meaning any act of withdrawal. The exclusively political connotations that govern the term today are peculiarly American, and do not appear in English until the early nineteenth century.[2] Prior to then, one could speak of the soul seceding from the body; or of seceding from one room of a building to another; or of seceding from any sort of human fellowship. The latter is how "secession" was defined in Samuel Johnson's *Dictionary* in the mid-eighteenth century. But Johnson did not capture the Scottish use of the term.

The Church of Scotland split in 1733. Those who left called themselves "seceders" and the resulting Church the "Secession Church." The Church went by this name for more than a century, during which time it split again, but was reunited in 1829 under the disarming name of the "United Secession Church." The seceding self-governing religious community paved the way for the

[1]Lee Buchheit, *Secession: The Legitimacy of Self-Determination* (New Haven, Conn.: Yale University Press, 1978). This book is an excellent discussion of the debate over whether a right of secession can be recognized in international law.
[2]*The Compact Edition of the Oxford English Dictionary* (New York: Oxford University Press, 1971), the articles on "secede" and "secession."

seceding self-governing political community and the term as we understand it today. One of the first to use the term in this new and exclusively political way was Thomas Jefferson, who, in 1825, retrospectively described the colonies as having seceded from the British Union.[3]

The word "secession," for us, not only has exclusively political connotations, it is a term that marks out a peculiarly modern political act. But this is not obvious, for it might be thought that as long as there have been large-scale political regimes, peoples have sought to withdraw from them. It could be said that the Israelites seceded from Egypt, or that Melos unsuccessfully sought to secede from the Athenian League. We can, of course, speak in this way, but the concept of secession, as understood in contemporary political discourse, is more specific in its meaning. Secession, for us, presupposes the background of the *modern state*, and this sort of state is only about two centuries old. So secession is not just any kind of political action; it is the withdrawal of a people from a modern state under the moral principle of the right of self-government, and such that the separation requires the territorial dismemberment of that state. The Israelites and Melots were not separating from a modern state, and their withdrawal would not have resulted in the territorial dismemberment of such a state.

The modern state has been theorized in such a way as to entail a strong presumption against secession. It has been said that the sovereignty of a modern state cannot be divided, and that sovereignty is co-extensive with territory. There has been no difficulty in allowing that a modern state can *expand* its territory and sovereignty, but it cannot allow itself to be dismembered by a supposed right of a people to self-government. Anyone who takes secession seriously as a possibility is necessarily throwing into question the legitimacy of the modern state.

At the time of William the Conqueror, Europe was composed of thousands of independent political units; today there are only a few dozen. This massive centralization and consolidation was accomplished mainly by conquest. The result was that dukedoms, margraviates, small republics, principalities, free cities, and baronies, (not to mention peoples speaking different languages, having different cultures and religions, and pursuing different visions of the human good) were crushed together into the modern state. This state was inherently unstable. A solution was theorized by Hobbes, who postulated a sovereign office whose task

---

[3]Ibid.

was to establish a rule of law which allowed individuals to pursue their own power and glory in that domain in which the law is silent. In time, a modern state came to be seen as an association to protect the rights of individuals, and this added a stronger presumption against secession, because any right of a people to secede could only be the aggregate right of a set of individuals. But if one set could secede, any other set or subset—down to one individual—could secede. An acknowledged right of secession would mean the unravelling of the modern state.

But to affirm a right of secession is not to say that secession is morally justified under *any* conditions, but only that there can be conditions under which it is justified, and even then there might be reasons for not exercising the right. But those philosophers who first theorized the modern state (Hobbes, Locke, Rousseau, and Hegel) do not so much as raise the question of whether such conditions are possible. Their main task is to understand and legitimate the modern state; the problem of secession simply never occurs to them. And political philosophers since have followed in their steps. John Rawls, for instance, dismisses the possibility of secession without argument.[4] Secessionist discontent, though a pressing fact of contemporary political life, is the most under-theorized concept in political philosophy. Political scientists and international jurisprudence have taken up the question, but philosophers have not. There is only one book length study by a philosopher on the question of whether secession is ever morally legitimate.[5]

One indication of this under-theorized character of secession is its being confused with revolution. Three conceptions of revolution have dominated in modern political speech. The first derives from the Glorious Revolution of 1688. This is revolution as restoration, and its image is the revolution of a wheel. According to eighteenth-century English Whiggism, the Glorious Revolution was a bloodless restoration of a liberty-loving Protestant regime from the attempted usurpations of the Catholic James II. The second form is Lockean revolution. Here a sovereign people recall the powers they have delegated to a government that has violated its trust in protecting life, liberty, and property. The government is overthrown and a new government instituted. The third form is Jacobin revolution. This is not Lockean revolution for the sake of preserving property but an attempt to subvert and

---

[4]Allen Buchanan discusses Rawls on secession in *Secession: The Morality of Political Divorce: From Fort Sumter to Lithuania and Quebec* (Boulder, Colo.: Westview Press, 1991), pp. 5–6.

[5]Ibid.

to totally transform an entire *social* and *political* order in accord with an egalitarian philosophical theory. A Lockean revolution leaves the social order intact, whereas Jacobin revolution aims at a root-and-branch transformation. Marxian revolution is Jacobin, as are many other forms of contemporary political criticism. Gloria Steinem once said that to talk about reforms for women is one thing, to talk about the total transformation of society is feminism. So conceived, feminism is a species of Jacobin revolution.

Secession is quite distinct from these dominant conceptions of revolution. All presuppose the theory of sovereignty internal to the modern state and the prohibition against dismembering its territory. Secession is not revolution in the sense of eighteenth-century Whiggism because it is not the restoration of anything. It is the dismemberment of a modern state in the name of self-government. Nor is it Lockean revolution. A seceding people does not necessarily claim that a government has violated its trust. And even if the claim is made, there is no attempt to overthrow the government and replace it with a better one. Indeed, a seceding people may even think that the government is not especially unjust. What they seek, however, is to be left alone to govern themselves as they see fit. Finally, secession is not Jacobin revolution because it does not seek to totally transform the social and political order. Indeed, it seeks to preserve its social order through secession and self-government.

We may, of course, continue to call secession "revolution" if we like, but the danger is that there will be a tendency to confuse it with the dominant meanings of revolution. A seceding people may indeed be said to be in a state of revolt in so far as they resist being coerced back into an established modern state, but this sort of revolt is quite different from revolution. And the moral considerations that would legitimate such resistance are categorically different from that which would legitimate revolution in the above senses, all of which seek, for different reasons, to overthrow an established regime. A seceding people is happy leaving the existing regime exactly as it is. It seeks only to limit its territorial jurisdiction. This, of course, is a serious matter, but it is not revolution in any of the traditional senses. Its name is secession.

Nowhere is the under-theorized character of secession and the confusion that results from failure to distinguish it from revolution more evident than in the habit of describing the conflict with Britain and the North American colonies as the "American Revolution." It is true that there were whiggish themes from the ideology of 1688 about restoring the rights of Englishmen, and there were Lockean themes about self-government. But the act of the British colonists in America was an act of secession. It was neither whiggish, nor Lockean, nor Jacobin revolution. The colonists did not seek to overthrow the British government. Commons, Lords, and Crown were to remain exactly as before. Indeed, many of the colonial leaders, such as Adams and Hamilton, admired the British constitution and government, and sought to imitate its best features. They wished simply to limit its jurisdiction over the territory they occupied. They wished to be let alone.

Much has been made of the influence the Lockean idiom of self-government had on the Founders. But it is important to realize that, though Locke allows the overthrow of a corrupt regime, he does not allow secession in the form of dismembering the territory of a modern state. And for citizens of a regime who have given their express consent, he does not even allow the right to exit, much less the right to carry territory with them.[6] There is every reason to believe that Locke, like the "friends of America" (Burke, Pitt, Shelburne, Barré), would have supported reforms on behalf of the Americans, but would have stopped short of secession.

The case is quite otherwise with David Hume, who supported complete independence for the colonies as early as 1768, before the idea had occurred to most Americans. In this he stood virtually alone among major British thinkers. The Edinburgh literati were overwhelming in their support for strong measures against the Americans. Hume, however, staunchly defended secession of the colonies from 1768 until his death on 25 August 1776, five days after the Declaration of Independence was published in Edinburgh's *Caledonian Mercury*. To the disappointment of his "oldest and dearest friend," Baron Mure, who had asked him to write a letter on behalf of the county of Renfrewshire advocating military measures against the Americans, Hume wrote: "I am an American in my Principles, and wish we would let them alone to govern or misgovern themselves as they think proper."[7]

In this statement, Hume put into words, for the first time, an ideology of "Americanism," the thought that there are political principles specifically American. What were those principles?

[6]John Locke, *Two Treatises of Government*, Peter Laslett, ed. (London: Cambridge University Press, 1988), p. 349.
[7]David Hume, *The Letters of David Hume*, John Y.T. Greig, ed. (Oxford: Clarendon Press, 1969), vol. 2, pp. 302–3.

They were free trade and the corporate liberty of a people to govern themselves. Hume argued that if the ports of America were open to free trade, it would result in only a trifling temporary loss of revenue, and would, in the long run, benefit British commerce.

> Let us, therefore, lay aside all Anger; shake hands, and part Friends. Or if we retain any anger, let it only be against ourselves for our past Folly; and against that wicked Madman Pitt; who has reduced us to our present Condition.[8]

This Humean notion of Americanism that acknowledges the right of a self-governing people to secede is framed in the Declaration of Independence. The Declaration is primarily a document justifying secession, but it has been thoroughly corrupted by Lincoln's reading of it and the ritualistic repetition and expansion of that reading. The Lincoln tradition reads the Declaration as affirming a metaphysical doctrine of individual rights (all men are created equal) and takes this to be the fundamental symbol of the American regime, trumping all other symbols, including the symbol of moral excellence internal to those inherited moral communities protected by the reserved powers of the states under the Tenth Amendment. Indeed, this tradition holds that the Declaration of Independence is superior to the Constitution itself, for being mere positive law, the Constitution can always be trumped by the "higher" metaphysical law of equality.

The Constitution of the United States was founded as a federative compact between the states, marking out the authority of a central government, having enumerated powers delegated to it by sovereign states which reserved for themselves the vast domain of unenumerated powers. By an act of philosophical alchemy, the Lincoln tradition has transmuted this essentially federative document into a consolidated nationalist regime having as its *telos* the instantiation of an abstract metaphysical proposition about equality. Such a proposition, in so far as it is taken seriously, must give rise to endless antinomic interpretations, and being metaphysical, these interpretations must stand in ultimate and implacable opposition. In this vision, the reserved powers of the states vanish, and the states themselves are transformed into resources for and administrative units of a nationalist political project "dedicated to the proposition that all men are created

---

[8]Ibid., pp. 300–1. Pitt had sought to establish a mercantile empire of managed trade which Hume thought required constant war for its maintenance and an increase in the public debt. For an in-depth study of Hume on secession and America, see my *Philosophical Melancholy and Delirium* (Chicago: University of Chicago Press, 1998).

equal." So well established has this inversion become that Mortimer Adler could write a book on the Constitution using for the title not the words of the Constitution, but those of the Lincolnian Declaration: "We Hold These Truths. . . ."[9]

Lincoln's vision of a consolidated nationalism in pursuit of an antinomic doctrine of equality had its roots in the French Revolution, which sought to unify the decentralized traditional order of France into a consolidated nationalism in pursuit of the rights of man. But Lincoln's vision was also forward looking. By the 1830s, the forces of nationalism and industrialism were sweeping Europe, and had begun to have an impact on an industrial North all too eager to compete on the world stage with the empires of Europe. For this project, centralization and consolidation were necessary. Lincoln's vision of consolidating the states into a nationalist regime was of a piece with that of Garibaldi in Italy, Bismarck in Germany, Lenin in Russia, and the general consolidating, industrializing, and imperializing forces on the move in the nineteenth and twentieth centuries.

But the Declaration was published before the forces of industrialism and nationalism had appeared. Rhetorically, the document is a lawyer's brief designed to justify breaking the "bands" that had tied one people politically to another. And the people in question were not (as Story, Webster, and Lincoln would claim) the American people in the mass, but the peoples of the former colonies now declared to be separate and independent states but united in their resolve to resist coercion back into the British empire. Overall, the Declaration is an argument designed to justify the secession of the new self-proclaimed American states from the British state. The rights asserted are not the rights of individuals in a continental nationalist political society, but the corporate right of the "people" of the several states to govern themselves. And the equality mentioned is the equality of the people of the separate states, now grown to maturity, to take their place among the nations of the world; in a word, that the people of Virginia, Massachusetts, New York, etc., are equal to the people of Holland or France or Britain, and are to be recognized as such.

The Declaration, then, is a document justifying the territorial dismemberment of a modern state in the name of the moral right of a people to self-government. It is not primarily an argument for individual rights, but rather an argument for the corporate rights of distinct moral and political societies. This theme of

---

[9]Mortimer Adler, *We Hold These Truths: Understanding the Ideas and Ideals of the Constitution* (New York: MacMillan, 1987).

corporate liberty shaped the first constitution Americans made for themselves, the Articles of Confederation, which styled itself a "league of friendship" between sovereign states. No mention was made of individual rights, as the Articles had no authority to enforce them. Individual rights, of course, were very important to Americans, but what those rights were and how they were to be protected were the prerogatives of the states and were clearly specified in their respective Constitutions.

The new Constitution, ratified in 1789, delegated enumerated powers to a central government whose laws would be supreme on matters of foreign treaties, defense, and regulation of foreign and interstate commerce. The Bill of Rights was added not as a massive grant of power to the central government to enable it to police supposed violations of individuals' rights by the states (as it is corruptly interpreted today), but primarily to protect the moral and political societies of the states from the inevitable tendency of the central government to engross more power than had been granted to it. The capstone and meaning of the Bill of Rights is the Tenth Amendment, which affirms the sovereignty of the states in declaring the powers of the central government to be enumerated and "delegated."

The *Oxford English Dictionary* identifies the first political meaning of "secession" in the secession of the southern states from the American Union. The Australian Constitution was formed with the American experience of federation and secession in mind.[10] And contemporary attempts to frame a theory of secession often return to the secession of the southern states as the primal scene in which the modern concept first appears and from which theorizing takes its bearings. But the term secession in this exclusively political and modern sense is used much earlier. Throughout the antebellum period secession was used, North and South, to describe a moral and legal action available to an American state. In this American speech, the modern concept of the right of a people to self-determination and the right of secession is theorized for the first time and publicly explored. This act, as we have seen, was spiritualized by Hume into what he called an American principle, namely the right of a people "to govern or misgovern themselves as they think proper." Neither Hume nor the Americans, at this time, used the term secession in its exclusively political and modern sense. But by the early nineteenth century, Americans were describing the break with Britain as secession, and they began to raise the question of the conditions

[10]Gregory Craven, *Secession: The Ultimate States Right* (Carlton, Vic.: Melbourne University Press, 1986).

under which an American state could legally secede. But speech and theorizing about secession as the last moral and legal right available to an American state and the vibrant federal life it made possible abruptly ended with the defeat of the Confederacy and the triumph of a consolidated nationalist Union that began the adventure of empire building in competition with the European empires. During this period of "manifest destiny," "the big stick," and empire building, few in America, or Europe, would be interested in thinking about the self-determination of peoples or the right of secession.

Thought about secession and self-determination did not occur again until Woodrow Wilson brought the issue before the League of Nations. The results were not always happy, but the agenda stuck. It was revived after World War II in the United Nations, and is the primary form under which the self-determination of peoples is discussed in the world today. The concept of legitimate secession, first framed and explored by Americans, is very much alive and is throwing into question the modern consolidated Leviathan. United States government policy, however, unhappily has been on the side of the *status quo*. The government of the United States has resisted every secession movement in the world since World War II, and was among the last to recognize the seceding states of the Soviet Union.

One reason why Americans have difficulty even thinking about secession is that since 1865, they have been taught and have come to believe the triumphant Unionist theory of their own constitutional order. According to that theory, the break with England threw the colonists into a state of nature from which they spontaneously formed the political society of the American people in the aggregate. This body was sovereign and created a central government. This government, in turn, authorized the formation of thirteen state governments as administrative units through which the sovereign will could be best expressed. In this view, an American state never possessed the attributes of sovereignty and so could not legally secede from the Union any more than a county could legally secede from a state. The classic formulation of the nationalist theory was given by Justice Story in the 1830s; it was eloquently defended by Webster and was established in the world with a writ of fire and sword by Lincoln.[11] Despite this distinguished pedigree, however, the theory is not only false, but spectacularly so.

[11]Joseph Story, *Commentaries on the Constitution of the United States* (Boston: Little, Brown, 1851), vol. 1, bk. 3, chap. 3. Also, *The Writings and Speeches of Daniel Webster* (Boston: Little, Brown, 1903), vol. 6, pp. 196–221.

The main error of the Unionist theory is the claim that the states were never sovereign. Each state, however, declared its sovereignty and independence from Britain on its own, and during the war each engaged in acts of sovereignty. After the war, each state was recognized by name as sovereign by the British government. These sovereign states formed the Articles of Confederation in which, again, the sovereignty of each was asserted and mutually recognized. Although the Articles of Confederation were supposed to be perpetual and could not be changed without unanimous consent, a number of states nonetheless sought to dissolve the Union. It was agreed (though not unanimously, since Rhode Island vetoed the Convention) that if nine states seceded and ratified the proposed constitution, a new Union would obtain between the nine seceding states. This was done, and by an act of secession the Union was dissolved leaving North Carolina, Virginia, Rhode Island, and New York to form a new union or to remain separate and independent states. Eventually, though reluctantly, all four entered. But Virginia, New York, and Rhode Island declared in their ordinances of ratification that, being sovereign states, they individually reserved the right to secede, and they asserted this right for the other states. This did not have to be asserted, since everyone knew that secession was an action available to an American state.[12] If, at the time of ratification, Lincoln's theory had been stated that the states were not and had never been sovereign, and that once in the Union a state could not leave, there would have been no Union.

It has been said that the constitution of the Soviet Union was the first to recognize explicitly the legal right of secession in a modern state. Strictly speaking this is true. Article 17 of the Soviet Constitution declares that "the right freely to secede from the U.S.S.R. is reserved to every Union republic." A right of secession was not written into the U.S. Constitution, but the *authority* of the Constitution consists solely in acts of ratification by sovereign states. In writing into their ordinances of ratification

---

[12]The best defense of the thesis that the states were sovereign and that secession was a right available to an American state is to be found in Albert Taylor Bledsoe's *Is Davis a Traitor, or Was Secession a Constitutional Right Previous to the War of 1861?* (Charleston, S.C.: Fletcher and Fletcher, [1866] 1995). This was reprinted by Fletcher and Fletcher, Charleston, S.C., 1995. The first systematic refutation of Story's thesis that the states were never sovereign was given by Abel Upshur, a distinguished Virginia jurist and Secretary of State under Tyler, in *A Brief Enquiry into the True Nature and Character of our Federal Government, Being a Review of Judge Story's Commentaries* (Petersburg, Va.: E. and J.C. Ruffin, 1840). On the sovereignty of the states, see also C.H. Van Tyne, "Sovereignty in the American Revolution: An Historical Study," *American Historical Review* 12 (April, 1907): 529–45.

the right to withdraw those powers delegated to the central government, Virginia, New York, and Rhode Island may be said to have framed a right of secession in the constitutional compact. Marxist jurists from the former Soviet Union and the Warsaw Pact nations took the lead in the international forum in arguing for secession as a moral and legal right.[13] Much of this was hypocrisy at the service of Soviet policy, but it was no more hypocritical than Lincoln's Gettysburg Address that presents the conflict of 1861–65 as an earth-shaking war to make the world safe for self-government, when he was engaged in a total war aimed at the civilian population of the South, and designed to suppress their efforts at self-government. The irony is complete when we consider that the Soviets eventually did allow the secession of states (something that caused nervous tremors in the Bush administration). Perhaps over time, as sometimes happens, the Soviets were partially converted by their own hypocrisy.

From the very first, secession was conceived as the last check an American state had to an abuse of those enumerated powers that had been delegated out of its sovereignty to the central government. From its beginning until 1865, secession was invoked by every section of the Union. And the section that first and most often raised the threat of secession was not the South but New England. Secession was threatened over the Louisiana Purchase in 1803, the embargo of 1807–09, the War of 1812, and the Mexican War. New Englanders refused to send troops in the second war with England, and seriously considered forming a New England Confederacy at the Hartford Convention in 1815.[14] From the 1830s until 1861, New England abolitionists argued strongly for secession of the northern states from the Union. The following resolutions were passed by the American Anti-Slavery Society: "Resolved, that secession from the United States Government is the duty of every Abolitionist. . . ." And Resolved, "That the Abolitionists of this country should make it one of the primary objects of this agitation to dissolve the American Union."[15]

One of the early studies of the Constitution was *A View of the Constitution*, published in 1825 by William Rawle, a Federalist who was a leader of the Pennsylvania bar and had twice been offered the position of district attorney by George Washington, but had refused for personal reasons. Rawle raised the issue

[13]Buchheit, *Secession, The Legitimacy of Self-Determination*, pp. 100ff.
[14]See *Documents Relating to New-England Federalism, 1800–1815*, Henry Adams, ed. (New York: B. Franklin, 1905). This contains John Quincy Adams's narrative of the Hartford Convention and other New England secession movements.
[15]Quoted in Bledsoe, *Is Davis a Traitor?* p. 149.

of whether a state could form a hereditary monarchy. He answered that since the people of a state are sovereign, they could, but the state would have to secede from the Union, since the Constitution guarantees to each state a republican form of government. He then laid out the formal conditions under which a state could unilaterally and legally secede from the Union.[16] Rawle's work on the Constitution was widely respected, and was used as a textbook at West Point from 1825–1840.

In 1840, Abel Upshur, a distinguished Virginia jurist and Secretary of State under Tyler, published *A Brief Enquiry into the True Nature and Character of our Federal Government*. This was an unanswerable criticism of Judge Joseph Story's theory of federalism in *Commentaries on the Constitution of the United States* (1833). Story systematically inverted the received opinion that the Constitution is a compact between sovereign states creating a central government and delegating to it only enumerated powers. Story argued that sovereignty is vested in the American people in aggregate, that the states had never been sovereign, and that in fact it was the central government that had created the states. The inversion was breathtaking, and it was this aggressive nationalist theory that Webster (who began his career as a compact theorist and as a New England secessionist) would popularize by his eloquence, and that Lincoln would seek to establish by war. Upshur has no difficulty in demolishing it as a historical theory of the Constitution. He sees clearly where a centralized and consolidated regime in the vast territory of America, with its heterogeneous interests and cultures, must eventually lead; namely, to the destruction of the states as the only constitutional protection for those substantial moral communities, local attachments, and particularities in which virtue has its source and where alone it can be tested and lived out. In subverting Story's inversion and by re-establishing the traditional theory that the Constitution is a compact between the states, Upshur had occasion to argue that an American state could legally secede from the Union.

Foreign writers who had studied the Constitution concluded that a state could secede from the compact. Tocqueville wrote:

> The Union was formed by the voluntary agreement of the States; and in uniting together they have not forfeited their nationality, nor have they been reduced to the condition of one and the same people. If one of the States chooses to withdraw from the compact, it would be difficult to disprove its right of doing so, and the Federal Government would have no

---

[16]William Rawle, *A View of the Constitution* (Philadelphia: H.C. Carey and I. Lea, 1825), see especially the last chapter, "Of the Union."

means of maintaining its claims directly either by force or right.[17]

Lord Brougham, in his magisterial, multi-volume study of constitutions published in 1849, considered the Constitution as a compact from which a state could secede:

> There is not, as with us, a government only and its subjects to be regarded; but a number of Governments, of States having each a separate and substantive, and even independent existence originally thirteen, now six and twenty and each having a legislature of its own, with laws differing from those of the other States. It is plainly impossible to consider the Constitution which professes to govern this Union, this Federacy of States, as any thing other than a treaty.[18]

He accordingly refers to the Union as the "Great League." And Dr. Mackay, another English scholar of the Constitution, writing in the mid-nineteenth century, observed that

> The Federal Government exists on sufferance only. Any state may at any time constitutionally withdraw from the Union and thus virtually dissolve it. It was not certainly created with the idea that the states, or several of them, would desire a separation; but whenever they choose to do it, they have no obstacle in the Constitution.[19]

During the 1850s, this Great League was coming apart, and a movement arose among prominent national and state leaders in the mid-Atlantic states to form what was called a "Central Confederacy." This new Union would be composed of such states as Virginia, Maryland, Delaware, New Jersey, New York, Ohio, Indiana, Pennsylvania, Kentucky, Tennessee, and Arkansas. This section constituted the conservative core of the Union, it was argued, and had interests different from the radicals of New England and the Gulf states. The formation of a Central Confederacy could prevent war and could serve as a rallying point around which the disaffected states of the deep South could one day return should they secede.[20] It is interesting that the proponents of the new Union showed little interest in including the New England states. Perhaps part of the reason was disgust over the long history of secession movements that had arisen in that region.

[17]Alexis de Tocqueville, *Democracy in America*, Henry Reeve, trans. (New Rochelle, N.Y.: Arlington House), vol. 1, chap. 18, p. 381.

[18]Henry Lord Brougham, *Political Philosophy*, 2nd ed. (London, 1849), vol. 3, p. 336.

[19]Quoted in Bledsoe, *Is Davis a Traitor?* p. 155.

[20]William C. Wright, *The Secession Movement in the Middle Atlantic States* (Rutherford, N.J.: Fairleigh Dickinson University Press, 1973).

The mayor of New York, Fernando Wood, and others argued that if New York state seceded, the city should secede from the state and declare itself a free city. The mayor declared,

> As a free city, with but nominal duty on imports, the local Government could be supported without taxation upon her people. Thus we could live free from taxes, and have cheap goods nearly duty free.[21]

Right up to the firing on Fort Sumter, many abolitionists in the North, having long argued for northern secession, were prepared to allow the South peacefully to secede. This was the position in New York of the *Douglass Monthly*,[22] printed by Frederick Douglass, and of Horace Greeley, editor of the Republican *New York Tribune*, who declared 23 February 1861, *after* the Confederacy was formed,

> We have repeatedly said . . . that the great principle embodied by Jefferson in the Declaration of Independence, that governments derive their powers from the consent of the governed, is sound and just; and that if the slave States, the cotton States, or the gulf States only, choose to form an independent nation, They have a clear moral right to do so. Whenever it shall be clear that the great body of Southern people have become conclusively alienated from the Union, and anxious to escape from it, we will do our best to forward their views.[23]

And John Quincy Adams, though a staunch unionist, declared in 1839, in a speech celebrating the Jubilee of the Constitution,

> The indissoluble link of union between the people of the several states of this confederated nation is, after all, not in the *right* but in the *heart*. If the day should ever come (may Heaven avert it!) when the affections of the people of these States shall be alienated from each other; when the fraternal spirit shall give way to cold indifference, or collision of interests shall fester into hatred, the bands of political associations will not long hold together parties no longer attracted by the magnetism of conciliated interests and kindly sympathies; and far better will it be for the people of the disunited states to part in friendship from each other, than to be held together by constraint. Then will be the time for reverting to the precedents which occurred at the formation and adoption of the Constitution, to form again a more perfect Union by dissolving that which could no longer bind, and to leave the separated parts to be reunited by the law of political gravitation to the center.[24]

[21]Quoted in ibid., pp. 177–78.

[22]Ibid., p. 199.

[23]Quoted in Bledsoe, *Is Davis a Traitor?* p. 146.

[24]John Quincy Adams, *The Jubilee of the Constitution* (New York: Samuel Coleman, 1839), pp. 66–69.

Four years after this speech, the former President would sign a document with other New England leaders declaring that annexation of Texas would mean the dissolution of the Union.

Pondering the secessionist movements in New England, Thomas Jefferson wrote in 1816 with characteristic liberality: "If any state in the Union will declare that it prefers separation . . . to a continuance in union . . . I have no hesitation in saying, 'let us separate.'"[25] On the eve of the War Between the States, the majority of northerners appeared to have believed *either* that a state could legally secede *or* that one should acquiesce in peaceful *de facto* secession. How northern opinion quickly changed sufficiently to support invasion is a complicated story that cannot be told here, but it would contain the following themes.

First and most crucial was Lincoln's early decision to make war against the southern states should they secede. In 1856, he had told southerners who asserted their right to secede:

> *We won't let you.* With the purse and sword, the army and navy and treasury in our hands and at our command, *you couldn't do it.*[26]

President James Buchanan, who preceded Lincoln, had declared that the central government had no authority to coerce a seceding state, but Lincoln stated privately that he would retake the forts Buchanan had allowed to pass back to state control. In the first draft of his first inaugural address, Lincoln was prepared to make this intention public: "All the power at my disposal will be used to reclaim the public property and places that have fallen."[27] Lincoln refused to negotiate with Confederate commissioners to pay for federal property and to establish a trade treaty, and he, thus, encouraged the public impression that the Confederates were lawless aggressors who had stolen federal property and threatened invasion of the North.

Second, the ineptitude of southern leaders, and their bellicose speech and policies (such as allowing themselves to be lured into firing on Ft. Sumter), played into Lincoln's hands by inflaming northern nationalism.

Third was the venality of northern commercial classes, who were happy to have the South to fund some three-quarters of the

[25]Thomas Jefferson, letter to W. Crawford, 20 June 1816, in *The Writings of Thomas Jefferson*, Albert Bergh, ed. (Washington, D.C.: Thomas Jefferson Memorial Association of the United States, 1905), vol. 15, p. 27.

[26]Quoted in Ludwell Johnson, *Division and Reunion: America 1848–1877* (New York: John Wiley and Sons, 1978), pp. 76–77, emphasis added.

[27]Ibid., p. 77.

federal revenue, but were unwilling to allow a low-tariff zone on their southern border. The economic differences between North and South were stark. By 1860, agriculture still accounted for some seventy-five percent of American exports and most all of it came from the South. Trading on an unprotected world market, the South required a policy of free trade. The North, having just industrialized, was guided by a vision of a vast continental market for manufacturing, which required a policy of prohibitive tariffs. For three decades, southerners had complained about the injustice of tariffs protecting northern manufactures, because the tariffs resulted not only in a drain of wealth from the South to the North but also because southern trading partners, whose manufactures became prohibitively high for exchange for southern staples, were forced to find staples elsewhere. Once the northern industrial section got control of Congress, the average rate on goods subject to duties rose from the 1860 rate of 18.84 percent to a spectacular high of 46.56 percent in 1865. The tariff did not drop below 40 percent until World War I, except for two years when it was 38 percent. After the war, it rose again under Harding, Coolidge, and Hoover.[28] This brutal and unjust policy dealt a crippling blow to the southern agricultural export trade, which was vastly greater than what northern markets could absorb.

Interstate commerce regulations passed late in the nineteenth century discriminated against southern manufacturing by, among other things, fixing rail rates and steel prices so that goods manufactured in the South would not be able to undercut northern manufactures.[29] These were not abolished until the 1940s when the Supreme Court declared them unconstitutional. The National Banking Acts of 1863, 1864, and 1865 created a new national currency, secured by the public debt, and drove state bank notes out of circulation. Once the central government and its national banks had the authority to control the money supply, the financial destruction of American federalism was complete. This revolution in finance discouraged the formation of banks in farming communities and worked to transfer bank funds from agriculture to industry. As historian Robert Sharkey wrote,

> Human ingenuity would have had difficulty in contriving a more perfect engine for class and sectional exploitation: creditors finally obtaining the upper hand as opposed to debtors, and the developed East holding the whip over the undeveloped West and South.[30]

[28]Ibid., pp. 109–10.
[29]C. Vann Woodward, *Origins of the New South 1877–1913* (Baton Rouge: Louisiana State University Press, 1971), chap. 11, "The Colonial Economy."
[30]Johnson, *Division and Reunion*, pp. 113–15, and quotation from p. 115.

All of this turned out to be much worse than what John C. Calhoun predicted would happen if the American federation of republics was transmuted into a consolidated nationalism dominated by a northern industrial class.

The brief constitutional history I have sketched that views secession as part of the checks and balances system of American federalism is unknown to most Americans. The reason is that we have come to believe the absurd nationalist theory of the Constitution propounded by Story and Webster and used by Lincoln to legitimate invasion of the South. Lincoln said he had taken an oath to preserve the Union, but he was mistaken. He had taken not an oath to preserve the Union, but rather an oath to preserve the Constitution, and the Constitution did not in 1861, and does not now, prohibit the secession of an American state.

The consolidated nationalism that Story, Webster, and Lincoln put forth as the Constitution was not the Constitution they had *inherited*. That instrument was a compact between sovereign states creating a central government having only enumerated powers. The instrument they put forth was an imagined and constitution at the service of an emerging industrial class. In this view, the states were reduced to little more than counties in a nationalist regime, and the central government emerged as unlimited in power if supported by a majority. Such a government could not only interfere with slavery by taxing it out of existence, it could do much else besides. Tariffs to protect northern industry had drained the South of wealth for over than thirty years. Further, the South was the source of most of the federal revenue, and this was exploited by a northern majority for improving its infrastructure. The South had generally been opposed to internal improvements, claiming that such powers had never been granted to the central government, and it was thought that if such powers were assumed, a scene of endless patronage and corruption would ensue without parallel in history.

Southern colonies had seceded from Britain because they refused to be a source of revenue for a consolidated British empire centered in London. That act was still vivid in the historical memory of southerners (for example, "Lighthorse" Harry Lee, the father of Robert E. Lee, was a Revolutionary War hero and a friend of George Washington). As such, southerners in 1861 were not prepared to be a source of revenue for a northern industrial version of a consolidated empire centered in Washington. Indeed, the very idea of Washington as the "capital" came after the failure of the war for southern independence. In the antebellum period, Washington was generally thought of as the "seat" of the central government, as when one speaks of a town being the seat of the county government, or of Strasbourg and New York as the seats, respectively, of the European Union, and the United Nations. Washington was the seat of a central government having only enumerated powers; it was not the *capital* of anything.

Likewise it is wrong to describe the conflict of 1861–1865 as the "Civil War." The exemplar of a civil war is the English Civil War. That war was a struggle, within a modern state, by two factions (Crown and Parliament) for control of the same government. But the federation of American states was not itself a modern state any more than the European Union is a modern state. Its central government had only enumerated powers delegated to it by the sovereign states. But Virginia, New York, etc., *were* modern states, each of which contained the presumption against the secession of its parts. And the struggle that occurred was not between two factions seeking control of the same government. Rather, it was between one group of states exercising their federative power to withdraw from the federation and govern themselves, and another group of states seeking to conquer and govern them. The Great Seal of the Confederacy bears an equestrian statue of George Washington, the symbol of secession from the British empire. Just as the break with Britain was not a revolution but an act of secession, so the break with the North was not an act of treason issuing in civil war, but an act of secession issuing in conquest by the North. That both conflicts are frequently misdescribed points again to the under-theorized character of secession.

But there is another difference between the conflicts. During the American Revolution, the American colonies could appeal only to a moral argument to legitimate secession. Having more or less governed themselves for more than a century, and having acquired the character of a people, they claimed that they had acquired a title to full self-government. But the colonies were not and never had been recognized as sovereign states, either by others or even by themselves. At the time of the Civil War, however, the southern states had been and still were sovereign states, and so they could mount not only a moral argument but a legal one as well. And it was the legal argument they primarily insisted upon. Each state used the same legal form to secede from the Union that it had used to enter, namely, ratification in a convention of the people. In some cases, the decisions of these conventions were put to referenda. Of those southerners who were opposed to secession, including Robert E. Lee, the great majority of them recognized the legitimacy of the conventions and supported their states, to which, under the compact theory of the Constitution, they owed their primary allegiance.

With the orderly, legal secession of the southern states, the American genius for self-government reached its highest moral expression. Here was something unprecedented in history; a vast continental empire of republics torn by sectional, economic, and moral conflicts seeking to settle its differences not by war, but by peaceful secession of eleven contiguous republics, legitimated by the consent of the people. This was the very thing that, in 1840, John Quincy Adams said might be necessary in the future, and which the American commitment to self-government of peoples would legitimate, rather than a Union held together by bayonets. It was this also that President Buchanan had in mind when, although opposed to secession, he declared that the central government had no authority to coerce a seceding state. The same doctrine was asserted by Madison and Hamilton in the *Federalist*. Lincoln, however, like George III, was determined on coercion, but unlike the latter, he was also prepared to launch total war against the civilian population of the South to achieve the goal of a consolidated nationalism.

With Lincoln, then, a radical break occurs between the older Americanism that was grounded in the natural rights of substantial moral communities to govern themselves and a new Americanism grounded in the centralization and consolidation of power, and like the French Revolution, dedicated to an egalitarian doctrine of individualism. This doctrine, wherever it has been applied in the world, has required the destruction of independent social authorities and moral communities and the massive consolidation of power needed to achieve such destruction. Lincoln was a man of his age, and it was an age of unashamed empire building and of the coercion of independent political societies into consolidated unions. What Bismarck was accomplishing in Germany with a policy of "blood and iron," and what Lenin would accomplish in Russia, Lincoln had accomplished in America. Lincoln did not *preserve* an organic indivisible union from destruction because he did not inherit one; rather, like Bismarck, he created one.

Why did the southern states secede? This is a question best answered by examining closely the Constitution of the Confederacy, which bears not only the imprint of the southern conception of self-government but also their grievances against the North. Though there is no space to do that here, a few points are worth making. Southerners were loyal to the Constitution of the Founders. What they objected to was the northern interpretation of it which sought, by an act of philosophical alchemy, to transmute it from a compact between sovereign states creating a central government with enumerated powers to a consolidated nationalism with a central government having unlimited powers.

The Confederate Preamble makes clear that the parties to the compact are the people of the states and not the people of the confederacy in the aggregate. And each state is said to retain "its sovereign and independent character." In the Federal Constitution, the initiative to amend can come from either Congress or the states. The Confederate Constitution vests this power only in the states. Southerners considered secession a legal right available to a state under the Federal Constitution conceived as a compact between sovereign states. But they purposely did not put a right to secession in their own constitution because to do so would imply a change and would play into the hands of those northerners who held that secession was treason. However, the right of a confederate state to secede was thought to be self-evidently contained in the declaration that the states retain their sovereignty and independence.

A central government in a federative system cannot be unduly oppressive if its revenue is carefully restricted by consensus of the states, or by something approaching consensus. One of the main grievances against the northern conception of the consolidated Union was that the central government would become an uncontrollable center of patronage and corruption that would subvert the independent moral and political life of the states. The hated protective tariffs on imports were prohibited. Export tariffs, however, were allowed if passed by a two-thirds majority. Funding for internal improvements was severely restricted. With few exceptions, Congress could appropriate money only by a two-thirds majority or by a majority upon a request by the President.

As in the Federal Constitution, slavery was recognized. The Confederate Constitution outlawed the slave trade, but, unlike the Federal policy, required Congress to pass legislation that would enforce the law. Current American policy refused to cooperate with the British and French in allowing American ships to be boarded, and so the slave trade continued into South America under American flags up to the conflict of 1861–65. Jefferson Davis's first veto was over a bill that would allow the sale of slaves captured by the Confederate Navy. The Confederate Constitution allowed non-slaveholding states to join the Confederation, and left it up to the individual states whether they would abolish slavery. Many nations in the Indian Territory had treaties with the Confederates, and fought for it on the promise of creating a sovereign Indian state.

The central reforms enacted by the Confederate Constitution, which Lord Acton greatly admired, were designed to protect and strengthen the substantial moral and political communities of the states, and to limit the power of the central government by reducing its revenue, restricting its power to spend, and making it difficult to pass legislation for special interest groups.[31]

Just as their ancestors two generations earlier, acting as citizens of sovereign states, had seceded from the Articles of Confederation (even though the Articles were styled as "a perpetual union" and could not be legally changed without unanimous consent) in order to form a "more perfect union" (a union requiring only nine states), so eleven contiguous southern states sought to form a more perfect union, one grounded in the preservation of independent moral and political communities, their union by consent, and the right of secession.

From a philosophical point of view, the Confederate Constitution may be viewed as the highest expression of the adventure in self-government begun by the American colonists in 1776. That adventure began with an assertion of the right of substantial moral and political societies to self-government, and this right was secured by an act of secession. The Americans, in their most speculative moments, imagined a legal world, a rule of law, in which this right would be recognized.

The sort of consolidationism which the British had sought to impose on their North American possessions had been going on in Europe for centuries and is still going on. Of the thousands of independent territorial units that existed in Europe at the dawn of the modern era, only a few dozen remain, and there is an attempt to consolidate most of these into a European Union. The ideologies that have sought to legitimate these consolidations have usually been in the name of the individual. Liberals favor consolidation of power to secure the *liberty* of the individual, and Marxists have favored it in order to secure the *equality* of the individual and to build an egalitarian society. But both of these forms of consolidationism have been at the expense of substantial moral communities and traditional forms of life. Indeed, Enlightenment Liberalism and Marxism, in their different ways, have been the most destructive forces in history in respect to

[31]Ibid., pp. 72–73; see also *Selected Writings of Lord Acton*, J. Rufus Fears, ed. (Indianapolis, Ind.: Liberty Classics, 1985), pp. 216–79 and 361–67.

traditional moral communities. Some of this change has brought benefits with it and has been accepted, but much of it has been oppressive. In that case, a constitutional right of secession of one of the recognized political units in the union would provide a check against oppression, and an exit should the check fail. Although intimated in early American experience and strongly implied in the Constitution of 1787, the first constitution in history to recognize both the advantages of large political unions and to provide a remedy for their abuse in secession was the Constitution of the Confederate States of America.

With the collapse of European imperialism and the revival in the United Nations of the Wilsonian doctrine of the self-determination of peoples (which is itself merely a later expression of the secessionist doctrine of the Declaration of Independence), the consolidated leviathans of the modern world no longer have the legitimacy they once had. Secession movements are strong where identifiable political units remain, such as Quebec in Canada, the Scots in Britain, and the Basques in Spain. Experience has shown that secession does not lead to anarchy, as Lincoln insisted it would. Norway peacefully seceded from Sweden (1905), as did Singapore from Malaysia (1965). Likewise, the secession of Quebec from Canada should not lead to chaos or war.

Secession can no longer be dismissed *a priori* as proponents of the modern state have done. And it certainly cannot be dismissed out of hand in the case of federal unions such as Canada, the U.S., Britain, Brazil, and Germany, all of which have political units with the administrative machinery and skills for self-government. The recognition of a legal right of such units to secede, established at the formation of a union of vast scale (such as the Confederate Constitution recognized), would tend to preserve distinct cultures and ways of life, make the operation of such unions more just, and, if necessary, their dissolution more orderly and humane.

The debate over the European Union today resembles the debate of 1787–89 between the Federalists and Antifederalists, the latter of which feared that the Constitution would end in a consolidated nationalism, and the former who assured them that such could never happen. One hopes that this will not degenerate into something like the shouting match between southerners who claimed that the Constitution was not a consolidated regime and northern unionists who declared that it was and always had been. But it could. One already hears from the left the claim that the European Union is an instrument for achieving human rights and that the powers surrendered to the Union cannot be recalled. This was exactly Lincoln's doctrine. Unless the right of secession is thought through and faced squarely, one can imagine Europe re-enacting the melancholy history of the United States with a minority of states seeking to secede from a Union that has become oppressive in a way they could not have imagined, and a powerful majority prepared to coerce them back into the Union in the name of the "last best hope on earth" for protecting human rights.

The moral grandeur of Lincoln is rooted in the myth that he made a war on the South to abolish slavery. This is, at most, a Platonic noble lie designed to legitimate the Unionist regime. Lincoln thought that slavery was immoral, but so did Robert E. Lee. And Lee, at his own expense, freed the slaves he had inherited, through marriage, from the family of George Washington. Only around fifteen percent of southerners even owned slaves, and the great majority of these had holdings of one to six. Jefferson Davis was an enlightened slave holder who said that once the Confederacy gained its independence, it would mean the end of slavery. The Confederate Cabinet agreed to abolish slavery within five years after the cessation of hostilities in exchange for recognition by Britain and France. Southerners were not fighting to preserve slavery, but simply and solely because they were being invaded. And the North certainly did not invade to abolish slavery.

Nor should this be surprising considering the Negrophobia that prevailed everywhere in the North. It was assumed by the vast majority of Americans, North and South, that America was a white European polity, and that the Indian and African populations were not—and were never to be—full participants in that polity. For example, blacks were excluded from the western territories. Oregon became a state in 1859, and its constitution, which was passed by a vote of eight to one, declared that

> No free negro, or mulatto, not residing in this state at the time of the adoption of this constitution, shall ever come, reside, or be within this state, or hold any real estate, or make any contract, or maintain any suit therein; and the legislative assembly shall provide by penal laws for the removal by public officers of all such free negroes and mulattoes, and for their effectual exclusion from the state, and for the punishment of persons who shall bring them into the state, or employ or harbour them therein.[32]

---

[32]Quoted in Tol. P. Shaffner, *The War in America* (London: Hamilton, Adams, 1862), pp. 337–38.

The constitution of Indiana contained the same prohibition. Lincoln's state of Illinois prohibited the entrance of Africans unless they could post a bond of $1,000. Free Africans in northern states were severely regulated. The following regulation is from the Illinois revised statutes of 1833:

> If any person or persons shall permit or suffer any . . . servant or servants of colour, to the number of three or more, to assemble in his, her, or their out-house, yard, or shed, for the purpose of dancing or revelling, either by night or by day, the person or persons so offending shall forfeit and pay a fine of twenty dollars.

And it was the duty of all "coroners, sheriffs, judges, and justices of the peace" who learned of such assemblages to commit the "servants to the jail of the county, and on view of proof thereof, order each and every such . . . servant to be whipped, not exceeding thirty-nine stripes on his or her back."[33]

Emancipation laws in the antebellum North were designed to rid the North of its African population. They typically declared that the children of slaves born after a certain date would, upon reaching a certain age, be emancipated. This meant that adult slaves were not freed and that families could be sold South before children reached the age of emancipation. Emancipation led to a reduction of the African population in the North, not to an increase, as it did in the South. Lincoln's own solution to the race problem was mass colonization of Africans, and he proposed securing land in Africa and elsewhere for the purpose. Even abolitionists were careful to point out that it was not the slave they loved but the slaveholder they hated, and that emancipation did not at all mean social and political equality with whites.

Slavery was more secure in 1860 than it had ever been. The Supreme Court, in the Dred Scott decision, had declared that Africans were not citizens; and Congress approved a constitutional amendment that would take the regulation of slavery forever out of the hands of the central government. Lincoln said that he had no authority and no inclination to interfere with slavery in the states where it was legal. He could tolerate slavery as a means of controlling what nearly everyone saw to be an exotic and alien population. What he could not tolerate was a dissolution of the Union, loss of revenue from the South, and a low-tariff zone on his southern border. This was the consistent thread running through Lincoln's policy from 1860–1865. He would not recognize the conventions of the people of the southern states, and he

[33]Ibid., pp. 339–40.

would not negotiate with their commissioners. He would go to war immediately to coerce the states of the deep South back into the Union. And it was this act that Virginia, North Carolina, Tennessee, and Arkansas could not tolerate. They had been opposed to the radicalism of the deep South, and their legislatures had voted firmly to stay within the Union. But they would not answer Lincoln's call for troops to coerce a state into the Union; this they considered not only unconstitutional, but immoral. And in this they were correct. But so strong is the Lincoln myth and so interwoven with American self-identity that Americans have never been able to confront the stark immorality and barbarism of Lincoln's decision to invade the South and to pursue total war against its civilian population.

To this we may add that the modern prejudice against secession has also served to occlude the immorality of the invasion. Here was a union of sovereign states only seventy years old. These states had originally asserted their sovereignty in acts of secession from the British empire, and the Union itself had been formed by an act of secession from the Articles of Confederation. Virginia, New York, and Rhode Island reserved the right to secede in their ordinances ratifying the Constitution, and secession was a part of public discourse in all sections throughout the antebellum period. This union, through conquest, purchase, and annexation, had, in fifty years, swollen to some ten times its original size. The Republic of Texas, having seceded from Mexico, had been in the Union only fifteen years. Secession is destabilizing in that it suddenly produces new majorities and new minorities. But annexation is destabilizing in exactly the same way. Rapid expansion led to rapidly shifting majorities and minorities and to conflicts of great and important interests.

By 1860, a choice lay open between either re-negotiating the compact between the states in order to form more perfect unions, as John Quincy Adams counseled should happen, or a powerful section would have to conquer the whole and reconstruct it into its own image, subordinating all else to its own interests. Everything in the older American tradition of the self-government of peoples points to the former path. Lincoln chose the latter path, and in doing so was in step with the nineteenth- and twentieth-century trend of industrial society to consolidationism. Southerners, at great sacrifice, sought to defend that older American notion of self-government, a notion which was pushed to the margins of American consciousness after the Army of Northern Virginia surrendered at Appomattox. But it has not been extinguished, and has greater purchase in the world today than ever before as the consolidated leviathans of the nineteenth and twentieth centuries are being called into question. The Russian invasion of Chechenya is widely regarded as barbarous, but the Russians have a better title to rule Chechenya than Lincoln had to coerce eleven contiguous American states into the Union.

This broader experience enables us to take a fresh look at the morality of Lincoln's decision. It has been said that, although the Union was originally conceived as a compact between sovereign states entailing a right to secession, it evolved into the notion of an indivisible, organic Union from which secession was impossible. This notion, however, was late in arriving, and was not universally received by 1860. Southerners obviously did not believe it, nor did many northerners. There was tremendous opposition to Lincoln's invasion of the South. To maintain power, he was forced to suspend the writ of *habeas corpus* throughout the North for the duration of the war, netting tens of thousands of political prisoners. Some 300 opposition newspapers were closed down. Democratic candidates, critical of the war, were arrested by the military, and the military was used to secure Republican victories at the polls, including Lincoln's election in 1864.[34]

But the barbarism of suppressing eleven contiguous American states in 1861 can best be brought out by a thought experiment. Today, unlike 1861, everyone has taken the pledge of allegiance affirming an organic union. (It is significant that the origin of the pledge is to be found in the loyalty oaths Confederates were required to take to regain citizenship.) Suppose that California, over a dispute with the central government about immigration, affirmative action, abortion, or some other issue, should, in a legally held convention of the people of the state, claim sovereignty under the Tenth Amendment and withdraw those powers it had delegated to the central government and withdraw from the Union. California is an economic giant. Its population is larger than that of twenty-two American states. Suppose, then, that other states, originally pro-Union, should see it in their interest to enter into a confederacy with California, and that eventually eleven contiguous states should form a western confederacy and

---

[34]Johnson, *Division and Reunion*, pp. 123–28. See also Ann Norton's excellent book *Alternative Americas* (Chicago: University of Chicago Press, 1986). For studies of Lincoln as a gnostic figure, see M.E. Bradford, "Dividing the House: The Gnosticism of Lincoln's Rhetoric," *Modern Age* 23 (1979): 10–24; ibid., "The Lincoln Legacy: A Long View," *Modern Age* 24 (1980): 355–63; ibid., *A Better Guide than Reason: Studies in the American Revolution* (LaSalle, Ill.: Sherwood Sugden, 1979), pp. 29–57 and pp. 185–203; and ibid., *The Reactionary Imperative* (Peru, Ill.: Sherwood Sugden, 1990), pp. 219–27.

send commissioners to Washington to negotiate payment for federal property and to establish a treaty. Would the eastern states be justified in launching an aggressive war to "save the Union"? Perhaps it would be thought that a show of force would cause people to rethink. But if it became clear that the people, at great sacrifice, were determined to gain their independence, could a policy of war aimed now at the civilian population be morally justified merely to preserve the Union?

Or, to vary the thought experiment, northern abolitionists had argued since the 1830s that the northern states should secede from the Union. Secession movements had arisen off and on in New England since 1803. Suppose now that a few New England states seceded over slavery, the tariff issue, and national expenditures for internal improvements. Other states, reluctantly, might find it in their interest to join this union so that by the time Lincoln entered Washington in 1861 he would find himself confronted with the secession of northern states and President of a southern-dominated United States, a Union that would include the eleven states of the Confederacy and most certainly Kentucky, Missouri, Maryland, Delaware, and perhaps others. Would we expect Lincoln to ignore the commissioners of this Northern Confederacy and launch a war to "save the Union?" Would we be celebrating, under his leadership, Stonewall Jackson's scorched-earth march to the sea, the burning of Boston, and the surrender of Grant to Lee at Scranton, Pennsylvania?

None of this, of course, would have happened. First, it is unlikely that southerners, who had long argued that the Constitution is a compact between sovereign states entailing a right to secede, would have perceived northern secession as *treason*. Second, the Republican party was a purely sectional party openly hostile to southern interests. And Lincoln, as its leader, was the first and only sectional president in American history. He had received only thirty-nine percent of the popular vote, and had no support outside the North. His goal from first to last was to advance the political agenda of the Republican party, which could be called the New York–Chicago industrial axis. The sectional goal of the Republican party was openly asserted by its most eloquent leaders. Wendell Phillips declared:

> It is just what we have attempted to bring about. It is the first sectional party ever organized in this country. It does not know its own face, and calls itself national; but it is not national—it is sectional. The Republican Party is a Party of the North pledged against the South.[35]

[35]Quoted in Bledsoe, *Is Davis a Traitor?* p. 250.

Charles Adams has shown that the Republican agenda could not tolerate a low-tariff zone to the south, and that the North had become accustomed to the South's funding the bulk of the federal revenue through its export trade.[36] And it was just this horror of what an economically independent South would mean to northern industrial interests that Charles Bancroft, writing in 1874, presented as the justification for invading the South:

> While so gigantic a war was an immense evil; to allow the right of peaceable secession would have been ruin to the enterprise and thrift of the industrious laborer, and keen eyed business man of the North. It would have been the greatest calamity of the age. War was less to be feared.[37]

A million-and-a-half people were killed, wounded, or missing in the war. The defense of protective tariffs has seldom been so ferocious, or so crude.

Lincoln's conservative statesmanlike posture about preserving an indivisible union cannot be taken seriously. Not only did he not inherit such a union, the only union he was interested in preserving was a union which was dominated by northern industrial ambition. And it was exactly this that Lincoln, and the Republican party, after his death, accomplished.

But Lincoln also had a philosophical argument for making war on the southern states that brings out the prejudice against secession that is internal to the idea of a modern state. In a message to Congress on 4 July 1861, Lincoln justified his choice of war over a negotiated settlement that allowed the southern states to form their own union:

> This issue embraces more than the fate of these United States. It presents to the whole family of man, the question, whether a constitutional republic, or a democracy—a government of the people, by the same people—can, or cannot, maintain its territorial integrity, against its own domestic foes. . . . It forces us to ask: "Is there, in all republics, this inherent, and fatal weakness? Must a government, of necessity, be too strong for the liberties of its own people, or too weak to maintain its own existence?"[38]

Here we have the familiar argument that a modern state cannot allow territorial dismemberment by secession. This was, of course, the same argument that was used by George III to coerce

---

[36]Charles Adams, *For Good and Evil: The Impact of Taxes on the Course of Civilization* (New York: Madison Books, 1993), pp. 323–37.

[37]Charles Bancroft, *The Footprints of Time: A Complete Analysis of Our American System of Government* (Burlington, Iowa: R.T. Root, 1877), p. 646.

[38]Abraham Lincoln, *Speeches and Writings*, Don E. Fehrenbacher, ed., 2 vols. (New York: Literary Classics of the United States, 1989), p. 250.

the American colonies. But Lincoln had in mind not just any sort of modern state (which could include monarchy) but a modern *republican* state. Being founded in liberty, such states are more liable to dissolution. Thus, the war that is beginning is a dramatic struggle to see whether a modern republican state is really possible. The same theme would be sounded in the Gettysburg Address. If secession is allowed, anarchy follows. As Lincoln put it elsewhere, if a state can secede, then the county of a state can secede, and a part of that county can secede, etc. And, if the American experiment in self-government fails, the world must revert back to monarchy.

There are a number of confusions here. First, the government of the United States in 1861 was not the government of a modern state. Rather, it was a central government of a federative union of states. It was endowed with only enumerated powers and these were delegated to it by sovereign states. The central government was the agent of those states, and the states were the principals in the federative compact. The states themselves *were* modern states; they had asserted this status in the Declaration of Independence, and had been recognized by the world as such. As modern states, they contained the usual legal prohibition against secession. A county cannot legally secede from an American state, but there is no such prohibition against a state exercising its federative power and withdrawing from the Union.

To describe, as Lincoln did, Virginia and the other southern states as "domestic foes" threatening self-government and to be suppressed by war is not only a spectacular absurdity, it also reveals a hubristic impiety and moral blindness. The first self-governing assembly in the western hemisphere was founded in Virginia. More great statesmen and jurists had come from Virginia than any other state. The leadership of Virginia was crucial in winning the war with Britain, during the period of the Articles of Confederation, and in forming the Union. In her ordinance of ratification, Virginia as a sovereign state, asserted the right to secede, and affirmed this right for every other state. The man often called the "father of the Constitution," James Madison, always described the Constitution as being a compact between sovereign states. In 1830, Madison could say that it was still not certain that the Union would work. By 1861, it was clear that the Union, as a voluntary association of independent political societies, had failed.

What would the great Virginians, George Washington, Thomas Jefferson, James Madison, Patrick Henry, George Mason, John Randolph, John Taylor, and "Lighthorse" Harry Lee have done?

They all supported the Union, believed the Constitution was a compact between the states, and were Virginians first. So when the states of the deep South discussed secession, Virginia called a convention of the people to decide the question, and the convention voted firmly to stay in the Union. It was only after Lincoln had decided on war and called for troops that the convention reconvened and voted to secede. Madison had said in the *Federalist* that the central government could not coerce a state. To be sure that the will of the people was expressed, the judgment of the convention was put to the people of Virginia, who supported secession by a margin of five to one. Tennessee was also pro-Union, but, in a referendum of the voters, decided to secede by a margin of two to one after Lincoln's decision to wage war. The pro-Union states of North Carolina and Arkansas seceded for the same reason.

To treat, as Lincoln did, the peoples of entire states who had engaged in deliberate and legal acts of self-government as common criminals and as "domestic foes" aroused deep emotions of resentment and injustice that could be felt only by an American who had received with his mother's milk the principle, framed in the Declaration of Independence, of the self-government of independent moral and political societies. As the case of Robert E. Lee makes clear, this feeling of resentment had nothing to do with slavery, an institution he thought was on its way to oblivion. It was this deeply felt *American* resentment that enabled the entire South, 85 percent of whom did not own slaves, to mobilize and to make spectacular sacrifices to keep out an invading army, the government of which was intent on destroying, and did destroy, the corporate liberty of their political societies. It was this sense of state honor that Hamilton had in mind when he said in the *Federalist* that the central government could never make war against an American state, and which he again asserted again before the New York State convention: "To coerce a state would be one of the maddest projects ever devised. No state would ever suffer itself to be used as the instrument of coercing another." One cannot imagine the great Virginians of his time disagreeing.

Herman Melville, who had a good eye for the hypocrisy of northern industrial unionism, wrote:

> Who looks at Lee must think of Washington
> In pain must think and hide the thought
> So deep with grievous meaning is it fraught.[39]

---

[39]Herman Melville, "Lee in the Capitol," in *Battle-Pieces* (Amherst: University of Massachusetts Press, 1972), p. 232.

To this conservative and backward-looking image, we should add the forward-looking and "progressive" image: he who looks at Lincoln has seen the consolidationists Bismarck and Lenin.

So Lincoln's inversion of the original American conception of self-government must itself be inverted. As H.L. Mencken cynically observed of the Gettysburg Address, it was not the Union forces that were fighting for government of the people, by the people, and for the people (a phrase Lincoln borrowed from Webster), but the people of the southern states. And the war was not a dramatic contest to see whether a modern republican state was possible. Virginia and the rest of the southern states were stable, self-governing modern republics whose citizens were loyal and well skilled in the art of self-government. If not conquered, there is every reason to think they would have lasted indefinitely.

All of them were, in fact, conquered, and self-government was destroyed. Virginia was divided and her western counties made into the new state of West Virginia. What Lincoln had presented as the absurdity of allowing a state to secede, namely that counties of that state could also secede, was legitimate after all, provided that it served northern industrial interests. After Lee had surrendered, and unionist governments had been formed in each southern state, and the Thirteenth Amendment outlawing slavery had been ratified by the southern states, they suddenly found themselves, by an arbitrary and unconstitutional act of Congress, expelled from the union and declared "conquered provinces."

The argument of Lincoln and the Republican party that secession was unthinkable because the Union was indivisible now appeared as the self-serving hypocrisy it was. States could not *secede* from the Union, but they could be expelled, or more precisely, obliterated. It was during this period of "Reconstruction" that the Fourteenth Amendment was floated. This amendment, since the 1950s, has been manipulated by the Supreme Court to affect a vast transfer of power from the states to the central government, making it virtually impossible for the states to maintain those independent substantial moral communities protected by the powers reserved in the Tenth Amendment. It is fitting that this amendment, which had a corrupt and illegal origin in Congress, was *never ratified* by the states, and is, thus, not a part of the Constitution! It was simply declared by Congress to have been enacted, something Congress had no authority to do.[40] This shows

[40]Forrest McDonald, "Was the Fourteenth Amendment Constitutionally Adopted?" *The Georgia Journal of Southern Legal History* 1, no. 1 (Spring–Summer 1991): 1–20.

just how far some Americans had wandered from the original conception of self-government.

The conflict of 1861–1865 was not, as Lincoln said it was, a struggle to see if a modern republican state could survive, but a struggle to see if a vast union of federative republics could survive without the consolidation and consequent destruction of independent moral life that a dominant faction will inevitably seek to impose on the rest. The American experience suggests that it is unlikely, but it must be admitted that our experience with such vast-scale federations is limited, so the question is still open. Since there are obvious advantages to federative unions, the only remedy is to acknowledge a legal right of secession for republics joining the federation. The American failure to achieve a genuine federalism of self-governing moral communities must stand as a challenge to the European Union. It was in recognition of this challenge that Nobel laureate James Buchanan has urged that a right of secession be written into the constitution of the European Union. With the benefit of over a century of experience, the Constitution of the Confederate States of America as an instrument of federalism appears well ahead of its time.

The brief constitutional history I have sketched that views secession as part of the checks and balance system of American federalism is completely unknown to most Americans. The reason is that we have come to believe the nationalist theory of the origin of the Constitution that Lincoln used to legitimate coercing the southern states back into the Union. Plato taught that the guardians of the republic may have to tell a noble lie about its origins. Whether the nationalist theory is a noble lie or an ignoble lie I shall not say. My point is that it is false. It has been said that the War of 1861–1877 decided once and for all the question of whether an American state could secede. But this is only another way of saying that might makes right, a principle that cannot sit well with the American doctrine of government by consent. The great Scottish philosopher David Hume taught a deeper truth; namely, that political authority is founded not on power but on opinion. A change in opinion at a strategic point can transform, in time, an entire political order.

To give an example, America began as a highly decentralized regime of independent moral and political communities jealous of their liberty. These political societies created a central government as their agent and endowed it with enumerated powers. This government was only a speck on the political landscape and its presence was scarcely felt in everyday life. From 1865 to

1965 it underwent a transformation, emerging as the most consolidated and centralized military and financial power in history. Moral and political societies with a life of their own independent of regulation and control by the central government (especially the Supreme Court) are today virtually impossible. By contrast, Canada began as a highly centralized regime under monarchy and has developed into a decentralized regime in which secession as a means of protecting independent moral and political life is part of public debate. There is a tradition in Canada that this change was due in part to Judah Benjamin, the former Secretary of State of the Confederate States of America who, after the war, fled to England and became a distinguished barrister. In a number of cases before the Imperial Parliament, he argued successfully for measures that gave the Provinces more autonomy, thereby setting Canadian federalism on the path to decentralization.[41] Asserting the right to secede, Quebec has already secured rights making it virtually an independent country, thereby making secession perhaps unnecessary.

Let me close with this question. If Hume is right that the authority of government is founded on opinion, and if acceptance of the absurd nationalist theory of the origin of the Constitution advanced by Story, Webster, and Lincoln could serve to legitimate the spectacular change from a decentralized federalism to a consolidated imperial nationalism, what would happen if Americans were taught and came to believe the truth about their own constitutional history?

---

[41]Claudius O. Johnson, "Did Judah P. Benjamin Plant the States Rights Doctrine in the Interpretation of the British North America Act?" *The Canadian Bar Review* 15, no. 3 (September 1967): 454–77.

2
WHEN IS POLITICAL DIVORCE JUSTIFIED?

Steven Yates

This essay has two bold aims: first, to identify the conditions which justify secession, and second, to conclude that since those conditions were effectively met in 1860s America, the secession of those parts of the United States desiring freedom from the central government was justified on both moral and legal grounds.

Secession here means the process of political divorce and formation of at least one new sovereign unit through a formal declaration of independence. Secession can take at least two forms. In the first, a section of a larger political entity (such as a state or a group of states) separates from the whole (the Union) and formally declares itself a sovereign, independent unit. While this may change geographical borders, the political structure and legal apparatus of the original unit is left mostly intact. For Americans, the best known successful instance of the first of these is, of course, the separation from Great Britain of the original Thirteen Colonies, and the formation of the first Union under the Articles of Confederation. The best known failed attempt is that of the Confederacy which led to the War for Southern Independence (called by most historians the "Civil War," a term I have elected not to use here).

In the second, all (or most) regions of the larger unit secede at once. The larger unit is dissolved, sometimes to be replaced with a new and improved model, sometimes not. The best example of this is the dissolution of the Union as defined by the Articles of Confederation, and its reformation in 1787 under the Constitution. The most significant recent example is the collapse of the Soviet Union.

It is extremely important to note that a secession need not necessarily involve violence. The replacement of the Articles of Confederation with the Constitution was non-violent. The secessions of the Baltic States from the Soviet Union were relatively bloodless in comparison to previous attempts by satellite states to free themselves of Communism (think of Czechoslovakia in 1968, Hungary in 1956, and so on). The dissolution of Czechoslovakia into Slovakia and the Czech Republic took place peacefully. It is possible that the Confederacy might have separated peaceably had Confederate troops not erred tragically by firing on Fort Sumter. Thus, political divorce might be accomplished peacefully if the larger power either is willing to let the smaller one go, or is incapable of preventing a formal declaration of independence which is recognized as legitimate by other nations.

The literatures of moral, political, legal, and economic philosophy have surprisingly little to say about secession.[1] Major figures in the history of political philosophy neglect it regardless of their orientation. Until recently, there was little reason for scholars other than specialized historians to study secession. Today, though, the topic is crying out for sustained philosophical attention. The above list of secessions is hardly exhaustive, and more may very well be on their way. The Azerbaijanis want to secede from Armenia. The Chechens have fought a valiant, if so far unsuccessful, struggle for freedom from Russian domination. The Kurds have long wanted freedom from Iraqi control. Quebec is moving to secede from the rest of Canada.[2]

The grounds which I use to defend a right of secession are fundamentally moral, incorporating a Constitutionalism holding that a Constitution is a morally binding contract between citizens and a government they created. Both contemporary libertarian philosophy and Austrian-school economics have provided compelling arguments for individualism and economic liberty. Together, they supply a broader philosophical and socioeconomic context in which neosecessionist arguments are at home. While secessionist movements are occurring all over the world, to keep the subject matter down to manageable size, I will limit this discussion to cases which have occurred on American soil.

Two final introductory comments are in order.

(1) There are some who prefer to bypass non-economic arguments for liberty and secession. I consider this shortsighted. It implies that a choice must be made between individualism, economic liberty, and political freedom on the one hand and morality on the other. Since many of those we must convince respect

---

[1]The only two book-length works on the topic are Allen Buchanan, *Secession: The Morality of Political Divorce from Fort Sumter to Lithuania and Quebec* (Boulder, Colo.: Westview Press, 1991), and Lee C. Buchheit, *Secession: The Legitimacy of Self-Determination* (New Haven, Conn.: Yale University Press, 1978). The first is marred by its subsuming self-determination in a collectivist ethos. For why this is a fault, see Steven Yates, *Civil Wrongs: What Went Wrong With Affirmative Action* (San Francisco: ICS Press, 1994), pp. 97–102.

[2]Lansing Lamont, *Breakup: The Coming End of Canada and the Stakes for America* (New York: W. W. Norton, 1994).

moral considerations and are suspicious of purely economic arguments, this effectively cedes a crucial element of the discussion to the collectivists and centralists. It is necessary, therefore, to show that individualism, political freedom, and economic liberty are morally superior to collectivism, centralization, and servitude. Without each of these elements, no defense of liberty, whether to justify secession or for any other purpose, is complete.[3]

(2) Late in this essay, I will reach the conclusion that secession is a live option both morally and legally; government by consent of the governed includes the right to secede, and to form a new government. I do not infer from this that any state or group of states *ought* to secede. Secession, as we shall see, is a procedure with enormous and potentially grave consequences—military, economic, and otherwise. Consequently, my conclusion is that secession ought to be considered as an absolute last resort, to be attempted only after every reasonable effort to restore government to its original functions has been blocked, every avenue closed off, every effort to discuss issues met with disdain or silence. Anything less would be irresponsible.

The argument of this essay—what I will call the neosecessionist argument—is in this case straightforwardly deductive:

(1) Government has legitimate—but strictly limited—functions which can be identified and shown to be such.

(2) If government has legitimate but strictly limited functions which can be identified and shown to be such, and if a given government develops in such a way that it ignores its legitimate functions and instead undertakes tasks it cannot reasonably perform or should not perform (because they violate its legitimate functions), then individuals living under the given government are morally justified in taking action to restore limited government, including, as a last resort, secession.

(3) The federal government of the United States sometimes developed in ways that ignored its legitimate functions, and instead undertook tasks it could not reasonably perform or should not perform (because they violated its legitimate functions).

Therefore:

(4) American citizens are morally justified in taking action to restore limited government, including, as a last resort, secession.

---

[3]For a more complete statement of this position, see Tibor Machan, *Individuals and Their Rights* (LaSalle, Ill.: Open Court, 1989).

LIMITED GOVERNMENT

The role of Premise (1) in the neosecessionist argument is to underscore the fact that neosecessionists are not closet anarchists motivated by hatred of government as such and opposed to it *tout court*—propaganda to the contrary notwithstanding. Human nature being what it is, we cannot live in society without rules, or without a legitimate authority to recognize and administer them when necessary. One of James Madison's most famous observations was, "If men were angels, government would not be necessary." Such realizations show why the institution is legitimate.

Yet, history shows all too well that this institution cannot really be trusted; not all of its participants behave morally and responsibly. Moreover, government, once established, is almost exclusively an agency of coercion (or threat thereof). Madison went on: "If angels were to govern men, neither external nor internal controls on government would be necessary." Thus, there is the need to limit government somehow, as a condition of its legitimacy. Madison then put his finger on the central problem in political morality: "In framing a government, which is to be administered by men, the great difficulty lies in this: You must first enable the government to control the governed; and in the next place, to control itself." The tendency of some to accumulate power and privileges at the expense of others and at the expense of the liberties they have been entrusted to uphold must somehow be checked.

A contractarian view of limited government proposes to do this: in a free society, government results from a contract between governors and governed; it derives its moral and its legal justification from the consent of the governed. The government of a free society is accountable to its citizens. It serves rather than rules them. If it ceases to serve and becomes a master (or in some other way fails to fulfill its role), then citizens have a right to do something about it: change it from within, leave its jurisdiction, or void their contract with it. Our concern here is with the third.

But first, let us be as clear as we can about what limited government is. What is this ideal on which our own country was founded, from which we contend it has departed, and to which neosecessionists (among others) desire to return? And what is its basis? What makes it superior to other options? Frederic Bastiat, the great nineteenth-century economist, statesman, and author, wrote:

> We hold from God the gift that includes all others. This gift is life: physical, intellectual, and moral life.

But life cannot maintain itself alone. The creator of life has entrusted us with the responsibility of preserving, developing, and perfecting it. In order that we may accomplish this, He has provided us with a collection of marvelous faculties. And He has put us in the midst of a variety of natural resources. By the application of our faculties to these natural resources we convert them into products, and use them. This process is necessary in order that life may run its appointed course. Life, faculties, production, in other words, individuality, liberty, property, this is man. And in spite of the cunning of artful political leaders, these three gifts from God precede all human legislation and are superior to it. Life, liberty, and property do not exist because men have made laws. On the contrary, it was the fact that life, liberty, and property existed beforehand that caused men to make laws in the first place.

. . . Each of us has a natural right—from God—to defend his person, his liberty, his property. These are the three basic requirements of life, and the preservation of any one of them is completely dependent on the preservation of the other two. For what are our faculties but the extension of our individuality? And what is property but an extension of our faculties?[4]

John Locke, of course, had presented the classic formulation of the doctrine of a natural right to property over a century-and-a-half earlier:

God, who hath given the world to all men in common, hath also given them the reason to make use of it to the best advantage of life and convenience. . . .

Though the earth and all inferior creatures be common to all men, yet every man has a property in his own person; this nobody has any right to but himself. The labour of his body and the work of his hands, we may say, are properly his. Whatsoever then he removes out of the state that nature hath provided and left it in, he hath mixed his labour with, and joined to it something that is his own, and thereby makes it his property. It being by him removed from the common state nature hath placed it in, it hath by this labour something annexed to it that excludes the common right of other men.[5]

Some twentieth-century defenders of these same basic ideas, Ayn Rand, for example, eliminate the theistic component:

The source of rights is man's nature. . . . The source of man's rights is not divine law or congressional law, but the law of

[4]Frederic Bastiat, *The Law* (Irvington-on-Hudson, N.Y.: Foundation for Economic Education, [1850] 1950), pp. 5–6.
[5]John Locke, *Second Treatise on Government* (New York: Hafner, [1690] 1969), p. 134.

identity. A is A—and Man is Man. *Rights* are conditions of
existence required by man's nature for his proper survival. If
man is to live on earth, it is *right* for him to use his mind, it is
right to act on his own free judgment, it is *right* to work for
his values and to keep the product of his work. If life on
earth is his purpose, he has a *right* to live as a rational being: nature forbids him the irrational.[6]

Murray Rothbard argued along similar Aristotelian lines:

"Natural rights" is the cornerstone of a political philosophy
which, in turn, is embedded in a greater structure of "natural
law." Natural law theory rests on the insight that we live in
a world of more than one—in fact, a vast number—of entities, and that each entity has distinct and specific properties,
a distinct "nature," which can be investigated by man's reason, by his sense perception and mental faculties. . . . The
species *man* . . . has a specifiable nature, as does the world
around him and the ways of interaction between them. . . .
[T]he nature of man is such that each individual person must,
in order to act, choose his own ends and employ his own
means in order to attain them. Possessing no automatic instincts, each man must learn about himself and the world, use
his mind to select values, learn about cause and effect, and
act purposively to maintain himself and advance his life.
Since men can think, feel, evaluate, and act only as individuals, it becomes vitally necessary for each man's survival
and prosperity that he be free to learn, choose, develop his
faculties, and act upon his knowledge and values. This is the
necessary path of human nature; to interfere with and crip-
ple this process by using violence goes profoundly against
what is necessary by man's nature for his life and prosperity.[7]

Rothbard thus enumerates a basic axiom, one's right to self-
ownership: "the absolute right of each man, by virtue of his (or
her) being a human being, to 'own' his or her own body; that is, to
control that body free of coercive interference."[8] From this he derives a right to justly acquired property in a way which inter-
sects with Locke's view above.

These remarks all point to the task of limited government.
The task of limited government is to serve as an institutional vehicle for recognizing and protecting the antecedent rights of individuals to life, liberty, the non-coercive and non-fraudulent pursuit of happiness, the non-coercive and non-fraudulent pursuit of
property, the retention of legitimately-acquired property, and

[6]Ayn Rand, "Man's Rights," in *The Virtue of Selfishness* (New York: Signet, 1964),
pp. 94–95.
[7]Murray N. Rothbard, *For a New Liberty: A Libertarian Manifesto* (New York: Collier,
1973), pp. 27–28.
[8]Ibid., p. 28.

the enforcement of mutually-agreed-upon contracts. It also serves as the agency of punishment against individuals who transgress these rights, according to an explicit body of laws. Bastiat again:

> If every person has a right to defend—even by force—his person, his liberty, and his property, then it follows that a group of men have the right to organize and support a common force to protect these rights constantly.... The law is the organization of the natural right of lawful defense. It is the substitution of a common force for individual forces. And this common force is to do only what the individual forces have a natural and lawful right to do: to protect persons, liberties, and properties; to maintain the right of each, and to cause *justice* to reign over us all.[9]

The world into which we are born does not sustain us. For all known plant species and nearly all animal species, built-in processes and instincts ensure their survival. Human beings, I would maintain, have a survival instinct as well—but it does not operate in the same way as that of other animals. For human beings have a capacity no other living thing has, so far as we know: the ability to think, or reason. Thought—rationality—does not work automatically. Hence, we must learn to think, to identify regularities in our surroundings. Then we must take specific courses of action. As Rand puts it, we survive by means of our minds. Minds, moreover, come one to an individual; "there is no such thing as a collective brain."[10] Hence, we are essentially individual human beings.[11] Thought being a condition for human action, it follows that all human action is individual action; references to collective actions are metaphorical at best. This should not be taken to preclude communication and voluntary interaction with others, the development of team efforts in which a number of individuals have come to agreement on a specific course of action, the formation of organizations, and the divisions of labor which result when all realize that more can be accomplished when people work together than when they work alone.

Given the indifference of the physical–biological universe, we must work; that is, we must produce the means of our survival amidst scarce resources, either producing for ourselves or producing for others, trading with them things they value for things we value. Clearly, we must be free to initiate and conduct such exchanges, whose details are only evident to the participants in

---

[9]Bastiat, *The Law*, pp. 6–7.

[10]Ayn Rand, "What Is Capitalism?" in *Capitalism: The Unknown Ideal* (New York: Signet, 1967), p. 16.

[11]Machan, *Individuals and Their Rights*, pp. 21–22.

the exchange. We must be free to develop such organizational arrangements as make such exchanges more efficient. Outside interference with such development can have only one result—to slow
it down, or worse, to stop it altogether, or even to prevent it from
occurring in the first place.

Historically, the institution which has most often interfered
with the capacities of human beings to acquire knowledge, act
freely in the world, identify what others value, and set about to
provide it either singularly or as a member of some institutional
entity, is government. Here is where trouble threatens, and why
we should attempt to limit government. Let us state our moral
premises clearly: since action is a necessary condition for the survival and self-improvement of an individual, it is morally proper that every individual be regarded as the sole owner of his own
mind, his own life, the fruits of his own labors, and the fruits of
honorable transactions with others. Conversely, no individual
has a moral claim on the mind, life, labor, or transactions of another individual (unless the two have come to a specific contractual arrangement). Hence, no individual has the right to forcibly
interfere with or defraud another individual.

The idea behind limited government is the idea that government should protect these basic principles, which are taken as
more basic than any legal arrangements since they derive from
the conditions for human survival and self-improvement in this
life. The principles themselves can be understood either theisti-
cally or non-theistically. Though we have refrained from going
into the issue here, many writers have argued that a theistic understanding of the universe and of the foundations of freedom is
both reasonable and provides a greater moral impetus to take
correct and morally responsible actions than any non-theistic account. Be this as it may, limited government still emerges as the
greatest of political ideals, supporting those who defend natural
rights. It establishes the responsibility of government as an institution enforcing the rule of law which protects rights understood as antecedent to its legal apparatus. Advocates of limited
government, therefore, necessarily reject the idea that governments can invent rights by legislative fiat. They see government-
manufactured rights as leading away from the rule of law, and
toward rule by politicians and bureaucrats who, more and more,
come to wield arbitrary and unpredictable force to advance their
own causes. Advocates of limited government see the latter as one
of the key developments behind the slow erosion of individual
freedoms in the United States.

LIMITED GOVERNMENT VERSUS HUMAN NATURE

Bastiat observed a tendency among people which ought to make every defender of limited government pause a moment:

> When they can, [people] wish to live and prosper at the expense of others. This is no rash accusation. Nor does it come from a gloomy and uncharitable spirit. The annals of history bear witness to the truth of it: the incessant wars, mass migrations, religious persecutions, universal slavery, dishonesty in commerce, and monopolies. This fatal desire has its origin in the very nature of man—in that primitive, universal, and insuppressible instinct that impels him to satisfy his desires with the least possible pain.[12]

Eighty-five years later, Albert Jay Nock would elaborate:

> There are two methods . . . whereby man's needs and desires can be satisfied. One is the production and exchange of wealth; this is the economic means. The other is the uncompensated appropriation of wealth produced by others; this is the political means. . . . The State . . . whether primitive, feudal, or merchant, is the organization of political means. Now since man tends always to satisfy his needs and desires with the least possible exertion, he will employ the political means whenever he can—exclusively, if possible; otherwise, in association with the economic means. He will, at the present time that is, have recourse to the State's modern apparatus of exploitation: the apparatus of tariffs, concessions, rent-monopoly, and the like.[13]

History, indeed, testifies that actual governments have never accepted the limited role assigned to them by the tradition of natural-rights. Our own system of federalism had its critics, the Antifederalists, who held that the Constitution delegated too much power to the central government. Even those who accept limitations on their authority tend to abrogate those limitations and increase their power until open rebellion results. The problem, Bastiat and Nock suggest, lies not so much with government *per se* but with human nature itself.

This suggests that—aside from the possibility of intervention by the Almighty—limited government will never be more than either a temporary, unstable arrangement or a regulative ideal. Human beings must produce the means of their survival, and they can do this only through individual action, through the re-arrangement of raw materials supplied by nature into useful

[12]Bastiat, *The Law*, pp. 9–10.
[13]Albert Jay Nock, *Our Enemy, The State* (New York: Libertarian Review Foundation, [1935] 1973), pp. 26–27.

materials, useful either for one's own purposes or for the purpose of trade with others. This, of course, is Nock's economic means. But most human beings, as Bastiat observed, tend to want to satisfy their needs and desires in the most expedient fashion, with the least amount of effort. So if a political means of obtaining the means of their survival is made readily available, they will seize on it. Hence, the origin of plunder, as opposed to production, as a means of satisfying one's wants: "[S]ince man is naturally inclined to avoid pain—and since labor is pain in itself—it follows that men will resort to plunder whenever plunder is easier than work."[14] An expansion of government (e.g., to extend a subsidy or protect some local enterprise with a tariff), if made available, will come to look very attractive as a means of insuring a "short cut" to success and prosperity. Certain forms of plunder will be entirely legal: Bastiat calls them "legal plunder."

In addition, government tends to attract people more interested in the political than in the economic means of getting things done. Conversely, those more content with the economic means tend to be uninterested in government—unless relying exclusively on the economic means becomes inconvenient or places them at an automatic disadvantage. Consequently, governments have found it easy to seize control of the economic means. In our society, this has occurred in increments. The history of America's railroads shows conclusively that the process was already underway by the 1820s[15]; the trajectory of modern "public education" reveals another government usurpation which began in the 1850s.[16] With the Federal Reserve System, adopted in 1913, the federal government began to assume control of money, banking, and credit, eventually leading to the destabilizations which produced the Great Depression[17]—its inroad to control over more and more of the economy via the creation of New Deal entitlements which now constitute the lion's share of the federal budget.

The mixture of political means with economic means typically results in special privileges for some at the expense of others. There is an automatic incentive to compromise, since the person who resists political temptations while others make full use of them automatically ends up at a competitive disadvantage. It is

[14]Bastiat, *The Law*, p. 10.

[15]Clarence B. Carson, *Throttling the Railroads* (Irvington-on-Hudson, N.Y.: Foundation for Economic Education, 1971).

[16]George Roche, *The Fall of the Ivory Tower: Government Funding, Corruption, and the Bankrupting of Higher Education* (Washington, D.C.: Regnery, 1994).

[17]Murray N. Rothbard, *America's Great Depression*, 4th ed. (New York: Richardson and Snyder, 1983).

easy to forget Jefferson's remark that "eternal vigilance is the price of liberty." Thus, we must restate the basic problem of political morality: if government does not restrain its nature itself, and if it has a natural tendency to expand, accumulate power, and become increasingly tyrannical, then how do citizens restrain it? Of course, government is just people. It isn't a mysterious entity standing above them.

Remember, our government is still representative; people have the right to vote, and can get rid of presidents and representatives they find unsatisfactory. Even the fact that some representatives have vastly more money and resources than their would-be challengers doesn't abrogate the fact that they can be voted out of office. In practice, of course, this doesn't always happen; today it doesn't even happen that often. A politician can retain his position by making promises to constituent groups—special interests—thus using the political means. Many citizens with interests of one sort or another seem to be easily tempted by such promises, and special interest groups have multiplied during the twentieth century; it would be easy to list several dozen special interest groups now influential in politics. So given that those who control government come from the citizenry (where else can they come from?), and must be supported by at least some of them, our question has an important corollary: how can citizens restrain their own temptations to pursue political as opposed to economic means of satisfying their needs and desires? Bastiat, as usual, framed the problem well:

> Generally, the law is made by one man or one class of men. And since law cannot operate without the sanction and support of a dominating force, this force must be entrusted to those who make the laws. This fact, combined with the fatal tendency that exists in the heart of man to satisfy his wants with the least possible effort, explains the almost universal perversion of the law. Thus it is easy to understand how law, instead of checking injustice, becomes the invincible weapon of injustice.[18]

It is important not to underestimate the formidable nature of this problem, which may be the biggest source of the corruption of free markets and free societies. Both Rand's and Rothbard's denials that human beings have any "automatic instincts" is probably false if meant literally; if human beings have any instincts, they are for security, which they easily choose over freedom when maintaining freedom requires more effort than being

---

[18]Bastiat, *The Law*, pp. 10–11.

safe (as it so often does).[19] If anything, Bastiat's and Nock's remarks are acknowledgements that human nature includes what
we may call, however Nietzschean this rings, a will to security
—perhaps born of the fact that the universe around us is indiffer-
ent to our needs and ends and, viewed from a limited perspective,
may often seem to openly thwart them. Different people derive a
sense of security from different things. Some people pursue security by pursuing political power over others—these people are
naturally attracted to positions in government. Others pursue security by pursuing special advantages to avoid open competition—
these people are easily tempted by the political means offered
by those in government.

These pursuits, arguably, corrupt the very language: rights
become not individual rights to pursue one's interests without coercive interference from others, but entitlements to specific goods,
often on the basis of a collective identity—requiring coercive interference with others. Liberty does not mean economic freedom
from coercion but political empowerment. Free action and personal responsibility become alien concepts. Actions become possible
only given certain institutional arrangements—to be supplied by
political means. Responsibility is shifted from the individual to
the individual's environment (socioeconomic, etc.). Justice itself
comes to mean advantages for us (my interest group).

Yet the core truth remains that human beings are not necessarily slaves to this will to security or to any other alleged
instinct. We can overcome such natural inclinations with our intelligence. This, I maintain, is a necessary truth; were it not so,
the mere identification of this or any other natural inclination
would be a cognitive impossibility. Overcoming them has been
done; the existence of our sciences, our technologies, our industries, and many other facets of twentieth-century life show that
human beings are capable of overcoming their wills to security
with a wide variety of intellectual, technological, and economic
achievements.

Today, however, philosophies which emphasize security
over truth and liberty have risen to power. Egalitarianism, for
example, stresses the moral imperative of making all individuals and groups as economically equal as possible—automatically placing moral and political shackles on anyone who tends
to soar ahead of the pack. Socioeconomic determinism regards an

---

[19]As H.L. Mencken puts it in his cynical *Notes on Democracy*, "The common man
does not want to be free. He simply wants to be safe" (New York: Alfred A. Knopf,
1926), p. 148.

individual as a product of immediate circumstances—automatically placing his capacity for independent thought, action, and personal responsibility in doubt. The social sciences of the past 150 years have been a great impetus to these developments, as well as having benefited directly from them as established disciplines in modern public universities. Since the various features of the socioeconomic environment can be observed, categorized, and to some extent manipulated politically, many political intellectuals have contributed directly to an expanded government, ideally with themselves (or their protegés) at the helm. Such people believe that they constitute an elite which alone has the knowledge, wisdom, and motivation to redress social inequalities, and to build, from the center outward, a progressively more egalitarian state. Of course, a moment's thought should make it clear that egalitarianism is an illusion; no citizen or group of citizens would be equal, either politically or economically, to the egalitarians themselves, who would remain a powerful political elite. Nevertheless, promises of cradle-to-grave security have often proven irresistible. Though overcoming the will to security with intelligence is possible, this is no more automatic than any other act of human cognition; it takes effort. For many people today, making this effort will be very hard—some have almost a lifetime of false promises to overcome.

The genuine elite in a free society is an elite of talent, ability, and achievement. Its members have obtained their standing through work and accomplishment, not through coercive interference with the honest labors of others. An elite of achievement must be contrasted with the elite of privilege which develops from increased use of the political means under an expanding central government, requiring coercive interference with others and making it more and more difficult for honest, hardworking citizens to function economically. When an elite of privilege takes power, individuals showing evidence of genuine talent, ability, and the capacity for achievement become a threat. Eventually, the latter must take action. Among their possible courses of action may be organization and secession from the geographical domain controlled by the elite of privilege. We therefore turn to the question of a right of secession itself.

FROM INDIVIDUAL RIGHTS TO A RIGHT OF SECESSION

Premise (1) of the neosecessionist argument thus emerges triumphant; it is up to human beings to conquer their weaknesses. When their governments get dictatorial enough, people will rise to the occasion. For whenever elites of privilege seize the helm of government, individuals of ability—or merely uncorrupted integrity—will begin first to chafe with discomfort and, when not recognized, engage in more and more active forms of rebellion. The will to security, after all, is not simply an impulse to legislate oneself into political slavery; under conditions of political repression it can be re-tooled into a servant of liberty. In practice, a government-supplied cradle-to-grave security becomes less and less distinguishable from repression—meaning that there is more security in both political and economic freedom than in bondage.

In addition, there remain those individuals, however few in number, who realize through their own force of intellect that economic liberty is superior to political bondage, and that an expanding government is therefore not to be trusted. These individuals will maintain the ideals of individuals' rights to life, liberty, and justly acquired property, and to the belief that government should be limited to recognizing and protecting these rights. Some of these individuals will write down their thoughts where they will be available for anyone motivated to seek them out. Hence, despite the natural tendency of governments to accumulate power, a belief in liberty and its benefits will survive—despite lack of official recognition, and even in the face of opposition (witness the survival of Ayn Rand's ideas in the face of the open hostility of the twentieth-century intellectual establishment). Among the resulting notions will be major alterations in government, ranging from secession to complete dissolution.

John Locke addressed the problem of when the "dissolution of governments" is justified:

> The constitution of the legislative is the first and fundamental act of society, whereby provision is made for the continuation of their union under the direction of persons and bonds of laws made by persons authorized thereunto by the consent and appointment of the people, without which no one man or number of men amongst them can have authority of making laws that shall be binding to the rest. When any one or more shall take upon them to make laws, whom the people have not appointed so to do, they make laws without authority, which the people are not therefore bound to obey; by which means they come again to be out of subjection and may constitute to themselves a new legislative as they think best, being in full liberty to resist the force of those who without authority would impose anything upon them.[20]

Locke believed, in other words, that citizens have a fundamental right to abolish a government which oversteps its legislative bounds and abuses its authority. Locke discusses a number

[20]Locke, *Second Treatise on Government*, pp. 229–30.

of circumstances under which governments are dissolvable, but not all pertain to a right of secession. For example, Locke discusses the right of a citizenry to dissolve a government which is neglectful. Other circumstances *do* raise the question of secession, such as what happens when governments betray their trust: "The legislative acts against the trust reposed in them when they endeavour to invade the property of the subject, and to make themselves or any part of the community masters or arbitrary disposers of the lives, liberties, or fortunes of the people."[21] The trust of government is the protection of rights, e.g., the right to justly-acquired property. Those in government who substitute their own agendas have abrogated this trust. Locke goes on:

> Whenever the legislators endeavour to take away and destroy the property of the people, or to reduce them to slavery under arbitrary power, they put themselves into a state of war with the people who are thereupon absolved from any further obedience, and are left to the common refuge which God hath provided for all men against force and violence. Whensoever, therefore, the legislative shall transgress this fundamental rule of society, and either by ambition, fear, folly, or corruption, endeavour to grasp themselves, or put into the hands of any other, an absolute power over the lives, liberties, and estates of the people, by this breach of trust they forfeit the power the people had put into their hands for quite contrary ends, and it devolves to the people who have a right to resume their original liberty, and by the establishment of a new legislative, such as they shall think fit, provide for their own safety and security, which is the end for which they are in society.[22]

The same applies to what Locke called individual "supreme executors":

> He acts also contrary to his trust when he either employs the force, treasure, and offices of the society to corrupt the representatives and gain them to his purposes, or openly pre-engages the electors and prescribes to their choice such whom he has by solicitations, threats, promises, or otherwise won to his designs, and employs them to bring in such who have promised beforehand what to vote and what to enact. Thus to regulate candidates and electors, and new-model the ways of election, what is it but to cut up the government by the roots, and poison the very fountain of public security?[23]

Locke nowhere mentions secession as such. But his discussion opens the door to the issue at one crucial juncture. Virtually no

[21]Ibid., p. 233.
[22]Ibid., p. 233.
[23]Ibid., p. 234.

government explicitly states in any official document that one or more of the regions under its authority may secede or that it may not; the issue is simply never breached. Locke tells us:

> If a controversy arise betwixt a prince and some of the people in a matter where the law is silent or doubtful, and the thing be of great consequence, I should think the proper umpire in such a case should be the body of the people; for in cases where the prince hath a trust reposed in him and is dispensed from the common ordinary rules of the law, there, if any men find themselves aggrieved and think the prince acts contrary to or beyond that trust, who so proper to judge as the body of the people—who, at first, lodged that trust in him—how far they meant it should extend? . . .
>
> [If the people] have set limits to the duration of their legislative and made this supreme power in any person or assembly only temporary, or else when by the miscarriages of those in authority it is forfeited, upon the forfeiture, or at the determination of the time set, it reverts to the society, and the people have a right to act as supreme and continue the legislative in themselves, or erect a new form, or under the old form place it in new hands, as they think good.[24]

Thus, for Locke, a given government, headed by a given sovereign, was not a permanent and unalterable institution. The citizenry had the right to replace their sovereign, and even replace their government. Does this include the right to organize and divorce themselves from a government which has betrayed its trust? The suggestion here is that where the law itself is silent, the people decide. Thus, if a group of people has a serious complaint against their sovereign, and they wish to secede, they have every right to do so.

Locke, again, does not say this explicitly, and it would be putting words in his mouth to attribute to him any unqualified claim of a right of secession. Thomas Paine, however, picked up a century later where Locke left off, defending the rights of the then-flourishing thirteen colonies against abusive British elites of privilege. Paine endorsed essentially the same natural-rights philosophy as Locke. In Paine's *The Rights of Man*, we read:

> Natural rights are those which always appertain to man in right of his existence. Of this kind are all the intellectual rights, or rights of the mind, and also all those rights of acting as an individual for his own comfort and happiness, which are not injurious to the rights of others.[25]

[24]Ibid., p. 246–47.

[25]Thomas Paine, *The Rights of Man* (Buffalo, N.Y.: Prometheus Books, [1787] 1987), p. 43.

In *Common Sense*, Paine, having lived in the colonies only a few months, forcefully attacked the British elite of privilege, and argued on behalf of American colonists that:

> A government of our own is our natural right: And when a man seriously reflects on the precariousness of human affairs, he will become convinced, that it is infinitely wiser and safer, to form a constitution of our own in a cool deliberate manner while we have it in our power, than to trust such an interesting event to time and chance.[26]

Such sentiments bore fruit on American soil with the Declaration of Independence, which qualifies as a statement of secession if anything does. Thomas Jefferson, its author, picks up the idea where Paine leaves off:

> When, in the course of human events, it becomes necessary for one people to dissolve the political bonds which have connected them to another, and to assume, among the powers of the earth, the separate and equal station to which the laws of nature and of nature's God entitle them, a decent respect to the opinions of mankind requires that they should declare the causes which impel them to the separation.
>
> We hold these truths to be self-evident: that all men are created equal; that they are endowed, by their Creator, with certain unalienable rights; that among these rights are life, liberty, and the pursuit of happiness. That to secure these rights, governments are instituted among men, deriving their just powers from the consent of the governed; that whenever any form of government becomes destructive of these ends, it is the right of the people to alter or abolish it, and to institute new government, laying its foundation on such principles, and organizing its powers in such form, as to them shall seem most likely to affect their safety and happiness. . . . [W]hen a long train of abuses and usurpations . . . evinces a design to reduce them under absolute despotism, it is their right, it is their duty, to throw off such government, and to provide new guards for their future security.[27]

Thus, those men who inspired or led the founding of the United States held that a group of citizens is morally justified in leading a separation from a government which ceases to fulfill its proper functions, violates honorable agreements, or abandons the role of a servant and assumes that of a master.

We can find occasional statements today that a right of secession exists. Some of these are very heavily qualified. Allen Buchanan discusses the right of secession in the context of *group*

---

[26]Thomas Paine, *Common Sense* (New York: Penguin Classics, [1776] 1986), p. 98.

[27]Quoted in *Paine and Jefferson on Liberty*, Lloyd S. Kramer, ed. (New York: Continuum, 1988), pp. 63–64.

rights, explaining the relative neglect of the topic from the alleged neglect of group rights by liberalism:

> The views on secession advanced in this book . . . will . . . provide a strong case for revising liberal doctrine's apparent refusal to recognize *group* rights as fundamental moral or constitutional rights. This result in turn will help to explain why liberalism, in spite of its emphasis on self-determination, diversity, and consent, has not included a right to secede but has instead remained largely silent on secession. . . .
>
>   My hypothesis is that the issue of secession has been an embarrassment that liberals have sought to ignore because it challenges two fundamental tenets of liberalism: the *universalism* that is a chief part of liberalism's inheritance from the rationalism of the Enlightenment, and the preoccupation with *individual* rights to which liberalism has been led by its conviction that the ultimate unit in the moral universe is the individual person. . . .
>
>   Liberalism's conviction that what matters most, morally speaking, are individuals, and its hostility toward those who would devalue the individual in the name of the collective . . . make it at minimum suspicious of the very concept of a group right. This suspicion has led . . . some liberal thinkers to underestimate the role that group rights, *including a right to secession*, can play in protecting *individuals* and the values that they affirm in their lives—particularly the value . . . in being members of groups.[28]

Listening to Buchanan, one would think that the concept of group rights had played virtually no role in twentieth-century moral philosophy public policy. This, of course, is very strange.

    Let us consider the views of one of those liberals whom Buchanan would unquestionably reject as too individualistic, Austrian-school economist Ludwig von Mises. Mises was no proponent of group rights in any sense of this term; yet, for Mises, there is unquestionably a right of secession that can be derived exclusively from the rights of individuals, bypassing groups completely:

> If a democratic republic finds that its existing boundaries, as shaped by the course of history before the transition to liberalism, no longer correspond to the political wishes of the people, they must be peacefully changed to conform to the results of a plebiscite expressing the people's will. It must always be possible to shift the boundaries of the state if the will of the inhabitants of an area to attach themselves to a state other than the one to which they presently belong has made itself clearly known.

---

[28]Buchanan, *Secession*, pp. 7–8, emphasis added.

> Whenever the inhabitants of a particular territory, whether it be a single village, a whole district, or a series of adjacent districts, make it known . . . that they no longer wish to remain united to the state to which they belong at the time, but wish either to form an independent state or to attach themselves to some other state, their wishes are to be respected and complied with. This is the only feasible and effective way of preventing revolutions and civil and international wars.

> [This] right of self-determination . . . is not the right of self-determination of a delimited national unit, but the right of the inhabitants of every territory to decide on the state to which they wish to belong . . . , the right of self-determination of the inhabitants of every territory large enough to form an independent administrative unit.

> . . . If . . . one seeks to determine their political fate against their will by appealing to an alleged higher right of the nation, one violates the right of self-determination no less effectively than by practicing any other form of oppression.[29]

Mises takes the view that individuals may choose to separate themselves and their property from the territory claimed by an abusive government. At first glance, this sounds extreme. No doubt it runs contrary to today's prevailing opinions which owe more to Rousseau, Hegel, Marx, and Rawls, than to Locke, Paine, or the Austrian school. The former reject individualism, and see societies as quasi-organic entities in which it is the job of government, not communities of individuals, to resolve social problems in ways suitable to them. Still, the former (and their many disciples) hold that they, as intellectuals, have the knowledge and wisdom to reshape society to fit an intellectual ideal, using both the universities and expanded government—especially the powers of the courts—as the most convenient instruments.

It should be sufficient to show that this kind of thinking has generated a great deal of tragedy in our century. The two bloodiest tyrannies the world has ever seen, Nazism and Communism, are both variants of it. Our own society is, at present, heading in a similar direction partly due to a widespread acceptance among the influential elite that government is capable of fulfilling a myriad of tasks beyond its original purpose of protecting individuals' rights to life, liberty, and justly acquired property. The widespread relativism and nihilism (postmodernism) rampant in the universities is rapidly robbing the rest of society of its

[29]Ludwig von Mises, *Liberalism: In the Classical Tradition* (Irvington-on-Hudson, N.Y.: Foundation for Economic Education, and San Francisco: Cobden Press, [1962] 1985), pp. 108–11.

moral compass, which would be its major weapon of resistance to the increasing control over their lives. Government, as Jefferson observed, tends to accumulate power. He wrote, "The natural progress of things is for liberty to yield and government to gain ground."[30]

Our government has proven to be as prone to this tendency as any, and now some fear we are progressing toward a home-grown, American brand of tyranny. This is the source of the current anti-government sentiment, and of the question of secession. Supposing that creating the government of a Constitutional republic means creating a contract between governers and governed, if either partner to the contract fails to hold up its end of the bargain, the contract may be dissolved, and the government loses legitimacy. A right of secession exists, in this case, if individual rights include the right to organize a new body politic to escape the reach of a repressive regime. These, of course, are still very general remarks. Let us turn to concrete applications.

ANOTHER LOOK AT THE WAR FOR
SOUTHERN INDEPENDENCE

The above material should establish the *moral* right of secession, that is, it should establish premise (2) above. Now we come to the all-important question: is (3) true? For while (2) establishes a right of secession in principle, (3) holds that secession is justified at specific times. This, of course, is a far more provocative claim. Thus, it might help to consider an earlier case of secession from the Union, and to consider the arguments its defenders provided, a case we may think of as

> a precedent which is cemented in our history, perhaps by the divine hand, for specific use in our day when evil and conspiring men would attempt to destroy the sovereignty of the 50 States along with the Constitution.[31]

Our present federal government was created when nine states ratified the Constitution, thus replacing the Articles of Confederation. The Constitution was the contract by which the states created the federal government, and limited its powers by creating specific branches of government, and by delegating specific

---

[30]Thomas Jefferson, "Letter to Colonel Edward Carrington of 1788," in *The Life and Selected Writings of Thomas Jefferson*, Adrienne Koch and William Peden, eds. (New York: Random House, 1994), p. 447.

[31]Joseph Stumph, *Saving Our Constitution From the New World Order* (Salt Lake City, Utah: Northwest Publishing, 1993), p. 213.

tasks to each, allowing each to check the powers of the others, in order to keep the whole on a short leash. *The Federalist Papers* were written to allay the fears of those who thought the Constitution would give too much power to the new federal government. While this got the Constitution ratified, it is doubtful that the new Union was ever as stable during its first century as the history books imply.

The Constitution explained how a territory could enter the Union as a state, but was unspecific regarding secession. It is suggestive, though, that the Articles of Confederation used the term *Perpetual Union* which appears nowhere in the Constitution. *The Federalist Papers* also avoid secession as a topic, but they contain numerous references to state sovereignty. Hamilton observes that "The State governments by their original constitutions are invested with complete sovereignty."[32] Madison adds: "The powers delegated by the proposed Constitution to the federal government are few and defined. Those which are to remain in the State governments are numerous and indefinite."[33] He chastised the critics of the Constitution for thinking of the two as rivals:

> the ultimate authority, . . . resides in the people alone, and . . . will not depend merely on the comparative ambition or address of the different governments whether either, or which of them, will be able to enlarge its sphere of jurisdiction at the expense of the other.[34]

Nevertheless, both Hamilton and Madison were convinced that there would be more danger to the Union from the states than to the states from the Union.[35] This seemed to make questions of secession moot.

Belief that states had the right to secede was nevertheless widespread. Secession movements stirred in 1798, 1801, 1811, and 1814 for various reasons.[36] A secession convention was actually held in Hartford, Connecticut, shortly after the War of 1812, to discuss the possibility of the secession of New England.[37] William Rawle, an attorney and early authority on the Constitution,

[32]*The Federalist Papers*, no. 32.

[33]Ibid., no. 45.

[34]Ibid., no. 46.

[35]Ibid., no. 45.

[36]Ashley Halsey, Jr., *Who Fired the First Shot?* (New York: Fawcett World Library, 1963), p. xiii.

[37]James Ronald Kennedy and Walter Donald Kennedy, *The South Was Right* (Gretna, La.: Pelican Publishing, 1994), p. 312.

was among the first to discuss secession from the constitutional point of view.

> It is not to be understood, that interposition would be justifiable, if the people of a state should determine to retire from the union, whether they adopted another or retained the same form of government, or if they should, with the express intention of seceding, expunge the representative system from their code. . . .
>
> It depends on the state itself to retain or abolish the principle of representation, because it depends on itself whether it will continue a member of the Union. *To deny this right would be inconsistent with the principle on which all our political systems are founded, which is, that the people have in all cases a right to determine how they will be governed.*
>
> *This right must be considered as an ingredient in the original composition of the general government, which, though not expressed, was mutually understood,* and the doctrine heretofore presented to the reader in regard to the indefeasible nature of personal allegiance, is so far qualified in respect to allegiance to the United States. It was observed, that it was competent for a state to make a compact with its citizens, that the reciprocal obligations of protection and allegiance might cease on certain events; and it was further observed, that allegiance would necessarily cease on the dissolution of the society to which it was due.
>
> *The States, then, may wholly withdraw from the Union,* but while they continue they must retain the character of representative republics.[38]

According to Rawle, then, there *is* an implied right of secession in the Constitution. But secession is not, in his view, a step which ought to be taken lightly and frivolously.

> The secession of a state from the Union depends on the will of the people of such state. The people alone as we have already seen, hold the power to alter their constitution. The constitution of the United States is to a certain extent incorporated into the constitutions of the several states by the act of the people.
>
> The state legislatures have only to perform certain organical operations in respect to it. To withdraw from the Union comes not within the general scope of their delegated authority. There must be an express provision to that effect inserted in the state constitution. This is not at present the case with any of them, and it would perhaps be impolitic to confide it to them. A matter so momentous ought not be entrusted to those who would have it in their power to

---

[38]William Rawle, *A View of the Constitution* (Baton Rouge, La.: Land and Land, [1825] 1993), pp. 234–35, emphasis added.

exercise it lightly and precipitately upon sudden dissatisfaction, or causeless jealousy, perhaps against the interests
and the wishes of a majority of their constituents.

But in any manner by which a secession is to take
place, nothing is more certain than that the act should be deliberate, clear, and unequivocal. The perspecuity and solem-
nity of the original obligation require correspondent quali-
ties in its dissolution. The powers of the general government
cannot be defeated or impaired by an ambiguous or implied
secession on the part of the state, although a secession may
perhaps be conditional. The people of the state may have
some reasons to complain in respect to acts of the general
government, they may in such cases invest some of their own
officers with the power of negotiation, and may declare an
absolute secession in case of their failure. Still, however, the
secession must in such case be distinctly and peremptorily
declared to take place on that event, and in such case—as in
the case of an unconditional secession, the previous ligament
with the Union, would be legitimately and fairly destroyed.
But in either case the people is the only moving power.[39]

Rawle was not alone in thinking of secession as a Constitutional right. The history of the period is replete with other such
remarks. Daniel Webster commented that "If the Union was
formed by the accession of the States, then the Union may be dissolved by the secession of the States." He added that

The Union is a Union of States founded upon a Compact.
How is it to be supposed that when different parties enter
into a compact for certain purposes either can disregard one
provision of it and expect others to observe the rest? If the
Northern States willfully and deliberately refuse to carry
out their part of the Constitution, the South would be no
longer bound to keep the compact. A bargain broken on one
side is broken on all sides.[40]

Horace Greeley wrote in the *New York Tribune*:

If the Declaration of Independence justified the secession of
3,000,000 colonists in 1776, I do not see why the Constitution ratified by the same men should not justify the secession
of 5,000,000 of the Southerners from the Federal Union in
1861.

We have repeatedly said, and we once more insist that
the great principle embodied by Jefferson in the Declaration
of Independence that government derives its power from the
consent of the governed is sound and just, then if the Cotton
States, the Gulf States or any other States choose to form an
independent nation they have a clear right to do it.

[39]Ibid., pp. 238–39.
[40]Quoted in Kennedy and Kennedy, *The South Was Right*, p. 313.

> The right to secede may be a revolutionary one, but it exists nevertheless; and we do not see how one part can have a right to do what another party has a right to prevent. We must ever resist the asserted right of any State to remain in the Union and nullify or defy the laws thereof; to withdraw from the Union is another matter. And when a section of our Union resolves to go out, we shall resist any coercive acts to keep it in. We hope never to live in a Republic where one section is pinned to the other section by bayonets.[41]

Even Abraham Lincoln, in 1847, had said that "any people whatever have a right to abolish the existing government and form a new one that suits them better."[42] It is clear, then, that secession was considered a live option, as was shown by additional stirrings in the years 1832, 1845, and 1856—some in northern states—all prior to South Carolina's actually putting the idea to official test in December of 1860 with the Ordinance of Secession.

Many historians have contended that the southern states seceded mainly to preserve slavery. If this is true, then since any moral code taking its starting point from the individual's right to life, liberty, and justly acquired property requires the rejection of slavery, this would cast doubt on the moral legitimacy of the Confederacy. But it is doubtful there was any intent on the part of Confederate authorities to preserve slavery. First, and most obviously, the institution only affected a small percentage of the white population (under ten percent owned slaves). It seems unlikely that thousands would have gone willingly to their deaths against a numerically and militarily superior foe just to help a handful of plantation owners keep their slaves.[43] Slavery was, in fact, dying out on its own. Jefferson Davis even observed that regardless of the outcome of the War for Southern Independence, the slave property of southerners "will eventually be lost."[44] As Dowdey also notes:

> Slavery was passing. With no importations to replace the slaves being sold south, as large plantations continued to cease the slave-system operation and few yeomen held aspirations to slave ownership, the time would come when there would be no more slaves.[45]

Finally, it is clear from Lincoln's own words—unfortunately mostly unknown—that despite his publicly stated purpose "To

[41]Quoted in ibid., pp. 313–14.
[42]Quoted in ibid., p. 313.
[43]Ibid., pp. 34–35.
[44]Quoted in ibid., p. 35.
[45]Clifford Dowdey, *The History of the Confederacy: 1832–1865* (New York: Barnes and Noble Books, 1955), p. 62.

free the slaves," legal equality between whites and blacks was hardly a motive force of the War. In 1858, Lincoln had stated unequivocally:

> I will say, then, that I am not, nor ever have been, in favor of bringing about in any way the social and political equality of the white and black races—that I am not, nor ever have been, in favor of making voters or jurors of negroes, nor of qualifying them to hold office, nor to intermarry with white people; and I will say in addition to this that there is a physical difference between the white and black races. . . . I, as much as any other man, am in favor of having the superior position assigned to the white race.[46]

In a similar context, Lincoln wrote that "If I could preserve the Union without freeing the Negro, I would do so."[47] He also had doubts about the feasibility of doing away with slavery: "I think no wise man has yet perceived how it could be at once eradicated without producing a greater evil even to the cause of human liberty itself."[48] In other words, contrary to prevailing opinions, freeing the slaves wasn't the reason the North went to war at all!

What created the acute dilemma over slavery was the fact that while the institution was widely perceived to be immoral, it was nevertheless understood as Constitutionally acceptable. In 1857, Supreme Court Chief Justice Roger B. Taney wrote, in *Dred Scott v Sanford*, that "the right of property in a slave is distinctly and expressly affirmed in the Constitution."[49] Taney went on to describe "negroes" as an "inferior race" whose members could not be citizens of the United States. The southern economy, moreover, had come to depend in large measure on slavery; freeing slaves all at once threatened enormous dislocation. Too, in light of the Nat Turner rebellion in 1831, many white southerners—rightly or wrongly—feared the growing black population too much to trust it with freedom. As a result, southern states perceived attacks on slavery as attacks on southern culture and their right of self-determination. Nevertheless, there was no special attachment to slavery as definitive of southern culture.

Lest there be any doubts as to where Jefferson Davis actually stood, the Confederate Constitution explicitly forbade importing any more African slaves, and he once vetoed a bill which he deemed in conflict with this:

[46]Ibid., p. 55.
[47]Cited in ibid., p. 219.
[48]Cited in ibid., p. 6.
[49]Quoted in Halsey, *Who Fired the First Shot?* p. 18.

> Gentlemen of Congress: With sincere deference to the judgment of Congress, I have carefully considered the bill in relation to the slave trade, and to punish persons offending therein, but have not been able to approve it, and therefore do return it with a statement of my objections. The Constitution (Art. I, §7) provides that the importation of African negroes from any foreign country other than slave-holding States of the United States is hereby forbidden, and Congress is required to pass such laws as shall effectually prevent the same.... This provision seems to me to be in opposition to the policy declared in the Constitution—the prohibition of the importation of African negroes—and in derogation of its mandate to legislate for the effectuation of that object.[50]

In other words, Davis knew the institution would gradually die out as more and more slaves were able to buy their freedom or die and not be replaced.

The reason the southern states gave for secession was their desire for a self-determination they saw themselves losing in the face of both government intrusions and broken agreements—in short, to escape a federal government which had already stepped outside its bounds. In 1831, the federal government unilaterally imposed high tariffs on imports which automatically favored northern states at the expense of southern ones. South Carolina resisted, nullifying the tariff and creating the Nullification Controversy.[51] The nullifiers spoke of seceding right then and there, threatening a confrontation with President Andrew Jackson which would have started the War for Southern Independence in 1831 instead of 1861. The tension was exemplified in Jackson's toast at a large dinner party: "Our Union must be preserved," to which Vice President John C. Calhoun, a South Carolinian, replied, "To our Union, next to our liberties, most dear." Jackson made it clear he would not tolerate Nullification and threatened to send troops into South Carolina if it seceded.[52] South Carolina blinked, as there was as of yet no Confederacy or anything like it, meaning that the state would have been entirely on its own. But from that time forward, the northern states and the southern ones were on a collision course.

Matters began to come to a head in 1846 when territory purchased from Mexico—what became New Mexico, Arizona, and southern California—came with a "proviso" forbidding slavery in those states, in violation of the Missouri Compromise of 1820

[50]Quoted in Kennedy and Kennedy, *The South Was Right*, p. 332.

[51]William W. Freehling, *Prelude to Civil War: The Nullification Controversy in South Carolina 1816–1836* (New York: Oxford University Press, 1965).

[52]Dowdey, *The History of the Confederacy*, p. 38.

which had established the legality of slavery in all new states south of the lateral from the southern boundary of Missouri extending west to the Pacific.[53] Clay's Compromise of 1850 admitted California as a non-slave state and allowed New Mexico and Utah to choose—offering the progressively outnumbered southern states nothing. Southerners saw northerners as using the slavery issue for political and economic gain, as a means of extending their manufacturing economy. What southerners feared was not so much the end of slavery but the destruction of their agrarian way of life in the face of the growing industrialization of the North. Days before his death in 1851, Calhoun predicted that "The Union is doomed to dissolution. . . . The probability is that it will explode in an election within twelve years."[54]

He was right. The election of Lincoln directly precipitated South Carolina's decision to secede. The situation had deteriorated to the point where physical violence was breaking out between northerners and southerners, often with the tacit support of the northern states. The worst such incident was the murderous assault in Northern Virginia by a group of abolitionists led by John Brown in October of 1859. Southerners, offended by such actions, and even more by the North's refusal to repudiate them, were looking for an opportunity to leave the Union. As Lincoln was perceived as more hostile to southern interests than was his opponent Stephen Douglas, his election gave them the opportunity, and on 17 December 1860, South Carolinians convened to secede from the Union. Three days later, they adopted the Ordinance of Secession:

> We, the people of the State of South Carolina in Convention assembled, do declare and ordain, and it is hereby declared and ordained, that the ordinance adopted by us in Convention on the twenty-third day of May, in the year of our Lord 1788, whereby the Constitution of the United States of America was radified, and also all acts and parts of acts of the General Assembly of this State ratifying amendments of the said Constitution, are hereby repealed; and that the union now subsisting between South Carolina and the other States, under the name of the "United States of America," is hereby dissolved.
>
> Done at Charleston the twentieth day of December, in the year of our Lord, 1860.[55]

[53]Ibid., p. 31.

[54]In ibid., pp. 350–51.

[55]In *South Carolina: A Documentary Profile of the Palmetto State*, Elmer D. Johnson and Kathleen Lewis Sloan, eds. (Columbia: University of South Carolina Press, 1983), pp. 350–51.

Tracts with names like *The South Alone Should Govern the South* appealed to other southern states to leave the Union and form what would become the Confederacy, and by April of 1861, six more states had seceded. Soon-to-be Confederate President Jefferson Davis made some remarks which are worth our attention. In January of 1861, prior to his leaving, he told the U.S. Senate:

> It is known to Senators who have served with me here, that I have, for many years, advocated, as an essential attribute of State sovereignty, the right of a State to secede from the Union. . . . Secession . . . is to be justified upon the basis that the States are sovereign. There was a time when none denied it. I hope the time may come again, when a better comprehension of the theory of our government, and the inalienable rights of the people of the States, will prevent anyone from denying that each State is sovereign, and thus may reclaim the grants from which it has made to any agent whomsoever.[56]

References to slavery are conspicuous by their absence. In his 18 April 1861 address to the Confederacy at Montgomery, Alabama, Davis stated that secession and formation of a new country were justified for the same reason that the breakaway of the thirteen original colonies from Great Britain had been justified:

> Our present political position . . . illustrates the American idea that governments rest on the consent of the governed, and that it is the right of the people to alter or abolish them at will whenever they become destructive of the ends for which they were established. The declared purpose of the compact of the Union from which we have withdrawn was to "establish justice, insure domestic tranquillity, provide for the common defense, promote the general welfare, and secure the blessings of liberty to ourselves and our posterity": and when, in the judgement of the sovereign States composing this Confederacy, it has been perverted from the purposes for which is was ordained, and ceased to answer the ends for which it was established, a peaceful appeal to the ballot box declared that, so far as they are concerned, the Government created by that compact should cease to exist.[57]

In an address at Richmond, Virginia, on 22 February 1862, after the North had begun waging war, Davis added:

> The people of the States now confederated became convinced that the Government of the United States had fallen into the hands of a sectional majority, who would pervert that most sacred of all trusts to the destruction of the rights which it

[56]Quoted in Kennedy and Kennedy, *The South Was Right*, pp. 316–17.
[57]Quoted in ibid., p. 322.

was pledged to protect. They believed that to remain longer in the Union would subject them to continuance of a disparaging discrimination, submission to which would be inconsistent with their welfare, and intolerable to a proud people. They therefore determined to sever its bounds and established a new Confederacy for themselves. . . . The experiment instituted by our revolutionary fathers, of a voluntary Union of sovereign States . . . had been perverted by those who, feeling power and forgetting right, were determined to respect no law but their own will. The Government had ceased to answer the ends for which it was ordained and established. . . . True to our traditions of peace and our love of justice, we sent commissioners to the United States to propose a fair and amicable settlement . . . but the Government at Washington, denying our right to self-government, refused even to listen to any proposals for peaceful separation. Nothing was then left to do but to prepare for war. . . . We are in arms to renew such sacrifices as our fathers made to the holy cause of constitutional liberty.[58]

In short, Davis believed his cause was the same as those who originally formed the Union: to create and preserve an ideal of government by consent of the governed, an ideal he accused the North of having systematically violated. In the case of those states in the second wave of secessions—Virginia, North Carolina, Tennessee, and Arkansas—this was clearly the reason.

To sum up, it seems clear that on any reasonable interpretation of the Declaration of Independence and the Constitution, the South was right! If the Declaration of Independence was morally legitimate, then so was South Carolina's Ordinance of Secession and other such declarations. The peoples of the southern states were within their rights to secede from the Union and form a new sovereign unit. Premise (3) of the argument was true during the period 1830–1861; and therefore (4), the statement that secession was then justified, is also true.

---

[58]Quoted in ibid., pp. 328–29.

3
THE ETHICS OF SECESSION

Scott Boykin

T he moral status of secession should be a significant issue in
contemporary political theory. Various secessionist movements around the globe have had a tremendous impact on
world politics, and the fluidity of power relations in many parts
of the world suggests that they will continue to have such an effect for some time. Moreover, secession addresses the fundamental problem of political theory: namely, the moral basis for the
state's authority.

Modern political thought has produced three main types of
argument for the state's legitimacy. One, found in Kant, grounds
the state's authority on the purported rightness of its institutions
and aims. A right of secession challenges this position if it allows a group to legitimately withdraw from a just state. Another, found in Locke, holds that consent, whether explicit or tacit,
is the source of the state's authority. A right of secession challenges this position in maintaining that consent may be legitimately withdrawn in favor of an alternative political arrangement. The third, found in Hume, bases the state's authority on its
usefulness in producing order, which facilitates the individual's
pursuit of self-chosen ends. A right of secession challenges this
position in negating the general Humean duty to support a historical or conventional state and morally permitting a group to
transfer its loyalties to one it expects to find more useful.

A right of secession does not demand that we reject any of
these positions; indeed, I employ each in defending secession. If
secession is morally justifiable, however, it calls for qualifications to each of these three accounts of political obligation.
Given its practical and theoretical import, it is surprising that
only one recent work in academic political theory, Allen Buchanan's *Secession*, has approached the subject at length.[1] Buchanan
seeks to establish a framework for considering the ethical issues
surrounding secession, and some key parts of what follows are
written with a view to his arguments.

In this essay, I make a moral case for secession. The argument
is concerned solely with secession by groups; while individual

---

[1]Allen Buchanan, *Secession: The Morality of Political Divorce from Fort Sumter to Lithuania and Quebec* (Boulder, Colo.: Westview, 1991).

secession is an interesting idea, I will not pursue it here.[2] In the first section, I lay the ethical grounds for a right of secession. An indeterminate contractualist argument, which eliminates specific rules or principles as elements of a just political order, can justify a right of secession. No state, I argue, can justly prohibit secession under all circumstances. The second section defines the right of secession and specifies the moral limits on the exercise of the right. Though secession as a right is exercised collectively, it is an individual and not a group right. This is important because it renders unnecessary a group claim to have shared ethnic or cultural attributes, and thus removes one obstacle to the right to secede. All that counts is whether the group wishes to define itself as a political unit. The right of secession is a limited one in that secessionists must, first, be able to establish a viable political order, and second, protect private property and the market. I argue that any group of persons that meets these criteria cannot be justly prohibited from seceding. The upshot of this section is that any political system ought to provide for a constitutional right of secession subject only to these limits. Buchanan sets further restrictions on the right of secession, which I criticize and reject in the final section.

NORMATIVE INDIVIDUALISM AND A RIGHT OF SECESSION

In this section, I develop a normative foundation for a right of secession consisting of two basic elements. The first is a treatment of value from the perspective of normative individualism. Under normative individualism, values are exclusively personal in nature, or agent-relative. The agent-relativity of all values places strict constraints on the moral claims individuals can legitimately make on one another, and thus limits the depth of social or political obligation. The second element is a contractualist ethical argument that establishes a moral presumption favoring a constitutional or procedural right of secession, which I define later in the chapter.

Normative Individualism

Under normative individualism, all values are agent-relative. An agent-relative value is a value for a particular person. A value is agent-relative if and only if its description must refer

---

[2]But see Lysander Spooner, *No Treason: The Constitution of No Authority*, in *The Lysander Spooner Reader* (San Francisco: Fox and Wilkes, 1992), pp. 49–111.

to the valuing agent.[3] For agent A_1 and states of affairs S_1 and S_2, S_1 possesses agent-relative value for A_1 if and only if A_1 ranks S_1 over S_2. With this ranking, A_1 has an agent-relative motivation to act so as to realize S_1, but no reason to promote S_2. An agent-neutral scale of value, as found in cardinal-comparable utilitarianism, yields an ordering that all agents must value and promote—without regard to their personal disposition—the highest-ranked state of affairs. If A_2 and A_3 prefer S_2, A_1 must value and promote S_2 in spite of his preference for S_1; A_1's life thus becomes shackled to others' preferences. The individualist theory of value rejects the validity of agent-neutral scales and their moral implications.[4]

Normative individualism entails that the value of a social and political order, like that of anything else, lies in its usefulness to the individual. Order facilitates the individual's pursuit of his plans and projects, collaboration with other individuals, and the emergence of competitive social processes that serve to coordinate individuals' actions. Rational agents have reason to participate in and observe the rules of a social and political order because, and only because, that order is useful to them. If a political arrangement is advantageous to A_1 and disadvantageous to A_2, it is not a value for A_2, and A_2 lacks reason to support it. A political arrangement has value for all the agents concerned, and provides them with motivation to support it, if and only if it is mutually advantageous.

Because normative individualism indicates that the value of political order lies in its capacity to facilitate the self-chosen plans and projects of individuals, it can play a key justificatory role in political argument. As James Buchanan argues, the principle supplies the

> normative premise that individuals are the ultimate *sovereigns* in matters of social organization, that individuals are the beings who are entitled to choose the organizational-institutional structures under which they will live. In accordance with this premise, the legitimacy of social-organizational structures is to be judged against the voluntary agreement of those who are to live or are living under the arrangements that are judged. The central premise of *individuals as*

[3]Thomas Nagel, *The View from Nowhere* (Oxford: Oxford University Press, 1986), pp. 152–53.

[4]For criticism of agent-neutrality, see Eric Mack, "Moral Individualism: Agent-relativity and Deontic Restraints," *Social Philosophy & Policy* 7 (Autumn 1989): 81–111; Loren Lomasky, *Persons, Rights, and the Moral Community* (New York: Oxford University Press, 1987), pp. 16–55; J.J.C. Smart and Bernard Williams, *Utilitarianism: For and Against* (Cambridge: Cambridge University Press, 1973), pp. 108–18.

> *sovereigns* does allow for the delegation of decision-making authority to agents, so long as it remains understood that individuals remain as *principals*. The premise denies legitimacy to all social-organizational arrangements that negate the role of individuals as either sovereigns or principals.[5]

Normative individualism, then, offers a critical perspective from which we can evaluate political institutions. Political institutions possess value only if they serve the interests of the persons subject to them. A model of voluntary agreement enables us to ascertain whether individuals can be expected to refuse assent to a rule. If they would do so, the rule in question cannot be justified.

Contractualism and Secession

A contractualist ethics can appraise political arrangements by considering whether they contain elements that anyone seeking a rational agreement on public institutions could reasonably reject.[6] This test is a variant of the principle of universalizability, and it narrows the range of individual interests considered morally significant. An agent, for example, might value his committing robbery and murder, but other persons could legitimately reject a rule permitting him to do so. An indeterminate contractualism evaluates particular principles and institutions, but does not fully determine the structure and contents of a worthy political order.[7] That some rules can be eliminated as alternatives does not indicate which remaining proposals individuals will accept. Contractualism can, and indeed must, take into account the indeterminacy of its conclusions with regard to the rules actual persons will approve. While contractualism cannot specify what people will accept, it can place moral constraints on actual political systems by showing that some rules should always be rejected. A rule that fails the contractualist test cannot be justly imposed on anyone.

With these constraints in mind, we can ask whether anyone could reasonably reject a political order that prohibits secession under any circumstances. Because normative individualism implies that institutions possess value only insofar as individuals ascribe value to them, it invalidates arrangements that benefit

[5]James M. Buchanan, *The Economics and the Ethics of Constitutional Order* (Ann Arbor: University of Michigan Press, 1991), p. 227, emphasis in original.

[6]Here I am following T.M. Scanlon, "Contractualism and Utilitarianism," in *Utilitarianism and Beyond*, Amartya Sen and Bernard Williams, eds. (Cambridge: Cambridge University Press, 1982), pp. 103–28.

[7]See John Gray, *Post-Liberalism* (New York: Routledge, 1993), pp. 48–50.

some persons at others' expense. When a subset of a group has determined that a new arrangement, which requires an act of secession to establish, would serve them better than the *status quo*, the subset can claim that forceful opposition to their secession on behalf of the interests of the remainder of the group benefits the latter at the prospective secessionists' expense. A constitutional or a procedural right of secession enables individuals to reveal their preferences over alternative arrangements by offering a means of disclosing whether, in the judgment of a subset of a larger group, present conditions are in fact a disvalue to them. Anyone, then, who suspects that at some point he may become dissatisfied with a set of political institutions could reasonably object to a rule prohibiting secession under any circumstances. Anyone, moreover, who considers it possible that he may, at some future time, judge secession a means by which he could participate in forming a new political unit which would better serve his interests could reasonably reject a rule prohibiting secession. All that is required is an assumption of uncertainty over the long-term consequences of life under a political arrangement.[8] Given this uncertainty, it is clear that anyone could reasonably reject a rule prohibiting secession under all circumstances. Contractualism, then, yields an ethical presumption favoring a right of secession.

Whether anyone could legitimately oppose a particular act of secession is another matter. In the following section, I examine the conditions under which secession might be justifiably prohibited, and show that the right of secession is a limited one.

DEFINING THE RIGHT OF SECESSION

The moral considerations advanced in the previous section support a right of secession that grounds a duty on the part of any state to refrain from prohibiting secession under all circumstances. This specifies the action which the right protects, and who is obliged to respect the right. Any state should provide a legal or constitutional means for secession. A complete right-statement must also define the bearer of the right and detail any limits on its exercise. In this section, I fill in these blanks.

Who Bears the Right of Secession

Allen Buchanan argues that because only groups may secede, secession must be a group right. Group rights, as he puts it,

---

[8]See Geoffrey Brennan and James M. Buchanan, *The Reason of Rules* (Cambridge: Cambridge University Press, 1985), pp. 28–31.

are ascribed to collections of individuals and can only be exercised collectively or at least on behalf of the collective, usually through some mechanism of political representation whereby a designated individual or subset of the group purports to act for the group as a whole. In addition, the good secured by the right is most often a collective good in the sense that if it is secured it will be available to all or most members of the group. Moreover, if we think of rights as serving certain interests, we may also say that the interests served by group rights are individuals' interests, *qua* members of the group, in the collective goods of the group—that is, their interests in participating in the common activities and in pursuing the shared goals of the group.[9]

There are two distinct flaws in Buchanan's treatment of secession as a group right. First, it unduly restricts the good secured by secession to the benefits of common activities and goals. Clearly, members of a group may wish to secede for the sake of pursuing private goals more effectively, and it is not apparent that such goals are a less legitimate basis for secession than are collective ones. Even if those interests that individuals have only as members of a group are a necessary condition of their collectively possessing a group right, such interests are not necessary to a right of secession.

Second, the fact that collective action is required to exercise a right of secession does not entail that it is a group right. Procedural rights of due process, for example, require collective action to establish reliable judicial and law enforcement institutions, but the goods they secure are inextricably bound to interests individuals possess *qua* individuals.[10] Collective action here is necessary to exercise the individual right to be treated justly by others. While collective action may be a necessary condition for a group right, it may also be a necessary condition for the exercise of some individual rights, hence it does not follow that the requirement of collective action makes secession a group right.

Treating secession as an individual right eliminates a complex of moral and practical problems, such as establishing group rights in heterogeneous populations.[11] It becomes unnecessary to identify and defend the group interests to which Buchanan refers. A group need not possess shared cultural or ethnic attributes, or assert historical claims to territory which they could justify only as a recognized group.

[9]Buchanan, *Secession*, p. 75. He discusses this idea further on pp. 75–80.
[10]See Robert Nozick, *Anarchy, State, and Utopia* (New York: Basic Books, 1974), pp. 96–101.
[11]See Buchanan's comments, *Secession*, pp. 139–43.

The right of secession, as an ethical constraint on any political order, establishes the conditions for actual contracts, because it permits individuals to establish new political arrangements through collective action. The actual contracts made possible by a right of secession promote an ideal of the self-defined political community, which is a variant of the principle of national self-determination. If self-determination applies only to identifiable cultural or ethnic groups, a right of secession that is defined in these terms is a group right, in that individuals may claim to exercise it only by virtue of group membership. If we interpret the right of secession as an individual right, this constraint on its exercise is unnecessary. Where political communities are self-defined by the expressed preferences of their members, their cultural or ethnic characteristics are irrelevant; the value ascribed to existing or proposed institutions by the several individuals is the only significant factor to be taken into account. Self-determination here is the individual's freedom to choose between existing and alternative arrangements. As Mises puts it, "The totality of freedom-minded persons who are intent on forming a state appears as the political union."[12]

As on Mises's analysis, political unity is the other side of the argument from self-determination.[13] A constitutional right of secession is exercised through the expressed preferences of those concerned. If a group opts for secession, its members express their dissatisfaction with existing institutions, and their favorable expectations of the alternative before them. It is quite likely, then, that the seceding group will be highly unified with respect to the procedures and aims of the alternative they choose. Having rid itself of at least some dissidents, moreover, the state that loses some fragment of its population due to secession will likewise be more unified than before. As preferences approach unanimity, of course, the more closely will collective choices on institutions correspond to individual preferences. From this perspective, again, secession promotes self-determination, and is defensible as a value in accordance with normative individualism.

Buchanan suggests that it may be desirable to make secession difficult by imposing special taxes on a seceding group or requiring extremely large majorities in favor of secession, because a society may have good reasons for opposing a particular act of secession.[14] I examine and criticize these in the next section. On the

---

[12]Ludwig von Mises, *Nation, State, and Economy*, Leland B. Yeager, trans. (New York: New York University Press, 1983), p. 34.

[13]Ibid., pp. 36–37.

[14]Buchanan, *Secession*, pp. 132–39.

basis of the argument so far, however, it is clear that no special difficulties should be placed in the way of a group who wishes to secede. Indeed, the individualist conception of the value of political order and the ideal of the self-defined polity suggest that it would be unjust to hedge about a constitutional provision for secession with obstacles the purpose of which is to make the right difficult to exercise. Procedural barriers to secession should, in principle, be no greater to secession than to other types of constitutional changes or legislative acts. Provisions for initiative to propose an act of secession should, then, be no more difficult than those currently in effect to propose constitutional amendments in the American states that allow for initiative. A referendum in which a three-fifths, two-thirds, or simple majority of citizens vote for secession should be sufficient for enactment.

A Limited Right

Ethical limits on the right of secession are part of the moral input associated with the right's justification, and are established in the same manner as the right itself. The seceding group must be capable of forming a viable state; the contractualist standard would allow anyone to reject an act of secession which would subject individuals to an inviable and thus useless state. The population of a seceding group must be large enough to support institutions that perform the fundamental governing functions of rule-making, enforcement, and adjudication. The newly-created state must be capable of penetrating the entire territory it will claim, otherwise individuals could claim that their property and liberty will not be adequately protected. Whether it must be shown that the new state can defend itself against external aggression is an entirely different matter. International affairs are rather unpredictable, and it is conceivable that almost any state might at some point be threatened by more powerful adversaries. Certainly a state must be able to defend itself to be viable and thus useful to individuals. It is difficult, however, to imagine how one could formulate a general constitutional principle that could be applied to all cases. The relative power and expected intentions of a state's neighbors are not good guides because these are subject to change. Moreover, states show a poor record of defending themselves. Aggressor states have won 69.2 percent of the international wars involving major powers over the last two centuries.[15] Given this record, it is unreasonable to

---

[15]Kevin Wong and James Lee Ray, "The Initiation and Outcome of International Wars Involving Great Powers" (paper presented to the International Studies Association Convention, Washington, D.C., April 1990).

demand that secessionists show they can provide an ironclad defense of their territory. Because of the greater unpredictability of international as opposed to domestic affairs, and the unimpressive performance of states in defense matters, the requirements for demonstrating this aspect of viability should not be too stringent. Provided the secessionists are capable of raising revenue to support defensive forces, or maintaining diplomatic institutions to form defense agreements with other states, they can legitimately claim viability.

Proposed or expected economic policies are the basis for a second limit on the right of secession. Socialism is ruled out as an alternative, and this exclusion can be reduced in part to the viability requirement. As Mises demonstrated, rational economic calculation is impossible under socialism.[16] In light of this theoretical critique and the subsequent failure of socialist economies, anyone could reasonably reject being made subject to a socialist state on account of its known inviability. The contractualist standard, however, also eliminates many forms of market intervention. Individuals have reason to support a social and political order only if it permits them to pursue their own plans and projects. Anyone could reasonably refuse their assent to rules that prohibit or otherwise render impossible the pursuit of goals that would not be excluded by contractualism. Interventionist economic policies that upset individual planning, or prohibit actions that are morally permissible by the contractualist standard, could be reasonably objected to by anyone.[17] Anything other than the unhampered market is an unjust imposition by the state, secessionist or not.[18]

In summary, the right of secession may be defined as follows. First, it is an individual right to engage in collective action for the purpose of secession. There is no need for the seceding group to show that it possesses common ethnic or cultural characteristics. As long as the group follows constitutional procedures, such as those suggested here, it may justly secede. Second, the seceding group must be able to erect a viable political order. Finally, the secessionists must refrain from engaging in unjust forms of market

[16]Ludwig von Mises, *Socialism*, J. Kahane, trans. (Indianapolis: Liberty Fund, 1981).

[17]For an account of interventionism and its effects, see Ludwig von Mises, *Human Action*, 3rd rev. ed. (New York: Henry Regnery, 1966), pp. 716–861.

[18]This is a stronger version of an argument presented by John Gray, who maintains that the liberal neutrality implied by contractualism excludes a socialist economy but does not require laissez faire. See John Gray, *Liberalism* (New York: Routledge, 1989), pp. 161–98. Surely, though, interventionism must fail to be neutral with respect to individuals' plans and projects, even if as an unintended consequence.

intervention. These are the demands of a just constitutional right of secession. In the next section, I examine and criticize additional limits on the right proposed by Allen Buchanan.

DEFENDING THE RIGHT OF SECESSION

The limits on the right of secession give citizens of a prospective secessionist state grounds for objection. The following objections would be lodged by the remainder state or its citizens. Buchanan discusses each of these and grants them a moral weight that justifies limiting the right of secession further than I have thus far. I shall argue that these objections are without merit, and that the only limits on the right of secession are those discussed in the previous section. Though the right of secession is a limited one, it is much less limited than Buchanan believes.

Secession and State Property

Buchanan argues that secessionists ought to compensate the remainder state for its loss of property and investment in the seceding territory, and that failure to make such an offer provides grounds for resisting an act of secession.[19] This is indeed a tangled problem, but it is by no means clear that secessionists must compensate anyone. If public expenditure is universally beneficial prior to an act of secession, it need not be the case that citizens of the remainder state are to be deprived of its benefits afterwards. A highway system, for example, may facilitate trade in both pre- and post-secession periods. If a public facility or construction project benefits an entire group prior to an act of secession, there is no obvious reason why it will fail to do so afterward. The justification for such appropriations is that they promote productivity and economic growth. The remainder state, then, would be deprived of benefits only if the secessionists close their market to the former. Since the right of secession is limited by the claims of property and the market, the secessionists are precluded from cutting off the free exchange which, in this case, would enable citizens of the remainder state to benefit from these public expenditures.

Actual states, of course, do not limit their fiscal decisions to the generally beneficial. Political institutions empowered to appropriate funds for purposes that are not universally beneficial are demonstrably unjust by the contractualist standard; anyone

---

[19]Buchanan, *Secession*, pp. 104–6.

may reasonably reject rules which allow some to benefit at others' expense. Pork-barrel projects are not only wasteful, but unjust as well. Unless it can be shown that the secessionists themselves are responsible for unjust public expenditures from which they have benefited, no compensation is necessary. Pork and logrolling are games played by politicians subject to the pressures of a political system that establishes the game. In the politicians' view, the game is positive-sum, since they benefit through vote trading and claiming to get their constituents a "fair share" of public booty. From the citizens' perspective, it is a prisoner's-dilemma game in which there is no rational incentive to refuse exploitative benefits, and all are worse off as a result. Unless the secessionists themselves can be assigned responsibility for this situation, they owe no compensation.

The "Threat" of Strategic Bargaining

Buchanan suggests that the threat of secession as an instrument of strategic bargaining justifies limiting the right by requiring extremely large majorities (e.g., three-fourths) or a special secession tax.

> In conditions in which the majority views secession by a group G as a prohibitive cost, G's threat to secede can in effect serve as a veto. G can use the *threat* of secession to ensure that the majority's will does not prevail, even when the majority's decision would respect constitutional limits.[20]

In light of normative individualism, majority rule is valuable only insofar as it provides a useful means for collective decision; it has no intrinsic value whatever. If a minority is so intensely opposed to a majority view that they are willing to secede, there is no legitimate interest in majority rule that justifies limiting the right of secession. The fact that a majority wishes to impose its position on a recalcitrant minority does not morally privilege the majority. Here again, the right to secede appears as a way to limit public power, and since anyone could expect to be in the minority at some point, anyone could reasonably reject restrictions of the right to secede which impose high costs on those wishing to escape a majority hostile to their interests.

Territorial Sovereignty

The violation of a state's territorial sovereignty is a *prima facie* objection to an act of secession. Buchanan defines territorial sovereignty as a

[20]Ibid., p. 100.

relationship among the state (the agent), the territory, and the
people (the principal), with the state acting on the people's
behalf to preserve the territory not only for the present but
for future generations as well. Territorial sovereignty is best
understood as a set of *jurisdictional* powers over territory,
conferred upon the state.[21]

Buchanan's definition suggests that the state's jurisdictional
powers are conferred upon it by the people. He argues, then, that
a withdrawal of consent can "demonstrate the conditions under
which the state no longer has authority over people," but that it
"cannot show when the state no longer has control over territory."[22] It is plain, though, that the state's territorial claim must
be dependent on persons, rather than on territory. Its jurisdictional powers obviously cannot be conferred by the territory itself.
Buchanan continues:

> A sound justification for secession has two territorial com-
> ponents: an argument to show that the state either never had
> or had but has lost territorial sovereignty over the seceding
> land, and an argument to show that the seceding group either
> has had or ought now to have territorial sovereignty.[23]

As Buchanan recognizes, the simple fact that nearly all actual states were created through conquest puts their territorial
claims on shaky moral ground, though he suggests that a "moral
statute of limitations" seems to "favor adopting a convention
that accords substantial weight to existing boundaries."[24] Even if,
however, we absolve a state of past injustices committed by officials no longer among us, it is not clear why we should adopt
Buchanan's convention as a reason to limit the right of secession.
An act of secession is an explicit rejection of the state's jurisdictional powers. Once most of the people in some portion of a state's
territory (who meet the criteria previously enumerated) have
shown, by wishing to secede, that they disvalue the state, it has
lost its claim over that piece of territory. The state's territorial
claim has no meaning, and hence no validity, apart from the value ascribed to it by citizens.

Buchanan muddies the waters considerably by invoking other moral questions concerning whether the seceding group can lay
claim to the territory. He argues that they must show that they
have been targeted by the state for unjust treatment not directed
against other groups, and that the other groups have not come to

[21]Ibid., p. 108, emphasis in original.
[22]Ibid., p. 73.
[23]Ibid., p. 113.
[24]Ibid., p. 110.

the aid of the group discriminated against. If everyone is unjustly treated, or if other groups try to help the victimized one, secession is not legitimate because it is government officials, not the people at large, who are responsible for the acts which justify secession.[25] Secession, however, is not an act of punishment; it falls in the category of procedural rather than rectificatory justice. Those who secede are punishing neither their former state nor its citizens; they are simply expressing their desire to govern themselves. This preference for self-government is the only significant issue, once the limitations discussed earlier are taken into account. That other groups are treated unjustly, or come to their aid, need not give the secessionists reason to ascribe value to the state they are trying to leave. No matter the disposition of other groups, the right of self-government under liberty, that is, the right of secession, cannot be justly opposed.

Judging Alternatives to Secession

A final issue to consider is whether the alternative constitutional provisions of nullification or group veto (Calhoun's concurrent majorities principle) are suitable replacements for a right of secession. If they are, a right of secession is not an essential element of a just constitution, provided one of these alternatives is in place. Buchanan suggests three criteria for weighing the alternatives: the independence the right offers its bearer, the strategic bargaining value of the right, and the disruption which the exercise of the right presents to others. On the first two criteria, secession ranks higher than group veto and nullification, because it grants greater independence and strategic value to its bearer. On the third criterion, the rights of nullification and group veto are ranked over secession because secession causes greater disruption in the remainder state's affairs. Buchanan argues that the choice among the three rights is indeterminate because differing circumstances affect how heavily we should weight the three criteria (e.g., how disruptive an act of secession will prove). Consequently, there is no sure means of deciding whether a right of secession must be part of a just constitution.[26]

If we can weight the criteria, however, they yield a determinate ranking. The criteria of independence and strategic value are lexically prior to that of disruption, because normative individualism morally permits individuals to afford greater weight to their own plans and projects than to those of others. A ranking

---

[25]Ibid., pp. 111–14.
[26]Ibid., pp. 143–48.

that failed to grant priority to independence and strategic value would lock individuals into a political order they disvalue, and this is what contractualism enables them to reject. Since the criteria of independence and strategic value are prior to that of disruption, the ranking they yield is determinate. Secession is ranked over group veto and nullification, so the latter are not suitable replacements for a constitutional right of secession.

4

NATIONS BY CONSENT: DECOMPOSING THE NATION-STATE

Murray N. Rothbard

L ibertarians tend to focus on two important units of analysis: the individual and the state. And yet, one of the most dramatic and significant events of our time has been the re-emergence—with a bang—in the last few years of a third and much-neglected aspect of the real world, the "nation." When the nation has been thought of at all, it usually comes attached to the state, as in the common word nation-state, but this concept takes a particular development of recent centuries and elaborates it into a universal maxim. In recent years, however, we have seen, as a corollary of the collapse of communism in the Soviet Union and in Eastern Europe, a vivid and startlingly swift decomposition of the centralized state or alleged nation-state into its constituent nationalities. The genuine nation, or nationality, has made a dramatic re-appearance on the world stage.

THE RE-EMERGENCE OF THE NATION

The nation, of course, is not the same thing as the state, a difference that earlier libertarians and classical liberals, such as Ludwig von Mises and Albert Jay Nock, understood full well. Contemporary libertarians often assume, mistakenly, that individuals are bound to each other only by the nexus of market exchange. They forget that everyone is necessarily born into a family, a language, and a culture. Every person is born into one or several overlapping communities, usually including an ethnic group, with specific values, cultures, religious beliefs, and traditions. He is generally born into a country; he is always born into a specific historical context of time and place, meaning neighborhood and land area.

The modern European nation-state, the typical major power, began not as a nation at all, but as an imperial conquest of one nationality—usually at the center of the resulting country, and based in the capital city—over other nationalities at the periphery. Since a nation is a complex of subjective feelings of nationality based on objective realities, the imperial central states have had varying degrees of success in forging among their subject nationalities at the periphery a sense of national unity incorporating submission to the imperial center. In Great Britain, the

English have never truly eradicated national aspirations among the submerged Celtic nationalities, the Scots and the Welsh, although Cornish nationalism seems to have been mostly stamped out. In Spain, the conquering Castilians, based in Madrid, have never managed—as the world saw at the Barcelona Olympics—to erase nationalism among the Catalans, the Basques, or even the Galicians or Andalusians. The French, moving out from their base in Paris, have never totally tamed the Bretons, the Basques, or the people of the Languedoc.

It is now well known that the collapse of the centralizing and imperial Russian Soviet Union has lifted the lid on the dozens of previously suppressed nationalisms within the former U.S.S.R., and it is now becoming clear that Russia itself, or rather the Russian Federated Republic, is simply a slightly older imperial formation in which the Russians, moving out from their Moscow center, forcibly incorporated many nationalities including the Tartars, the Yakuts, and the Chechens. Much of the U.S.S.R. stemmed from imperial Russian conquest in the nineteenth century, during which the clashing Russians and British managed to carve up much of central Asia.

The nation cannot be precisely defined, since it is a complex and varying constellation of different forms of communities, languages, ethnic groups, and religions. Some nations or nationalities, such as the Slovenes, are both a separate ethnic group and a language; others, such as the warring groups in Bosnia, are the same ethnic group whose language is the same but who differ in the form of alphabet, and who clash fiercely on religion (the Eastern Orthodox Serbs, the Catholic Croats, and the Bosnian Muslims, who, to make matters more complicated, were originally champions of the Manichaean Bogomil heresy).

The question of nationality is made more complex by the interplay of objectively existing reality and subjective perceptions. In some cases, such as Eastern European nationalities under the Habsburgs or the Irish under the British, nationalisms, including submerged and sometimes dying languages, had to be consciously preserved, generated, and expanded. In the nineteenth century, this was done by a determined intellectual elite, struggling to revive peripheries living under, and partially absorbed by, the imperial center.

THE FALLACY OF "COLLECTIVE SECURITY"

The problem of the nation has been aggravated in the twentieth century by the overriding influence of Wilsonianism on U.S.

and world-wide foreign policy. I refer not to the idea of national self-determination, observed mainly in the breach after World War I, but to the concept of collective security against aggression. The fatal flaw in this seductive concept is that it treats nation-states by an analogy with individual aggressors, with the world community in the guise of a cop-on-the-corner. The cop, for example, sees A aggressing against, or stealing the property of, B; the cop naturally rushes to defend B's private property, in his person or possessions. In the same way, wars between two nations or states are assumed to have a similar aspect: State A invades, or aggresses against, State B; State A is promptly designated the aggressor by the international policeman or his presumptive surrogate, be it the League of Nations, the United Nations, the U.S. President or Secretary of State, or the editorial writer of the august *New York Times*. Then the world police force, whatever it may be, is supposed to swing promptly into action to stop the principle of aggression, or to prevent the aggressor, be it Saddam Hussein or the Serbian guerrillas in Bosnia, from fulfilling their presumed goals of swimming across the Atlantic and murdering every resident of New York City or Washington, D.C.

A crucial flaw in this popular line of argument goes deeper than the usual discussion of whether or not American air power or troops can really eradicate Iraqis or Serbs without too much difficulty. The crucial flaw is the implicit assumption of the entire analysis: that every nation-state *owns* its entire geographical area in the same just and proper way that every individual property owner owns his person and the property that he has inherited, worked for, or gained in voluntary exchange. Is the boundary of the typical nation-state really as just or as beyond cavil as your or my house, estate, or factory?

It seems to me that not only the classical liberal or the libertarian, but anyone of good sense who thinks about this problem, must answer a resounding "No." It is absurd to designate every nation-state, with its self-proclaimed boundary as it exists at any one time, as somehow right and sacrosanct, each with its territorial integrity to remain as spotless and unbreached as your or my bodily person or private property. Invariably, of course, these boundaries have been acquired by force and violence, or by inter-state agreement above and beyond the heads of the inhabitants on the spot, and invariably these boundaries shift a great deal over time in ways that make proclamations of territorial integrity truly ludicrous.

Take, for example, the current mess in Bosnia. Only a few years ago, Establishment Opinion, Received Opinion of the Left,

Right, or Center, loudly proclaimed the importance of maintaining the territorial integrity of Yugoslavia, and bitterly denounced all secession movements. Now, only a short time later,
the same Establishment, only recently defending the Serbs as
champions of the Yugoslav nation against vicious secessionist
movements trying to destroy that integrity, now reviles and
wishes to crush the Serbs for aggression against the territorial
integrity of Bosnia or Bosnia-Herzegovina, a trumped-up nation
that had no more existence before 1991 than does the "nation of
Nebraska." But these are the pitfalls in which we are bound to
fall if we remain trapped by the mythology of the nation-state
whose chance boundary at a given time must be upheld as a prop-
erty-owning entity with its own sacred and inviolable rights, in
a deeply flawed analogy with the rights of private property.

To adopt an excellent strategem of Ludwig von Mises in ab-
stracting from contemporary emotions, let us postulate two contiguous nation-states, Ruritania and Fredonia. Let us assume that
Ruritania has suddenly invaded eastern Fredonia, and claims
the area as its own. Must we automatically condemn Ruritania
for its evil act of aggression against Fredonia, and send troops,
either literally or metaphorically, against the brutal Ruritan-
ians and in behalf of brave, little Fredonia? By no means is this
necessarily the case. For it is very possible that, say, two years
ago, eastern Fredonia had been part and parcel of Ruritania, was
indeed western Ruritania, and that the Rurs, ethnic and national
denizens of the land, have been crying out for the past two years
against Fredonian oppression. In short, in international disputes
in particular, in the immortal words of W. S. Gilbert:

> Things are seldom what they seem,
> Skim milk masquerades as cream.

The beloved international cop, whether it be Boutros Boutros-
Ghali or U.S. troops or the *New York Times* editorialist, had
best think more than twice before leaping into the fray.

Americans are especially unsuited for their self-proclaimed
Wilsonian role as world moralists and policemen. Nationalism
in the U.S. is peculiarly recent, and is more of an idea than it is
rooted in long-standing ethnic or nationality groups or struggles.
Add to that deadly mix the fact that Americans have virtually
no historical memory, and this makes Americans peculiarly unsuited to barreling in to intervene in the Balkans, where who
took what side at what place in the war against the Turkish
invaders in the fifteenth century is far more intensely real to
most of the contenders than is yesterday's dinner.

Libertarians and classical liberals, who, in particular, are well-equipped to rethink the entire muddled area of the nation-state and foreign affairs, have been too wrapped up in the Cold War against communism and the Soviet Union to engage in fundamental thinking on these issues. Now that the Soviet Union has collapsed and the Cold War is over, perhaps classical liberals will feel free to think anew about these critically important problems.

RETHINKING SECESSION

First, we can conclude that not all state boundaries are just. One goal for libertarians should be to transform existing nation-states into national entities whose boundaries could be called just, in the same sense that private property boundaries are just; that is, to decompose existing coercive nation-states into genuine nations, or nations by consent.

In the case, for example, of the eastern Fredonians, the inhabitants should be able to secede voluntarily from Fredonia and join their comrades in Ruritania. Again, classical liberals should resist the impulse to say that national boundaries "don't make any difference." It's true, of course, as classical liberals have long proclaimed, that the less the degree of government intervention in either Fredonia or Ruritania, the less difference such a boundary will make. But even under a minimal state, national boundaries would still make a difference, often a big one to the inhabitants of the area. For *in what language*—Ruritanian or Fredonian or both?—will be the street signs, telephone books, court proceedings, or school classes of the area?

In short, every group, every nationality, should be allowed to secede from any nation-state and to join any other nation-state that agrees to have it. That simple reform would go a long way toward establishing nations by consent. The Scots, if they want to, should be allowed by the English to leave the United Kingdom, and to become independent, and even to join a Gaelic Confederation, if the constituents so desire.

A common response to a world of proliferating nations is to worry about the multitude of trade barriers that might be erected. But, other things being equal, the greater the number of new nations, and the smaller the size of each, the better. For it would be far more difficult to sow the illusion of self-sufficiency if the slogan were "Buy North Dakotan" or even "Buy 56th Street" than it now is to convince the public to "Buy American." Similarly, "Down with South Dakota," or *a fortiori*, "Down with

55th Street," would be a more difficult sell than spreading fear or hatred of the Japanese. Similarly, the absurdities and the unfortunate consequences of fiat paper money would be far more evident if each province or each neighborhood or street block were to print its own currency. A more decentralized world would be far more likely to turn to sound market commodities, such as gold or silver, for its money.

THE PURE ANARCHO-CAPITALIST MODEL

I raise the pure anarcho-capitalist model in this paper not so much to advocate the model *per se* as to propose it as a guide for settling vexed current disputes about nationality. The pure model, simply, is that no land areas, no square footage in the world, shall remain "public"; every square foot of land area, be it part of a street, square, or neighborhood, is privatized. Total privatization would help solve nationality problems, often in surprising ways, so I suggest that existing states, or classical-liberal states, try to approach such a system even while some land areas remain in the governmental sphere.

Open Borders, or the Camp-of-the-Saints Problem

The question of open borders, or free immigration, has become an accelerating problem for classical liberals. This is, first, because the welfare state increasingly subsidizes immigrants to enter and receive permanent assistance, and second, because cultural boundaries have become increasingly swamped. I began to rethink my views on immigration when, as the Soviet Union collapsed, it became clear that ethnic Russians had been encouraged to flood into Estonia and Latvia in order to destroy the cultures and languages of these peoples. Previously, it had been easy to dismiss as unrealistic Jean Raspail's anti-immigration novel *The Camp of the Saints,* in which virtually the entire population of India decides to move, in small boats, into France, and the French, infected by liberal ideology, cannot summon the will to prevent economic and cultural national destruction. As cultural and welfare-state problems have intensified, it has become impossible to dismiss Raspail's concerns any longer.

However, on rethinking immigration on the basis of the anarcho-capitalist model, it became clear to me that a totally privatized country would not have open borders at all. If every piece of land in a country were owned by some person, group, or corporation, this would mean that no immigrant could enter there unless invited to enter and allowed to rent, or purchase, property.

A totally privatized country would be as closed as the particular inhabitants and property owners desire. It seems clear, then, that the regime of open borders that exists *de facto* in the U.S. really amounts to a compulsory opening by the central state, the state in charge of all streets and public land areas, and does not genuinely reflect the wishes of the proprietors.

Under total privatization, many local conflicts and external- ity problems—not merely the immigration problem—would be neatly settled. With every locale and neighborhood owned by private firms, corporations, or contractual communities, a true di- versity would reign, according to the preferences of each commu- nity. Some neighborhoods would be ethnically or economically diverse, while others would be ethnically or economically homo- geneous. Some localities would permit pornography or prostitu- tion or drugs or abortions, while others would prohibit any or all of them. The prohibitions would not be state imposed, but would simply be requirements for residence or for use of some person's or community's land area. While statists, who have the itch to im- pose their values on everyone else, would be disappointed, every group or interest would at least have the satisfaction of living in neighborhoods of people who share its values and preferences. While neighborhood ownership would not provide Utopia or a panacea for all conflicts, it would at least provide a second-best solution that most people might be willing to live with.

Enclaves and Exclaves

One obvious problem with the secession of nationalities from centralized states concerns mixed areas, or enclaves and exclaves. Decomposing the swollen central nation-state of Yugoslavia into constituent parts has solved many conflicts by providing inde- pendent nationhood for Slovenes, Serbs, and Croats, but what about Bosnia, where many towns and villages are mixed? One solution is to encourage more of the same, through still more de- centralization. If, for example, eastern Sarajevo is Serb and west- ern Sarajevo is Muslim, then they become parts of their respec- tive separate nations.

But this of course will result in a large number of enclaves, parts of nations surrounded by other nations. How can this be solved? In the first place, the enclave/exclave problem exists right now. One of the most vicious existing conflicts, in which the U.S. has not yet meddled because it has not yet been shown on CNN, is the problem of Nagorno-Karabakh, an Armenian ex- clave totally surrounded by, and therefore formally within, Az- erbaijan. Nagorno-Karabakh should clearly be part of Armenia.

But how, then, will Armenians of Karabakh avoid their present fate of blockade by Azeris, and how will they avoid military battles in trying to keep open a land corridor to Armenia?

Under total privatization, of course, these problems would disappear. Nowadays, no one in the U.S. buys land without making sure that his title to the land is clear; in the same way, in a fully privatized world, access rights would obviously be a crucial part of land ownership. In such a world, then, Karabakh property owners would make sure that they had purchased access rights through an Azeri land corridor.

Decentralization also provides a workable solution for the seemingly insoluble permanent conflict in Northern Ireland. When the British partitioned Ireland in the early 1920s, they agreed to perform a second, more micro-managed partition, but they never carried through on this promise. If the British would permit a detailed parish-by-parish partition vote in Northern Ireland, most of the population, which has a Catholic majority, would probably hive off and join the Republic, including such counties as Tyrone and Fermanagh, southern Down, and southern Armagh, for example. The Protestants would likely be left with Belfast, county Antrim, and other areas north of Belfast. The major remaining problem would be the Catholic enclave within the city of Belfast, but again, an approach to the anarcho-capitalist model could be attained by permitting the purchase of access rights to the enclave.

Pending total privatization, it is clear that our model could be approached, and conflicts minimized, by permitting secessions and local control down to the micro-neighborhood level, and by developing contractual access rights for enclaves and exclaves. In the U.S., it becomes important, in moving toward such radical decentralization, for libertarians and classical liberals—indeed, for many other minority or dissident groups—to begin to lay the greatest stress on the forgotten Tenth Amendment and to try to decompose the role and power of the centralizing Supreme Court. Rather than trying to get people of one's own ideological persuasion on the Supreme Court, its power should be rolled back and minimized as far as possible, and its power decomposed into state, or even local, judicial bodies.

Citizenship and Voting Rights

One vexing current problem centers on who becomes the citizen of a given country, since citizenship confers voting rights.

The Anglo–American model, in which every baby born in the country's land area automatically becomes a citizen, clearly invites welfare immigration by expectant parents. In the U.S., for example, a current problem is illegal immigrants whose babies, if born on American soil, automatically become citizens and therefore entitle themselves and their parents to permanent welfare payments and free medical care. Clearly, the French system, in which one has to be born to a citizen to become an automatic citizen, is far closer to the idea of a nation-by-consent.

It is also important to rethink the entire concept and function of voting. Should anyone have a "right" to vote? Rose Wilder Lane, the mid-twentieth-century U.S. libertarian theorist, was once asked if she believed in women's suffrage. "No," she replied, "and I'm against male suffrage as well." The Latvians and Estonians have cogently tackled the problem of Russian immigrants by allowing them to continue permanently as residents, but not granting them citizenship or therefore the right to vote. The Swiss welcome temporary guest-workers, but severely discourage permanent immigration, and, *a fortiori*, citizenship and voting.

Let us turn for enlightenment, once again, to the anarcho-capitalist model. What would voting be like in a totally privatized society? Not only would voting be diverse, but more importantly, who would really care? Probably the most deeply satisfying form of voting to an economist is the corporation, or joint-stock company, in which voting is proportionate to one's share of ownership of the firm's assets. But also there are, and would be, a myriad of private clubs of all sorts. It is usually assumed that club decisions are made on the basis of one vote per member, but that is generally untrue. Undoubtedly, the best-run and most pleasant clubs are those run by a small, self-perpetuating oligarchy of the ablest and most interested, a system most pleasant for the rank-and-file non-voting member as well as for the elite. If I am a rank-and-file member of, say, a chess club, why should I worry about voting if I am satisfied with the way the club is run? And if I am interested in running things, I would probably be asked to join the ruling elite by the grateful oligarchy, always on the lookout for energetic members. And finally, if I am unhappy about the way the club is run, I can readily quit and join another club, or even form one of my own. That, of course, is one of the great virtues of a free and privatized society, whether we are considering a chess club or a contractual neighborhood community.

Clearly, as we begin to work toward the pure model, as more and more areas and parts of life become either privatized or micro-decentralized, the less important voting will become. Of course, we are a long way from this goal. But it is important to begin, and particularly to change our political culture, which treats democracy, or the right to vote, as the supreme political good. In fact, the voting process should be considered trivial and unimportant at best, and never a right, apart from a possible mechanism stemming from a consensual contract. In the modern world, democracy or voting is only important either to join in or ratify the use of the government to control others, or to use it as a way of preventing one's self or one's group from being controlled. However, voting is, at best, an inefficient instrument for self-defense, and it is far better to replace it by breaking up central government power altogether.

In sum, if we proceed with the decomposition and decentralization of the modern centralizing and coercive nation-state, deconstructing that state into constituent nationalities and neighborhoods, we shall at one and the same time reduce the scope of government power, the scope and importance of voting, and the extent of social conflict. The scope of private contract, and of voluntary consent, will be enhanced, and the brutal and repressive state will be gradually dissolved into a harmonious and increasingly prosperous social order.

5
SECESSION: THE LAST, BEST BULWARK OF OUR LIBERTIES

Clyde N. Wilson

What might have been and what has been
Point to one end, which is always present.
– T.S. Eliot, "Burnt Norton"

I am convinced 'twas Calhoun who divined
How the great western star's last race would run.
– Allen Tate, "Fragments of a Meditation"

My subject is our lost and stolen heritage of states' rights; my goal is to point out a few home truths that were clear to our Founders and forefathers but that we have lost. Just a few years ago, we had a bicentennial celebration of the Constitution. As far as I am aware, republicanism and federalism, the two most salient features of the Constitution, were never mentioned. Instead, we had a glorification of multiculturalism.

Federalism implies states' rights, and states' rights imply a right of secession. The cause of states' rights is the cause of liberty; they rise or fall together. If we had been able to maintain the real union of sovereign states founded by our forefathers, then there would not be, could not be, the imperial central state that we suffer under today. The loss of states' rights is mirrored by the rise of the American empire, where a vast proportion of the citizens' wealth is engrossed by bureaucracy; where our personal and local affairs are ever more minutely and inflexibly managed by a remote power; where our resources are squandered meddling in the affairs of distant peoples.

That happy old Union was a friendly contract—the states managing their own affairs, joining together in matters of defense, and enjoying free trade among themselves, and indeed, enjoying free trade with the world, because the Constitution, as is sometimes forgotten, required all taxes to be uniform throughout the Union and absolutely forbade taxation of the exports of any state. The federal government was empowered to lay a modest customs duty to raise revenue for its limited tasks, but otherwise had no power to restrict or assist enterprises.

That is what the States United meant to our Founders—a happy Union of mutual consent and support. It did not mean a government that dictated the arrangement of every parking lot in every public and private building in every town, and the kind of grass that a citizen must plant around his boat dock. It did not mean the incineration of women and children who might have aroused the ire of a rogue federal police force, unknown to the Constitution and armed as for a foreign enemy. It did not mean that billions would be spent (as in Kuwait) restoring an oriental despot to his throne; or that a hero would be made out of the successful general who killed more women, children, soldiers trying to surrender, and his own men than he did armed enemies. Had George Washington been confronted with these things, he would have reached for his sword.

The founding fathers knew that republican societies were fragile—that they tended to degenerate into empires if extended beyond a small state, though they hoped the federal principle would block this tendency in America. Their definition of self-government was the superiority of the community to its rulers. In a reversal of the age-old pattern of mankind, the rulers (a necessary evil) became delegates of the community temporarily assigned to take care of some part of the public business. In an empire, like the one from which they had seceded, the community existed for the support and gratification of the rulers. A republican America was to be governed in the interest of the communities that made it up; its rulers were "responsible." An empire, to the contrary, was governed by the needs, ideas, interests, even whims, of the rulers. A republic passes over into empire when political activity is no longer directed toward the well-being of the people (mostly by leaving them alone), but becomes a mechanism for managing people for the benefit of their rulers. That is to say, an empire's government reflects management needs, and reflects the desires and will of those who control the machinery, rather than the interests and will of those being governed. Who can doubt that we are now an empire? The American people no longer think of the government as theirs, but as a hostile, manipulative, unjust, and unresponsive distant ruler.

A republic goes to war to defend itself and its vital interests, including possibly its honor. Empires go to war because going to war is one of the things irresponsible rulers do. The point of reference for a republic is its own well-being. An empire has no point of reference except expansion of its authority. Its foreign policy will be abstract, and will reflect on the vagaries of mind of the rulers, who might, for instance, proclaim that it is their subjects' duty to establish a New World Order, whatever the cost to their own blood and treasure. Who can doubt that the once-proud republican Union of the states is now an empire?

An empire contains not free citizens, but subjects, interchangeable persons having no intrinsic value except as taxpayers and cannon fodder. So, if the governors of an empire should feel that it is easier for them to placate criminals than to punish them, they will turn over the neighborhoods and schools of their subjects to criminals, and even punish officers of the law for acting too zealously against the criminal class, thus violating the first rule of good government, which is the preservation of order. A people's culture may be changed by imperial edict to reflect a trumped-up multiculturalism (a sure sign of an empire), or their religion persecuted. And, of course, violating one of the essential rules of republicanism, that the laws be equal to all, the imperialists exempt themselves from the commands they lay down for the rest of us. The republican right of self-government and the right of self-determination both necessarily incorporate the right of secession—that a people may withdraw from an imperial power to defend its liberty, property, culture, and faith.

We know the problems. Where should we look for solutions? Changing the personnel of the White House, the Congress, and the Supreme Court has been of little avail. Thomas Jefferson gives us the answer: our most ancient and best tradition, states' rights. In his first inaugural address, Jefferson remarked that in most ways Americans were very happily situated, and then asked:

> What more is necessary to make us a happy and prosperous people? Still one thing more, fellow citizens—a wise and frugal government, which shall restrain men from injuring one another, which shall leave them otherwise free to regulate their own pursuits . . . and shall not take from the mouth of labor the bread that it has earned. This is the sum of good government.[1]

But how to preserve this form of government? What should we do, or not do? Jefferson answered: preserve elections (not the party system), maintain equal justice under the law, rely on the militia, avoid debt, maintain the freedoms of speech, religion, and trial by jury, and avoid entangling alliances. And most important: "the support of the state governments in all their rights, as the most competent administrations for our domestic concerns and the surest bulwarks against anti-republican tendencies."[2]

---

[1]*The Life and Selected Writings of Thomas Jefferson*, Adrienne Koch and William Peden, eds. (New York: Modern Library, 1944), pp. 323–24.
[2]Ibid.

There is a large sophistical literature which tells us that states' rights was for Jefferson just a temporary expedient for other goals. This is false. For his own generation and several following, it was understood that the state sovereignty of the Kentucky resolutions was Jefferson's primary platform as an American leader.

John C. Calhoun, speaking in exactly the same tradition a generation later, said:

> The question is in truth between the people and the supreme court. We contend, that the great conservative principle of our system is in the people of the States, as parties to the Constitutional compact, and our opponents that it is in the supreme court. . . . Without a full practical recognition of the rights and sovereignty of the States, our union and liberty must perish. . . . State rights would be found . . . in all cases of difficulty and danger [to be] the only conservative principle in the system, the only one that could interpose an effectual check to the danger.[3]

By conservative principle he means not a political position of right as opposed to left—he means that which conserves and preserves the Constitution as it was intended. Contrast that with our present position. Forrest McDonald, our greatest living Constitutional scholar, writes:

> Political scientists and historians are in agreement that federalism is the greatest contribution of the Founding Fathers to the science of government. It is also the only feature of the Constitution that has been successfully exported, that can be employed to protect liberty elsewhere in the world. Yet what we invented, and others imitate, no longer exists on its native shores.[4]

Why are states' rights the last best bulwark of our liberties? It is a question of the sovereignty of the people—in which we all profess to believe. Every political community has a sovereign, an ultimate authority. The sovereign may delegate functions (as the states did to the federal government) though it may not alienate authority. It may not always rule from day to day, but it is that place in the society that has the last word when all else is said and done.

All agree that in America the people are sovereign—we are republicans, not monarchists or aristocrats. But what people?

[3]*The Essential Calhoun*, Clyde N. Wilson, ed. (New Brunswick, N.J.: Transaction, 1992), pp. 299–302.

[4]Forrest McDonald, "Federalism in America," in *Requiem: Variations on Eighteenth Century Themes*, Forrest McDonald, ed. (Lawrence: University Press of Kansas, 1989).

The term is not self-defining, any more than is the term liberty. What do we mean by the people? How do we know when the people have spoken? A simple electoral majority, which can shift the next day, is insufficient in bottom-line questions of sovereignty. By people, do we mean that if a million Chinese wade ashore in California and out vote everybody else, then they are sovereign? I think not.

In American terms, the government of the people can only mean the people of the states as living, historical, corporate, indestructible, political communities. The whole of the Constitution rests upon its acceptance by the people acting through their states. The whole of the government reflects this by the representation of the states in every legitimate proceeding. There is no place in the Constitution as originally understood where a mere numerical majority in some branch of the federal government can do as it pleases. The sovereign power resides, ultimately, in the people of the states. Even today, three-fourths of the states can amend the Constitution—that is, they can abolish the Supreme Court or the income tax, or even dissolve the Union. In no other way can we say the sovereign people have spoken their final word. States' rights *is* the American government, however much in abeyance its practice may have become.

The alternative to state sovereignty, as Calhoun pointed out, is to give the final say-so to the black-robed deities of the Court, who go into their closets, commune with the gods, and tell us what *our* Constitution means and what orders we must obey, no matter how absurd their interpretation may be. But this is to abandon the sovereignty of the people, that is, to abandon democracy or republicanism and to abandon constitutional government for oligarchy—and for an oligarchy based upon mystification rather than reason. James Madison, thought to be the Constitution's father, tells us that the meaning of the Constitution is to be sought "not in the opinions or intentions of the body which planned and proposed it, but in those of the state conventions where it received all the authority which it possesses."[5] *All the authority which it possesses!*

The sovereignty of the people, in which we all believe, can mean nothing except, purely and simply, the people of each state acting in their sovereign constitution-making capacity—as they did in the American Revolution when they threw off their king and assumed their own sovereignty, making their own constitutions. This was a revolution in the sense of a transfer of the

[5]James Madison, *Writings of James Madison*, Gaillard Hunt, ed. (New York: G.P. Putnam's Sons, 1900–1910), vol. 9, p. 372.

locus of sovereignty, not in the sense of social upheaval. The people of each state ratified the Constitution as freely consenting sovereigns, agreeing to make an instrument, limited and precise, for some of their common business.

The case of South Carolina is illustrative but not unusual. The people of South Carolina were sovereign and independent before the Declaration of Independence. Through their own governor, legislature, courts, and armed forces they were exercising every sovereign power—taxation, war, treaty-making, and the execution of felons. The week before the Declaration of Independence, Colonel Moultrie and the South Carolina forces, from their palmetto log fort on Sullivan's Island, repulsed and defeated a British fleet that threatened to supress their sovereign self-government.

The question is not altered by the fact that the Union has been expanded to fifty states. The Founding Fathers wisely made the Union expansible. The Congress may *admit* new states (or not), but the federal government does not *create* new states. States create themselves. The federal government may administer the territory, the land, before statehood, but only the sovereign people can adopt a constitution and incorporate themselves into a political society. Only by a sovereign act of free consent can a state ratify the U.S. Constitution—if we believe in government of the people. This is as true of the new states as the old, of Montana as of South Carolina—if we believe the people are sovereign.

Americans are natural republicans, not monarchists or aristocrats. That is, we believe government rests upon consent of the governed—this is the key phrase of the Declaration of Independence. Government is legitimate in just so far as it rests upon consent, that is, the people accede to the government. The opposite of accede is secede—the withdrawal of consent. The right to self-government rests on the right to withdraw consent from an oppressive government. That is the only really effective restriction on power, in the final analysis.

The American Revolution was not seen by our Fathers as a one-time event after which we were bound forever by the government. Of course, they did not wish to encourage so decisive a proceeding as secession for "light and transient causes," but it remained, in the final analysis, an option. Jefferson referred specifically to the "secession" of the colonies from Britain, and he was willing to entertain the idea that in the future there might be two or more confederacies among the Americans (just as there had been many states and confederacies among the freedom-loving Greeks). The point was to preserve the right of self-government. What was sacred was not the Union but the consent of the governed, to which the Union might or might not be of assistance. Jefferson and the other Founders were patriots, not nationalists.

Anyone who has studied, with any degree of depth and honesty, the founding years and the period which followed understands that the idea of states' rights was considered obvious by our forefathers, however wildly irrelevant it may seem today. Centralizers were always on the defensive, and always compelled to conceal their intent. The United States were universally spoken of in the plural. It was clearly understood that the Bill of Rights meant the states binding the federal government to stay out of certain areas. ("Congress shall make no law. . . .") To most people at the time, and for several generations thereafter, the electoral victory of Jefferson and his friends in 1800 meant primarily the putting to rest of a too-assertive idea of national power. General Hamilton was sent home and his schemes of centralization were put to rest, and so it remained until the War Between the States. But even that, though it fatally compromised the idea of states' rights, did not destroy it.

The states'-rights interpretation of the Constitution was not, as its enemies have alleged, a mere theoretical rationalization made up for the defense of slavery. It is, rather, a living heritage of great power, absolutely central to the understanding of the American liberty. It was the fundamental issue of the most bloody war in which Americans have been involved. Lost and stolen as the idea may be, American history cannot be understood without it.

Alexis de Tocqueville, the French historian thought by many to be the most profound foreign observer of America, wrote this in the 1830s:

> The Union was formed by the voluntary agreement of the states; and these, in uniting together, have not forfeited their nationality, nor have they been reduced to the condition of one and the same people. If one of the states chose to withdraw its name from the contract, it would be difficult to disprove its right to do so.[6]

Tocqueville was merely expressing what everyone already knew.

Lord Acton, the great British historian who devoted his life to the study of liberty and to what was conducive to and inimical

[6]Alexis de Tocqueville, *Democracy in America* (New York: Vintage Books, 1990), vol. 1, pp. 387–88.

to the establishment and preservation of liberty, wrote shortly after the war that the defeat at Appomattox was a greater setback for genuine liberty than Waterloo had been a victory. Waterloo ended an empire; Appomattox established one. Acton wrote also:

> The theory which gave to the people of the states the same right of last resort against Washington as against Great Britain possessed an independent force of its own, northern statesmen of great authority maintained it, its treatment by Calhoun and Stephens forms as essential a constituent in the progress of democratic thinking as Rousseau or Jefferson.[7]

Here is a very simple proposition that our forefathers understood—that indeed governed everything they did. The only way to preserve civil liberty is to check government power. The only way to check power is to disperse and divide it. Some of the Founders hoped that a federal system would allow growth without centralization (or "consolidation" as they called it). This, the main check, has failed. It was also hoped that the division of legislative, executive, and judicial power in the general government would help. Let us be clear—these checks and balances do not work. They ceased to work a long time ago. The Supreme Court does not check the Congress, or the President—it checks us. There is no serious conflict of power among the federal branches. The acts of all of them are directed toward checking the people of the states.

The federal government will never check itself—that is the *raison d'etre* of federalism. It must be checked by the states. And this ultimately is of no avail unless it is backed by the right of secession. Curiously, recognition of the right of secession often obviates its use, because where it is a real possibility, Power is motivated, has incentive, to check itself and be responsible.

Federalism is one of the least understood, both theoretically and practically, of all political forms. The habit of not even thinking about it, as in the Constitution bicentennial, provides a great obstacle, which there are signs today of a tendency to overcome. We must beware of phony forms of top-down federalism that will be invented by cornered politicians. Federalism is not when the central government graciously allows the states to do this or that; that is just another form of administration. True federalism is when the people of the states set limits to the central government.

[7]*Selected Writings of Lord Acton.* J. Rufus Fears, ed. (Indianapolis: Liberty Press, 1985), vol. 1. pp. 170–71, 363.

States' rights has fallen into disuse not because it is unsound in history, in constitutional law, or in democratic theory. It remains highly persuasive on all these grounds to any honest mind. It has fallen into disuse because it presented the most powerful obstacle to the consolidation of irresponsible power—that consolidation which our forefathers decried as the greatest single threat to liberty. For that reason, states' rights had to be covered under a blanket of lies and usurpations by those who thought they could rule us better than we can rule ourselves. At the most critical time, the War Between the States, states' rights was suppressed by force, and the American idea of consent of the governed was replaced by the European idea of obedience. But force can only settle questions of power, not of right.

States' rights are historically sound, constitutionally sound, ethically sound, and sound from the point of view of democracy. Where they fall short is simply in the realm of political will and agenda—the practical effort to implement them. That can change.

The people of the states have a *right* to protect themselves against an out-of-bounds federal government, and to determine when the proper bounds have been passed—or to interpose their sovereignty, as Jefferson said, as Madison said, as Calhoun said. Proclaiming a right, of course, does not make it prevail. For a long time now, a century at least, the course of history has been moving in the direction of consolidation, the gathering of concentrated power in one central, irresponsible, imperial government.

But there is hope. We now see, all over the Western world, a ferment of people against consolidation, in favor of regionalism, devolution, secession, break-up of unnatural states, and the return to historic identities in preference to universal bureaucracies. You know the signs in the break-up of the Soviet Union and Czechoslovakia, and you can see the signs in the secessionist movements in Britain, Italy, Canada, and many other countries.

There is reason to believe that the consolidation phase of history may be coming to an end. We may be ready for a new flowering of freedom for families and communities. We know that the great periods of Western history have been not those of powerful states but of multiple and dispersed sovereignty—flourishing liberty for small communities. We know that such freedom equals creativity in wealth, art, intellect, and every other good thing. And we now have an asset that the Founders did not, the great comprehensive wisdom of Austrian economics, which is federal in its essential spirit. All over the Western world, once again people are thinking of liberty—the most characteristic and unique of Western values—and are doubting the central state that has been worshipped since the French Revolution.

I know there are many moral and social problems that are not solved by political arrangements, and that the level of statesmanship in the states is not much higher, if at all, than in the federal government. But if we are to speak of curbing the central power, the states are what we have got. They exist. They are historical, political, cultural realities, the indestructible bottom line of the American system.

It would be a shame if, in this world-historical time of devolution, Americans did not look back to an ancient and honorable tradition that lies readily at hand. To check power, to return the American empire to republicanism, we do not need to resort to the drastic right of revolution nor to the destructive goal of anarchic individualism. We have in the states ready-made instruments. All that is lacking is the will. Our goal should be the restoration of the real American Union of sovereign states in place of the upstart empire under which we live.

6
REPUBLICANISM, FEDERALISM, AND SECESSION IN THE SOUTH, 1790 TO 1865

Joseph R. Stromberg

REPUBLICANISM IN AMERICAN HISTORY

In recent decades, as historians have come to an enhanced understanding of the importance of republican ideas in American history, the so-called "republican synthesis" has increasingly established itself. In what follows, I hope to describe how republican ideas entered into combination with classical-liberal ideas to create an ideology which gave meaning to American political thought and action, with special emphasis on how republican thought in the southern states gave rise to an anticentralist theory of the Constitution and Union, a theory which included the right of secession—a peculiarly American variation of social contract.

In America, republicanism was never the mere reflex of material interest. Instead, it was a complete theory of civil society in history. The widespread use of republican categories and their considerable overlap with those of classical liberalism long obscured the character and importance in American history of republicanism.[1]

CIVIC HUMANISM, REPUBLICANISM AND REVOLUTION

The roots of republicanism run deep. Some trace its remote ancestry to Aristotle and Polybius, whose Renaissance interpreter was Nicolo Machiavelli. Florentine Republicanism, restated in 1656 by James Harrington and reinterpreted by neo-Harringtonians, served English political oppositions from Bolingbroke to the Chartists. Classical-republican themes found constant employment after 1688 by a series of Anglo-American "Rights" and "Lefts." The centerpiece of civic humanism (the oldest stratum of republicanism) was the independent proprietor able to bear arms on his own account. Established on the land with their families

---

[1]For overviews see Robert E. Shalhope, "Toward a Republican Synthesis," *William and Mary Quarterly*, 3rd ser. 29, no. 4 (January 1972): 49–80; J.G.A. Pocock, "Machiavelli, Harrington and English Political Ideologies in the 18th Century," ibid., 3rd ser. 22, no. 4 (October 1965): 549–83; and Bernard Bailyn, *The Ideological Origins of the American Revolution* (Cambridge, Mass.: Belknap Press, 1967).

and retainers, such freeholders were ideal republican citizens. Republican liberty required their existence; otherwise, social struggle between the rich few and the poor multitude would cause political degeneration.[2] Republican writers from Polybius to John Adams favored combining the features of monarchy, aristocracy, and republic (in the narrow sense). In time, the mixed constitution would enter the American Constitution as the balance or separation of powers among a trinity of executive, legislature, and judiciary.[3]

Preventing the engrossment of power and property by an oligarchical "Court Party" was the key to preserving a free society. Republicans believed that standing armies had historically been the chief engine with which Court Parties subverted liberty. The armed citizens organized as militia, conversely, were a defense force compatible with constitutional stability and ordered liberty.[4]

Harrington theorized that the passing of the "Gothick order"—feudalism—had left England a balanced republic. His successors inverted his historical analysis. For them, the post-1688 financial revolution was undermining the constitution. The Whig Oligarchy, a Court Party of stock-jobbers, placemen, and pensioners, were unbalancing society through taxes, monetized national debt, and the standing army which the debt helped make possible.

It was for the "Country Party," the virtuous land owners who were the real political nation, to oppose this corruption of the constitution.[5] On both sides of the Atlantic the Country-Party concept took in an ever wider spectrum of independent men until in the land-rich United States it included all farmers and planters. In eighteenth-century Britain there were two broad groups of

[2]On all this see J.G.A. Pocock, *The Machiavellian Moment* (Princeton: Princeton University Press, 1975).

[3]For the prehistory of political "trifunctionalism" see John E. Tashjean, "Indo–European Studies and the Sciences of Man," *History of Political Thought* 2, no. 3 (November 1981): 447–67; and C. Scott Littleton, "Toward a Genetic Model for the Analysis of Ideology: The Indo–European Case," *Western Folklore* 24 (1967): 37–47.

[4]The armed people entered the U.S. Constitution in the Second Amendment. See Stephen P. Halbrook, *That Every Man Might Be Armed: The Evolution of a Constitutional Right* (Albuquerque: University of New Mexico Press, 1984). For a modern Harringtonian statement in the spirit of the original, see Vo Nguyen Giap, *People's War, People's Army* (New York: Frederick A. Praeger, 1962).

[5]On Harrington's "revisionist" followers see J.G.A. Pocock, *The Ancient Constitution and the Feudal Law* (New York: Norton, 1967). "Virtue" refers to manly, patriarchal, even Spartan attributes of character; "corruption" refers to unbalancing or subversion of republican constitutions.

Country ideologists. The first, led by Henry St. John, Viscount Bolingbroke, combined attacks on Court Party-sponsored monopolies with anticommercial rural nostalgia.[6] On the Left, a bourgeois Country Party appeared which was antimercantilist, anti-Court and antimonopolist, but pro-commercial. Because these opposition movements shared rhetoric and enemies, they give the appearance of agrarians opposing capitalism—a traditional but very misleading interpretation.[7] An understanding of republican ideological developments allows us to sort this out. Bourgeois writers like the "True Whigs" simply set Bolingbroke and Locke side by side without bothering to reconcile them in detail. As one writer says:

> One can be both a bourgeois radical and a thinker concerned with themes important to the civic humanist tradition. A new language of public discourse can be acquired alongside continued use of older words and concepts.[8]

Late-eighteenth- and early-nineteenth-century British radicals redefined such key concepts as independence and virtue, and broadened the appeal of republicanism for tradesmen and enterprisers.[9] Landed gentry no longer had the Country Party to themselves. In revolutionary North America, broad ownership of land and firearms already had brought Country ideas into a plausibly close relationship with social reality.[10]

Americans read the English opposition writers thoroughly, if not critically. They drew upon English law (especially Coke and Blackstone), Locke, the True Whigs, Bolingbroke, and the French and Scottish Enlightenments to create the ideology of the Revolution.[11] The contrast between Court and Country gave way to that of Power and Liberty. Americans took "a negative view of

---

[6]Isaac Kramnick, *Bolingbroke and His Circle* (Cambridge, Mass.: Harvard University Press, 1968), and "An Augustan Reply to Locke," *Political Science Quarterly* 82, no. 4 (December 1967): 571–94.

[7]On this issue see Leonard P. Liggio, Review of *Tom Paine and Revolutionary America* by Eric Foner, *Libertarian Review* 6, no. 3 (July 1977): 38.

[8]"English Middle Class Radicalism in the 18th Century," *Literature of Liberty* 3, no. 2 (Summer 1980): 32–33. On the True Whigs, see Caroline Robbins, *The Eighteenth Century Commonwealthmen* (Cambridge, Mass.: Harvard University Press, 1959).

[9]John Brewer, "English Radicalism in the Age of George III," in J.G.A. Pocock, ed., *Three British Revolutions: 1641, 1688, 1776* (Princeton: Princeton University Press, 1980), pp. 323–67.

[10]See Jackson Turner Main, *The Social Structure of Revolutionary America* (Princeton: Princeton University Press, 1965).

[11]Trevor Colbourn, *The Lamp of Experience* (Chapel Hill: University of North Carolina Press, 1965); Bailyn, *Ideological Origins*; and Forrest McDonald, "A Founding Father's Library," *Literature of Liberty* 1, no. 1 (January–March 1978): 4–15.

government," and saw "rulers and ruled" as antagonistic forces.[12] In effect, the American republicans had their British mentors' revolution for them, a revolution for which their colonial self-government experiences had partially prepared them.[13]

REPUBLICANISM AND THE CONSTITUTION MOVEMENT

A reasonably coherent libertarian republicanism informed the American Revolutionary outlook. The new states' first federal constitution and their first territorial legislation reflected the revolutionary generation's experience and ideas.[14] Having only just fought the English Court Party, many in the revolutionary coalition rejected energetic government for the new confederacy. Only the belief that the United States were facing a historical crisis—a Machiavellian moment—overcame this reluctance. The heightened sense of crisis drew on republican historical pessimism. True to Florentine thinking, the revolutionary generation held a cyclical view of history. Nations followed an invariable course of rise, greatness, and decline; constitutional forms inevitably degenerated into their baser counterparts.[15]

Whatever the role of their material interests,[16] a coalition of able men, concerned for the future of American republican liberty and the stability which secured private property, worked creatively within an ideological consensus to solve the problems facing the United States. By linking the idea of popular sovereignty to their proposed Constitution, the Federalists made an

[12]Shalhope, "Towards a Republican Synthesis," pp. 64–65. At this "moment," individualist libertarianism came close to subordinating civic humanist republicanism and retaining it as its own living history. Most Americans drew back, preferring to live with the philosophical imprecision of the Revolutionary–Republican synthesis.

[13]On local self-government, see Michael Zuckerman, *Peaceable Kingdoms* (New York: Vintage Books, 1965); Charles S. Sydnor, *American Revolutionaries in the Making* (New York: Free Press, 1965); and Clinton Rossiter, *The First American Revolution* (New York: Harcourt, Brace and World, 1956).

[14]Merrill Jensen, *The Articles of Confederation* (Madison: University of Wisconsin Press, 1966); idem, *The New Nation* (New York: Vintage Books, 1965); and Robert F. Berkhofer, Jr., "Jefferson, the Ordinance of 1784 and the Origins of the American Territorial System," *William and Mary Quarterly*, 3rd ser. 29, no. 2 (April 1972): 231–62.

[15]Pocock, "English Political Ideologies," pp. 568–69. Also Neal Riemer, "James Madison's Theory of the Self-Destructive Features of Republican Government," *Ethics* 64 (1954): 34–43.

[16]On this issue see Charles A. Beard, *An Economic Interpretation of the Constitution of the United States* (New York: Free Press, 1965); Forrest McDonald, *We the People* (Chicago: University of Chicago Press, 1963); and Lee Benson, *Turner and Beard* (New York: Free Press, 1960).

end run around their opponents. They sought to "retard the thrust of the Revolution with the rhetoric of the Revolution," and in the process invented "a distinctly American political theory, but only at the cost of eventually impoverishing later American political thought."[17] While all agreed that the people were sovereign and the ultimate source of political power, the ratification debates left unresolved the potentially disruptive question of whether there was One People or Thirteen Peoples of the several states.[18]

On their side, the misnamed Antifederalists brought an array of republican arguments against the new Constitution, stressing the time-honored truism that only small states could remain republics. Over time, an enlarged general government would necessarily become unrepublican. Focusing on the taxing power in the new charter, they revived the pre-revolutionary distinction between external and internal taxes—to the detriment of the new document. As cautious republicans, the Antifederalists could not justify the leap into an untried form of government, whatever the inconvenience of the Articles of Confederation.[19]

THE "COURT" IN POWER: 1789–1800

With ratification, a stronger general government came to life, led by those who had led the Constitution movement. The Federalist quickly embarked upon a program of American mercantilism, epitomized in the fiscal measures of Treasury Secretary Alexander Hamilton. They wanted to consolidate the Union, and to bind mercantile and landed wealth to the new regime.[20] To do this, they levied a combination of internal and external taxes, created a National Bank and a monetized national debt, began redeeming Revolutionary War bonds above market value, and addressed the issue of the western lands. This program soon excited the opposition of former Antifederalists and

[17]Gordon S. Wood, *The Creation of the American Republic, 1776–1787* (Chapel Hill: University of North Carolina Press, 1969), p. 562.

[18]Claude H. Van Tyne, "Sovereignty in the American Revolution," *American Historical Review* 12, no. 3 (April 1907): 529–45.

[19]Jackson Turner Main, *The Antifederalists* (Chapel Hill: University of North Carolina Press, 1961), pp. 226–27; and Michael Lienisch, "In Defense of the Antifederalists," *History of Political Thought* 4, no. 1 (February 1983): 65–87. On the external–internal tax issue, see Thomas P. Slaughter, "The Tax Man Cometh," *William and Mary Quarterly*, 3rd ser. 41, no. 4 (October 1984): 566–91.

[20]See William Appleman Williams, "The Age of Mercantilism," in idem, *The Contours of American History* (New York: New Viewpoints, 1973), pp. 77–223.

other republican ideologues.[21] "The Federalist party found itself in the awkward position of fostering what amounted to traditional 'court' policies . . . in a nation of 'country' ideologues."[22] In such a landscape, politics was not the art of the possible but was a life-and-death struggle for the soul of the republic. The American Country Party, which soon took the name of Republicans, cast Hamilton as a Walpole bent on the corruption of the constitutional order.

The seriousness of this struggle emerges from inflammatory rhetoric employed during the crises occasioned by the excise tax on whiskey and the Alien and Sedition Acts.[23] The excise seemed an attack on the sturdy yeomanry for the benefit of northeastern commercial interests; the Alien and Sedition Acts direct subversion of the Constitution. Reacting swiftly, the Republicans undertook the organization and propaganda which brought them—the self-defined American Country Party—to power in 1800.

THE "COUNTRY PARTY" IN POWER: 1800–1824

With the election of Thomas Jefferson as president, Republicans thought they had rescued liberty and free institutions. The Country Party was in power; republican ideas would now define policy. To a surprising degree, the Republicans did follow their pre-election program of retrenchment, reduction of military establishments, and repeal of internal taxes.[24] For some historians, it is precisely the Republicans' ideological purity that caused their major problems. By reducing federal debt and taxation— even at the expense of the army and navy, it is argued—Jefferson and his successor James Madison rendered themselves unable to

[21]On the rough continuity between the Antifederalists and the Republicans see Main, *Antifederalists*, p. 281; and Charles A. Beard, *The Economic Origins of Jeffersonian Democracy* (New York: Free Press, 1965).

[22]Rowland Berthoff and John M. Murrin, "Feudalism, Communalism, and the Yeoman Freeholder," in Stephen G. Kurtz and James H. Hutson, eds., *Essays of the American Revolution* (Chapel Hill: University of North Carolina Press, 1973), p. 277.

[23]On these crises, see John R. Howe, Jr., "Republican Thought and the Political Violence of the 1790s," *American Quarterly* 19 (1967): 147–65; Lance Banning, "Republican Ideology and the Triumph of the Constitution, 1789 to 1793," *William and Mary Quarterly*, 3rd ser. 31, no. 2 (April 1974): 167–88; Mary K. Bonsteel Tachau, "The Whiskey Rebellion in Kentucky," *Journal of the Early Republic* 2, no. 3 (Fall 1982): 239–59; James Morton Smith, "The Grass Roots Origins of the Kentucky Resolutions," *William and Mary Quarterly*, 3rd ser. 27, no. 2 (April 1970); 221–45, and Murray N. Rothbard, "The Whiskey Rebellion," *The Free Market* 12, no. 9 (September 1994): 1f.

[24]See Forrest McDonald, *The Presidency of Thomas Jefferson* (Lawrence: University of Kansas Press, 1976), chap. 2, pp. 29–52.

deal effectively with foreign policy. Hemmed in by the European empires and faced with the Napoleonic Wars in Europe, the Republic faced a serious threat to its independence. Having thrown away their sword (as these historians would have it), the Republicans now drew it at home to enforce an unpopular embargo designed to coerce Britain and France economically. In an attempt to enforce the embargo, "the government resorted to repressive measures so severe as to endanger the Republicans' reputation as friends of limited government and guardians of civil rights."[25]

An even harsher judgment comes from a modern Hamiltonian who writes

> The embargo, then, both as a bankrupt foreign policy and a reign of domestic oppression, was not a sudden aberration but the logical and virtually certain outcome of the Jeffersonian ideology put into practice: the ideology's yield was dependence rather than independence, oppression rather than liberty.

Caught in a self-created crisis, the Senate Republicans took up what "might be styled totalitarian libertarianism." The Republicans'

> view of Jefferson's mission as president did not differ substantively and significantly from Bolingbroke's idea of Patriot King: a head of state who would rally the entire nation to his banner, and then, . . . voluntarily restrain himself and thus give vitality and meaning to the constitutional system.[26]

This was an interesting development, particularly in relation to the similar charges which were to be made against "King Andrew" Jackson, who became heir to a portion of the Republican legacy.

In the throes of an economic depression caused by the "cursed Ograbme," as they called the embargo, and by a Republican war they had not wanted, New England Federalists met at Hartford, Connecticut, to consider drastic measures. With some irony, men who had figured as Court Party demons for the Republicans now attacked the Madison government in pure Country-ideological terms. They toyed with secession, but called instead for constitutional amendments to diminish federal power. James M. Banner, Jr., credits the Hartford group with "a consistent vision of republicanism" and adds that if they "are to be arraigned by

[25]Lance Banning, *The Jeffersonian Persuasion* (Ithaca, N.Y.: Cornell University Press, 1978), p. 293.
[26]McDonald, *Presidency of Jefferson*, pp. 128–29, 162, and 165.

history, they must be arraigned for their fidelity to the Republican faith."[27]

While some have blamed the troubles of Jefferson and Madison on fidelity to unworkable ideology, other writers question the consistency of Republican practice and ideology and accuse them of abandoning their own program. The Republicans swept away much of the Federalist "achievement," but the temptations—or "responsibilities"—of power resulted in "the Jeffersonian compromise" in which a "Federalized Jefferson" perpetuated much of the Federalists' statecraft.[28] This was perhaps even more the case under Madison who, as "father of the Constitution," was closer to the Federalists than to many in his own party; he was therefore a consistent force for compromise within the Republican movement. "Mr. Madison's war" strengthened the general government, as wars do, and John Randolph of Roanoke complained:

> We had vaunted of paying off the national debt, of retrenching useless establishments; and yet had now become as infatuated with standing armies, loans, taxes, navies, and war, as ever were the Essex Junto. What Republicanism is this?[29]

Mercantilist political economy also accounts for Madison's resistance to the laissez-faire liberal ideas which so many of his party saw as applied republicanism. As a mercantilist thinker, Madison consciously fashioned a rationale for an American empire; this was the inner meaning, as he saw it, of the Constitution to which he contributed so much, and was the key to his 10th Federalist Paper with its argument for an extensive federal republic whose free institutions would actually become more secure as new territory accrued to its domain.[30]

This raises the question of the relationship of individualism and laissez-faire economics to republicanism in the Early Republic. Jefferson and John Taylor represent one end of a continuum. They were conversant with the works of Adam Smith, Jean-Baptiste Say, and Destutt de Tracy.[31] Thus, it is not altogether fair

---

[27]James M. Banner, Jr., *To the Hartford Convention* (New York: Alfred A. Knopf, 1970), p. 350.

[28]Arthur A. Ekirch, Jr., *The Decline of American Liberalism* (New York: Atheneum, 1969), chap. 5, "Jeffersonian Compromise," pp. 55–72.

[29]Ibid., p. 66.

[30]Williams, *Contours*, pp. 157–62. The 10th Federalist was Madison's reply to Antifederalists who reasoned that republics could avoid Harringtonian corruption only by remaining small and cohesive.

[31]See William D. Grampp, "John Taylor: Economist of Southern Agrarianism," *Southern Economic Journal* 11, no. 3 (January 1945): 255–68; and idem, "A Re-examination of Jeffersonian Economics," *Southern Economic Journal* 12, no. 3 (January 1946): 263–82.

for William Appleman Williams to dismiss them as "physio-crats" yearning for a "feudal utopia."[32] In adopting classical-lib-eral economics, Republicans sought a policy consistent with the "left-wing" individualism which had emerged in the Revo-lution. This modernization of Country ideology paralleled the course of bourgeois radicalism in Great Britain.

Republican virtue now coexisted with thrift and industry, and less-genteel social strata could aspire to being ideal repub-lican citizens.[33] Later divergences within the libertarian repub-licanism so reformulated are nicely illustrated in the differences in the American careers of those two English ideologues Thomas Paine and Thomas Cooper.

The old civic humanist ideal of the agrarian proprietor with his servants on the land held its own in the southern states be-cause it corresponded to social reality. Relative to northern de-velopments, this circumstance allows the appearance of a "re-countrification" of southern republicanism. This is largely an op-tical illusion, since southerners were about as pro-commercial as their northern counterparts. If republican ideology is put in the picture, the contrast between an "agrarian South" and a "capi-talist North" recedes to its proper dimensions.[34] What William Marina writes of one wing of the English Country Party—and that party's reaction to the eighteenth-century state financial revolution—applies here:

> They understood the virtue of the agrarian life: the apparent political stability of a nation of independent yeomen. But they realized the potential benefits from an urban-market sector within the society. They were also disenchanted with the long-range corruption of a state-financial system based upon great extremes of wealth and the creation of an urban proletariat without property. Whatever their ambivalences, they opposed the Court's alliance of State and private in-terests.[35]

The mercantilism or crypto-Federalism of Republican admin-istrations from Jefferson to Monroe led to the secession from the party of self-proclaimed purists like Nathaniel Macon, Thomas

[32]Williams, *Contours*, pp. 152–55.

[33]On this growing individualism, see John Brewer, "English Middle Class Rad-icalism," pp. 33–34; and Cecilia Kenyon, "Republicanism and Radicalism in the American Revolution," in Sidney Fine and Gerald S. Brown, eds., *The American Past* (New York: Macmillan, 1970), vol. 1, pp. 139–64.

[34]On Southern republicans and commerce, see Robert E. Shalhope, *John Taylor of Caroline: Pastoral Republican* (Columbia: University of South Carolina Press, 1980), pp. 185–88 and 204–8.

[35]William F. Marina, "Revolution and Social Change: The American Revolution as a People's War," *Literature of Liberty* 1, no. 2 (April–June 1978): 14.

Ritchie, and John Randolph,[36] while the disillusioned John Taylor took no part, writing his ponderous tomes instead. Randolph emerged as the most extreme critic of his own party's policies in office, and was a pivotal figure in passing on the principles of "Old Republicanism." To John C. Calhoun he bequeathed the dogmas of limited government and states' rights, both now explicitly linked to defense of the South's "peculiar institution."[37]

Despite the complaints of the Quids, as the Old Republican remnant was known, the Republicans did play the part of a Country Party relative to the ambitious mercantilism of the Federalists and their successors, the Whigs. Taking into account the importance of the South in the Republican and (later) Democratic Party, and in the Union itself, the Country Party—broadly conceived—did remain in power from 1800 to 1860. Southern Republicans and their northern allies prevented both federal interference with slavery and the centralization of power which might have made it possible. Only in the Supreme Court did the original American Court Party retain a foothold.[38]

The collapse of the Federalist Party after 1800 left a political vacuum. Apparent Republican dominance gave way to internal factionalism. The presidency of John Quincy Adams as a National Republican was the high-water mark of American mercantilism (up to that point). It came to an abrupt end. Andrew Jackson, a frontier general, slaveholder, and "primitive republican," became president with the support of those groups opposed to American mercantilism (at least at the national level). Jackson and the Democrats were heirs to republican ideology, and to much of the Republican Party's constituency. Nonetheless, his presidency saw republicanism fragment along sectional and functional lines.[39]

THE FRAGMENTATION OF REPUBLICANISM IN AN AGE OF EGALITARIANISM: 1828–1860

Political and social equality for white males was the hallmark of Andrew Jackson's Age of Egalitarianism. Revolutions in

---

[36]On Randolph and the Quids, see Norman K. Risjord, *The Old Republicans* (New York: Columbia University Press, 1965); and David A. Carson, "That Ground Called Quiddism," *Journal of American Studies* 20, no. 1 (1986): 71–92.

[37]See Russell Kirk, *John Randolph of Roanoke* (Chicago: Henry Regnery, 1964), pp. 93–94, 141–42, and 187–88.

[38]John M. Murrin, "The Great Inversion, or Court versus Country: A Comparison of the Revolution Settlements in England (1688–1721) and America (1776–1816)," in Pocock, *Three British Revolutions*, pp. 368–453.

[39]For an overview see Williams, *Contours*, pp. 204–83.

communications and transportation, the effects of which rami-
fied throughout American society and culture, intensified the dy-
namism of a society with a largely open-market economy and
huge reserves of cheap land.[40] In most states, party politics replaced eighteenth-century gentry-led politics. Equality—understood as an equal chance in a laissez-faire marketplace—created
an individualist and anti-institutionalist drift which Americans
offset by inventing the intermediate social networks and institutions that Alexis de Tocqueville found so fascinating.[41]

In this unsettling period of "creative disorder," republicanism functioned less and less as a basis of national consensus. Sec-
tionalists, interest groups, and radical reformers exposed the different possibilities latent in the Revolutionary synthesis. Jackson's coalition came in with a program of laissez-faire liberalism
and undid much of "political capitalism" at the federal level.[42]
They destroyed the National Bank and blocked the so-called
internal improvements put forward by mercantilists like Henry
Clay. At the state level, the Jacksonians made for somewhat-
less-consistent laissez faireists.

The Jackson men were agreed on Indian removal, territorial
expansion, states' rights, slavery, and a strong "democratic" executive. This last point resembled Jefferson's actual practice, and
contradicted the anti-monarchist rhetoric of Revolutionary republicans. Jackson's opponents got together as "Whigs" and attacked his executive style, while bringing forward decidedly
Federalist economic projects. Nonetheless, sound republican theorists could be found in both parties (e.g., Alexander H. Stephens,
a southern Whig). Jackson's coalition first ran aground on the tariff. The South Carolina nullification movement of 1831–1832 divided even strong states'-rights men. Jackson, who was always a
strong states'-rights advocate, drew the line at nullification and
secession. He won his point, but the rising northern anti-slavery
movement drove many southerners to look on secession as a last
resort in defense of their interests.[43]

[40]See Lee Benson, *The Concept of Jacksonian Democracy* (Princeton: Princeton
University Press, 1961).

[41]Robert H. Wiebe, *The Opening of American Society* (New York: Vintage Books,
1985); and John Lukacs, "Alexis de Tocqueville," *Literature of Liberty* 5, no. 1 (Spring
1982): 11–17.

[42]Robert V. Remini, *Andrew Jackson and the Course of American Freedom, 1822–1832*
(New York: Harper and Row, 1981). For a definition of "political capitalism" see
Gabriel Kolko, "Max Weber on America," in George H. Nadel, ed., *Studies in the Phi-
losophy of History* (New York: Harper and Row, 1965), pp. 180–97.

[43]On the connection with slavery, see Richard H. Brown, "The Jacksonian Pro-
Slavery Party," in Edward Pessen, ed., *New Perspectives on Jacksonian Parties and*

REPUBLICAN THEORY AND SECESSION IN THE SOUTH

Between 1789 and 1860, southern particularists derived doctrines of nullification and secession from republicanism, constitutional law, and social contract theory. In effect, they elaborated
an American variant of the social contract theory. Drawing on
the Lockean portion of the Revolutionary heritage, they described the Union as a compact terminable by any single state if external forces threatened its rights and local sovereignty. In his
first inaugural address, Abraham Lincoln said that "Plainly, the
central idea of secession is the essence of anarchy." It is worth our
while to see how the states'-rights theorists of the Old South
developed this "anarchistic" position. First of all, in America,
law, as embodied in the Constitution, serves as a secular social
cement and a source of values. Lacking the kind of value base an
established church could provide, Americans have subscribed to
a cult of the Constitution.[44] Hence Americans often make moral
questions into constitutional ones, a habit reinforced by the heritage of English legalism. Except for a few higher-law advocates, most American political thinkers have been eager to appear as good constitutionalists.

Thus, when southerners defended slavery and when they resolved on a separatist revolution, they argued as constitutional
lawyers and republican theorists. When the southern states seceded, they possessed a complete theory which legitimized
their actions. Southern political thinkers from Thomas Jefferson
and John Taylor of Caroline to Jefferson Davis and Alexander H.
Stephens further elaborated this states'-rights or compact theory of the Constitution and Union. Nullification of (or "interposition" against) an unconstitutional federal law, and secession,
withdrawal by a sovereign state from a federation voluntarily
entered, were the devices which the states'-rights school put
forward as bulwarks against majoritarian centralization or empire.

Because legality and morality coincide so much in Anglo-
American thought, the constitutional rationale for an action is of
no small importance. When war came, it was critical. As Chief
Justice Salmon P. Chase admitted in *Texas v White* (1869), if secession had been constitutional, the struggle "must have become a

---

Politics (Boston: Allyn and Bacon, 1969), pp. 272–89; and Charles S. Sydnor, *The
Development of Southern Sectionalism, 1819–1848* (Baton Rouge: Louisiana State University Press, 1968).

[44]Hannah Arendt, *On Revolution* (New York: Viking Press, 1965), pp. 152, 156; and
Williams, *Contours*, p. 158.

war for conquest and subjugation" on the part of the federal government.[45] This was precisely the view urged after 1865 by former Confederate President Davis and Vice President Stephens. Seeking to win the post-war legal argument, at least, they provided the final summaries of received secessionist dogma.[46]

According to the mature states'-rights viewpoint, the Constitution was a compact between the states (including those formed later out of the common territory of the states), each of which remained fully sovereign. Since no common judge existed to decide ultimate constitutional questions—John Marshall claims for the Supreme Court being rejected by the states'-rights school—each state, as a party to the compact, had a residual right to exercise judgment. This right extended as far as nullification and secession if the Constitution were violated by the common agent of the states—the federal government—or by the other parties. These remedies were not to be undertaken lightly, but they were within the reserved rights of the states.

The compact theory was articulated at various times of crisis and gradually refined. The Kentucky and Virginia Resolutions of 1798, drafted by Thomas Jefferson and James Madison respectively, were an early expression of it. The Kentucky Resolutions, although watered down somewhat from Jefferson's rough draft, began with the ringing declaration that

> the several states composing the United States of America, are not united on the principle of unlimited submission to their general government; but that by a compact . . . they . . . delegated to [that government] certain definite powers, reserving . . . the residuary mass of right to their own self-government.

Each state "acceded as a State" to the constitutional compact, and was "an integral party." There being no common judge, each state had *"an equal right to judge for itself, as well of infraction as of the mode and measure of redress."*[47]

The Kentucky Resolution and the Virginia Resolution each declared that the Alien and Sedition Acts, which were passed

[45]*Texas v White*, in Charles G. Fenwick, ed., *Cases on International Law* (Chicago: Callaghan, 1951), p. 58.

[46]See Jefferson Davis, *The Rise and Fall of the Confederate Government* (reprint; New York: Thomas Yoseloff, 1958), vol. 1; and Alexander H. Stephens, *A Constitutional View of the Late War Between the States*, 2 vols. (Philadelphia: National Publishing, 1868 and 1870). Stephens is one of our most brilliant, if neglected, political thinkers.

[47]Henry Steele Commager, ed., *Documents of American History* (New York: Appleton-Century-Crofts, 1963), vol. 1, pp. 178–79.

when the Federalists were in power to cow the republican movement, were "altogether void and of no force." Citing instances of the Federalists' drift toward arbitrary power, the resolutions warned that such acts "may tend to drive these States into revolution and blood." Government by confidence was dangerous, for "free government is founded in jealousy."[48]

The Resolutions were sent to the other states in the hope that they would join in resisting federal usurpation. The Virginia Resolution attributed all federal power to "the compact to which the States are parties." When the federal government exceeded its delegated powers, the states were "duty bound to interpose for arresting the progress of the evil." The Virginia Assembly declared the Alien and Sedition Acts "unconstitutional" and called on the other states to act against them.[49]

Madison's resolutions had used the word "interposition," but the Kentucky Resolutions of 1799, drawn up by John Breckinridge, first introduced the term "nullification." The Kentucky Resolutions, asserting that the "sovereign and independent" parties to the federal compact possessed final judgment, stated that "*a nullification of those sovereignties, of all authorized acts done under color of* [the Constitution] *is the rightful remedy.*"[50]

Liberal historians, eager to claim Jefferson for the tradition of democratic nationalism, hesitate to admit that he held extreme states'-rights views. They tend to present the Resolutions as emergency rhetoric inspired solely by concern for freedom of expression. But the crisis went deeper. One historian notes that Hamilton's circle "talked of marching into Virginia and dividing it into smaller States," while "Virginians openly considered secession."[51]

John Taylor, the Jeffersonian theorist *par excellence*, was in the forefront of the disunionists, and as matters worsened Jefferson became willing to consider secession. When Breckinridge hurriedly drew up the Kentucky Resolutions of 1799, he consulted Jefferson's draft resolutions.[52] Jefferson had written that "every State has *a natural right* in cases not within the compact . . . to nullify of their own authority all assumptions of power by others

---

[48]Ibid., pp. 179–81.

[49]Ibid., pp. 182–83.

[50]Ibid., p. 184.

[51]Williams, *Contours*, p. 176.

[52]Merrill D. Peterson, *Thomas Jefferson and the New Nation* (New York: Oxford University Press, 1970), p. 624.

within their limits."[53] Later, because of the other states' unfavorable replies to the 1798 resolutions, Jefferson favored a more radical protest. Writing to Madison on 23 August 1799, he suggested declaring that Kentucky and Virginia would "sever ourselves from that union we so much value, rather than give up the rights of self-government which we have reserved."[54] Clearly, nullification and secession were not inventions of later southern "fire-eaters." Madison's Report on the Resolutions, written for the Virginia Assembly in 1800, affirmed that if the Constitution was a compact, states could determine what questions "require their interposition."[55]

Once in power in Washington, the Jeffersonian Republicans found new merit in federal activity, including the Louisiana Purchase, which Jefferson admitted was of dubious constitutionality. The War of 1812, derided by the Federalist remnant as "Mr. Madison's War," was very unpopular in New England. Of the older Republican party, John Randolph battled almost alone for peace. Northeastern spokesmen, particularly the "Young Federalists," took up, temporarily anyway, the states'-rights arguments of their enemies. Massachusetts spent the war as a virtual neutral power, supplying few soldiers for it. Disaffected Federalists met in convention at Hartford, Connecticut in 1814 to protest the war. Some of them favored a separate New England confederacy. Before any drastic measures were taken, the war ended. The convention recommended several constitutional amendments and adjourned.[56]

States'-rights positions were again put forward during the fight over the protective tariff in 1828–1833. South Carolina became the focal point of southern resentment directed at the protection of northern manufacturers. Under the covert leadership of Vice President John C. Calhoun, South Carolina reasserted the right of state interposition against unconstitutional federal laws. After South Carolina formally nullified the tariff in 1832 and prepared to arrest federal collectors, President Andrew Jackson wanted to march troops in to reduce the state to obedience. The Carolinians prepared to resist with state forces. To avoid bloodshed, the state rescinded its Nullification Ordinance; at the same time Congress lowered the tariff rates.

[53]Nathan Schachner, *Thomas Jefferson: A Biography* (New York: Thomas Yoseloff, 1957), p. 616. Italics added.

[54]Ibid., p. 626; see also Peterson, *Jefferson*, p. 623.

[55]J.W. Gough, *The Social Contract* (Oxford: The Clarendon Press, 1967), p. 235.

[56]See Ekirch, *Decline of American Liberalism*, pp. 65–69; and Banner, *To the Hartford Convention*.

Calhoun, now senator for South Carolina, led the states'-rights forces in the debate. His rigidly logical mind was responsible for the first advances in states'-rights theory in some time. In his *Disquisition of Government* he sought to ground his conception of federalism in political philosophy. Paradoxically, he severed his position from any Lockean connections while attempting to vindicate particularist rights with his notion of the "concurrent majority."[57]

One South Carolinian innovation was to call a convention directly expressing the sovereignty of the people to nullify the tariff, and later, the Force Bill. Like a constitutional convention, this body was deemed to be more qualified to pass on such matters than was the sitting state legislature, itself a creature of the people. The Nullification Ordinance also directly threatened secession.[58]

The idea of states' rights cut across the growing North–South "cold war" over slavery and slavery expansion. At the time of the Mexican War, threats of secession were heard in New England.[59] In 1859, the Supreme Court of Wisconsin nullified a U.S. Supreme Court decision enforcing the Fugitive Slave Act, and quoted Jefferson's language of 1798.[60] Radical abolitioist William Lloyd Garrison advocated northern secession, crying "No Union with slaveholders." As the South became a "conscious minority," more was heard of leaving the Union. After 1850, proslavery radicals held conventions almost yearly; at these meetings fire-eaters like William Lowndes Yancey and Robert Rhett agitated for a southern confederacy.[61] In 1860, South Carolina led the way: the state seceded by repealing in convention the act of an earlier South Carolina convention ratifying the U.S. Constitution.[62]

THE HISTORICAL BASIS OF THE THEORY

Was the secessionist case a sound one? In many ways it was. The secessionist contention that the states were sovereign, subject

[57]See John C. Calhoun, *A Disquisition on Government*, R.K. Cralle, ed. (New York: Peter Smith, 1943); and August O. Spain, *The Political Theory of John C. Calhoun* (New York: Octagon Books, 1968).

[58]For the Ordinance, see Commager, *Documents*, vol. 1, pp. 261–62.

[59]Davis, *Rise and Fall*, vol. 1, p. 76.

[60]Carl Brent Swisher, *Roger B. Taney* (Hamden, Conn.: Archon Books, 1961), pp. 526–33.

[61]On the "fire-eaters" see Ronald T. Takaki, *A Proslavery Argument* (Glencoe, Ill.: Free Press, 1971).

[62]For the secession ordinance, see Commager, *Documents*, vol. 1, p. 372.

to no higher final authority, during and after the Revolutionary War, is strong indeed. Despite generations of Federalist propaganda and nationalist razzle-dazzle, it is clear that the thirteen colonies fought for their separate sovereignty and independence, albeit in loose concert.[63] During the war, the Continental Congress—in which nationalists have always espied the germ of unitary national sovereignty—was a standing committee of the states which coordinated the common struggle. The Declaration of Independence proclaimed the colonies "Free and Independent States." Twelve colonial delegations awaited instructions from home before consenting to it (New York abstained). Even then, seven legislatures separately confirmed it: Connecticut, for example, announced that it was "a free and independent State." Virginia, in fact, had declared its independence several days before 4 July 1776.[64]

The Declaration of Independence asserted that the new states could "levy War, conclude Peace, contract Alliances" and exercise all other sovereign powers. Virginia's independent foreign-policy activities illustrate state exercise of these powers.[65] With the Articles of Confederation, which took more than three years to ratify, the states created "a firm league of friendship" and a "confederacy." Article II reserved to each state "its sovereignty, freedom, and independence, and every Power, Jurisdiction, and right, which is not by this confederation expressly delegated to the United States, in Congress assembled." Most of the revolutionary generation believed in the sovereignty of *"the people organized as states."*[66] They were certainly not fighting to replace one strong central government, that of King George III and Parliament, with another strong central government, simply based in America.

---

[63]On this, see Jensen, *Articles*, esp. pp. 161–76; and Van Tyne, "Sovereignty," pp. 529–45.

[64]Ibid., p. 538. See also John Richard Alden, *The South in the Revolution* (Baton Rouge: Louisiana State University Press, 1957), p. 212; and Julian F. Boyd, ed., *The Papers of Thomas Jefferson* (Princeton: Princeton University Press, 1950), vol. 1, pp. 377–83, for the Virginia constitution adopted on 29 June 1776 which—in a preamble written by Jefferson—directly repudiated the rule of George III.

[65]Van Tyne, "Sovereignty," p. 540. See also James Jackson Kilpatrick, *The Sovereign States* (Chicago: Henry Regnery, 1957); Thomas Jefferson, *Papers of Thomas Jefferson* (Princeton: Princeton University Press, 1950), vol. 2, pp. 128, 181–82, 200, 348–49, 364–67, 375–81, 476–79, and 589–91; and ibid. (Princeton: Princeton University Press, 1951), vol. 3, pp. 10–13, 162–67, 208–9, and 624–637 (for various exercises of sovereignty in foreign affairs); and Michael H. Shuman, "Courts v. Local Foreign Policies," *Foreign Policy* 86 (Spring 1992): 158–77.

[66]Jensen, *Articles*, p. 165.

The right wing of the Revolutionary coalition was appalled by democracy in the states and sought to curtail it. Crying up a crisis—which may have existed only in their pocketbooks—a coalition of northern merchants and southern planters engineered the Constitutional Convention at Philadelphia, and secured ratification of a new Constitution. Despite the nationalism of the proponents of a stronger Union, prevailing opinion forced them to compromise—perhaps only rhetorically in their minds—with state sovereignty to get the new charter approved.[67]

Because of this compromise, the Constitution lent itself to a states'-rights interpretation, especially since social contract had been one of the rhetorical models in use at the Convention. Gouverneur Morris, no friend of neighborhood control, wanted "to form a compact for the good of America."[68] Elbridge Gerry protested the plan to let nine states establish the Constitution, saying, "If nine out of thirteen can dissolve the compact, Six out of nine will be just as able to dissolve the new one hereafter."[69] References to Locke, Priestley, Vattel, and other writers abounded.[70] On the extremes, Luther Martin and Alexander Hamilton used the Lockean and republican terminology but with radically different intentions.

The nationalists probably believed that they were making a proper, irrevocable Whig compact, a pure Lockean contract creating a new sovereign *over* the states. But during the ratification struggle, Madison and Hamilton argued in *The Federalist Papers* that the new Constitution was at once federal and national. States's-rights men, or "Antifederalists," stressed the dangers of a monarchical presidency, imperial consolidation, and the decline of the states—and were borne out by events.[71]

From the standpoint of states'-rights theory, much of the argument over ratification seems opportunistic. States'-rights men, wishing to retain the Articles, asserted that the existing constitution could not be broken. The Nationalists, contemplating a constitutional *coup d'état*, had to claim that the Union could be dissolved and recreated by as few as nine states. Madison, who

[67]For evidence that things were not falling apart under the Articles, see Jensen, *The New Nation*. On Madison's (and others') backpedaling, see M.E. Bradford, "The Constitutional Convention as Comic Action," in *Original Intentions* (Athens: University of Georgia Press, 1993), pp. 1–16.
[68]Charles C. Tansill, ed., *Documents Illustrative of the Formation of the Union of the American States* (Washington, D.C.: Government Printing Office, 1927), p. 364.
[69]Ibid., p. 698.
[70]See Luther Martin's remarks, ibid., pp. 815–16.
[71]Main, *Antifederalists*, pp. 226–27.

denied the sovereignty of the states at this time, argued that the Confederation was not a proper compact precisely because a majority could not bind the remainder: it was a "convention" and could be dissolved by any single party.[72]

Given the need to reassure the states, Madison and Hamilton pitched their arguments to the objections of states'-rights men like Patrick Henry. Hamilton called the proposed system "a Confederate Republic," defining it—after Montesquieu—as "an assemblage of societies." Such a confederacy secured to its members the advantages of strength in foreign affairs without annihilating their individual characters.[73] Answering charges of consolidation, Madison emphasized that ratification was "the act of the people, as forming so many independent States, not as forming one aggregate nation"; otherwise, the majority of the whole could bind the rest. Each state was "a sovereign body" only "bound by its voluntary act."[74] Denying that the new government was novel in operating on individuals, Madison remarked that the existing Confederation did so already. Hence, the new plan was merely "the expansion of principles which are found in the articles."[75]

These admissions from the centralizing camp, founded in political reality, greatly assisted later states'-rights men. Jefferson Davis could write that "a more perfect union was accomplished by the organization of a government more complete in its various branches . . . and by the delegation . . . of certain additional powers."[76] The changes did not alter the principles of a federal compact and the sovereignty of the states. Accepting Hamilton's terminology in his secessionist *summa*, Alexander H. Stephens, perhaps the foremost republican thinker of the Old South, called the American system "a pure Confederated Republic, upon the model of Montesquieu." The general government was "*an entirely artificial* or conventional *State or Nation*," "a Political Corporation" created by a compact between states.[77] Externally, it did appear to be a nation. In its metaphysical essence, however, it was a sort of political joint-stock venture, whose shareholders could withdraw for cause.[78] With such theoretical innovations,

---

[72]Tansill, *Documents*, pp. 226–27.

[73]*The Federalist* #9 (New York: Modern Library, 1937), pp. 50–53.

[74]Ibid., #39, pp. 246–47.

[75]Ibid., #40, pp. 254–55.

[76]Davis, *Rise and Fall*, vol. 1, p. 169.

[77]Stephens, *Constitutional View*, vol. 1, p. 483. His italics.

[78]Ibid., p. 496. For the entire discussion see pp. 167–70 and 477–522.

secessionist thought almost transcended its liberal and republican origins.

In his celebrated "Reply to Hayne" in 1830, Daniel Webster denied that terms like "compact" and "accede" (the counterpart to "secede") had been in use at the Constitutional Convention; states'-rights men had invented them. Since these were typical eighteenth-century terms, Webster's opponents easily refuted him.[79] As for "We the People" in the preamble, the original draft had begun "We the People of the States of New Hampshire" *et cetera*.[80] Since as few as nine states could enact the Constitution, it would have been awkward to name them all. Most of the prohibitions on the states (Article I, §10) existed in the Articles, which acknowledged the states' sovereignty. Finally, Rhode Island and North Carolina remained aloof from the Union in 1789–1790 after eleven states had instituted the new government. This would seem to demonstrate beyond question that "the people" who ratified were the peoples of the several states, and not Americans in the aggregate.[81]

If the states were arguably sovereign before 1789, and if sovereignty cannot pass by mere implication (as Jefferson Davis put it), then they remained sovereign under the new constitutional

---

[79]Davis, *Rise and Fall*, vol. 1, pp. 137–39.

[80]Tansill, *Documents*, p. 471.

[81]Davis, *Rise and Fall*, vol. 1, pp. 124–26. Of late, Samuel H. Beer has attempted to nail down a neo-Unionist case for national sovereignty *ab initio foederis* in *To Make a Union: The Rediscovery of American Federalism* (Cambridge, Mass.: Belknap Press, 1993), and does about the best one could from that perspective. He argues that the continental Whig movement was the constituent power of a new national sovereignty over the states (or colonies), and a new people. Accepting provisionally the somewhat Hegelian metaphysic invoked by Beer, one has to wonder why, if the Whigs were consciously reinventing government *à la* Al Gore, they weren't a bit more *explicit* about it. Why, then, did the former Whigs we call the Antifederalists not accept the reasonings of Hamilton and James Wilson? Beer's position, well argued as it is, rests on the shaky foundations of James Wilson's and Justice Joseph Story's fantasies in which the Continental Congress represented the sovereignty of a single new people. The idea that the states, heirs of separate colonial political communities whose origins reached back into the seventeenth century, had to be "authorized" by the Continental Congress to set up new governments (and were, therefore, somehow the "creatures" of the Congress) is such a palpable absurdity as to warrant laughter or tears. For a realistic view of the imbecilities and unsovereign character of that body, see Edmund Cody Burnett, *The Continental Congress* (New York: W.W. Norton, 1964), *passim*. For the important insight that the handful of nationalists in the Congress (including Wilson) were interested in *any* government that could protect their large-scale land speculations, see Murray N. Rothbard, *Conceived in Liberty* (New Rochelle, N.Y.: Arlington House, 1979), vol. 4, pp. 369–72.

compact.[82] Constitutional scholars are wont to lose much sleep over the framers' intentions in such matters, especially Madison's. Although the potentially radical notion of "consent of the governed" remains an ideological prop of the present empire, little attention is paid, oddly, to the intentions of those who *ratified* the document. Ratification gave the Constitution all the "validity it ever had."[83] The temper of the ratifying conventions may be gauged by their words. Massachusetts, South Carolina, New Hampshire, Virginia, North Carolina, and Rhode Island all called for an amendment along the lines of the second Article of Confederation, reserving to the states all powers not "delegated" to the general government. (This, of course, was the basis of the Tenth Amendment.) In their ratifications, South Carolina and Rhode Island mentioned state "sovereignty," North Carolina and Virginia invoked natural rights, the latter even listing the rights men retain in their own hands when they form a "social compact."[84]

Most significantly, perhaps, Virginia, New York, and Rhode Island declared that "the powers of government" may be "resumed" or "reassumed" by the people when perverted or abused.[85] Since each convention spoke only for the people of its own state, Davis's and Stephens's idea that three states by this language explicitly reserved the right of secession in their very ratifications is not unwarranted. In addition, New York and South Carolina declared all undelegated powers to be reserved; Virginia, New York, North Carolina, and Rhode Island stated that clauses restricting Congress were exceptions to delegated powers or inserted "for greater caution."[86] In other words, restrictions on Congress were not limits on an otherwise vague and voluminous mass of power somehow granted (as Hamilton and others later argued from the "necessary and proper" clause). Given these sentiments, it is not surprising that ten amendments passed quickly, including the much neglected ninth and tenth.

PHILOSOPHICAL ROOTS AND OUTCOME

Granting the sovereignty of the states *arguendo*, some would say that withdrawal by a single state on its own motion requires

[82]Davis, *Rise and Fall*, vol. 1, pp. 170–76.
[83]Madison as quoted by Davis, *Rise and Fall*, vol. 1, p. 105.
[84]Ibid., vol. 1, pp. 103–11; Tansill, pp. 1018, 1023, 1025, 1028–31, 1044–47, and 1056.
[85]Ibid., pp. 1027, 1034–35, and 1052. John Locke speaks of the people's "Right to resume their original Liberty" in *Two Treatises of Government*, Peter Laslett, ed. (New York: New American Library, 1963), p. 461.
[86]For full texts of the ratifications, see Tansill, *Documents*, pp. 1009–59.

further justification. Even Lincoln, though, conceded that by general agreement the states could dissolve the Union. Southern republicans of the states'-rights school found justification for single-state secession from more than one source. According to Vernon Lewis Parrington, the great historian of American thought, secession ultimately rests on "the doctrine which Paine and Jefferson derived from the French school, namely, that a constitutional compact is terminable."[87] Paine argued, as against Whig theory, that the people are always entitled to alter their government. Strict Lockeanism seemed to hold that a people may only change a government after a long chain of abuses and then only if a substantial majority of them support the rebellion. In this, Paine agreed with Priestley and Price. Jefferson, too, believed that "No society can make a perpetual Constitution, or even a perpetual law."[88]

If the people are sovereign-as-states, a right of secession follows if one accepts the radical version of social contract theory. Parrington comments:

> However deeply it might be covered over by constitutional lawyers and historians who defended the right of secession, the doctrine [of terminable compact] was there implicitly, and the southern cause would have been more effectively served if legal refinements had been subordinated to philosophical justification of this fundamental doctrine.[89]

Parrington clearly overstated the French influence on the thought of Jefferson and other southerners. There also existed an Anglo-American natural law school whose ideas the French had in large measure borrowed upon.[90] As the slave controversy grew in intensity, southerners tended to shy away from overtly natural-law underpinnings for their political theory. Finally, in defending unilateral state secession, southerners could draw on commercial contract law and the analogous rules of international law.[91] Unwilling to follow natural-law thinking in the direction

[87]Vernon Lewis Parrington, *Main Currents in American Thought* (New York: Harcourt, Brace, 1954), Book Two, p. 88.

[88]Ibid., Book One, pp. 334–35 and Book Two, p. 12.

[89]Ibid., Book Two, p. 12.

[90]Staughton Lynd, *Intellectual Origins of American Radicalism* (New York: Pantheon, 1968), pp. 55–61; Jensen, *Articles*, p. 165; and Murray N. Rothbard, *Conceived in Liberty* (New Rochelle, N.Y.: Arlington House, 1975), vol. 2, pp. 186–98.

[91]Edmund Burke rather famously wrote that "the state ought not to be considered as nothing better than a partnership agreement in a trade of pepper and coffee, calico, or tobacco, or some other low concern, to be taken up for a little temporary interest, and to be dissolved by the fancy of the parties" (Peter J. Stanlis, ed., *Edmund Burke: Selected Writings and Speeches* [Garden City, N.Y.: Anchor Books, 1963],

of slave emancipation, southerners thus refrained from developing this particular potential basis of support for the idea of secession. The Virginia debate of 1830 was the last open discussion
of emancipation in the South until 1864–1865 (at which point it
was too late to do anything about it on southern terms). Determined to defend their rights and interests, southerners turned in-
ward in the context of what Clifford Dowdey once called the 30-
year "cold war" between North and South (1830–1860). Conscious
of their gradual transformation into a political minority, southerners developed a *laager* mentality which, combined with their
traditional legalism, led them to present secession as a legal,
constitutional, and procedural right.

All this was a legitimate reading of the Constitution, but not
the only possible one.[92] Jefferson and Madison had expressed similar views in the Kentucky and Virginia Resolutions. Spencer
Roane, John Taylor, and many others produced a coherent case for
states' rights and made it integral to southern republicanism. To
achieve the Revolutionary–republican aims of taming power and
securing liberty, Taylor went beyond the balanced constitution
and separation of powers, and proposed to so thoroughly divide
power as to render it relatively harmless.[93]

This antifederalist republicanism, which Taylor read into
the Constitution (not without substantial justification), became a
key fixture in southern thought. There were indeed Unionists and
"integral nationalists" in the South, but by 1850 they were outside the southern mainstream.[94] As North and South came into

p. 471). It is ten times obvious to me that when it came to the federal union,
Southerners were not good Burkeans. The theme of the Constitution as an inter-
national agreement or a business partnership runs all through the works of Bledsoe,
Davis, Stephens, and others. For Southerners the union was of *instrumental* value.

[92]Cf. Gough, *The Social Contract*, pp. 234–43.

[93]On Taylor's celestial mechanics of government, see M.J.C. Vile, *Constitutionalism
and the Separation of Powers* (Oxford: Clarendon Press, 1976), pp. 161–72; on this
and other aspects of Taylor's republicanism see also Shalhope, *John Taylor*; Grant
McConnell, "John Taylor and the Democratic Tradition," *Western Political Quarterly*
4, no. 1 (March 1951): 17–31; Joseph R. Stromberg, "Country Ideology, Republicanism, and Libertarianism: The Thought of John Taylor of Caroline," *Journal of Libertarian Studies* 6, no. 1 (Winter 1982): 35–48; and Manning J. Dauer and Hans Ham-
mond, "John Taylor: Democrat or Aristocrat?" *Journal of Politics* 4, no. 4 (November
1944): 381–403. For Taylor's influence on the Jacksonians, see Williams, *Contours*,
pp. 227–33.

[94]For Southern integral nationalism see Jackson's "Proclamation to the People of
South Carolina," 10 December 1832, in Commager, *Documents*, vol. 1, pp. 262–68.
Two other integral (U.S.) nationalists in the South are treated in Herbert J. Do-
herty, *Richard Keith Call: Southern Unionist* (Gainesville: University of Florida Press,
1961); and Llerena B. Friend, *Sam Houston: The Great Designer* (Austin: University of
Texas Press, 1969).

collision over slavery, slavery expansion, and the question of which section would benefit most from the huge *ager publicus* bought from France and seized from Mexico, southern anti-federalism ran head-on into growing northern democratic integral nationalism.

DEMOCRATIC INTEGRAL NATIONALISM IN THE NORTH

After the Hartford Convention (1815), northerners made little use of the idea of secession. The Fugitive Slave Act led to several cases of northern judicial nullification (or interposition), but in the North, the main drift was the marriage of the Federalist judiciary's theory of an organic American nation with the majoritarianism unleashed in the Age of Egalitarianism.[95] The new majoritarianism carried forward an egalitarian trend set in motion by the Revolution but at the cost of weakening institutional barriers the Founders had thought necessary for ordered republican liberty.

Northern majoritarians postulated the sovereignty of the "people of the United States in the aggregate,"[96] and stood opposed to the southern view of the Union as a compact between states whose people were severally "sovereign." In this way, egalitarian democracy, which the Federalists had abhorred, completed their project of a consolidated empire. (In this, the democratic ideologues were greatly assisted by the theoretical end run which the Federalists made around traditional republican theory back during the ratification struggle, as noted earlier.) Integral nationalism represents an interesting (one could even say dialectical) counterpoint to the pervasive anti-institutionalism of the period. Already, the Dorr War had shown that, however democratic their politics, post-Revolutionary Americans had lost touch with some fundamental values of 1776. Instead of republicans primed to rebel, they were becoming a democratic Party of Order.[97] This, too, held danger for the future.

[95]On the relation between democracy, egalitarianism, and Northern unionism, see Wiebe, *Opening of American Society*, chap. 12, "The Jacksonian Revolution," pp. 234–52.

[96]This phrase comes from Davis, *Rise and Fall*, vol. 1, p. 142; he, in turn, was paraphrasing Madison (*Federalist*, #246).

[97]George Dennison, *The Dorr War: Republicanism on Trial, 1831–1861* (Lexington: University Press of Kentucky, 1976), "Epilogue: The 'Precedent of 1842,'" pp. 193–205. For the way that Northerners developed a theology of the Union in stark contrast to the instrumental valuation of the Union in earlier generations, see Paul C. Nagel, *One Nation Indivisible: The Union in American Thought, 1776–1861* (New York: Oxford University Press, 1964).

More in tune, perhaps, with the disorder of the "Middle Period" was the anti-institutional stance of the Transcendentalists and Abolitionists. In the wake of the unraveling of left-wing Protestantism in New England, Henry David Thoreau, William Lloyd Garrison, and Lysander Spooner took the natural-rights theory of the Revolutionary generation all the way into individualist anarchism.[98] (George Fitzhugh had a case of sorts when he wrote that "with inexorable sequence 'Let-Alone' is made to usher in No-Government."[99]) For all its inherent appeal, the anti-Constitutional dissent of northern radicals put them outside any possible American consensus.

Mainstream northern political life featured Democrats, some of whom were "northern men with southern principles,"[100] and—following the collapse of the Whig Party—Free Soilers, and later the new Republican Party. Drawing on the time-honored republican tradition of unearthing conspiratorial threats to liberty, anti-slavery northerners pointed with some justification at the southern "Slave Power."[101] With the breakdown of the tacit national consensus to keep slavery out of politics the Free Soilers developed an "ideology of free labor" which gave temporary new life to the Revolutionary values of liberty and independence. This outlook held great appeal for northern farmers who did not want to share the western public lands with slaveholders or Negroes.[102]

[98]On the anarchism and near-anarchism of the Abolitionists see Eric Foner, "Radical Individualism in America: Revolution to Civil War," *Literature of Liberty* 1, no. 3 (July–September 1978): 5–31; Lynd, *American Radicalism*, pp. 56–63; Lewis Perry, *Radical Abolitionism: Anarchy and the Government of God in Antislavery Thought* (Ithaca, N.Y.: Cornell University Press, 1973); and Aileen S. Kraditor, *Means and Ends in American Abolitionism* (New York: Pantheon Books, 1969). For critical assessments see Williams, *Contours*, pp. 250–55; and Stanley M. Elkins, *Slavery: A Problem in American Institutional and Intellectual Life* (New York: Universal Library, 1963), pp. 140–93.

[99]Harvey Wish, ed., *Ante-Bellum: Writings of George Fitzhugh and Hinton Rowan Helper on Slavery* (New York: Capricorn Books, 1960), p. 154.

[100]For one of these Jeffersonian–Jacksonian Northerners, see Robert Kelley, *The Transatlantic Persuasion: The Liberal–Democratic Mind in the Age of Gladstone* (New York: Alfred A. Knopf, 1969), chap. 7, "Samuel Tilden: The Democrat as Social Scientist," pp. 238–92.

[101]See Larry Gara, "Slavery and the Slave Power: A Crucial Distinction," *Civil War History* 15, no. 1 (March 1969): 5–18. For the republican habit of finding conspiracies see Richard Hofstadter, *The Paranoid Style in American Politics and Other Essays* (New York: Vintage Books, 1967), pp. 3–40. On the other hand, Hofstadter cannot prove that there are never "conspiracies" against liberty.

[102]See Eric Foner, *Free Soil, Free Labor, Free Men: The Ideology of the Republican Party Before the Civil War* (New York: Oxford University Press, 1970). Banning, *Jeffersonian Persuasion*, tries to connect these northern republicans with the broader republican

SLAVERY, SOUTHERNISM, AND "RECOUNTRIFICATION"

The Age of Egalitarianism was an experience common to North and South. Jackson himself was a "new man" whose political success heralded the decline of gentry politics. As a Scotch–Irish frontiersman, slaveholder, slave trader, and Indian-removing general, Jackson symbolized for many the rise of the common man and equal opportunity for white males. As a Revolutionary War veteran, Jackson was a direct link to the older republicanism.

As in the North, the democratic reforms in the South swept away barriers to popular political participation state-by-state. In states like Alabama, Georgia, and Mississippi, a vigorously democratic politics took hold.[103] Except in Virginia and South Carolina, gentry politics was on the wane. Egalitarian individualism characterized many areas of white southern life.

Egalitarianism within the white community was intimately connected with slavery. All white men shared a common superiority to Negroes, but few of them would concede another white man's inherent superiority.[104] Slavery was the bottom line in southern society and politics, and provisionally, at least, white southerners were united on the necessity of maintaining it.[105] As Stanley Elkins writes,

> [t]he underlying egalitarianism in Southern values was such, and the South's faith in barriers between classes was so limited, that once the Negro's bonds of chattel slavery were removed and once he was redefined as human, the first thing he was likely to do, for all anyone knew, was to marry somebody's daughter.[106]

tradition (p. 302, n. 54). On the Free-Soilers' lack of sympathy for Negroes, slave or free, see Williams, *Contours*, p. 291. Foner's book is quite clear on the racism of the Northern antislavery coalition.

[103]Sydnor, *Southern Sectionalism*, chap. 12, pp. 275–93.

[104]Kenneth P. Vickery, "'Herrenvolk' Democracy and Egalitarianism in South Africa and the U.S. South," *Comparative Studies in Society and History* 16, no. 3 (June 1974): 309–28; Robert E. Shalhope, "Race, Class, Slavery and the Ante-bellum Southern Mind," *Journal of Southern History* 37, no. 4 (November 1971): 557–74; and Eugene D. Genovese and Elizabeth Fox-Genovese, *Fruits of Merchant Capital: Slavery and Bourgeois Property in the Rise of and Expansion of Capitalism* (New York: Oxford University Press, 1983), ch. 9, "Yeoman Farmers in a Slaveholders' Democracy," pp. 249–64.

[105]For the fragility of this consensus, see Ralph E. Morrow, "The Proslavery Argument Revisited," *Mississippi Valley Historical Review* 48, no. 1 (June 1961): 79–94.

[106]Stanley M. Elkins, "On Eugene D. Genovese's *The Political Economy of Slavery*," in Allen Weinstein and Frank O. Gatell, eds., *American Negro Slavery: A Modern Reader* (New York: Oxford University Press, 1973), p. 391.

Racially specific chattel slavery created some ideological problems for southern whites, but solved others. The presence of a distinct subject race, unassimilable on any terms acceptable to white Americans—northerners included—was a dilemma for republican theory, which presupposed a homogeneous citizenry; the treatment of ethnic minorities was not its strong point.[107] Faced with this issue, southerners played down concepts of natural or inherent rights.

At the same time, slavery solved a problem that had plagued the English Country Party thinkers, i.e., how to prevent anti-republican forces from using "unvirtuous men"—the lazy, the idle, and dependent unpropertied men—to overturn the constitution. One answer was to enslave the unreliable element. It is a bit jarring to find otherwise-libertarian writers drawing this conclusion, but it does underline the way in which republicanism and libertarianism overlap without being identical.[108]

Slavery solved this problem for nineteenth-century white southerners before they were born. As real historical actors, white southerners were able to live with inconsistencies which critical reason—had they been its devotees—would have revealed to them. Untheoretical though they were, southerners saw daily the difference between freedom and slavery, and this knowledge increased their personal libertarianism.[109]

"African slavery" set limits to the universalism of southern conceptions of liberty; it thereby kept southern republicanism frozen in the mold of the Revolutionary synthesis as understood by their libertarian slaveholding forefathers. Thereafter, innovations and refinements in southern republicanism took the form of political-institutional analysis of the rights of the constituent states in a federal Republic; a retreat from the analysis of individual rights accompanied the complex reasonings of John Taylor and John C. Calhoun. At the same time, defense of slavery worked against the ideal of integral nationalism.

Just as slavery made southerners assert states' rights out of fear of anticipated northern interference, so too did the presence

[107]On the rather fruitless deliberations of Jefferson, Taylor, and others, who conceded that slavery was unrepublican and unlibertarian but could not conceive of any workable solution for it, see Winthrop Jordan, *White Over Black: American Attitudes Toward the Negro, 1550–1812* (Baltimore: Penguin Books, 1969), pp. 429–81 and 542–69; Duncan MacLeod, *Slavery, Race and the American Revolution* (New York: Cambridge University Press, 1974); and Robert McColley, *Slavery and Jeffersonian Virginia* (Urbana: University of Illinois Press, 1973).

[108]Shalhope, *John Taylor*, p. 149; and Lynd, *American Radicalism*, p. 35.

[109]See Edmund S. Morgan, *American Slavery, American Freedom: The Ordeal of Colonial Virginia* (New York: W.W. Norton, 1975), pp. 380–87.

of the slaves themselves tend to make white society more cohesive. Southern individualism necessarily coexisted with a strong sense of white community.[110] A pre-modern code of honor and a strong "folk culture" among the "plain folk"—subsistence farmers and herdsmen with few or no slaves—likewise set bounds to individualist theorizing, if not to southern individualism and "personalism" themselves.[111]

Southern individualism had a strong social context. On the other hand, material, ideological, and cultural limitations on southern libertarianism and individualism can be overstated. As Eugene D. Genovese has argued, the great slaveholding planters enjoyed political and ideological "hegemony." For Genovese, the planters were a confident, class-conscious ruling elite whose position was so secure that they were beginning to develop their own organicist and anti-bourgeois ideology.[112] A few writers did indeed present a self-consistent pro-slavery argument but for the most part this "reactionary Enlightenment" proved abortive.[113]

For one thing, southerners were not given to theoretical consistency; for another, they already had an outlook, that of their forefathers. As we have seen, republicanism, in its classical versions, was compatible with slavery.[114] If southerners felt the need for an ideology to sustain their practical libertarianism for whites and justify chattel slavery for blacks, the necessary materials were on hand. It was a matter of shifting emphases. A relative recountrification was possible, even likely, if by country we

---

[110]See Richard M. Weaver, "Two Types of American Individualism," in George M. Curtis III and James J. Thompson, Jr., *The Southern Essays of Richard M. Weaver* (Indianapolis: Liberty Press, 1987), pp. 77–103. For reflections on the present-day status of Southern values, see the interesting comments of John Shelton Reed, "The Same Old Stand?" in Fifteen Southerners, *Why the South Will Survive* (Athens: University of Georgia Press, 1981), pp. 13–34.

[111]On Southern personalism, see Bertram Wyatt-Brown, "The Ante-bellum South as a 'Culture of Courage,'" *Southern Studies* 20, no. 3 (Fall 1981): 213–46.

[112]Eugene D. Genovese, *The World the Slaveholders Made* (New York: Vintage Books, 1971); and idem, *The Political Economy of Slavery* (London: MacGibbon and Kee, 1964).

[113]Louis Hartz, *The Liberal Tradition in America* (New York: Harcourt, Brace and World, 1955), chap. 6 and 7, pp. 145–200.

[114]James Oakes stresses that white liberty and Negro slavery had been juxtaposed with little theoretical anguish since the Revolution. See Oakes, *The Ruling Race* (New York: Alfred A. Knopf, 1983), pp. 30–31. Religion or economic theory were the usual starting points for the corporal's guard of white Southern abolitionists. See, for example, Jeffrey Brooke Allen, "Were Southern White Critics of Slavery Racists? Kentucky and the Upper South, 1791–1824," *Journal of Southern History* 44, no. 2 (May 1978): 169–90.

mean an appeal to the Bolingbrokean side of the republican heritage.

Men could take republicanism in a "seigneurial" or "revolutionary capitalist" direction according to their needs. With John Taylor, republicanism stood balanced between its bourgeois and pre-bourgeois possibilities. John C. Calhoun tried working backwards into pre-eighteenth-century civic humanism (with an eye on ancient Athens), but remained a republican. Louis Hartz observes that "Calhoun betrayed the Reactionary Enlightenment when he based the sectional defense of the South on the liberalism it tried to destroy."[115] But political liberalism in a modern sense had never been at issue.

Those like Abel Upshur and Benjamin Leigh who wanted a more socially conservative ideology brought Burke and Blackstone into the mixture—*and stopped*. Wealthy planters who argued in this way were more concerned with political extremism emerging from the plain folk than with refining theory. Fred Siegel draws two conclusions. First, the planters *did not* have hegemony and *could not* impose a new class ideology on society. Second, they had to argue *within* republicanism precisely because their adversaries did.[116] Third, I would add, they themselves believed in it. Bertram Wyatt-Brown confirms Siegel's analysis when he writes that "secession was a complex movement involving social intimidations of lesser men against the wealthiest and generational strains that cannot be adequately defined as 'planter hegemony' no matter how broadly conceived."[117]

What stands out from the interplay of democracy and aristocracy in the antebellum South is the stark fact of a monolithic republican consensus reaching back into the Revolutionary era as experienced in the South.[118] Planters and yeomen used republicanism, interpreting it here and there, adding a racist codicil to its social applications, but they never departed far from its

[115]Hartz, *Liberal Tradition*, p. 159.
[116]Fred Siegel, "The Paternalist Thesis: Virginia as a Test Case," *Civil War History* 25, no. 3 (1979): 246–61.
[117]Wyatt-Brown, "Ante-bellum South," pp. 217–18.
[118]For a thorough demonstration of this consensus and the persistence of republicanism in the South, see W.K. Wood, "The Union of the States: A Study of the Radical Whig–Republican Ideology and Its Influence Upon the Nation and the South, 1776–1861" (Ph.D. Diss., University of South Carolina, 1978). For the complexity of the ante-bellum South, see Emory M. Thomas, *The Confederate Nation* (New York: Harper and Row, 1979), chap. 1, "The Social Economy of the Old South," pp. 1–16.

fundamentals. This is why George Fitzhugh put himself entirely outside southern discourse when he wrote that "[a] Constitution, strictly construed, is absolutely incompatible with permanent national existence."[119]

One illiberal innovation was the suppression of free speech on the slavery question.[120] Even here, southerners were on republican ground, but not libertarian ground, since, strictly speaking, the Bill of Rights only applied against the general government. Even the suppression of debate does not prove planter hegemony, but only reflects racial consensus; white southerners simply did not know what to do about blacks in southern society except to keep them as they were. The bottom line was race, not the "mode of production."[121]

If slavery limited the universal application of libertarian ideals, the latter (as part of republicanism) limited aristocratic tendencies in politics and thought, and thwarted the emergence of an internally consistent pro-slavery ideology. We can accuse antebellum southerners of compartmentalizing liberty and slavery, or we can understand that their ideology was a form of premodern republicanism which had already done their compartmentalizing for them. Many southerners chose to stop where John Taylor had in the development of republican ideas. Others, especially on the frontier or in the lower South, went in for a more egalitarian, individualist, and libertarian ideology.[122]

THE PERSISTENCE OF REPUBLICANISM IN THE SOUTH AND THE ROAD TO SECESSION

It appears, then, that a better case can be made for the persistence of Revolutionary republicanism in the South than can be

[119]George Fitzhugh, *Cannibals All! Or Slaves without Masters* (reprint; Cambridge, Mass.: Belknap Press, 1960), p. 249.
[120]See Clement Eaton, The Freedom-of-Thought Struggle in the Old South (Durham, N.C.: Duke University Press, 1940).
[121]See John W. Cell, *The Highest Stage of White Supremacy: The Origins of Segregation in South Africa and the American South* (Cambridge: Cambridge University Press, 1982).
[122]Wyatt-Brown's description of the familial near-anarchism of Southern white society begs for comparison with stateless societies organized around kinship relations ("Ante-bellum South," pp. 239–40). For the contribution of immigrants from Britain's Celtic fringe to the character of Southern society, see Forrest McDonald and Grady McWhiney, "The South from Self-Sufficiency to Peonage," *American Historical Review* 85, no. 5 (December 1980): 1095–118; and idem, "The Ante-bellum Southern Herdsman," *Journal of Southern History* 41, no. 2 (May 1975): 147–66; and Grady McWhiney, *Cracker Culture: Celtic Ways in the Old South* (Tuscaloosa: University of Alabama Press, 1988).

made for its persistence in the North. Indeed, some recent inter-
preters of southern political life down to 1860 lay heavy emphasis on just this circumstance. Attacking the notion that a "Great
Reaction" away from liberalism and democracy took place in the
southern states between 1776 and 1860, W.K. Wood writes:

> This liberal consensus makes sense only if the United States
> began its career with the same beliefs in democracy, capi-
> talism, and nationalism that we share today. As is becoming
> increasingly evident, early Americans were the heirs of a
> distinctly antistatist, antidemocratic, anticapitalistic, anti-
> urban, and anti-industrial political philosophy (republican-
> ism) that they inherited not from the liberal Enlightenment
> but rather from the radical Whigs and opposition writers of
> seventeenth and eighteenth century England. . . . Not until the
> thought of the founding generation was overturned could
> America hope to become democratized and nationalized,
> which is precisely what happened during the Middle Peri-
> od.[123]

In the North, democratization and nationalization ran parallel to one another. In the South, republican ideology persisted
via the Old Republican–Jacksonian connection even as political
life became more democratic in form. At the same time, the
structural logic of the North–South conflict over slavery in the
western territories made southerners increasingly true to an anti-
federalist theory of the Constitution and union.

As the national political consensus broke down in the 1850s,
southerners began expressing fears of political "enslavement" to
the North. The issue of slavery in the territories came to symbol-
ize the South's rights within the union. Just as the Free Soilers
had pointed to a Slave Power "conspiracy," southerners sensed a
"Black Republican" plot to subordinate them within the union
and interfere with slavery. In this, they seriously underestimat-
ed western farmers' racism and overestimated their "abolitionism."[124] It seemed clear to many southerners that northern anti-
slavery men were threatening their constitutional rights and
liberties. The election of Abraham Lincoln galvanized southern
separatists into action to secure their republican liberties in their
own confederacy.

That slavery and slavery expansion, as going *economic* prop-
ositions, were not the central issues to most white southerners is

[123]W.K. Wood, "Rewriting Southern History: U.B. Phillips, the New South, and
the Ante-bellum Past," *Southern Studies* 22, no. 3 (Fall 1983): 240–41, footnote 38.
(For "anticapitalist" I would suggest the term "antimercantilist.")
[124]James A. Rawley, *Race and Politics: "Bleeding Kansas" and the Coming of the Civil
War* (Lincoln: University of Nebraska Press, 1979), esp. chap. 9, pp. 223–56, and
Epilogue, pp. 257–74.

shown by the appeals which secessionists presented to the voters. J. Mills Thornton III's study of politics in Alabama is very suggestive in this connection.[125] Writing of Alabama's post-secession Constitutional Convention, he observes that:

> [I]n Alabama there was always only one question which really mattered: how to maintain one's freedom. The genuine factions in the convention were ideological groupings determined by convictions upon this all-important subject.[126]

Thornton distinguishes three factions in the Convention:

> [W]higgish members, who believed that the path to freedom lay through the energetic intervention by the political structure to assist the growth of commerce and industry; Jacksonians, who thought that the essence of the struggle for freedom was the destruction of any institution which had the power to coerce obedience from the citizenry; and younger politicians—the group which constituted the backbone of the Yanceyite faction and which shared many of its ideals with the emerging school of laissez-faire radicals in England—who accepted the need for industrialization, but felt that real freedom required that government involve itself in the economy and in the society as infrequently as possible.[127]

The laissez-faireists and neo-Jacksonians were strong enough together to prevent the local mercantilism of the whiggish faction from being written into the Alabama Constitution in any important way. Both factions worked within the individualist and libertarian republicanism of the lower South. Their persistent republicanism explains the appeal of secession as a means of escaping anticipated northern tyranny.

This interpretation appears to hold true for Georgia as well. Michael P. Johnson writes:

> When secessionists tied their hopes to the ideas of the Founding Fathers rather than to the proslavery argument, they implicitly acknowledged the limited hegemony of slaveholders. The ideology of 1776 did what proslavery ideology apparently could not do. . . . If there had been a broad consensus on the proslavery view that slavery was the fundamental basis of Southern society, secessionists would have had to demonstrate only that the Lincoln administration had threatened slavery. By using instead the rhetoric of a national independence movement and emphasizing that the

---

[125]J. Mills Thornton III, *Politics and Power in a Slave Society: Alabama, 1800–1860* (Baton Rouge: Louisiana State University Press, 1978), esp. chap. 6, "Secession," pp. 343–461.

[126]Ibid., p. 437.

[127]Ibid., p. 436.

rights of all Georgians were threatened by a Republican president, secessionists implicitly suggested that any consensus about the social necessity of slavery was not strong enough to rest their case on.[128]

Republicanism in its various forms—Jeffersonian in Virginia, Bolingbrokean in South Carolina,[129] and largely Jacksonian elsewhere (i.e., more democratic)—was the ideology that served the vast majority of white southerners. Despite the best efforts of George Fitzhugh and a few others, the great slaveholders could not free themselves from this outlook, if indeed they saw any need to. Charles Grier Sellers, Jr. remarks that "Robert Barnwell Rhett, declaimed on 'liberty' so constantly and so indiscriminately that John Quincy Adams could call him 'a compound of wild democracy and iron bound slavery.'"[130]

It can be argued that republicanism leads to extremism unless restrained by a strong two-party electoral tradition. This helps explain the salience and priority of secession movements in the Gulf states and South Carolina. South Carolina still practiced the republican but undemocratic gentry politics of a Bolingbrokean Country-Party-in-power, while Mississippi, Florida, and Alabama had not developed viable two-party systems.[131] Ideology, it appears, is not as manipulable or "superstructural" as some students of history would have it.

Republicanism persisted in the South partly because of, and partly despite, southern social, political, and economic realities. Republicanism continued as a "structure of thought," exerting its own pressure on southern political behavior, permitting southerners—in the eyes of outsiders—constantly to contradict themselves. The (whites-only) libertarianism of the South varied in intensity by geography, white ethnic origins (Celtic fringe vs. home counties), religious affiliation, income level, and status, perhaps, but it was characteristic of southern society as a whole.

These political and social values affected the history of the South on topics ranging from secession to Confederate military

[128]Michael P. Johnson, *Toward a Patriarchal Republic: The Secession of Georgia* (Baton Rouge: Louisiana State University Press, 1977), pp. 33–34.

[129]See Robert M. Weir, "'The Harmony We Were Famous For': An Interpretation of Pre-Revolutionary South Carolina Politics," *William and Mary Quarterly*, 3rd ser. 26, no. 4 (October 1969): 473–501.

[130]Charles Grier Sellers, Jr., "The Travail of Slavery," in idem, ed., *The Southerner as American* (Chapel Hill: University of North Carolina Press, 1960), p. 42.

[131]See Michael F. Holt, *The Political Crisis of the 1850s* (New York: W.W. Norton, 1983), chap. 8, "Politics, Slavery, and Southern Secession," pp. 219–59.

organization.[132] As General L.M. Keitt, CSA, wrote in early 1864:

> Countries like ours are not fit for revolution. . . . What is the
> cause of this? Our political institutions. In peace they make
> us great through our individuality; in war they make us
> weak through want of harmony and complete obedience to
> routine.[133]

So given were southerners to their values of independence
and liberty—both local and individual—that the attempts of
the Davis administration to regiment them for war led to considerable disaffection.[134] Republicanism as a coherent *Weltanscha-
uung* persisted after 1790 and survived in the South down to the
1860s. Appomattox marked a great historical defeat of the Anglo-American Country Party. Thereafter, republicanism survived
in the constitutional framework of American federalism but it
withered rapidly as an ideology. New issues replaced the old
ones, and new ideologies arose around them. In Old Republican
terms, northern Republican dominance after 1865 intensified a
resurrected American mercantilism. In the 1930s, this northern
mercantilist Court Party gave way before its own logical outcome: a bureaucratic Court Party—a sort of leveling Oriental
despotism and Asiatic mode of production in the name of radical
egalitarianism and with actual production somewhat lost in the
shuffle—which even organized corporatist interest groups could
not entirely abide.

The republicanism of the South found its final expression in
the various post-war Confederate *apologiae*.[135] These works are
largely neglected because of their authors' claims that issues of
liberty and self-determination were as important, or more important, to white southerners than chattel slavery itself. The belat-
ed debate over Confederate emancipation gives some support to
the Confederate apologetic.[136] Southern republicanism was the
inheritance the South received from its Revolutionary forefathers and, whether right or wrong, the South had remained truer to

[132]David Donald, "Died of Democracy" in David Donald, ed., *Why the North Won
the Civil War* (New York: Collier Books, 1960), pp. 79–90.

[133]Quoted in Bell Irvin Wiley, *The Road to Appomattox* (New York: Atheneum,
1971), chap. 3, "Failures That Were Fatal," p. 117.

[134]Robert L. Kerby, "Why the Confederacy Lost," *Review of Politics* 35, no. 3 (July
1973): 326–45; and Paul D. Escott, *After Secession: Jefferson Davis and the Failure of
Confederate Nationalism* (Baton Rouge: Louisiana State University Press, 1978).

[135]Albert Taylor Bledsoe, *Is Davis a Traitor? Or Was Secession a Constitutional Right
Previous to the War of 1861?* (Lynchburg, Va.: J.P. Bell, 1915); Davis, *Rise and Fall*;
and Stephens, *Constitutional View*.

[136]Robert F. Durden, *The Gray and the Black* (Baton Rouge: Louisiana State University Press, 1972).

the original understanding of it than had the North. The English liberal historian Lord Acton understood this well. Writing of the Confederate Constitution he said:

> These were the political ideas of the Confederacy, and they justify me, I think, in saying that history can show no instance of so great an effort made by Republicans to remedy the faults of that form of government. Had they adopted the means which would have ensured and justified success, had they called on the negroes to be partners with them in the perils of war and in the fruits of victory, I believe that generous resolution would have confirmed in all future ages incalculable blessings on the human race.[137]

After 1860, the American Country Party had not the time, the resources, nor the vision—until it was far too late—to carry through the sort of revolution Acton sketched out. As Vernon Louis Parrington observed, it was no small tragedy that in America the causes of local self-government and decentralization had become bound up with the defense of chattel slavery.[138] If republicanism still has any meaning for us, it should remind us that something more than slavery died in 1865.

---

[137]J. Rufus Fears, ed., *Selected Writings of Lord Acton* (Indianapolis: Liberty Classics, 1984), vol. 1, chap. 21, "The Civil War in America," p. 278.

[138]Parrington, *Main Currents*, Book Two, pp. 92–93.

7

YANKEE CONFEDERATES:
NEW ENGLAND SECESSION MOVEMENTS
PRIOR TO THE WAR BETWEEN THE STATES

Thomas J. DiLorenzo

An insurrection once every twenty years
is a wholesome feature of national life.

– Thomas Jefferson

C ontrary to standard accounts, the birthplace of American secessionist sentiment was not Charleston, South Carolina in 1860, but the heart of the New England Yankee culture—Salem, Massachusetts—more than half a century before the first shot was fired at Fort Sumter. From 1800 to 1815, there were three serious attempts at secession orchestrated by New England Federalists, who believed that the policies of the Jefferson and Madison administrations, especially the 1803 Louisiana Purchase, the national embargo of 1807, and the War of 1812, were so disproportionately harmful to New England that they justified secession.

If these New England Federalists had been southerners and said the things they said in 1861 rather than in 1803, they would have long ago been denigrated by historians as maniacal "fire eaters" or traitors. "I will rather anticipate a new confederacy, exempt from the corrupt and corrupting influence and oppression of the aristocratic Democrats of the South," wrote the prominent Massachusetts Federalist politician and U.S. Senator, Timothy Pickering, in 1803. "There will be . . . a separation," he predicted, and "the white and black population will mark the boundary."[1] His colleague, Senator James Hillhouse, agreed, saying, "The Eastern States must and will dissolve the Union and form a separate government."[2] "The Northern States must be governed by Virginia or must govern Virginia, and there is no middle ground," warned the conspiratorial Aaron Burr, who joined the New England Federalists in a secessionist plot (discussed below).[3]

---

[1]Letter of Timothy Pickering to Richard Peters, in Henry Adams, *Documents Relating to New-England Federalism, 1800–1815* (Boston: Little, Brown, 1877), p. 338.

[2]Cited in Claude G. Bowers, *Jefferson in Power: The Death Struggle of the Federalists* (Boston: Riverside Press, 1936), p. 235.

[3]Ibid., p. 243.

These "Yankee Confederates" were not an isolated band of radicals. They were among the leaders of the Federalist Party, many of whom had participated in the Revolutionary War and had even helped write the U.S. Constitution. John Hancock and Samuel Adams are among the best known of the New England Federalists who, by the early nineteenth century, were reaching their twilight years. The push for secession came primarily from the younger generation of Federalist leaders, including George Cabot, Elbridge Gerry, Theophilus Parsons, Timothy Pickering, Theodore Sedgwick, John Quincy Adams, Fisher Ames, Harrison Gray Otis, Josiah Quincy, and Joseph Story, among others.

Their cause, moreover, was virtually identical to the southern Confederacy's, a half century later: they were defending the principles of states' rights and self-government from an overbearing federal government. They condemned the Jefferson administration as being plagued by "falsehood, fraud, and treachery," which induced "oppression and barbarity" and "ruin among the nations."[4]

They believed that the South—especially Virginia—was gaining too much wealth, power, and influence, and was using that influence against New England politically. Their complaints are virtually identical to John C. Calhoun's concerns, decades later, about the unjust regional impacts of excessive federal power.

RATIONALES OF THE
NEW ENGLAND SECESSION MOVEMENT

In 1800, Thomas Jefferson's Republican Party took control of the presidency as well as the Congress. To the Federalist party, this was nothing but apocalyptic, for most party leaders absolutely abhorred Jefferson and all that he stood for. New England clerics, who were extremely influential, likened Jefferson to Beelzebub, and talked of a "moral putrefication that covers the land" because of Jefferson's ascent to the presidency.[5] To the Federalists, Jefferson was not just a political opponent who had defeated them; he was the personification of evil.

Jefferson was intolerable to the Federalists because his philosophy, policies, and even religious beliefs were fundamentally incompatible with the Federalist worldview. An essential, if not

---

[4]Cited in James Banner, *To the Hartford Convention: The Federalists and the Origins of Party Politics in Massachusetts, 1789–1815* (New York: Alfred A. Knopf, 1970), p. 35.
[5]Ibid.

primary, element of the Federalist worldview, notes historian James Banner, was that "public and private virtue" were requir-ed for a successful republic.[6]

But "virtue" implied dedication to organized religion, and Jefferson was "known to be deeply hostile to the Congregational clergy and the long-rooted religious sensibilities of the majority of New England's inhabitants."[7] More than any other public figure of his time, Jefferson insisted on the strict separation of church and state. Because of this, writes Jefferson biographer Claude Bowers, he "had been habitually denounced as an anti-Christ by the political preachers of his time" and "in the New England states, where the greater part of the ministers were militant Federalists, he was hated with an unholy hate. More false witness had been borne by the ministers of New England and New York against Jefferson than had ever been borne against any other American publicist."[8] Many Federalists apparently could not countenance the fact that Jefferson, whose party con-trolled the federal government, stood in the way of state-spon-sored Puritanism.

ETHNIC HOMOGENEITY

The Federalists also believed strongly that homogeneity of race, and "ethnic purity," were essential ingredients of a success-ful republic. These New Englanders thought of themselves as "choice offspring of the choicest people, unpolluted by foreign blood."[9]

New England Federalists were almost universally of English descent. Most of them agreed with William Smith Shaw that "the grand cause of all our present difficulties may be traced . . . to so many *hordes of Foreigners* immigrating to America."[10] "Our progenitors were choice scions from the best English stock," add-ed Federalist William Cunningham. Their "natural wants" did not "force them here for subsistence, like the wild *Irish* and sour *Germans in Pennsylvania*."[11] And, in a widely cited if not cele-brated remark, William Stoughton stated that "God sifted a

[6]Ibid., p. 26.

[7]Ibid.

[8]Bowers, *Jefferson in Power*, p. 145.

[9]Banner, *To the Hartford Convention*, p. 90.

[10]Letter from William Smith Shaw to Abigail Adams, 20 May 1798, cited in Banner, *To the Hartford Convention*, p. 90, emphasis in original.

[11]William Cunningham, *An Oration* (Leominster, Mass.: n.p., 1803), cited in Ban-ner, *To the Hartford Convention*, p. 91, emphasis in original.

whole Nation that he might send choice Grain over into this wilderness."[12]

Given these strong feelings about the primacy and importance of ethnic purity, the Jeffersonian policy of expansionism—especially the Louisiana Purchase which incorporated "hordes of foreigners" into the U.S.—was an abomination to the Federalists. Josiah Quincy was one of the most respected and influential of the Federalists. He warned that the Louisiana Purchase obligated the nation to assimilate "a number of French and Spanish subjects, whose habits, manners, and ideas of civil government are wholly foreign to republican institutions."[13] Quincy felt so strongly about this that he clearly stated that if the purchase were consummated the only recourse for New England would be secession. For the purchase meant that

> the bonds of this Union are virtually dissolved; that the States which compose it are free from their moral obligation; and that, as it will be the right of all, so it will be the duty of some, to prepare definitely for a separation, amicably if they can, violently if they must.[14]

The Federalists, as well as the Jeffersonians, understood that the Constitution was a carefully considered compact between the states which formed the union for certain well-defined reasons. Any measure that would fundamentally alter its relationships without a formal amendment would require consent of the parties to the compact. But the Louisiana Purchase was carried out by Jefferson and twenty-six senators—without consulting Congress, and without first attaining any such agreement among the states. Many of the Federalists considered this to be a gross violation of the compact that made a mockery of states' rights.

It was at this point in history—in 1803—that the New England Federalists began discussing secession. The ring leader was Pickering, who was among the most prominent of the Federalists. He had been elected colonel of the Essex County (Massachusetts) Militia at the outset of the American Revolution, and later served as adjutant general and quartermaster general of the Revolutionary Army. After the revolution, he was a member of Congress, Secretary of War, and U.S. Senator from Massachusetts.

---

[12]William Stoughton, *New England's True Interest* (Cambridge, Mass.: n.p., 1670), quoted in Perry Miller, *The New-England Mind: From Colony to Province* (Cambridge, Mass.: Harvard University Press, 1962), p. 135.

[13]Cited in Banner, *To the Hartford Convention*, p. 94.

[14]Cited in Daniel Wait Howe, *Political History of Secession* (New York: Negro Universities Press, 1914), p. 13.

In a letter to George Cabot, Pickering wrote of the "depravity" of Jefferson's "plan of destruction" and concluded that "the principles of our Revolution [the Revolution of 1776] point to the remedy—a separation. That this can be accomplished, and without spilling one drop of blood, I have little doubt."[15] Pickering believed that the different cultures of the North and South were inherently incompatible and would only lead to perpetual political conflict, if not violence. "The people of the East cannot reconcile their habits, views, and interests with those of the South and West."[16]

Pickering undoubtedly had in mind the clear cultural differences among different sets of British immigrants that historian David Hackett Fischer outlined in his treatise, *Albion's Seed*.[17] Fischer charts four distinct migrations to the U.S. from England: the exodus of Puritans from the east of England to Massachusetts from 1629–1640; the migration, from 1642 to 1675 of "a small Royalist elite and large numbers of indentured servants" to Virginia; a movement from the North Midlands of England and Wales to the Delaware Valley between 1675–1725; and the flow of English-speaking people from North Britain and Ireland to Appalachia from 1718–1775.

These four groups had much in common, but were also very different in their religion, social ranks, history, language or dialect, folkways, and perhaps most importantly, their conceptions of "order, power, and freedom."[18] And these were just the differences among the four British cultures in Colonial America. Dutch, Spanish, French, and other immigrants created even more diversity. The Federalists, however, were stridently opposed to multicultural assimilation. They thought secession and a truly federal system of government was necessary to avoid violent clashes among these incompatible cultures. These men, being of European ancestry, understood fully how ethnic divisions had historically been the source of much slaughter and strife, as indeed they still are today.

But this cultural incompatibility need not extend to *commercial* relationships. Pickering and other Federalists thought the creation of a northern confederacy would be economically beneficial to both North and South, while eliminating much of the

[15]Letter from Timothy Pickering to George Cabot, 29 January 1804, published in Adams, *Documents Relating to New-England Federalism*, p. 338.

[16]Ibid.

[17]David Hackett Fischer, *Albion's Seed: Four British Folkways in America* (New York: Oxford University Press, 1989).

[18]Ibid., p. 6.

political conflict that would inevitably occur under a more centralized governmental regime. "A Northern confederacy would
unite congenial characters, and present a fairer prospect of public
happiness; while the Southern States, having a similarity of
habits, might be left to manage their affairs in their own way."
Secession would "render a friendly and commercial intercourse"
between North and South, for the southern states would probably
want to contract out for such things as naval protection by the
northern confederacy, while the products of the South would "be
important to the navigation and commerce of the North."[19]

Some historians have portrayed Pickering and his colleagues
as crackpots or traitors because of their secessionist views, but all
they were really advocating is an American continent organized
more along the lines of modern Switzerland, with its twenty-six
cantons, than the highly-centralized mega-state the U.S. has
become. In Switzerland, there are "long-standing and deep linguistic, cultural and religious divisions—French, Swiss–German,
Italian, and a local language, Romansh, plus several dialects."[20]
These differences are typical of Europe and have been the source
of violence and bloodshed there for centuries.

What is unique about Switzerland is that despite these differences, it has enjoyed a much higher degree of peace, harmony,
and prosperity than most of the rest of Europe over the past 150
years. One likely reason for this is that the Swiss have in common "their political will to lead a free and independent life and
to resist the imposition of foreign laws—and especially foreign
taxes."[21] The Swiss system of highly decentralized and auton-
omous cantons greatly facilitates this goal. Something like the
Swiss system seems to be exactly what the New England secessionists had in mind.

In 1804, the New England Federalists began plotting their
strategy. In a letter to Theodore Lyman, Pickering explained
that Massachusetts would "take the lead" in secession, upon
which time "Connecticut would instantly join," as would New
Hampshire, Rhode Island, Vermont, New York, New Jersey, and
Pennsylvania "east of the Susquehanna River."[22]

Pickering and his associates decided that New York was the
key to persuading *all* New England states to secede as a block.

[19]Adams, *Documents Relating to New-England Federalism*, p. 338.
[20]Arnold Beichman, "What's the Swiss Secret of Serenity?" *The Washington Times*
(2 January 1995): A–15.
[21]Ibid.
[22]Letter from Timothy Pickering to Theodore Lyman, 11 February 1804, published
in Adams, *Documents Relating to New-England Federalism*, p. 338.

They struck a deal with Aaron Burr: the party apparatus would do all it could to help Burr get elected governor of New York, and in turn, Burr would see to it that New York promptly seceded and became part of the northern confederacy.

The election was very close, with Burr losing by only 7,000 votes, and exceptionally bitter, with Burr's opponent, Alexander Hamilton, denouncing him as lacking in integrity, dangerous, intemperate, profligate, and dictatorial.[23]

After the election, Burr demanded an apology, and when Hamilton refused, Burr challenged him to a duel. Burr won the duel, killing his adversary with one shot, and became a pariah. Hamilton was so well liked and respected throughout the United States that Burr could barely appear in public. The entire nation mourned the death of one of its founding fathers as "more memorial services were held in New England than ever had been held for a native son."[24] Because of Burr's association with the Federalists, the death of Hamilton discredited and temporarily stopped the New England secession movement.

All during this episode, virtually no one questioned the right of any state to secede. Any objections that were raised were strictly utilitarian—the timing was not right, the economic benefits might have been overestimated, and so on. Jefferson himself announced in his first inaugural address that "if there be any among us who wish to dissolve the Union or to change its republican form, let them stand undisturbed, as monuments of the safety with which error of opinion may be tolerated where reason is left free to combat it."[25]

Jefferson was the co-author (with James Madison) of the Virginia and Kentucky Resolutions of 1798, which suggested that "where powers were assumed by the national government which had not been granted by the States, nullification is the rightful remedy" and that every state has an original, natural right "to nullify of its own authority all assumptions of power by others, within its limits."[26] Thus, both major political parties believed in the *inviolable* states' rights of nullification and secession in the early nineteenth century.

[23]Bowers, *Jefferson in Power*, p. 245.

[24]Ibid., p. 252.

[25]Cited in Edward Powell, *Nullification and Secession in the United States* (New York: Putnam's Sons, 1897), p. 128.

[26]Ibid., p. 63.

CALHOUNISM

John C. Calhoun, the fierce southern partisan of the early- and mid-nineteenth century, has been called the "architect of nullification" because of his role, while he was a U.S. Senator from South Carolina, in getting the federal government to reduce the 1828 "Tariff of Abominations." South Carolina and other southern states relied heavily on foreign trade, and believed that high tariffs benefited the northern industrialists by diminishing their competition, while harming the South by causing European governments to retaliate with tariffs of their own on imports from the Southern United States. Moreover, the South hardly benefited at all from the revenues collected by the tariffs, thus rendering the 1828 tariff law "an instrument of monopoly and oppression."[27]

Calhoun orchestrated a South Carolina nullification convention that voted in 1832 to nullify the tariff. To avoid a confrontation, the federal government compromised by sharply reducing the tariff rates. After the compromise was reached, Calhoun reiterated Jefferson's thoughts on nullification when he declared that nullification should always remain a tool of the states because it was the best known vehicle for arresting "the alarming growth of political corruption and to save the Constitution, the Union and Liberty of these states."[28]

Nearly thirty years before the South Carolina nullification crisis, the New England Federalists were out-Calhouning Calhoun (who at the time was a twenty-year-old student at Yale). Throughout the published letters of the New England Federalists, one reads of the complaints of an over-reaching federal government that was disproportionately harming their region. The Federalists, however, were more radical than Calhoun: they wanted to secede, not to merely nullify misbegotten laws.

The Federalists were convinced that the federal government "had fallen into the hands of infidel, anti-commercial, anti-New England Southerners."[29] They believed there was a conspiracy among the "Virginia faction" to "govern and depress New England," in the words of Stephen Higginson.[30] John Lowell, Jr., declared that in any conflict between their state and the federal government, "it is our duty, our most solemn duty, to vindicate the

---

[27]Irving H. Bartlett, *John C. Calhoun: A Biography* (New York: W.W. Norton, 1993).

[28]Ibid., p. 201.

[29]Banner, *To the Hartford Convention*, p. 48.

[30]Ibid., p. 100.

rights, and support the interests of the state we represent."[31] Timothy Pickering added that his loyalties possessed a "natural order toward Salem, Massachusetts, New England, and the Union at large."[32]

These statements are strikingly similar to the justifications of secession given by so many of the most prominent southern Confederates in 1861. They are especially reminiscent of Robert E. Lee's response to General Winfield Scott when Scott offered him command of the Union Army just days before Virginia officially seceded. "If the Union is dissolved and the government disrupted," Lee said, "I shall return to my native state and share the miseries of my people and save in defence will draw my sword on none."[33]

Roger Griswold, the governor of Connecticut, sounded exactly like Calhoun if one were only to transpose the words "North" and "South." "The balance of power under the present government is decidedly in favor of the Southern States. . . . The extent and increasing population of those States must for ever secure to them the preponderance which they now possess." He also complained that New Englanders were paying "the principal part of the expenses of government" without receiving commensurate benefits, which led him to conclude that "there can be no safety to the Northern States without a separation from the confederacy" [the Union].[34]

THE EMBARGO

Clearly, the New England Federalists believed that southern politicians, who dominated the federal government, were intentionally harming the New England states. Considerable credence was lent to this conspiracy theory—at least in the minds of the Federalists—in 1807, when Jefferson declared an embargo on all foreign trade. The embargo rekindled the fires of secession that had been cooled by the Hamilton–Burr episode. The Federalists commenced planning a convention that they hoped would lead to the creation of a northern confederacy.

In 1807, Great Britain was at war with France, and announced that it would "secure her own seamen wherever found," which

[31]Ibid., p. 117.

[32]Ibid.

[33]Douglass Southall Freeman, *Lee* (New York: Charles Scribner's Sons, 1991), p. 110.

[34]Letter from Roger Griswold to Oliver Wolcott, 11 March 1804, in Adams, *Documents Relating to New-England Federalism*, p. 376.

included U.S. ships. After a British war ship captured the USS *Chesapeake* off Hampton Roads, Virginia, Jefferson imposed the embargo as a temporary expedient.

This abolition of legal international commerce crushed the national economy and hurt New England disproportionately, for at that time the region was very heavily trade dependent. However, it has been estimated that about half of all the trade with England and France during the embargo was continued by smugglers, ameliorating some of the harmful economic effects of the policy.

When Jefferson left office in January, 1809, his successor, James Madison, imposed an "Enforcement Act" which allowed for a war-on-drugs-style seizure of goods on the mere suspicion that they were intended for export. The army and navy were empowered to enforce the embargo, doing to American merchants in peace time what our enemies would want to do during war. This radicalized the secessionists who no longer plotted behind closed doors but began to *publicly* call for secession. They issued a public proclamation reminding the nation that the U.S. Constitution was "a Treaty of Alliance and Confederation" and that the central government was an association of states, so that "whenever its provisions are violated, or its original principles departed from by a majority of the states or of their people, it is no longer an effective instrument, but that any state is at liberty by the spirit of that contract to withdraw itself from the union."[35]

The Massachusetts legislature formally condemned the embargo, demanded that Congress repeal it, and declared the Enforcement Act "not legally binding." This was an act of nullification, virtually identical to South Carolina's twenty-five years later. A New England convention was scheduled where the strategy for secession was to be worked out.

The New England public was just as outraged as the Federalist politicians were over the embargo. The people "peppered Washington with protests" and of the five New England states, Madison carried only tiny Vermont in the 1808 election.[36]

Madison won the election, but the embargo generated so much animosity toward him that he ended it in March 1809. Ironically, that action took some of the wind out of the sails of the planned secession convention—at least temporarily.

---

[35]Banner, *To the Hartford Convention*, p. 301.
[36]Powell, *Nullification and Secession in the United States*, p. 203.

EARLY YANKEE ATTITUDES TOWARD SLAVERY

In the early nineteenth century, the Constitution allowed that five slaves could be counted as three whites for the purpose of determining congressional representation. This procedure provided the "Yankee Confederates" with yet another rationale for secession: they believed this arrangement artificially stacked the electoral decks against them. As Josiah Quincy claimed,

> The slave representation is the cause of all the difficulties we labor under. . . . [Because of this arrangement,] the southern states have an influence in our national councils, altogether disproportionate to their wealth, strength, and resources.[37]

The Federalists never voiced *moral* objections to the three-fifths clause. In fact, they argued that blacks should be counted as zero, rather than three-fifths of a white man, for purposes of congressional representation. Further, they did not make any case whatsoever that southern slavery should be ended.

Their insensitivity toward slavery should not be surprising, considering the Federalists' strongly held beliefs regarding the primacy of ethnic homogeneity and their belief in the superiority of English descendants. Even though slavery itself was abolished in Massachusetts in the 1780s, Massachusetts communities had, by the turn of the century, "tightened their poor laws, warned more Negroes from their boundaries, and established segregated schools and churches."[38] The Federalist leaders also lectured free blacks that they should not try too hard to climb up the social and economic ladder: "Be contented in the humble station in which Providence has placed you," Federalist cleric Jedidiah Morse lectured the Negro Congregation of Boston's African Meeting House in 1808.[39]

If the Federalists thought the three-fifths clause of the Constitution was oppressive, they would have considered the abolition of slavery in the South—and the extension of the franchise to blacks—an unmitigated disaster. As historian James Banner has concluded: "Freed, it appeared, the Negro was more of a political threat than enslaved. What the Federalists wanted, and what their assaults upon the three-fifths clause were designed to gain, was not the abolition of slavery but the abolition of Negro representation."[40] Because of their belief that the

---

[37]Banner, *To the Hartford Convention*, p. 102.
[38]Mary Stoughton Locke, *Anti-Slavery in America From the Introduction of African Slaves to the Prohibition of the Slave Trade, 1619–1808* (Boston: n.p., 1901).
[39]Banner, *To the Hartford Convention*, p. 106.
[40]Ibid., p. 107.

political power of the South was perpetual, the Federalists saw no prospect of ever eliminating the three-fifths clause—at least not in their lifetimes. Secession was the only sensible course.

THE WAR OF 1812

Virginia statesman John Randolph was a far more consistent proponent of limited government than his fellow Virginian Thomas Jefferson. He frequently pilloried Jefferson on such issues as the embargo, and eventually became a close friend and political collaborator of Federalist icon Josiah Quincy. Randolph teamed up with the Federalists in opposing Jeffersonian interventionism, including the War of 1812. In the last moments of congressional debate before war was declared, Randolph argued with Calhoun against going to war until he was ruled "out of order" by Speaker of the House and war proponent Henry Clay. Calhoun then prepared a bill declaring war on Great Britain which passed by a 79 to 49 vote, with New York, New Jersey, Delaware, and all the New England states voting for peace.[41]

To the Federalist leaders, this was the last straw. "We are to be taxed beyond our means, and subjected to military conscription," an alarmed Governor George Morris of New York wrote to Timothy Pickering.[42] "We cannot exist, but in poverty and contempt, without foreign commerce," wrote Pickering, and "by a war of any continuance with Great Britain, that commerce will be annihilated."[43]

The Massachusetts legislature declared the war "needless and unwise" and denounced it as "a wanton sacrifice of the interests of New England."[44] Dozens of town meetings were organized in New England to denounce the war. The Massachusetts legislature even instructed its citizens not to volunteer: "Let there be no volunteers except for defensive war."[45] When the federal government came to New England to enlist recruits, those who did enlist were routinely arrested on (mostly) fictitious charges of not having paid their debts. The Federalist courts then ruled that, as debtors, these men were the "property" of creditors and therefore could not leave the state.

[41]Bartlett, *John C. Calhoun*, p. 75.

[42]Letter from George Morris to Timothy Pickering, 1 November 1814, in Adams, *Documents Relating to New-England Federalism*, p. 390.

[43]Letter from Pickering to Edward Pennington, 12 July 1812, in Adams, *Documents Relating to New-England Federalism*, p. 390.

[44]Powell, *Nullification and Secession in the United States*, p. 208.

[45]Ibid.

The Supreme Courts of Massachusetts and Connecticut also ruled that the states had a right to decide whether exigencies existed that warranted the calling up of the state's militia, effectively nullifying the declaration of war by the national government. Thus, by refusing to fight any war that did not directly take place on its own soil, New England effectively seceded.

President Madison responded to this *de facto* secession by repudiating his old friend Jefferson's policy of opposition to a standing army "which will grind us with public burdens and sink us under them."[46] He announced that he would need to institute "those large and permanent military establishments which are forbidden by the principles of free government," thereby validating the fears of war opponents such as John Randolph.[47]

The U.S. Treasury was soon bankrupted by the war, so the government doubled all import duties, harming the U.S. economy even further. Little revenue was raised, however, since international trade was virtually at a standstill.

This policy of protectionist extremism did artificially stimulate some domestic industries which sprung up to compensate for the loss of goods previously provided more efficiently through international trade. Being protected from international competition, they quickly organized politically to assure the continuation of that protection after the war. And they got the protection because, according to economist Frank Taussig, "the men who had brought about the war . . . felt in a measure responsible for its results."[48]

Thus, the War of 1812 created dozens of protected industries, especially in the more industrialized North, that would form the core of political support for protectionist trade policies for decades to come. These protectionist interests helped precipitate the nullification crisis of 1832 and, eventually, the War Between the States. It should not be forgotten that Fort Sumter was, after all, a customs house where federal authorities collected tariffs and fees that interfered with southern commerce. That most of the revenues collected in this way were spent in the North infuriated southern secessionists.

THE HARTFORD CONVENTION

On 24 August 1813, the British captured Washington, and "New England was practically in rebellion. It had seceded from

[46]Ibid., p. 121.
[47]Ibid., p. 212.
[48]Frank Taussig, *Tariff History of the United States* (New York: Putnam's Sons, 1931), p. 18.

national action, and had set up a war confederacy."[49] Governor Strong of Massachusetts called a special session of the legislature in October to declare that the national government had failed to fulfill the terms of the Constitution and to protect New England from invasion. The time had come, he told them, for a separate New England alliance. The legislature agreed that the Constitution "must be supplanted."[50]

President Madison's mind was said to be "full of the New England sedition" and, as further evidence of the similarity of views between the New England Federalists and John C. Calhoun, there was even "a proposition ... discussed in New England to form an alliance with South Carolina to resist Virginia, so strong was the similarity of the two sections in temper, religion, and trading instincts."[51]

The rank-and-file members of the Federalist Party, if not the leadership, were demanding a separate peace with England, secession, and Madison's resignation. Newspapers throughout New England were "largely in favor of prompt action" with regard to these demands, and were complaining bitterly about foot-dragging by the state legislatures.[52] There were threats of internal rebellion within the Federalist Party. The language of the public was becoming "high toned and menacing," Harrison Gray Otis wrote to Daniel Webster.[53] Something had to be done to calm the public, and a convention was the chosen vehicle.

The convention was held in Hartford in December, 1814, and was attended by twenty-six representatives from Massachusetts, Connecticut, Rhode Island, New Hampshire, and Vermont. But the delegates—all professional politicians and party leaders—turned out to be considerably more moderate and less radical than the rank-and-file of New England Federalism. Secessionist John Lowell, Jr., realized this when he forecast that the convention "would not go far enough."[54] Lowell ascribed this likely result to the fact that the party leaders feared that something as radical as secession would threaten their careers and standing in national politics. "Separation would have severed their last chance for preferment at the national level."[55]

[49]Powell, *Nullification and Secession in the United States*, p. 219.
[50]Ibid.
[51]Ibid., p. 220.
[52]Ibid., p. 221.
[53]Cited in Banner, *To the Hartford Convention*, p. 322.
[54]Ibid., p. 325.
[55]Ibid., p. 343.

Nathan Dane, a delegate to the convention, explained conde-
scendingly that when "the multitudes" are "excited and highly
dissatisfied with their rulers' conduct, often they can be moder-
ated . . . only when they know not" what their rulers are up to.[56]
Even though the New England Federalist public, and quite a few
of its political leaders, were calling for secession, Dane thought
of his job as essentially to "prevent mischief."[57]

The convention did issue a published report which contained
several key recommendations. First, it called for the elimination
of the three-fifths clause. Second, it called for a two-thirds vote
of both houses of Congress to admit any new states. Third, it
advocated a limit on embargoes of sixty days and a two-thirds
vote of Congress for their enactment to protect states against "the
sudden and injudicious decisions of bare majorities."[58]

A two-thirds vote was also demanded before declaring war,
and the convention wanted to prohibit a president from succeed-
ing himself (i.e., executive branch term limits), and to outlaw
the election of a president from the same state in successive
terms. The convention also argued for block grants to the states
from the national government, earmarked for state armies for
self-defense purposes.

The secretive conventioneers tried to appease the Federalist
public by proposing a second convention in Boston if their recommendations were not implemented by the national government.
But a small group of delegates gave themselves the authority to
reconvene such a convention without the assistance of the legislatures so as to "divert any movement for a second and more radical gathering."[59]

The Washington-based Federalists, such as Pickering, complained bitterly that the convention had been "captured" by the
political careerists and "moderates," but to no avail. Very little
came of the convention's proposals and the delegates were determined to have "not done as much as was expected of them by the
great Body of the people of this State," complained Federalist
Theodore Dwight, the president of Yale College and John C.
Calhoun's academic mentor.[60]

[56]Ibid., p. 332.
[57]Ibid.
[58]A text of the convention report is found in Powell, *Nullification and Secession in the
United States*, pp. 234–40.
[59]Banner, *To the Hartford Convention*, p. 343.
[60]Ibid., p. 345.

Federalist radicals like Pickering and Massachusetts Governor Strong were bitterly disappointed, but they still thought the union would not last. The western states "will soon prefer a government of their own," predicted Strong.[61] When the war finally ended, so did the Federalist effort to secede from the union.

THE SECESSIONIST LEGACY OF NEW ENGLAND FEDERALISM

Throughout these episodes, historian Edward Powell has written, "the right of a State . . . to withdraw from the Union was . . . not disputed."[62] There was indeed virtually universal support—from Republicans and Federalists alike—for the right of secession. Moreover, this belief in the right to secession was alive and well *in the North* at the outset of the War Between the States. Contrary to what most Americans have been taught, many—perhaps most—northerners believed the South should have been permitted to peacefully secede, however unwise they thought secession might have been for the South. This belief is the legacy of the early-nineteenth-century New England secessionists.[63] It will be useful to cite just a few examples.

On 10 November 1860, the *Albany (New York) Atlas and Argus* editorialized that "we sympathize with and justify the South" because "their rights have been invaded to the extreme limit possible within the forms of the Constitution." If the South wanted to secede, the editors wrote, "we would applaud them and wish them God-Speed."

The *Chicago Daily Times and Herald* declared, eleven days later, that "like it or not, the cotton States will secede." The government will not then "go to pieces," but Southerners will be allowed to regain their "sense of independence and honor."

On 24 November 1860, the *Concord (New Hampshire) Democratic Standard* complained of "fanatics and demagogues of the North" who "waged war on the institutions of the South" and appealed for "concession of the just rights of our Southern brethren."

Two days later, the *New York Journal of Commerce* condemned the "meddlesome spirit" of people of the North who wanted to "seek to regulate and control" people in "other communities."

---

[61]Powell, *Nullification and Secession in the United States*, p. 232.

[62]Ibid.

[63]These beliefs are chronicled in Howard Cecil Perkins, *Northern Editorials on Secession* (Gloucester, Mass.: American Historical Association, 1964). The following references to newspaper articles are all taken from this source.

On 13 November 1860, the *Bangor (Maine) Daily Union* defended southern secessionists by explaining that the Union "depends for its continuance on the free consent and will of the sovereign people" of each state, and "when that consent and will is withdrawn on either part, their Union is gone." If military force is used, then a state can only be held "as a subject province," and can never be "a co-equal member of the American Union."

On the same day, the *Brooklyn Daily Eagle* clearly explained that "any violation of the constitution by the general government, deliberately persisted in would relieve the state or states injured by such violation from all legal and moral obligations to remain in the union or yield obedience to the federal government." And while the editors saw "no real cause for secession on the part of the South, should any states attempt it there is nothing to be done but let them go."

The *Cincinnati Daily Commercial* echoed similar sentiments by advocating that the southern states be allowed to "work out their salvation or destruction in their own way" rather than "to attempt, through forcible coercion, to save them in spite of themselves."

The *Davenport (Iowa) Democrat and News*, on 17 November 1860, editorialized against secession, but in its editorial it noted that it was apparently in the minority in the North, where most of "the leading and most influential papers of the Union" believe "that any State of the Union has a right to secede."

One such paper was the *Providence (Rhode Island) Evening Press*, which wrote on that same day that sovereignty "necessarily includes what we call the 'right of secession'" and "this right must be maintained" unless we would establish "colossal despotism" against which the founding fathers "uttered their solemn warnings."

The *Cincinnati Daily Press* repeated this sentiment on 21 November 1860: "We believe that the right of any member of this Confederacy to dissolve its political relations with the others and assume an independent position is *absolute*—that, in other words, if South Carolina wants to go out of the Union, she has the right to do so, and no party or power may justly say her nay." This, the editors surmised, is what the Declaration of Independence means when it says that whenever government becomes destructive of the protection of lives, liberties, and the pursuit of happiness, then "it is the right of the people to alter or abolish" their government and "to institute a new government."

The *New York Daily Tribune* made the exact same point on
17 December 1860, adding that if tyranny and despotism justified
the American Revolution of 1776, then "we do not see why it
would not justify the secession of Five Millions of Southrons from
the Federal Union in 1861."

Once South Carolina seceded on 20 December 1860, dozens of
northern editorialists viewed it as a confirmation of the principle of sovereignty and self-government, while others, like the
Indianapolis Daily Journal, said "thank God that we have had
a good riddance of bad rubbish."

The *Kenosha (Wisconsin) Democrat* wrote on 11 January 1861,
that secession was "the very germ of liberty" and declared that
"the right of secession inheres to the people of every sovereign
state."

The *New York Journal of Commerce,* sensing the war fever in
Washington, reminded its readers on 12 January 1861, that by opposing secession, northerners would be changing the nature of government "from a voluntary one, in which the people are sovereigns, to a despotism where one part of the people are slaves.
Such is the logical deduction from the policy of the advocates of
force."

The *Washington (D.C.) Constitution* concurred, stating that
the use of force against South Carolina would be "the extreme of
wickedness and the acme of folly." It further opined the desire
"that all the Southern States will secede."

On 5 February 1861, the *New York Tribune* characterized
Lincoln's latest speech as "the arguments of the tyrant—force,
compulsion and power." "Nine out of ten of the people of the
North," the paper surmised, were opposed to forcing South Carolina to remain in the Union.

"We ought to let them go," said the *Greenfield (Massachusetts) Gazette and Courier,* once additional southern states began
to follow South Carolina's lead.

The *Detroit Free Press* declared on 19 February 1861, that "an
attempt to subjugate the seceded States, even if successful, could
produce nothing but evil—evil unmitigated in character and ap-
palling in extent."

The *New York Daily Tribune* argued once again that "the
great principle embodied by Jefferson in the Declaration . . . is
that governments derive their just power from the consent of the
governed." Therefore, if the southern states want to secede,
"they have a clear right to do so."

On 21 March 1861, the *New York Times* intoned "that there is a growing sentiment throughout the North in favor of *letting the Gulf States go.*"

"The people are recognizing the government of the Confederates," the *Cincinnati Daily Commercial* wrote on 23 March 1861, and "there is room for several flourishing nations on this continent; the sun will shine brightly and the rivers run as clear . . . when we acknowledge the Southern Confederacy as before."

"Public opinion in the North," said the *Hartford (Connecticut) Daily Courant* on 12 April 1861, "seems to be gradually settling down in favor of the recognition of the New Confederacy by the Federal Government." The thought of a "bloody and protracted civil war . . . is abhorrent to all."

There were, of course, northern papers that supported going to war over secession. The point of this section has been to illustrate how widespread was the view among important opinion makers *in the North* that to deny the right of secession was to deny the very essence of the Declaration of Independence itself. Lincoln had anything but strong public support when he decided to wage total war on the South. His war dictated the death of one of the most important rights of a free nation—the right to secession—as well as the deaths of 618,000 young men.

8

WAS THE UNION ARMY'S INVASION OF THE CONFEDERATE STATES A LAWFUL ACT? AN ANALYSIS OF PRESIDENT LINCOLN'S LEGAL ARGUMENTS AGAINST SECESSION

James Ostrowski

On 27 May 1861, the army of the United States of America (the Union)—a nation which had been formed by consecutive secessions, first from Great Britain in 1776, and then from itself in 1788—invaded the State of Virginia,[1] which had itself recently seceded from the Union, in an effort to negate Virginia's secession by violent force.

The results of the efforts begun that day are well known and indisputable: after four years of brutal warfare, during which 620,000 Americans were killed, the United States of America forcibly negated the secession of the Confederate States, and re-enrolled them into the Union. The Civil War ended slavery, left the South in economic ruins, and set the stage for twelve years of military rule.

Beyond its immediate effects, the Civil War also made drastic changes in politics and law that continue to shape our world 130 years later. Arthur Ekirch writes:

> Along with the terrible destruction of life and property suffered in four long years of fighting went tremendous changes in American life and thought, especially a decline in [classical] liberalism on all questions save that of slavery. . . .
>
> Through a policy of arbitrary arrests made possible by Lincoln's suspension of *habeas corpus*, persons were seized and confined on the suspicion of disloyalty or of sympathy with the southern cause. Thus, in the course of the Civil War, a total of thirteen thousand civilians was estimated to have been held as political prisoners, often without any sort of trial or after only cursory hearings before a military tribunal.[2]

---

[1]United States War Department, *The War of the Rebellion: A Compilation of the Official Records of the Union and Confederate Armies*, series 1 (Washington, D.C.: Government Printing Office, 1880), vol. 2, pp. 51ff.

[2]Arthur A. Ekirch, Jr., *The Decline of American Liberalism* (New York: Atheneum, 1980), pp. 122, 125.

The Civil War caused and allowed a tremendous expansion of the size and power of the federal government. It gave us our first federal conscription law, our first progressive income tax, and our first enormous standing army; it gave us a higher tariff, and it gave us greenbacks. James McPherson writes approvingly:

> This astonishing blitz of laws . . . did more to reshape the relation of the government to the economy than any comparable effort except perhaps the first hundred days of the New Deal. This Civil War Legislation . . . created the blueprint for modern America.[3]

Albert Jay Nock was more critical of the war's impact, especially on the Constitution:

> Lincoln overruled the opinion of Chief Justice Taney that suspension of *habeas corpus* was unconstitutional, and in consequence the mode of the State was, until 1865, a monocratic military despotism. . . . The doctrine of "reserved powers" was knaved up *ex post facto* as a justification for his acts, but as far as the intent of the constitution is concerned, it was obviously pure invention. In fact, a very good case could be made out for the assertion that Lincoln's acts resulted in a permanent radical change in the entire system of constitutional "interpretation"—that since his time, "interpretations" have not been interpretations of the constitution, but merely of public policy. . . . A strict constitutionalist might indeed say that the constitution died in 1861, and one would have to scratch one's head pretty diligently to refute him.[4]

This paper will attempt to explore Nock's thesis by examining the central constitutional issue of the war: was the Union Army's invasion of the Confederacy a lawful act? This will be done primarily by analyzing the legal arguments made by President Abraham Lincoln in support of the invasion and against the Confederate secession. This method is justified by several facts. First, the invasion of the Confederacy was ordered by President Lincoln. Second, President Lincoln was one of the most brilliant lawyers of his era. As such, it is safe to assume that his legal argument in support of the invasion was of the highest quality. Third, it is likely that President Lincoln read, thought, wrote, and spoke about the legal issues involving the Civil War more so than any other pro-Union lawyer of his era. He was aware of the pro-Union arguments made both by his predecessors as well as by

[3]James McPherson, *Abraham Lincoln and the Second American Revolution* (New York: Oxford University Press, 1990), p. 40.

[4]Albert Jay Nock, *Our Enemy, The State* (Caldwell, Idaho: Caxton Printers, 1950), p. 171, n. 16.

his contemporaries.[5] Finally, President Lincoln, a superb writer and speaker, had strong incentive to make his views against secession known to the American people in order to secure their support for the onerous war which was made necessary by his opposition to secession. From the above facts, we can conclude that if the invasion of the Confederacy was legally justified, such legal justification can be found in the writings and pronouncements of President Lincoln.

This paper will not address the *morality* of the Union's invasion of the Confederacy, except indirectly and only to the extent that certain moral principles were undoubtedly reflected in the framework of laws governing the Union in 1861. Thus, whether the Union's invasion of the Confederacy can be morally justified, even if found to be unlawful, will not be answered here.[6] It is the case, however, that the officials who launched the invasion, especially President Lincoln, made no such argument in 1861. He had previously indicated his views on that issue by criticizing John Brown's raid on Harper's Ferry.[7]

The issue of the right of a state to secede is of more than historical interest. Since the end of the Civil War in 1865, though several amendments giving the federal government greater power over the states have been ratified, there have been no textual changes to the Constitution which explicitly prohibit secession.

There was no attempt by either side in the Civil War to resort to federal courts or international arbitrators for a decision on the legality of secession. Nor has any state attempted to secede since the Civil War. As settled as secession may be as a political or historical issue to many, it has never been settled as a legal one. The recent revival of secession talk and practice worldwide makes the present undertaking a valuable one.

[5]Gary Wills, *Lincoln at Gettysburg* (New York: Simon and Schuster, 1992), pp. 124–33.

[6]A moral defense of the Civil War as a crusade to end slavery would have to begin by answering this question: how is it justified to use involuntary servitude (conscription), leading to the deaths of many of the "servants," as a means of ending the involuntary servitude of others? See Eugene Converse Murdock, *One Million Men: The Civil War Draft in the North* (Madison: State Historical Society of Wisconsin, 1971). For a view of the Civil War as an attempt to preserve a vital portion of the American Empire, see C. Adams, "The Second American Revolution: A British View of the War Between the States," *Southern Partisan* (1st Quarter 1994): 16. On p. 21, Adams states, "It seems clear that British war correspondents and writers saw the War Between the States as caused by the forces that have caused wars throughout history—economic and imperialist forces behind a rather flimsy facade of freeing the slaves."

[7]Abraham Lincoln, Address at Cooper Institute, 27 February 1860, *Abraham Lincoln: Speeches and Writings, 1859–1865* (New York: Library of America, 1989), p. 111.

WAS THE INVASION JUSTIFIED
BY THE SEIZURE OF FORT SUMTER?

In the context of a legal analysis of state secession, it was the Union's invasion of Virginia that is significant, and not the Confederacy's firing on Fort Sumter a month earlier. The Confederacy fired on Fort Sumter to expel what it believed were trespassers on South Carolina soil and territorial waters. By no means can the seizure of the fort be construed as a threat to the security of the states remaining in the Union, the closest of which was 500 miles away.

If South Carolina illegally seceded from the Union, then both the Union's initial refusal to surrender Fort Sumter and its subsequent invasion were lawful and constitutional. Conversely, if South Carolina had the right to secede from the Union, then indeed the Union soldiers in the Fort *were* trespassers and also a potential military threat to South Carolina. Thus, assuming the right of secession existed, the Union had no right to retaliate or initiate war against the Confederacy. Its subsequent invasion of Virginia then marks the beginning of its illegal war on the Confederacy.

The incident at Fort Sumter is largely significant as a political victory for the Union. President Lincoln, while holding a hostile military force on southern soil, was able to outmaneuver the Confederacy into firing the first shot of the war.[8] That the shot would be fired, however, was guaranteed by President Lincoln in his Inaugural Address when he disingenuously announced, "there shall be [no violence] unless it be forced upon the national authority." He then defined the term "national authority" in such a way as to insure that war would come:

> The power confided in me, will be used to hold, occupy, and possess the property, and places belonging to the government, and to collect the duties and imposts; but beyond what may be necessary for these objects, there will be no invasion—no using of force against, or among the people anywhere.[9]

Whatever one's legal, political, or moral views about President Lincoln or the Civil War, it should be obvious that Lincoln was being dishonest here. He was suggesting that he would not

[8]See Shelby Foote, *The Civil War: Fort Sumter to Perryville* (New York: Vintage Books, 1986), pp. 44–51; cf. Kenneth Stampp, *And the War Came: The North and the Secession Crisis 1860–1861* (Baton Rouge: Louisiana State University Press, 1950), pp. 284–86.

[9]President Abraham Lincoln, Inaugural Address, 4 March 1861, *Speeches and Writings*, p. 215.

resist secession, but would continue to tax the seceders and to hold hostile military installations on their property—an absurdity. Before becoming president, Lincoln had been more honest. He had simply said "we won't let you" secede. The truth is, the southern states wanted to go in peace, but Lincoln "wouldn't let them."[10]

LINCOLN'S LEGAL ARGUMENTS AGAINST SECESSION

Lincoln set forth his views on secession mainly in his First In-augural Address (4 March 1861), and his Special Message to Con-gress (4 July 1861). In the first speech, Lincoln made primarily *political* arguments against secession, apparently hoping to per-suade secessionists with his arguments. However, with secession already accomplished by 4 July 1861, Lincoln's Special Address to Congress focused on the alleged *illegality* of secession, to es-tablish the legitimacy of his intended military resistance to it. This paper will therefore first consider the Special Message's le-gal arguments against secession, then the First Inaugural's pol-itical arguments against secession.

In his Special Message to Congress, President Lincoln called the doctrine of the secessionists "an insidious debauching of the public mind." He said,

> They invented an ingenious sophism, which, if conceded, was followed by perfectly logical steps, through all the incidents, to the complete destruction of the Union. The sophism itself is, that any state of the Union may, *consistently* with the nat-ional Constitution, and therefore *lawfully*, and *peacefully*, withdraw from the Union, without the consent of the Union, or of any other state.

Ironically, it was not "fire-eating" southern rebels who had originated this "sophism," but the man Lincoln called "the most distinguished politician in our history"—Thomas Jefferson.[11] Jef-ferson, who called Virginia his "country," planted the seeds of the secession doctrine when he wrote his Kentucky Resolution of 1798, in protest to the Alien and Sedition laws:

> The several states composing the United States of America are not united on the principle of unlimited submission to their general government; but that, by compact, under the style and title of the Constitution of the United States, and of

[10]Abraham Lincoln, speech, 23 July 1856, Galena, Illinois, cited in *The Collected Works of Abraham Lincoln*, Roy Basler, ed. (New Brunswick, N.J.: Rutgers University Press, 1953), vol. 2, p. 353.

[11]Wills, *Lincoln at Gettysburg*, p. 85.

certain amendments thereto, they constituted a general government for general purposes, delegated to that government
certain powers, reserving, each state to itself, the residuary
mass of right to their own self-government; and that whensoever the general government assumes undelegated powers, its
acts are unauthoritative, void and of no effect.[12]

Hannis Taylor called Jefferson's compact doctrine the "Pan-
dora's Box" out of which flew the "closely related doctrines of
nullification and secession," which he notes, with less than perfect foresight, "were extinguished once and forever by the Civil
War."[13] Jefferson's biographer, Willard Sterne Randall agrees:

> [Jefferson] forthrightly held that where the national govern-
> ment exercised powers not specifically delegated to it, each
> state "has an equal right to judge . . . the mode and measure of
> redress." . . . He was, he assured Madison, "confident in the
> good sense of the American people," but if they did not rally
> round "the true principles of our federal compact," he was
> "determined . . . to sever ourselves from the union we so much
> value rather than give up the rights of self-government . . . in
> which alone we see liberty, safety and happiness."[14]

Lincoln, in reply to this "insidious debauching of the public
mind," constructs a straw man secessionist argument: "This sophism derives much—perhaps the whole—of its currency, from the
assumption, that there is some omnipotent, and sacred supremacy, pertaining to a *State*—to each State of our Federal Union."
No secessionist, including Jefferson, ever made such an argument,
though it sounds ominously like a description of Lincoln's own
feelings about the *Union*. Since the states *created* the Union, Lincoln's denigration of the states and glorification of the Union is
paradoxical.

Lincoln challenges the claim of reserved state powers by asserting that no state, except Texas, had ever "been a State *out* of
the Union." In fact, Lincoln argues that the states "passed into
the Union" even before 1776; united to declare their independence
in 1776; declared a "perpetual" union in the Articles of Confederation two years later; and finally created the present Union by

[12]Quoted in Hannis Taylor, *The Origin and Growth of the American Constitution* (Boston: Houghton Mifflin, 1911), p. 306.

[13]Ibid., p. 310. The violent tone in which many unionist writers proclaimed the
death of secession is perfectly appropriate given their ultimate means of dealing
with secessionists: "The inextricable knots which American lawyers and publicists
went on tying, down till 1861, were *cut by the sword* of the North in the Civil War
and need concern us no longer" (ibid., quoting James Bryce, *American Commonwealth* [New York: MacMillan, 1912], vol. 1, p. 322–3), emphasis added.

[14]Willard Sterne Randall, *Thomas Jefferson: A Life* (New York: Henry Holt, 1993),
pp. 534–36.

ratifying the Constitution in 1788. There are many problems with his argument.

Lincoln confuses no fewer than four different concepts of union. Prior to 4 July 1776, the colonies were united by their increasing concern over the violation of their rights by the British government. Their representatives met in a Continental Congress which ultimately issued the Declaration of Independence and organized the Revolutionary War effort. Prior to 1776, no issue of secession from a union could have arisen because the colonies still considered themselves part of Great Britain. Neither were there any legal documents agreed to by the Continental Congress which directly or indirectly addressed the issue of secession. Thus, any union that existed prior to 1776 is of no importance at all to the issue of secession.

Next comes the union created by the Declaration of Independence. The most notable fact in this context is that the Declaration announces a lawful *secession* by the colonies from Great Britain based on the right of the people to alter or abolish their form of government. It is thus apparent that the Declaration of Independence establishes that the right of secession is among the *inalienable* rights of men. The Declaration is, therefore, literally the last place on earth one would hope to find legal justification for a war against secession. It was adopted by representatives of the thirteen colonies, and declared that those colonies had become "Free and Independent States." However, the Declaration was not a constitution, establishing any particular type of union among the states, or specifying any duties binding on them other than a moral commitment to mutually defend their newly declared independence.

Ironically, the past "train of abuses" Thomas Jefferson cited in support of secession reads like a checklist of the tactics Lincoln and his successors used against the South to prevent secession:

> He has dissolved Representative Houses repeatedly, for opposing with manly firmness his invasions on the rights of the people. He has refused for a long time, after such dissolutions, to cause others to be elected. . . . He has made Judges dependent on his Will alone. . . . He has erected a multitude of New Offices, and sent hither swarms of Officers to harass our people, and eat out their substance. He has kept among us, in times of peace, Standing Armies without the consent of our legislatures. He has affected to render the Military independent of and superior to the Civil Power. He has combined with others to subject us to a jurisdiction foreign to our constitution, and unacknowledged by our laws, giving his Assent to their Acts of pretended Legislation: For quartering

large bodies of armed troops among us. For cutting off our Trade with all parts of the world. For imposing Taxes on us without consent. For depriving us in many cases, of the right of Trial by Jury. For taking away our Charters, abolishing our most valuable Laws and altering fundamentally our own legislatures, and declaring themselves invested with power to legislate for us in all cases whatsoever. He has abdicated Government here, by declaring us out of his Protection and waging War against us. He has plundered our seas, ravaged our Coast, burnt our towns, and destroyed the lives of our people. He is at this time transporting large Armies of foreign Mercenaries to compleat the works of death, desolation and tyranny.

The next union cited by Lincoln is the government established by the Articles of Confederation, which were ratified on 1 March 1781. Perhaps the most significant fact about the Articles is that they specify, both in the preamble and in the body, that the union thus created is "perpetual." Article XIII states:

> The Articles of this confederation shall be inviolably observed by every state, and the union shall be perpetual; nor shall any alteration at any time hereafter be made in any of them; unless such alteration be agreed to in a congress of the united states, and be afterwards confirmed by the legislatures of every state.

In contrast, however, Article II makes clear that "Each state retains its sovereignty, freedom and independence *and* every Power, Jurisdiction and right, which is not by this confederation expressly delegated to the United States, in Congress assembled."[15] This sentence is divided into two clauses, the first speaking of states retaining their sovereignty, freedom, and independence, and the second reserving to the states those powers and rights not expressly delegated to the United States.

Resolving the apparent conflict between Article II and Article XIII as it respects the issue of secession is unnecessary for our purposes. Suffice it to say that the Articles expressed a desire for perpetual union, while recognizing the independence of states, and omitting any clear mandate or enforcement mechanism that prevents state secession. They also established a decentralized federal system without a strong executive power which apparently failed to arouse any secessionist impulses in its short tenure.

The union established by the Articles of Confederation, in spite of its exhortation of perpetuity, was terminated by nothing other than a *secession!* The proposed Constitution provided that

[15]Emphasis added.

it would take effect upon ratification by nine states. On 21 June 1788, New Hampshire became the ninth state to ratify. On that date, a new union was formed, exclusive of Virginia, New York, North Carolina, and Rhode Island, which had not yet ratified. That new union *seceded* from the union formed by the Articles of Confederation in violation of Article XIII, which barred any alteration in the Articles save by unanimous consent.[16]

Significantly, the exhortation of perpetuity from the Articles—which was repeated five times—was dropped by the new Constitution. In response to this embarrassing fact, Lincoln argues that the phrase "a more perfect union" in the preamble implies at least the perpetuity of the Articles. Evidently, the Framers either disagreed or chose to be silent on the matter. (Indeed, common sense suggests that perpetual—forced—unions are *less* perfect than consensual ones, about which more later.) Their omission is especially significant since the term "perpetuity" was part of the full name of the Articles: "Articles of Confederation and Perpetual Union." Thus, the Framers could not have missed the term.

More importantly, a comparison of the two texts reveals, contrary to popular thought, that much copying was done by the Framers of the Constitution. Entire clauses from the Articles were imported virtually word for word into the Constitution. Examples include the following clauses: privileges and immunities, extradition, full faith and credit, congressional immunity while in session, ban on state treaties, and ban on state imposts and duties. The Framers were clearly conversant with the text of the Articles, yet no mention of perpetuity appears in the Constitution.

Neither does the Constitution explicitly say anything about state secession. The word "secession" does not appear in the Constitution. The Constitution neither prohibits a state from leaving the union nor explicitly authorizes a state to do so. Nor does it explicitly authorize the federal government to forcibly retain a state that has seceded.

[16]See James Garfield Randall, *Constitutional Problems Under Lincoln* (New York: D. Appleton, 1926), pp. 14–15. The secession of 1788 can probably not be justified by reference to Article VI: "No two or more states shall enter into any treaty, confederation or alliance whatever between them, without the consent of the united states in congress assembled, specifying accurately the purposes for which the same is to be entered into, and how long it shall continue." The new Constitution was an "alteration" which had the effect of abolishing the previous government. Thus, such a measure required the procedure set forth in Article XIII: consent of Congress plus the unanimous consent of each of the states.

Secession was apparently not discussed at the Constitutional Convention.[17] This may have been a deliberate omission:

> It would have been inexpedient to have forced this issue in 1787, when the fate of any sort of a central government was doubtful. But [this] subject [was] probably not even seriously considered at that time.[18]

President Buchanan later argued that if states had the right to secede, all that anti-federalist concern about potential federal tyranny was pointless.[19] This is a clever, but strange, legal argument. It uses circumstantial evidence to establish what certain *opponents* of the Constitution might have thought it meant on a point which was not widely discussed or considered at that time. Such a method of constitutional interpretation is tertiary at best. This article relies primarily on textual analysis and secondarily on consideration of the purposes of the drafters and ratifiers and their historical circumstances. It is not at all clear why what opponents of the Constitution might have thought it meant should be a criterion of interpretation.

Even if it is considered important, however, there are still problems with the argument, since many historians have concluded that most people of the time believed the states retained the right to secede.[20] Since the Constitution expanded the powers of the federal government, omission from it of any mention of secession or perpetuity certainly removes a potential source of opposition to ratification.

Another problem with Buchanan's argument is that its initial premise is dubious. That is, it assumes that if a right to secession existed under the proposed Constitution, opposition to it would have been less severe. However, even if the Constitution *explicitly* allowed states to secede, opponents of a strong federal government nevertheless had strong incentive to oppose it for the simple reason that the new Constitution meant the death of the minimalist Articles of Confederation. Finally, even if antifederalists believed that the states retained the right to secede under the new Constitution, they could well have thought—with

[17]Max Farrand, *The Framing of the Constitution* (New Haven, Conn.: Yale University Press, 1913), p. 206.

[18]Ibid.

[19]"Last Annual Message of President Buchanan," in *Great Debates in American History*, Marion Mills Miller, ed. (New York: Current Literature Publishing, 1913), vol. 5, p. 298.

[20]See Randall, *Constitutional Problems Under Lincoln*, pp. 15–16, n. 18; see also the classic by Alexis de Tocqueville, *Democracy in America* (New York: Harper and Row, [1835] 1969), p. 369.

perfect foresight—that the federal government would neverthe-less *ignore* that right, and use military force to prevent such a lawful secession. Thus, Buchanan's argument is mere sophistry.

This review of the legal history of the states contradicts Lincoln's claim that the states had *always* been part of a superior union which implicitly forbade secession. In fact, such a claim is preposterous. At various times, the states had been loosely joined for their common defense without a constitution, while at other times, certain states had been left entirely out of the union. The very birth of the states as independent entities took place when they ratified a Declaration of Independence which enshrined a right of secession as an inalienable right of the people of each of the states.[21]

We turn next to Lincoln's discussion of the Constitution as he believes it relates to secession. He argues that while states have reserved powers under the Constitution—presumably referring to, but not mentioning, the Tenth Amendment—secession is not such a power since it is "a power to destroy the government itself."[22] This, of course, is hyperbole and abuse of language. To depart from is to destroy, according to Lincoln. If the union government was destroyed by secession, what was the entity that put a million troops in the field during the subsequent war?

Secession does not destroy the federal government; it merely ends its authority over a certain territory and sets up a new gov-ernment to take its place in that territory. Nevertheless, even if we meet Lincoln halfway and concede that secession involves a partial destruction of the power and scope of the federal govern-ment, how does that fact alone prove its unconstitutionality?

It still remains for Lincoln to confront the limited and dele-gated nature of the powers of the federal government, and the Ninth and Tenth Amendments which transform those principles into positive law. He dodges:

> What is now combatted, is the position that secession is *con-sistent* with the Constitution—is lawful, and peaceful. *It is not contended that there is any express law for it*; and nothing should ever be implied as law, which leads to unjust, or ab-surd consequences.[23]

---

[21]It should be noted that, while several seceding states had not been part of the original thirteen, under the "equal footing doctrine," states later accepted into the Union share the same legal rights as the original thirteen. See H. Morse, "The Foun-dations and Meaning of Secession," *Stetson Law Review* 15 (1986): 419, 429–31.

[22]Lincoln, *Speeches and Writings*, pp. 353, 355.

[23]Lincoln, *Speeches and Writings*, p. 257, emphasis added.

Nowhere does Lincoln mention the Ninth and Tenth Amendments. Since those Amendments carry much of the load of the argument for secession, and were frequently cited by secessionists of the day, the failure of the brilliant lawyer to grapple with them is strong evidence of his inability to do so. Lawyers have often treated the weak points in their cases with silence there and much noise elsewhere.

Not only does Lincoln ignore the Ninth and Tenth Amendments, he simply replaces them with an amendment of his own: states have no rights that are not expressly stated in the Constitution. It was precisely the point of those amendments, however, to ensure that no serious lawyer would ever make such an argument.

The Ninth Amendment states:

> The enumeration in the Constitution, of certain rights, shall not be construed to deny or disparage others retained by the people.

The precise purpose of the Ninth Amendment was to respond to the argument Alexander Hamilton made against attaching a bill of rights to the Constitution. Hamilton argued that the expression of certain rights such as free speech and the right to bear arms would, by longstanding rules of legal interpretation, be construed to deny other possible rights.[24] The Ninth Amendment was added to the Bill of Rights to make clear that rights other than those specified were indeed retained by the people.

The most authoritative source for unenumerated rights is the Declaration of Independence. Bennett Paterson writes, "The Declaration of Independence was a forerunner of the Ninth Amendment."[25] As we have seen, in the context of announcing a secession from Great Britain, the Declaration explicitly supports the right to alter or abolish government. The author of the leading constitutional-law treatise of the early-nineteenth century wrote:

> To deny this right [secession] would be inconsistent with the principle on which all our political systems are founded, which is, that the people have in all cases, a right to determine how they are governed.[26]

[24]See Randy Barnett, "James Madison's Ninth Amendment," in *The Rights Retained by the People: The History and Meaning of the Ninth Amendment*, Randy Barnett, ed. (Fairfax, Va.: George Mason University Press, 1989), pp. 11–12.

[25]Bennett Paterson, "The Forgotten Ninth Amendment," in *The Rights Retained by the People*, p. 107.

[26]William Rawle, *A View of the Constitution of the United States* (Philadelphia: H.C. Carey and I. Lea, 1825).

Thus, the right of a people to secede from a larger polity would appear to be among the unenumerated rights which are protected by the Ninth Amendment.

The Tenth Amendment states:

> The powers not delegated to the United States by the Constitution, nor prohibited by it to the States, are reserved to the States respectively, or to the people.

The Tenth Amendment complements the Ninth[27] in providing a persuasive textual argument that the right of secession is reserved to the states.[28] The right to prevent secession is not delegated to the United States. In fact, the Constitutional Convention considered and rejected a provision that would have authorized the use of Union force against a recalcitrant state. On 31 May 1787, the Constitutional Convention considered adding to the powers of Congress the right

> to call forth the force of the union against any member of the union, failing to fulfil its duty under the articles thereof.[29]

The clause was rejected after James Madison spoke against it:

> A Union of the States containing such an ingredient seemed to provide for its own destruction. The use of force against a State, would look more like a declaration of war, than an infliction of punishment, and would probably be considered by the party attacked as a dissolution of all previous compacts by which it might be bound.[30]

Neither is the right to secede expressly prohibited to the states. Thus, under the plain meaning of the Tenth Amendment, the states retain the right to secede. This position is buttressed

---

[27]The Ninth Amendment "is a companion to and in a measure the complement of the Tenth Amendment," according to K. Kelsey, "The Ninth Amendment of the Federal Constitution," in *The Rights Retained by the People*, pp. 93–94.

[28]I note in passing the silly argument, advanced by the *New York Times* on 12 April 1861, that since the South claimed to be independent of the United States, it was no longer able to claim the protection of the Constitution (see Stampp, *And The War Came*, pp. 42–43). This is a disingenuous point, since the Union's entire justification for the war was that the Constitution remained in effect in the South. Furthermore, the Ninth and Tenth Amendments protected the right of the states to secede, *while they remained part of the union*. Thus, the act of ratifying secession was a constitutionally protected act. Since the states left the Union lawfully, the Union thereafter had no lawful authority over them. Thus, the invasion of the South was unlawful. Having left the union lawfully, the Southern states were no longer bound by the various constitutional clauses cited above.

[29]*The Records of the Federal Convention*, Max Farrand, ed. (New Haven, Conn.: Yale University Press, 1911), vol. 1, p. 47.

[30]Ibid., p. 54.

by the historical fact that the states had the right to secede in 1776 and did not expressly give up that right in ratifying the Constitution. To the contrary, New York and several other states, in their acts of ratification, noted that "the powers of government may be reassumed by the people, whensoever it shall become necessary to their happiness."[31] The Tenth Amendment also makes clear that a right or power need not be expressly granted to the states by the Constitution. Rather, the states are *irrebuttably presumed* to have such a power, unless that power is expressly taken from them by the Constitution.[32]

Since the acts of secession were approved by state legislatures, then ratified by conventions whose delegates were elected by the people of those states, there is no conflict between the Ninth and Tenth Amendments in authorizing Confederate secessions.[33]

Lincoln was therefore in error in suggesting that the right of secession had to be spelled out in the Constitution. He did, however, make an argument in the alternative that secession should not be "implied as law [because it] leads to unjust, or absurd consequences." Among the "unjust" consequences of secession Lincoln cites are the financial consequences. The federal government had borrowed money to purchase the territories of several seceding states, and had contracted to pay the debts of Texas when it entered the union. Also, the seceding states would allegedly escape their share of the national debt.

All these issues, however, are collateral to the issue of secession and are therefore to be regarded as red herrings. We *know* that even if the seceding states had hired an accountant, determined the *net* amount, if any, owed to the federal government and tendered payment in that amount, that President Lincoln would nonetheless have ordered the invasion. Furthermore, if the war was fought to recover a just debt, then the Union army would only have needed to confiscate a sufficient quantity of Confederate property to pay that debt, and leave in peace. That image is as absurd as Lincoln's argument. Since Lincoln's argument is not a *bona fide* argument against secession, we need not consider

[31]Quotation from the New York ratifying convention, cited in Randall, *Constitutional Problems under Lincoln*, p. 15, n. 18.

[32]For a remarkably similar discussion of the meaning of the Tenth Amendment, published after the initial presentation of this paper, see *U.S. Term Limits, Inc. v Ray Thornton*, United States Supreme Court, 115 S.Ct. 1842, 1875 (1995), p. 1876. (Dissenting opinion of Justice Thomas, joined in by Justices Renquist, O'Connor and Scalia): "the States can exercise all powers that the Constitution does not withhold from them."

[33]Morse, "The Foundations and Meaning of Secession," pp. 435–36.

the complex issue of whether the seceding states actually owed money to the federal government.[34]

Yet another part of the Bill of Rights that is ignored by Lincoln is the Second Amendment, which speaks of "the right of the people to keep and bear arms" and to form a "well regulated Militia" in order to protect the security of a "free State." A reasonable interpretation of this Amendment, based on its historical origins, is that the people of the states have the right to defend themselves against the tyranny of the federal government:

> The Second Amendment was designed to guarantee the right of the people to have "their private arms" to prevent tyranny and to overpower an abusive standing army or select militia.[35]

James Madison, writing before the ratification of the Second Amendment, commented:

> Let a standing army, fully equal to the resources of the country, be formed; and let it be entirely at the devotion of the federal government; still it would not be going too far to say, that the State governments, with the people on their side, would be able to repel the danger. . . . To these would be opposed a militia amounting to near half a million of citizens *with arms in their hands*, officered by men chosen from among themselves, fighting for their common liberties, and united and conducted by governments possessing their affections and confidence.[36]

If states have the right to protect themselves against federal tyranny by force, they would appear to have the right to do so by the peaceful means of secession. While the right of secession is not derived from the Second Amendment, the denial of such a right renders the Second Amendment incongruous. Lincoln not only ignored the Second Amendment, he perverted its intent—and undercut the premise of Madison's argument—by calling out the militias of the northern states to fight against the militias of the Confederate States. His agents violated the Second Amendment rights of citizens in border states by systematically seizing their muskets.[37]

---

[34]It has been argued that the North actually owed money to the South, due to the discriminatory effects of the tariff on imported goods. On this issue, see Allen E. Buchanan, *Secession: The Morality of Political Divorce from Fort Sumter to Lithuania and Quebec* (Boulder, Colo.: Westview Press, 1991), pp. 104–5.

[35]Stephen P. Halbrook, *That Every Man Be Armed: The Evolution of a Constitutional Right* (Albuquerque: University of New Mexico Press, 1984), pp. 76–77.

[36]*The Federalist Papers*, no. 46, emphasis added.

[37]Dean Sprague, *Freedom Under Lincoln* (Boston: Houghton Mifflin, 1965), pp. 55, 80, 90, 203, and 220.

Lincoln cites only two clauses in the Constitution in his argument against the legality of secession: the supremacy clause and the guarantee clause. Each argument shares the same logical defect. The supremacy clause, in Article VI, states:

> This Constitution, and the Laws of the United States which shall be made in Pursuance thereof . . . shall be the supreme Law of the Land; and the Judges in every State shall be bound thereby, any Thing in the Constitution or Laws of any State to the Contrary notwithstanding.

This clause could arguably be invoked to negate secessionist legislation as violative of federal laws against treason. Reliance on the supremacy clause, however, begs the question. The supremacy clause can be used as an argument against secession only if the Constitution requires a state to remain part of the union[38]; it does not apply otherwise, nor, obviously, does it apply to a state that has left the Union. Thus, arguments from the supremacy clause assume as a premise precisely what is in dispute: that the state is still part of the Union and thus bound by the supremacy clause. In light of the arguments previously made that the *Constitution* allows secession, one can just as easily argue that the supremacy clause barred the Union army's invasion of the South!

Article IV, §4, states that "The United States shall guarantee to every State in this Union a Republican Form of Government." This clause was cited by President Lincoln to justify a war to prevent secession:

> If a State may lawfully go out of the Union, having done so, it may also discard the republican form of government; so that to prevent its going out, is an indispensable *means*, to the *end*, of maintaining the guaranty mentioned; and when an end is lawful and obligatory, the indispensable means to it, are also lawful, and obligatory.[39]

John Adams once complained that "he 'never understood' what the guarantee of republican government meant; 'and I believe no man ever did or will.'"[40] Nevertheless, Lincoln's argument again begs the question. The clause itself applies only to a state in the Union. Thus, to apply the clause, one must first *assume* that a state may not lawfully secede.[41]

[38]See Morse, "The Foundations and Meaning of Secession," p. 425, n. 35.

[39]Lincoln, Special Message, *Speeches and Writings*, p. 261.

[40]Quoted in William M. Wiecek, *The Guarantee Clause of the U.S. Constitution* (Ithaca, N.Y.: Cornell University Press, 1972), p. 13.

[41]Since the seceding states ultimately formed a confederation, does the constitutional prohibition on states entering into a "confederation" [Art. I, §10] prohibit secession? Such an argument suffers from the same logical fallacy as resort to the

Those portions of the guarantee clause not cited by Lincoln are instructive: "The Unites States shall . . . protect each of them from Invasion; and on application of the Legislature, or of the Executive (when the Legislature cannot be convened) against domestic violence." Lincoln failed to cite the "invasion" clause, of course, since he himself was planning an invasion of the southern states. Nor could he very well justify the invasion on the grounds of preventing "domestic violence" since he lacked the consent of the legislatures of the Confederate states, to say the least. A plain reading of the Guarantee Clause as a whole suggests it was written for the benefit of the states, not to provide a pretext for invading them.

Lincoln's evasion of these critical portions of the guarantee clause are symptomatic of the central fallacy of his constitutional view of secession: his belief that the Constitution countenanced a military invasion of the South and resulting extended displacement of its civil authorities by military rule. To the contrary, the Constitution contemplates a structure of state–federal relations in which the states must take an active and *voluntary* part.[42] This contrasts sharply with Lincoln's view of the Union as little more than a prison from which unhappy states are not allowed to escape:

> The Union, in any event, won't be dissolved. We don't want to dissolve it, and if you attempt it, *we won't let you*. With the purse and sword, the army and navy and treasury in our hands and at our command, you *couldn't do it*.[43]

Lincoln believed that the Union would be fully preserved if that escape was prevented by force. But was it? The Constitution uses the word "State" over a hundred times. It does not establish a prison–inmate relation, but rather a complex political structure in which powers, duties, and rights are carefully split between

---

supremacy and guarantee clauses. This clause governs only states which are still part of the United States. Thus, to apply this clause to a state which has previously seceded, one must assume that the secession was invalid, which begs the question. Further, the United States did not invade the southern states because they had formed a confederacy; it invaded because of the alleged illegality of their secession. In fact, each state had seceded prior to joining the Confederacy. For example, by the time the first Confederate Constitution was passed on 8 February 1861, all the member states at that time had already seceded. See Edward Alfred Pollard, *Southern History of the War* (New York: Fairfax Press, 1866), pp. 44–45; Morse, "The Foundations and Meaning of Secession," p. 436.

[42]Cf. "Opinion on Secession by Attorney General Black," in *Great Debates in American History*, pp. 292–93; "Last Annual Message of President Buchanan," ibid., pp. 293–305.

[43]Lincoln, Galena speech, p. 355, emphasis added.

the federal government and the states. Even the Supreme Court, in two cases critical of secession, admitted this:

> The States are organisms for the performance of their appropriate functions in the vital system of the larger polity, of which, in this aspect of the subject, they form a part, and which would perish if they . . . ceased to perform their allotted work.[44]

> Without the States in union, there could be no such political body as the United States.[45]

The states were expected to choose members of the House of Representatives and elect representatives to "The Senate of the Unites States [which] shall be composed of two Senators from each State."[46] The states were also supposed to select electors who would then elect a president. In addition, the states would each maintain militia, which could be called upon by the President to defend the nation.[47] States were required to respect the "Privileges and Immunities" of the citizens of other states, give full faith and credit to the judicial proceedings of other states, and return fugitives from justice to other states.[48] The states were expected to actively participate in the process of amending the Constitution, such amendments requiring the consent of three-fourths of the states.[49] State courts were expected to be bound by the Constitution, treaties, statutes, and federal court decisions.[50]

Some of the state functions listed above are simply not subject to being effectively compelled by the federal government. Sending representatives to Congress and participating in the election of a president fall into this category. It is difficult to conjure an image of a state being forced at gunpoint to elect a Senator.

Other functions listed are subject to being compelled. Examples include recognition of the court decisions of other states and of the federal government. Such compulsion, however, in the presence of a recalcitrant state government, requires the establishment of a lasting federal military government in such state.

To an extent, the South's decision to seek secession through military resistance obscured this fact. The South, having been defeated militarily, and exhausted by war, reluctantly accepted

[44] *White v Hart*, 646, 650 (1871).
[45] *Texas v White*, 74 U.S. 718, 725 (1868).
[46] U.S. Constitution, Art. I, §3.
[47] U.S. Constitution, Art I., §8; U.S. Constitution, Art. II, §2; U.S. Constitution, Amend. II.
[48] U.S. Constitution, Art. IV, §1 and 2.
[49] U.S. Constitution, Art. V.
[50] U.S. Constitution, Art. VI.

federal authority in order to rid itself of military occupation. In contrast, if a state were to pursue secession by means of non-violent resistance and complete non-involvement with the federal government, an anti-secessionist federal government would have to *permanently* occupy and rule that state in the manner of a colonial power, exercising even greater authority than Great Britain held over the American Colonies prior to 1776![51] That ugly scenario, however, is precisely what anti-secessionist thinkers are obliged to assert was the intent of the ratifiers of the Constitution of 1788, that is, the intent of the thirteen states which had recently fought long and hard to escape colonial status.

While it may be true that some of the Framers intended the Union to be perpetual, it is unlikely that even those Framers believed the Constitution authorized the establishment of a military dictatorship to keep it so. Thus, it could be said that while the issue of secession was perhaps not contemplated by the Constitution, neither was forced union at the cost of the military occupation of recalcitrant states.[52] Such military occupation flatly contradicts the Guarantee Clause drafted by those same Framers.

From the moment federal troops occupied the South, the governments of those states could no longer be considered "republican." With apologies to John Adams, by republican I mean a government exercising limited powers delegated to it by the people, whose officials are answerable to the people in regular and free elections.[53] Since the very purpose of invading the South was to destroy the state governments established by the people, in militarily occupying those states, the federal government breached its obligation to guarantee to each state a republican form of government.[54] Since the federal government necessarily violated the Constitution's Guarantee Clause by waging war on the seceding

[51]The colonies, after all, did enjoy limited self-government through colonial legislatures.

[52]Gottfried Dietz argues that even Hamilton would not rule out secession under the Constitution. See *The Federalist: A Classic of Federalism and Free Government* (Baltimore: Johns Hopkins Press, 1960), pp. 283–85.

[53]"A state, in the ordinary sense of the Constitution, is a political community of free citizens, occupying a territory of defined boundaries, and organized under a government sanctioned and limited by a written constitution and established by the consent of the governed." *Texas v White*, 721.

[54]U.S. Constitution, Art. IV, §4. It is true that the South no longer considered itself governed by the Constitution, including the guarantee clause. The argument in the text does not rest on an assumption that the guarantee clause applies to states *after* they have successfully seceded. Rather, it merely points out that the federal government cannot constitutionally use military force to prevent secession in the first place.

states, it should be evident that it had no constitutional authority to prevent such secessions.

The strength of this argument is best seen by noting the absurd linguistic manipulations used to justify the constitutionality of military occupation. Andrew Johnson, whom President Lincoln appointed the military governor of Tennessee, and who, later, as President, would appoint other military governors in the South, said in 1862 that his authority to militarily rule Tennessee came to him by way of the *Guarantee Clause!*[55] The republicanism thus guaranteed by Johnson apparently consisted of forcing on the people of the state of Tennessee certain forms of government and policies they evidently did not desire. The rationale? "[The] right of self-government could be temporarily impaired but only for the purpose of assuring its eventual and permanent triumph."[56]

The other rationale for military occupation is also self-contradictory. In *Coleman v Tennessee*, the Supreme Court held military occupation lawful, not on constitutional grounds, but by resorting to international law principles which apply primarily to independent nations.

> Though the late war was not between independent nations, but between different portions of the same nation, yet having taken the proportions of a territorial war, the insurgents having become formidable enough to be recognized as belligerents, the same doctrine must be held to apply. *The right to govern the territory of the enemy during its military occupation is one of the incidents of war . . . and the character and form of the government to be established depend entirely upon the laws of the conquering State or the orders of its military commander.*[57]

Thus, to justify the otherwise unconstitutional military occupation of a state, the Supreme Court treats that state as if it were an independent nation, implicitly recognizing the validity of its secession.

What the Court did not cite was any constitutional provision which justified the war in the first place. Since the invocation of international law was based on the fact of war, and the Union's involvement in that war violated the Constitution, it is evident that the Constitution's supremacy clause[58] forbade any resort to

---

[55]See Wiecek, *The Guarantee Clause of the U.S. Constitution*, pp. 183–84.

[56]Ibid., p. 243.

[57]*Coleman v Tennessee*, 97 U.S. 509, 517 (1879) (emphasis added).

[58]"The Constitution . . . shall be the supreme Law of the Land." U.S. Constitution, Art. IV.

international law to override the Constitution. The unconstitutional and amoral nature of the Court's reasoning can be seen by assuming that the Confederacy, in violation of the Constitution, had conquered the North and set up a military government there. The Supreme Court, by the same logic they applied in *Coleman*, would be compelled to endorse the legality of that military dictatorship!

Much ink has been spilled over the ancient debate between those, such as Jefferson and Calhoun, who hold that the Constitution is a compact among the states, and those, including Marshall and Webster, who deem it "an instrument of perpetual efficacy" created by the people of the nation as a group.[59] The outcome of this debate can have no impact on the above conclusions, since those conclusions rest primarily on an analysis of the relevant texts and secondarily on the historical context in which those texts were drafted. Nevertheless, because of the historical association between this debate and the issue of secession, a brief evaluation is appropriate.

Ironically, reliance on the compact theory tends to weaken the case for secession by suggesting that it is not justified by the actual text of the Constitution. The main textual problem with the compact theory is that the Constitution does not read like a contract among the states. The main logical problem is that, while this theory claims that the Constitution is an implied contract among the states, that document creates a separate entity—the federal government—which would not appear to be bound by the contract because it is not a contracting party. Thus, secessionists erred in choosing poor ground on which to do battle with unionists. The compact theory also creates an insoluble procedural difficulty. If the Constitution is a compact, the violation of which allows a state to withdraw, who is to judge whether such a violation has occurred? However, reliance on the Ninth and Tenth Amendments, under which secession is a reserved power, eliminates this procedural obstacle to secession.[60]

[59]Cf. Taylor, *The Origin and Growth of the American Constitution*, pp. 296–341; D. Tipton, *Nullification and Interposition in American Political Thought* (Albuquerque: University of New Mexico Press, 1969); Randall, *Constitutional Problems Under Lincoln*, pp. 12–24; B. Samuel, *Secession and Constitutional Liberty* (New York: Neale Publishing, 1920); Daniel Wait Howe, *Political History of Secession to the Beginning of the American Civil War* (New York: G.P. Putnam's Sons, 1914), pp. 15–36; Eugene Gary, "The Constitutional Right of Secession," *Central Law Journal* 76: 165.

[60]While Jefferson clearly held the compact theory of the Constitution, which implies a need to justify a secession, he simultaneously held to the Ninth and Tenth Amendment approach of this article, which treats secession as an unconditional right of each state: "If any State in the Union will declare that it prefers separation

Nevertheless, the compact theory contains an essential element of truth. It takes the long way around the barn to arrive at the rather obvious conclusion that the states enacted the Constitution for their mutual benefit. Shifting then, from the quaint, complex, and controversial compact theory to the indisputable proposition that a constitution should be interpreted according to the purposes of its ratifiers, it becomes apparent that the purposes of the Constitution do not envision the use of armed force against a state that has concluded it is no longer benefiting from the Union. The Constitution may not be a literal compact among the states, but neither is it a sentence of perpetual imprisonment.

While unionists assert that the compact theory is nothing more than "scholastic metaphysics,"[61] their own view of the Constitution contains elements which fail to connect with reality at any point. Bryce wrote that the Constitution was "an instrument of perpetual efficacy, emanating from the whole people."[62] Yet, as already noted, it contains no such language, and, in fact, its Framers deliberately chose not to carry over the use of the term "perpetual union" from the Articles of Confederation to the Constitution.

Likewise, the Constitution did not "emanate from the whole people." Leaving aside the preamble for the moment, the actual language of the texts of Articles VII and V is to the contrary:

> The Ratification of the Conventions of nine States shall be sufficient for the Establishment of this Constitution between the States so ratifying the Same. . . . Done in Convention by the Unanimous Consent of the States present.

> [The Constitution may be amended] when ratified by the Legislatures of three fourths of the several States, or by Conventions in three fourths, thereof. . . .

Since the Constitution was proposed by a convention called by the states, was ratified by the states, and can only be amended by the states, any notion that "the government proceeds directly from the people,"[63] that it is "of the people" and "by the people,"[64] or that it "emanates from the whole people" can only

---

. . . I have no hesitation in saying 'let us separate.'" Letter of Jefferson to W. Crawford (20 June 1816), *The Writings of Thomas Jefferson*, Paul Ford, ed. (New York, G.P. Putnam's Sons, 1899), vol. 10, 1816–1826, pp. 34–35.

[61]Taylor, *The Origin and Growth of the American Constitution*, p. 310.

[62]Bryce, *American Commonwealth*, vol. 1, p. 322.

[63]*McCulloch v Maryland*, 4 Wheat 316 (1819).

[64]President Abraham Lincoln, Gettysburg Address, 19 November 1863, *Speeches and Writings*, p. 536.

be described as metaphysical nonsense invented by those who view the states as a mere inconvenience on the path to creating an all-powerful central government.

Much has been made by unionists of the Preamble:

> *We, the People of the United States,* in Order to form a more perfect Union, establish Justice, insure domestic Tranquility, provide for the common defense, promote the general Welfare, and secure the Blessings of Liberty to ourselves and our Posterity, do ordain and establish this Constitution of the United States of America.[65]

This reliance is understandable. If one lacks support for one's view in the *text* of the constitution, one seeks it in the *preamble.* The italicized phrase, however, has no unambiguous meaning. Its meaning depends on whether the word "United," an adjective, or "States," a noun, is given greater emphasis. However, there is no need to resolve this issue, because the presence in the Preamble of the phrase, "We, the People of the United States" was an accident! It originally read:

> That the people of the States of New Hampshire, Massachusetts, Rhode Island, Connecticut, New York, New Jersey, Pennsylvania, Delaware, Maryland, Virginia, North Carolina, South Carolina and Georgia do ordain, declare and establish the following constitution for the government of ourselves and our posterity.[66]

Judge Eugene Gary explains:

> It was amended, not for the purpose of submitting the constitution to the people in the aggregate, but because the convention could not tell, in advance, which States would ratify it.[67]

Even though unionists have placed great stock in the Preamble, their recitations rarely extend past the first 15 words. Nothing thereafter is particularly helpful to their cause. The Union's creation of martial law in the South can hardly be within the ambit of "establishing justice" or "securing the blessings of liberty." "Domestic tranquility" was clearly not insured by the bloodiest war ever fought in North America. The "general welfare" was not promoted when one section of the nation fought, subdued, and militarily ruled the other for 16 years.[68] And "Providing for

---

[65]Emphasis added.

[66]Gary, "The Constitutional Right of Secession," p. 171.

[67]Ibid.

[68]The political domination of the South lived well past the end of Reconstruction. "After the Civil War a century passed before another resident of the South was

the common defense" does not in any way sanction an attack on eleven states.

Ultimately, one must look beyond mere logic and the four corners of the Constitution to identify the unionist spirit that led to the Civil War:

> The union was . . . more than a mere compact between separate entities, separate states. It was rather a union of early history and future promise, of generations past and generations still to come, of agriculture and industry, of plains and seaboard, of the vast hosts of mystical and emotional forces which give to man a greater sense of belonging, a greater sense of community.[69]

Gary Wills denies the claim that Lincoln "did not really have *arguments* for union, just a kind of mystical attachment to it."[70] He argues that Lincoln got most of his pro-union legal arguments from Daniel Webster. Wills's discussion of those arguments (e.g., the Union is older than the states, and the Declaration of Independence sanctions war against seceding states) tends one to the view that Webster was a union mystic as well.

A THOUGHT EXPERIMENT

Those still harboring doubts about the constitutionality of secession in 1861 should attempt a sincere answer to the question: would the Constitution, as construed by President Lincoln and his allies in all eras, have been ratified in 1788? To answer this question, we must first make *explicit* those provisions Lincoln and his successors thought were *implicit* in the Constitution. For the sake of realism, these provisions will be organized in the form of an imaginary Eleventh Amendment to the Constitution.[71] Such an amendment would read as follows:

(Imaginary) Amendment XI

Section 1. Notwithstanding the Guarantee Clause and the Ninth and Tenth Amendments, no state may ever secede from the Union for any reason, except by an amendment pursuant to Article V.[72]

---

elected president. . . . For half a century after the war, *none* of the speakers or presidents *pro tem* [of the Senate] was from the South." McPherson, *Abraham Lincoln and the Second American Revolution*, p. 13.

[69]Alan Pendleton Grimes, *American Political Thought* (New York: Holt, Rinehart and Winston, 1960), p. 281.

[70]Wills, *Lincoln at Gettysburg*, pp. 125ff.

[71]The real Eleventh Amendment was not ratified until 1795.

[72]Which clauses in the Constitution would such an amendment violate?

Section 2. If any State attempts to secede without authorization, the Federal Government shall invade such State with sufficient military force to suppress the attempted secession.

Section 3. The Federal Government may require the militias of all states to join in the use of force against the seceding State.

Section 4. After suppressing said secession, the Federal Government shall rule said State by martial law until such time as said State shall accept permanent federal supremacy and alter its constitution to forbid future secessions.

Section 5. After suppressing said secession, the Federal Government shall force said State to ratify a new constitutional amendment which gives the Federal Government the right to police the states whenever it believes those states are violating the rights of their citizens.

Section 6. The President may, of his own authority, suspend the operation of the Bill of Rights and the writ of *habeas corpus*, in a seceding or loyal state, if in his sole judgment, such is necessary to preserve the Union.[73]

This imaginary amendment contains a fair summary of what Lincoln thought the Constitution, ratified in 1788, had to say implicitly about state secession. Would the Constitution have been ratified if it contained such an amendment? Would that amendment have been ratified at any time between 1788 and 1861? The answer to both questions, according to any intellectually honest historian or constitutional lawyer, must be a resounding "No!" If that is the case, however, then the dense fog made up of equal parts of Websterian metaphysics and Lincolnesque legalese disintegrates to reveal the truth of Albert Jay Nock's thesis: the Constitution of 1788 did indeed expire in 1861.

In 1861, the Constitution did not authorize the federal government to use military force to prevent a state from seceding from the Union. The Constitution established a federal government of limited powers delegated to it by the people, acting through their respective states. There is no express grant to the federal government of a power to use armed force to prevent a secession, and there is no clause which does so by implication. To the contrary, the notion of the use of armed force against the states, and the subsequent military occupation and rule of the states by the federal government, does violence to the overall

---

[73]For evidence that during the war the federal government violated most, if not all, of the first ten Amendments to the Constitution *in the Northern and border states*, see, generally, Sprague, *Freedom Under Lincoln*.

structure and purpose of the Constitution by turning the servant of the states into their master. Any doubts about whether the federal government had such a power must be resolved in favor of the states, since the Ninth and Tenth Amendments explicitly reserve the vast residue of powers and rights to the states and to the people of those states.

LINCOLN'S POLITICAL ARGUMENTS AGAINST SECESSION

While Lincoln the lawyer made a variety of legal arguments against secession, Lincoln the politician made two main political arguments against secession. He argued that the option of secession violated the principle of majority rule and that it led ultimately to anarchy.[74] However, the line between legal and political arguments is not precise. Further, it is undoubtedly true that considerations of policy and consequences do impact on judgments about what the law is and should be. Thus, a brief consideration of Lincoln's views on that issue is in order. It must be emphasized, however, that the distinction between what the law is and what it should be is a real one. Thus, the conclusions about Lincoln's *legal* arguments remain valid, regardless of the wisdom of his *political* arguments. In this context, Lincoln's arguments can be seen as points which should have been made at the Constitutional Convention of 1787, and incorporated into the Constitution, but were not.

Lincoln's central political arguments against secession are contained in the following passage from the First Inaugural Address, delivered on 4 March 1861:

> We divide upon [all our constitutional controversies] into majorities and minorities. If a minority . . . will secede rather than acquiesce [to the majority], they make a precedent which, in turn, will divide and ruin them; for a minority of their own will secede from them, whenever a majority refuses

---

[74]A full consideration of the political arguments for and against secession is beyond the scope of this article. On this, cf. Lee C. Buchheit, *Secession: The Legitimacy of Self-Determination* (New Haven, Conn.: Yale University Press, 1978); Buchanan, *Secession: The Morality of Political Divorce*; Allen E. Buchanan, "Self-Determination and the Right to Secede," *Journal of International Affairs* 45 (1992): 347; Allen E. Buchanan, "Toward a Theory of Secession," *Ethics* 101 (1991): 322; M. Kampelman, "Secession and Self-Determination," *Current* 5 (November 1993): 35; R. McGee, "A Third Liberal Theory of Secession," *Liverpool Law Review* 14 (1992): 45; Amitai Etzioni, "The Evils of Self-Determination," *Foreign Policy* 89 (Winter 1992/93): 21; Alexis Heraclides, "Secession, Self-Determination and Nonintervention: In Quest of a Normative Symbiosis," *Journal of International Affairs* 5 (1992): 399; Harry Beran, "A Liberal Theory of Secession," *Political Studies* 32 (1984): 21.

> to be controlled by such minority. . . . The central idea of se-
> cession, is the essence of anarchy.[75]

The argument contains two closely related elements:

(1) secession violates the principle of majority rule; and
(2) secession ultimately leads to anarchy.

Majority Rule[76]

If anything can be identified as the key axiom of Lincoln's thought, it is majoritarianism. He was devoted to the principle despite his numerous electoral losses and the rejection of his presidential candidacy by 60 percent of the electorate. Although Lincoln personally opposed slavery, before the war he had favored allowing the majority in each southern state to decide the issue.[77] For the sake of a majoritarianism which he believed was undermined by secession, he ordered the invasion of the South. What Lincoln never confronted was the fact that the Civil War was a war between two majorities.[78] In 1860, Lincoln did not receive a single vote in North Carolina, South Carolina, Georgia, Tennessee, Louisiana, Mississippi, Alabama, Arkansas, Florida, or Texas.[79]

The ultimate justification of majority rule is that it is better than minority rule. Its value is purely utilitarian—more people get what they want than if we let the minority rule. By its very nature, the utility of majority rule *increases* as the political unit is divided into smaller and more homogeneous units. For example, if the largely black Roxbury section of Boston seceded from the city,[80] its voters, currently outvoted by the majority white

[75]Lincoln, *Speeches and Writings*, p. 220.

[76]The discussion that follows was inspired by Murray Rothbard's analysis of the concept of democracy in *Power and Market: Government and the Economy* (Kansas City: Sheed Andrews and McMeel, 1970), pp. 189–99.

[77]See President Abraham Lincoln, First Inaugural Address, 4 March 1861.

[78]He had apparently forgotten his speech in Congress in 1848: "Any portion of such people that can, may revolutionize, and make their own of so much of the territory as they inhabit. More than this, a majority of any portion of such people may revolutionize, putting down a minority, intermingled with, or near about them, who may oppose their movements." Quoted in Alexander H. Stephens, *A Constitutional View of the War Between the States* (Philadelphia: National Publishing Company, 1867), vol. 1, p. 520.

[79]Howe, *Political History of Secession*, p. 446. The Republican Party was a purely regional party, and simply was not on the ballot across the South.

[80]As it has tried to do in recent years. See "Seceding From Boston?" *Newsweek* (3 November 1986): 30; "The Roxbury Rebellion," *Common Cause Magazine* (Winter 1992): 25.

population, could increase their utility by electing officials and policies they preferred, while the white majority would remain able to enact its own preferred policies.

Secession therefore, far from being hostile to majority rule, allows multiple satisfied majorities to be created out of large political units which can only satisfy one majority bloc at a time. The only difference, of course, is that the old majority is no longer able to impose its will on the old minority. It is this loss of *power* over the escaped minority and its territory, and not any devotion to majority rule, that so irks unionists of all eras, often leading them to start wars to retain power over the seceders. Evidence that such was the case with the Civil War is contained in the following passages from journals published at that time:

> [The North] fought . . . for all those delicious dreams of national *predominance* in future ages, which she must relinquish as soon as the union is severed.[81]

> We love the Union because . . . it renders us now the equal of the greatest European Power, and in another half century, will make us the greatest, richest, and most *powerful* people on the face of the earth.[82]

In examining these two quotes, it is remarkable to note that the first journal, which was British, pro-South, and post-War, saw the war in the same nationalistic and imperialistic terms as did the second journal, which was American, pro-North, and pre-War. It should be obvious that wars of this type are not sanctioned by the majority principle; they are condemned by it.

Anarchy

We have seen how the right of secession *and* the principle of majoritarianism each tends to create pressure for smaller political units. Lincoln argued that the principle of secession led by infinite regress to anarchy, as each minority seceded to become a majority. However, this theory is killed by an ugly fact—history shows that secessions, like revolutions, happen only seldom, because "mankind are more disposed to suffer, while evils are sufferable, than to right themselves by abolishing the forms to which they are accustomed." After all, it takes a "long train of abuses and usurpations" to instigate secessionist activities.

[81]*The Athenaeum* (6 May 1865), quoted in Adams, "The Second American Revolution," p. 19 (emphasis added).

[82]*New York Courier and Enquirer* (1 December 1860), quoted in *The Causes of the Civil War*, rev. ed., Kenneth Stampp, ed. (Englewood Cliffs, N.J.: Prentice-Hall, 1974), p. 55 (emphasis added).

The best example of this is, after all, the Civil War itself. Even though there were unionists in the South and secessionists in the North, no further secessions took place after the start of the war, even though those were times of great stress and social conflict. Evidently, the people on both sides used their common sense to put a brake on Lincoln's infinite regress.

Even in theory, an infinite number of secessions is unlikely because there is unlikely to be an infinite succession of major grievances which are clearly solvable by secession. Ireland, for example, solved its perceived major problem by getting rid of the British in 1922 (except in Northern Ireland). Evidently, no further significant political problem there is sufficiently connected to the option of further secession to stir any interest in the subject. Norway seceded from Sweden in 1905 by a vote of 368,208 to 272![83] Since then, little has been heard from Norway about further secession.

Lincoln was wrong in believing that the right of secession invariably leads to the break-up of nations. Rather, the recognition of such a right will tend to discourage the exploitation of states by the central government, which in turn will encourage states to remain in the Union. Applying that principle to 1861, can the possibility be denied that it was the Union's militant rejection, over several decades, of the right to secede that was itself the proximate cause of Confederate secession? That is, the seceding states knew their secession would be violently resisted—Lincoln had told them so—thus, they made a strategic decision to make this fight before the North grew any stronger, economically or militarily. Had Lincoln recognized a right of peaceful secession, the Confederate states may well have stayed in the Union and tried to work out their differences, knowing that if such attempt failed, secession remained a viable option. Jefferson himself believed that if the South ever broke off, it would eventually return to the Union, presumably after it had renegotiated its constitutional arrangement.[84]

In this sense, secession actually reduces anarchy by allowing a peaceful resolution of disputes between large political groups.[85] In contrast, Lincoln's policy of forced association led to four years

[83]Michael Hechter, "The Dynamics of Secession," *Acta Sociologica* 35 (1992): 267, 278.

[84]Jefferson, letter to Crawford.

[85]Those who blame secessionist movements for the violence associated with them are blaming the victims. See Kampelman, "Secession and Self-Determination," p. 8. The violence invariably is caused by the *opponents* of secession.

of anarchy and war in the South, followed by decades of sporadic violence and lawlessness.

The most interesting aspect of the topic of *secession* is how little attention or discussion there is about the obverse of secession: the *expulsion* of a portion of a nation by the larger and more powerful sector. It is always the case that the people living in a small part of a nation-state desire to secede; never that the larger part wants to kick them out. The very fact that a portion of the nation wants to secede, by the law of demonstrated preference,[86] proves that those citizens believe they are being harmed by being subjects of that nation. Similarly, the rarity of historical expulsions proves that governments benefit from ruling over and exploiting the various regions that are within their control. This fact is consistent with the view of the nation-state—developed by Oppenheimer, Nock, and Rothbard[87]—as the organization of the political (coercive) means of acquiring wealth:

> There are two methods, or means, and only two, whereby man's needs and desires can be satisfied. One is the production and exchange of wealth; this is the *economic means*. The other is the uncompensated appropriation of wealth produced by others; this is the *political* means. . . . The State is *the organization of the political means*.[88]

Another significant aspect of secession is that, by and large, the parties that urge various legal, political, and moral arguments for the right of secession, do so because they are less powerful than the majority block. If they were more powerful, they would simply secede and be done with it! In sum, a seceding group is generally the weaker and economically exploited junior partner in a nation-state. Thus, in general, we may say that in any given secession dispute, *right* is on the side of the proponents of secession, while *might* is on the side of their opponents. That being the case, Lincoln's political arguments against secession must be rejected.

[86]"Every action is always in perfect agreement with [a person's] scale of values or wants because these scales are nothing but an instrument for the interpretation of a man's acting." Ludwig von Mises, *Human Action*, 3rd rev. ed. (Chicago: Contemporary Books, 1966), p. 95.

[87]Cf. Franz Oppenheimer, *The State: Its History and Development Viewed Sociologically* (New York: Vanguard Press, 1926); Nock, *Our Enemy, The State*; Murray N. Rothbard, *The Ethics of Liberty* (Atlantic Highlands, N.J.: Humanities Press, 1982), pp. 161–72.

[88]Nock, *Our Enemy, The State*, pp. 59–60 (emphasis in original). Nock mentioned tariffs as one way the state appropriates the wealth of others (ibid., p. 61). There is reason to believe that the North gained economically at the South's expense as the result of the disproportionate impact of tariffs. See Adams, "The Second American Revolution," p. 20–22; Buchanan, *Secession*, p. 41.

LEGAL DEVELOPMENTS SINCE 1861

If states had the right of secession in 1861, have any developments subsequently removed that right? That is actually a complex question for which no entirely satisfactory answer exists. This is largely because of the eternal question: who has the final say on interpreting the Constitution?

One fallacy that can be quickly disposed of is that the Civil War answered the question of secession forever. We may call this fallacy the Ulysses S. Grant theory of constitutional law: "the right of a state to secede from the Union [has been] settled forever by the highest tribunal—arms—that man can resort to."[89] Questions of constitutional law, however, cannot be settled on the battlefield:

> Throughout history, force appears as the arbiter of the moment. . . . Reason, organically slow—reacting against force only when the ill effects of the latter become so general as to be inevitably obvious—finally confirms or annuls its judgement.[90]

If indeed secession was a state and people's right, all the Union victory proved was that the stronger party in a constitutional conflict may violate the law with impunity.

Neither was the issue of secession settled by various Supreme Court decisions resolving questions tangential to the issue itself.[91] First, in none of those cases was the Court asked to deal squarely with the issue of state secession when the outcome of the case impacted on the rights of the seceding states and those states were represented by counsel before the Court. Second, none of those cases contained a detailed and serious analysis of the issues, arguments, and constitutional clauses one would expect to see in a comprehensive treatment of the issue by the highest court in the land. Therefore, these cases carry little moral or legal authority.

Furthermore, if the issue of secession had been taken to the Supreme Court, for instance by the Confederacy seeking an injunction against President Lincoln, the Court would likely have responded by refusing to hear the case on the grounds that it dealt mainly with a political question, that is, a question which, although a legal one to be sure, is not suitable for resolution by the

---

[89]Quoted in Tipton, *Nullification and Interposition in American Political Thought*, p. 50.

[90]Samuel, *Secession and Constitutional Liberty*, p. 14.

[91]See, e.g., *The Prize Cases*, 67 U.S. 635 (1862), *Mississippi v Johnson*, 4 Wall. 475 (1866); *Texas v White*, 7 Wall. 724 (1868); and *White v Hart*, 13 Wall. 246 (1871).

Court.[92] Thus, secession is a question that has never been satisfactorily resolved by the Supreme Court, and is not likely to be addressed by the Court in the future.

Since the Civil War, there have been two main legal developments impacting on the issue of secession: the amendment of state constitutions to prohibit secession, and the passage of the Fourteenth Amendment. While under military control and occupation, the states of Arkansas, North Carolina, Florida, South Carolina, Mississippi, and Virginia each enacted new constitutions containing clauses prohibiting secession.[93] Soon thereafter, the troops were withdrawn.

Such clauses, however, did not in any way serve to abolish the right of those states to secede from the Union. First, these clauses were added only under duress. It is an ancient principle of law that agreements made under duress are voidable at the option of the aggrieved party. Second, those states remain free at any time to amend their constitutions to delete the ban on secession.[94] If they choose not to do so, that merely means they are choosing not to exercise a legal right, which is quite distinct from not possessing that right. Finally, since all states have equal rights in the Union,[95] the fact that other states have not relinquished their right to secede means that these southern states cannot be deemed to have relinquished theirs.[96]

The Fourteenth Amendment, however, poses a more serious problem for a constitutional doctrine of secession. That Amendment reads in relevant part:

> Section 1. All persons born or naturalized in the United States and subject to the jurisdiction thereof, are citizens of the United States and of the State wherein they reside. No State shall make or enforce any law which shall abridge the privileges or immunities of citizens of the United States; nor shall any State deprive any person of life, liberty, or property, without due process of law; nor deny to any person within its jurisdiction the equal protection of the laws.

The Amendment goes on to make apparent reference to the Civil War by prohibiting any military officer, who, having previously sworn to support the Constitution, engaged in "insurrection or

[92]See *Luther v Borden*, 48 U.S. 1 (1849) (a federal court could not competently decide which state government was in power).

[93]Morse, "The Foundations and Meanings of Secession," pp. 431–32.

[94]Relying on the doctrines of duress or equality of states.

[95]Morse, "The Foundations and Meanings of Secession," pp. 429–31.

[96]Ibid., p. 433, n. 64.

rebellion" against it, from serving as a federal official.[97] It further provides that no state shall assume or pay any debt "incurred in aid of insurrection or rebellion against the United States," but that no debts incurred in "suppressing insurrection or rebellion shall be questioned."[98]

The Amendment grants the federal government vast new powers over the states in the context of a concern over the post-Civil War welfare of the recently freed slaves. That fact, and the pejorative references to "insurrection and rebellion" quoted above, allow a persuasive argument to be made that the Fourteenth Amendment bars secession. If it did not, states could simply secede, thus defeating the purpose of the Amendment by avoiding federal regulation under §1 of the Amendment. Ironically, if this argument is correct, the pre-war case for secession is strengthened.[99] That is, if the Fourteenth Amendment bars secession, then presumably there was such a right before the Amendment was passed.

Is there any room for a secessionist argument to be made in the post-Fourteenth Amendment era? First, the obvious can be stated: the Fourteenth Amendment does not explicitly prohibit secession. One would have thought that the pro-unionists who controlled American politics after the War would have included such a provision. Their failure to do so, whatever the motive,[100] means that resort may still be had to the pro-secession arguments stated above. Unionists might respond by arguing that the Fourteenth Amendment *implicitly* bans secession, and, since it was passed after the other portions of the Constitution, it prevails over them in any conflict of meaning. That argument would be perfectly valid if the Amendment *explicitly* banned secession. However, since it does not, we are left with the need to resolve an apparent implicit conflict between the Fourteenth Amendment and the Ninth and Tenth Amendments. The best that can be said in this context is that any secession movement designed to restore blacks to their pre-Civil War political and economic status would be barred by the Fourteenth Amendment.

Second, the Fourteenth Amendment was ratified by the seceding states under the same type of duress which forced several of them to ban secession in their state constitutions. Indeed, ratification of the Fourteenth Amendment was made a pre-condition

---

[97]U.S. Constitution, Amend. XIV, §3.

[98]U.S. Constitution, Amend. XIV, §4.

[99]See Morse, "The Foundations and Meanings of Secession," p. 433.

[100]Not wanting to implicitly admit a pre-Fourteenth Amendment right to secede?

of readmission of the states into the Union by the Reconstruction Act of 1867.[101] It was only after such ratification that military rule was ended in those states. Thus, as it regards the issue of secession, the Fourteenth Amendment is tainted, having been enacted under the same duress which this article concludes was a violation of the right to secession, i.e, the invasion and occupation of the South by the Union army. Thus, any Fourteenth-Amendment-based argument against secession is self-negating, since it must implicitly concede a pre-Amendment right to secede, the violation of which led to the enactment of the Fourteenth Amendment.

Finally, in resolving any conflict between the Fourteenth and the Ninth and Tenth Amendments, reliance on the doctrine of inalienable rights would be useful. An inalienable right is one possessed by a human being that is so basic to his or her welfare that we do not enforce any contract or agreement in which a person relinquishes such a right.[102] As Murray Rothbard writes:

> There are certain vital things which, in natural fact and in the nature of man, are *inalienable*, i.e., they *cannot* in fact be alienated, even voluntarily. Specifically, a person cannot alienate his *will*, more particularly his control over his own mind and body. Each man has control over his own mind and body. Each man has control over his own will and person, and he is, if you wish, "stuck" with that inherent and inalienable ownership. Since his will and control over his own person are inalienable, then so also are his *rights* to control that person and will. That is the ground for the famous position of the Declaration of Independence that man's natural rights are inalienable; that is, they cannot be surrendered, *even if* the person wishes to do so.[103]

If the right of secession is inalienable, then that right, protected as it is by the Ninth and Tenth Amendments, survives any attempt to relinquish it through the Fourteenth Amendment. As such, the right to "alter or abolish" forms of government does appear to be a fundamental right that should be considered inalienable.[104] It is integral to the protection of those other rights which

[101]U.S. Statutes at large 153, 39th Cong. 2nd Sess. (1867): 428–29. Six Southern states, whose votes were necessary for ratification, ratified the Amendment after having first rejected it. See *The Constitution of the United States of America: Annotations of Cases Decided by the Supreme Court of the United States* (Washington, D.C.: U.S. Government Printing Office, 1973), p. 31.

[102]See Rothbard, *The Ethics of Liberty*, pp. 135–36, citing Williamson Evers, "Toward a Reformulation of the Law of Contracts," *Journal of Libertarian Studies* 1 (1977): 3.

[103]Rothbard, *The Ethics of Liberty*, p. 135 (emphasis in original).

[104]A United Nations resolution "the Granting of Independence to Colonial Countries and Peoples," states: "all peoples have an *inalienable* right to complete freedom, the exercise of their sovereignty and the integrity of their national territory."

Jefferson termed inalienable, such as the rights to life and liberty. Thus, it is a right that should survive regardless of its alleged implicit relinquishment under the Fourteenth Amendment.

CONCLUSION

The Union's invasion and subsequent military occupation of the Confederacy were illegal. Today, however, the Fourteenth Amendment arguably prohibits secession by implication. Nevertheless, that Amendment, insofar as it can be interpreted to bar state secession—is tainted. It is the direct result of the illegal invasion and subsequent military domination of the South. Even the Fourteenth Amendment does not explicitly outlaw secession, and there remains a conflict between the Fourteenth Amendment and the Ninth and Tenth Amendments in this regard. This conflict should be resolved by reference to the doctrine of inalienable rights, of which secession is one.

No doubt today's Supreme Court, if it took the case, would rule secession to be treasonous and illegal, not to mention highly politically incorrect. The Supreme Court, being an agency of the federal government, has, since John Marshall's day, usually given the Constitution that interpretation which increases the power of the federal government over states and persons.[105] Its continual abdication of its purported role of guaranteeing constitutionally limited government is in large part responsible for the recent revival of interest in the theory and practice of secession. However, far more important than what the Supreme Court would decide is the people's own understanding of the true meaning of the Constitution. The people retain the inalienable right to alter or abolish a government destructive to their liberties.

United Nations General Assembly, Fifteenth Session, Official Records, Supplement 16, Resolution 1514, A/4684 (1960) (emphasis added). While contemporary international law recognizes a vaguely defined right of self-determination of peoples, it does not as of yet recognize an absolute right of secession. See J. Falkowski, "Secessionary Self-Determination: A Jeffersonian Perspective," *Boston University International Law Journal* 9 (1991): 209; L. Brilmayer, "Secession and Self-Determination: A Territorial Interpretation," *Yale Journal of International Law* 16 (1991): 177; Note, "Secession: State Practice and International Law After the Dissolution of the Soviet Union and Yugoslavia," *Duke Journal of Competition and International Law* 3 (1993): 299; Note, "The Logic of Secession," *Yale Law Journal* 89 (1980): 802; Note, "The Law of Secession," *Houston Journal of International Law* 14 (1992): 521. Neither, however, does it prohibit secession when such secession is lawful under the constitution of a given nation.

[105]Henry Mark Holzer, *Sweet Land of Liberty?* (Costa Mesa, Calif.: Common Sense Press, 1983).

The existence of slavery in the Confederate States in 1861 cannot alter this truth. The Constitution did not forbid slavery prior to the passage of the Thirteenth Amendment in 1865, and since chattel slavery no longer exists in the United States, it can no longer be used to legally or morally justify war on a seceding state. That is as it should be, since, ultimately, a policy of violent opposition to secession is a policy of forced association. As with all forms of forced association, the stronger party will tend to exploit the weaker. Such is the case with the master–slave relationship. Such is the case when a state is forced to remain in the Union against its will. Both forms of forced association are immoral, and both should be—and are—forbidden by the Constitution.

Had the commander of the Union army, on entering Virginia on 27 May 1861, encountered the ghost of the finest American lawyer who had yet lived, and asked for advice on the legality of his mission, Thomas Jefferson would likely have replied, "Go back to your country, Sir."

9

THE ECONOMIC AND POLITICAL RATIONALE FOR EUROPEAN SECESSIONISM

Hans-Hermann Hoppe

U ntil very recently, the future of Europe seemed fairly certain: twelve individual nation-states would have their political, economic, and cultural identities submerged into a central government welfare–regulatory–monetary apparatus controlled by a bureaucratic elite operating out of Brussels, Belgium, under the authority of the European Parliament, and separated from the socialist East. However, obstacles have appeared that will probably prevent the completion of this seemingly preordained path. First is the collapse of socialism, which has introduced mass migration as an issue into European politics. Second is the appearance of nationalist and secessionist movements that are not only skeptical of European integration but that have also called for new varieties of smaller political arrangements. Although disparaged by the media and hated by all central governments, these movements are based on an economic, political, and cultural rationale that should be encouraged. The task now is to understand how the forces of separatism and secessionism can be the basis of a new Europe based on increasingly smaller governmental units that take account of the growing demand for political, cultural, and economic sovereignty and the classic liberal ideals of private property, free trade, and competition (cultural, economic, and political) that have been integral to the historical development of the Western world.

I

In the aftermath of the collapse of socialism in Eastern Europe, a mass migration set in which can be compared in direction and magnitude only to the great population movements after the fall of the Roman Empire during the fifth century. Millions of people moved westward: Albanians, Bulgarians, Hungarians, Rumanians, Slovenes, Croatians, Macedonians, Czechs, Slovaks, Armenians, Ukrainians, Balts, Poles, and Russians, and, in their wake, refugees from an even-greater multitude of Asian and African countries. In 1990, nearly one million reached Germany, Europe's most prosperous and hence attractive destination, but all of Western Europe, from Finland and the Scandinavian countries to

Greece, Italy, Spain, and Portugal, have been affected by the exodus. Moreover, the flood of East European immigrants is expected to grow still larger. Estimates of the number of Soviet emigrants during the next decade range from five to forty million.[1]

People stay where they are or migrate to distant locations for various reasons, one of which is the expected future income attainable at alternative locations. Other things being equal, people will move from lower- to higher-income areas. Hence, migration patterns are highly relevant in any comparative analysis of economic systems. However, migration statistics reveal the full extent to which one economic system is judged better or worse than another only so long as no migration restrictions exist. With migration controls in effect, such statistics only render a distorted picture. They remain of great significance if *any* migration exists, but they must be complemented by and re-evaluated in light of an analysis of existing anti-migration laws and their corresponding enforcement policies.

The recent exodus from Eastern Europe provides final dramatic proof of the inferiority of socialism as judged by those who are forced to experience it. Under socialism, almost all factors of production are owned collectively. With private ownership of productive assets essentially outlawed, no market, and hence no prices, for capital goods exists. Yet, without market prices for capital goods, cost accounting is impossible. The result is the permanent misallocation of capital goods.

Collective ownership, furthermore, socializes gains and losses from production, diminishing every single producer's incentive to increase the quantity or quality of his individual output, or to use production factors sparingly, which systematically encourages laziness and negligence. Moreover, with collectivized production factors, no one can determine independently of others what to do with any given factor of production (as can happen under a regime of private property). Instead, every decision as to what, how, and where to produce becomes a political affair, requiring a collective decision-making mechanism, and thereby creating *winners* and *losers*. The flight of the people of Eastern Europe is a flight from the impoverishment and total loss of independence from political control created by socialism.[2]

[1]According to surveys recently conducted in the Soviet Union, more than 30 percent of the population (close to 100 million people) expressed the desire to emigrate.

[2]The lack of democracy (multi-party elections), in fact, has essentially nothing to do with socialism's plight. It is obviously not the selection principle for politicians that causes socialism's inefficiencies. It is politics and political decision-making as

II

Judged by emigration statistics, practically no single day has passed since the inception of socialism in Russia, in 1917, and since 1945 on a larger scale in all of Eastern Europe, when socialism has not been proven a failure. The longer it lasted, the more obvious this failure became.

With no West German immigration controls directed against East Germans and language barriers nonexistent, the case of East Germany is the most instructive. After less than 15 years of socialism, nearly four million East Germans (about 20 percent of the population) had migrated westward. The growing flood of emigrants had risen to more than 1,000 per day (an annual population loss of almost 3 percent) when, on 13 August 1961, East Germany's socialist regime, to avoid crumbling under its own weight, had to seal off its borders to the West. Previously, emigration had been treated as a criminal offense (*Republikflucht*) and punished by the confiscation of all "abandoned" property. But escape remained possible, as the border between East and West Berlin had stayed wide open. Then, to keep its population from running away from socialism, the East German government built a border fortification system of walls, barbed wire, electrified fences, minefields, automatic shooting devices, watchtowers, and heavily armed military patrols—100 miles around West Berlin, and nearly 900 miles along the border to West Germany.

While somewhat less dramatic, the development of the other East European countries closely paralleled that of East Germany. Each socialist regime suffered migration losses, and by the mid-1960s, orchestrated by the Soviet government and in concert with the unique East German measures, all of Eastern Europe (with the partial exception of Yugoslavia) had been turned into a giant prison camp.[3]

---

such that are responsible. With socialized factors of production, each decision requires a collective's permission. It is irrelevant to a producer how those giving permission are chosen. What matters to him is that permission has to be sought at all. As long as this is the case, the incentive for producers to produce is reduced, and impoverishment will continue. The opposite of socialism is, thus, not democracy, but private property and capitalism as a social order built on the recognition of private property. Private property is as incompatible with democracy as it is with any other form of political rule. Private property implies a completely *de-politicized* society, or, in Marx's terms, an anarchy of production, in which no one rules anybody, and all producers' relations are voluntary and, hence, mutually beneficial.

[3]It is indicative of the quality of American textbooks dealing with the comparative analysis of economic systems that most do not even mention the terms "migration" and "migration restriction" in their index, and that hardly anyone gives systematic

For more than two decades, the problem could be repressed, and socialism's failure could be concealed. Emigration persisted even under the most adverse conditions, but the flood became a trickle. Yet, when, in the late 1980s, after continued economic decline that had increasingly eroded the Soviet government's position as a military super power, reformist forces gained control over the government apparatus in the Soviet Union, Hungary, and Poland, and ever-so-slightly liberalized their anti-emigration policies, the flood immediately resumed at levels higher than ever, and has continued to increase.[4]

III

If left alone, the current exodus would continue until the losses of productive individuals became such a burden and caused so much economic hardship that the governments of Eastern Europe, whether communist or welfare statist, would be toppled and socialism completely uprooted. Unfortunately, such a development is unlikely, as migration is not being left alone. However, this time it is not the governments of Eastern Europe that are taking the initiative. To be sure, they continue to hamper emigration. Yet the de-legitimization of governmental power in Eastern Europe has proceeded too far to allow them a return to the *status quo ante*. In fact, the means with which to accomplish such a return—the Warsaw Pact—no longer exist. Rather, it is the governments of Western Europe which are now determined to prevent such a development by tightening their own anti-immigration policies.[5]

---

consideration to international flows of population. From this fundamental miscomprehension, it is only a small step to conclusions as perverse as Paul Samuelson's (drawn until 1989) and many lesser known *experts*, that the economic development of the Soviet Union and Eastern Europe has by and large been a success story—all the while no government in Eastern Europe allowed its people the right to free emigration, requests for emigration permits were regarded as punishable offenses, and people trying to exit nonetheless faced the very real threat of being shot down without mercy.

[4]East Germany is again most instructive. Before the construction of the Wall, more than 1,000 people per day had fled. In the summer of 1989, when socialist Hungary began to open its borders to Austria, and since the breakdown of the Berlin Wall on 9 November 1989, the flood of East German emigrants rapidly increased to exceed 2,000 per day.

[5]While a complete-privatization-free-trade-no-tax policy cannot instantly create wealth, it instantly creates a reason not to emigrate. Even if wage rates in Western Europe remained higher for the time being (due to more past capital accumulation), future production would instantly be made less costly than in the highly taxed and regulated economies of Western Europe. By choosing instead a policy of

Immigration to the countries of Western Europe is already highly restrictive, and the further the process of West European integration has advanced and the more intra-West European migration has been liberalized, the more restrictive the admission standards toward non-West Europeans have become. Work permits are required, and foreigners have no right to such a permit (even if there is an employer willing to employ them, or if they possess the means for self-employment). Permits are granted at the governments' discretion, only in small numbers, and typically only to individuals classified as political asylants—as persons who can demonstrate political persecution in countries officially recognized as evil (whereas all economic reasons for asylum are considered invalid).[6] Despite these restrictions, all West European countries host a substantial number of illegal aliens who, under the constant threat of deportation, have been driven underground and form the growing West European *Lumpenproletariat*.

Faced with a rising tide of immigrants, the governments of Western Europe are now reacting with more restrictive measures. They all have dropped Poland, The Czech Republic, Slovakia, and Hungary from the official list of evil countries, so as to make their populations ineligible for political asylum and work permits. Austria has deleted Rumania from its list. Led by the signatories of the Schengen Accord—the governments of Germany, France, Belgium, the Netherlands, Luxembourg, and Italy—tourist visa requirements have been extended to include practically all non-Western nations in order to "harmonize" the West European immigration laws. Norway and Finland have tightened their controls at the border of the former Soviet Union. Austria has begun to employ military patrols on the Hungarian border.

---

gradually reducing the government sector from close to 100 percent to the standards of Western Europe (where total government expenditures, including social security payments, typically amount to around 50 percent of GNP), the current emigration wave may be somewhat reduced, but westward migration will actually be made permanent (as current and future income levels in Western Europe will remain higher than in the East). Once again, this is best illustrated by the German example. Since the currency unification on 2 July 1990 and the incorporation of East by West Germany on 2 October 1990, the number of emigrants fell as expected. However, because the government sector in former East Germany still remains far larger than that in the West (within one year of de-socialization, a mere 700 out of 9,000 East German "production units" had been privatized, while the West German tax and regulation structure was exported wholesale to the East), to this day, emigration from East to West has continued at a rate of more than 500 per day.

[6]This leads to the perverse result that men like Trotsky—a murderer and plunderer running away from another, more powerful one—can find refuge in the West more easily than men who have no other reason to emigrate than to be left alone by the murderers or plunderers.

The Italian navy now intercepts Albanian refugees crossing the Adriatic. Assisted by the West, the anti-immigration fervor has spread eastward. The Polish government has restricted access to Rumanians. In a treaty with the six member states of the Schengen Accord, it has further agreed to halt the influx of Soviet citizens (in exchange for exempting Poles from the standard West European travel visa requirements). Similarly, Czechoslovakia and Hungary have raised their entry requirements for Rumanians and Soviets, and the Czechoslovakian government has made it harder for Poles to travel to its country.

IV

It is easy to understand why governments should want to stop emigration, for every productive person lost is·a loss of taxable income. Why a government should want to prevent immigration is more obscure. For does not every additional producer represent an increase in government revenue? Indeed, a population influx in a given territory, while it would lower the nominal wage rates, would raise real income per capita as long as the population remained below its "optimum" size (and surely this would be the case for Western Europe, even if the most dramatic immigration estimates became reality). A larger population implies an expansion and intensification of the division of labor, a greater physical labor productivity, and thus, all-around higher living standards.

The early post-World War II development of Western Europe provides a perfect illustration of this. By the late 1960s, the population of West Germany and France had each grown by more than twenty percent, and that of Italy, the third major continental country, by about fifteen percent.[7] Accompanying this development, Italy, France, and West Germany experienced a period of unprecedented economic expansionism, with higher growth rates than any other major country (with the exception of Japan) and steadily increasing per capita incomes. During this period, West Germany, the most successful of all, integrated millions of southern European *Gastarbeiter* (guestworkers) and East German refugees. By the early 1960s, its labor force had grown by some eight million (more than 60 percent), while the unemployment rate fell from a peak of eight percent in 1950 to below one percent. From 1948 to 1960, the total wage sum tripled, wage rates more

---

[7]Still more spectacular was the growth in some smaller countries. During the same period, the population of Switzerland increased by close to 30 percent, and that of the Netherlands by more than 40 percent.

than doubled in constant terms, and the annual rate of economic growth increased to close to ten percent. Total industrial output was raised fourfold, GNP per capita tripled, and West Germans became one of the world's most prosperous peoples.[8]

By the late 1980s, however, the economies of Western Europe had gone through a complete transformation from their post-World War II beginnings. The former expansionism was replaced by economic stagnation, and instead of helping stimulate another leap forward, the latest population increases, besides revealing the bankruptcy of Russian-style socialism, also threatened to expose the bankruptcy of Western-style welfare democracies.

V

Throughout Western Europe, the inter-war period was characterized by economic stagnation brought on by money and credit expansion, monetary disintegration—the destruction of the gold exchange standard in the early 1930s—increased protectionism, business cartelization, labor legislation, socialized investment, and public sector growth.[9] World War II further accelerated this tendency, added large-scale destruction and millions of deaths, and left Western Europe severely impoverished.

Italy was essentially still a third-world country at the end of World War II, hardly touched by the industrial revolution and grimly poor. While its population had slightly increased during the period between the two World Wars, Italy's desperate economic conditions had produced a constant stream of overseas emigration (mostly to the Americas). In 1946, its GNP was 40 percent less than what it had been in 1938, and had reverted to its pre-World War I level. Wages in constant terms had fallen to about 30 percent of their value in 1913.

Although more industrialized and wealthier than Italy, France remained a rural society. For half a century, its population size had stagnated, and during the 1930s, it had actually decreased slightly, shrinking the extent of the division of labor. Half of the population lived in tiny rural communities, and almost one third of the labor force worked in agriculture, mostly on

[8]The West German performance was surpassed by Switzerland. With a larger proportion of foreigners—more than 15 percent—than any other country, by the mid-1960s, Switzerland had achieved the rank of the world's most prosperous country.

[9]By 1938, in all major countries—Germany, the United Kingdom, France, and Italy—government expenditures as a percent of GNP had more than doubled as compared to their pre-World War I level (from around 15 percent to somewhere between 30–40 percent).

small horse-and-buggy farms. In 1946, France's GNP had fallen to half of its pre-1938 level.

Germany, before World War I the most industrialized of the continental big three, strengthened its position during the inter-war period. Yet, Germany was devastated by the hyperinflation in the early 1920s and the Great Depression. Throughout this period until the second half of the 1930s, when the problem was administratively solved through the implementation of a command economy, Germany suffered from a severe unemployment problem peaking at more than 40 percent in 1932). The size of its population stagnated, and as late as 1938, real incomes had not yet reached their pre-World War I levels. In 1946, amidst massive physical destruction (25 percent of the housing had been destroyed), and with a quarter of the working population employed in agricultural production, GNP had fallen to less than a third of its 1938 level. More than half of the population was undernourished, and Germany had reverted to a barter economy.

Western Europe's quick recovery from World War II's destruction and—after three decades of stagnation—its return to the pre-World War I conditions of dynamic economic growth (rising population sizes combined with rising per capita incomes) was the result of a decisive reversal of economic policies. The inter-war period, shaped by international and national socialist, fascist, and corporatist ideas, saw a steady expansion of governmental control over the economy—a silent, but increasing nationalization of private ownership rights. But at the end of World War II, first in defeated Italy and West Germany, and with the founding of the Fifth Republic in France, pre-World War I ideas of hard money (the gold standard), monetary integration, free trade, deregulation, freedom of contract, and private-sector (not public-sector) growth temporarily regained controlling influence in the direction of economic policy, and significant steps toward de-nationalization, i.e., re-privatization, were taken.

In Italy, this return to liberal economic policies was initiated by Luigi Einaudi (1874–1961), who was the Governor of the Bank of Italy (1945), Deputy Prime Minister and Minister of the Budget (1947), and first President of the new Republic of Italy (1948–1955); in Germany, by Ludwig Erhard (1897–1977), Economic Director of the American and British Occupied Zones (1948), Economic Minister of the new Federal Republic of Germany (1949–1963), and Chancellor (1963–1966); and in France by Jacques Rueff (1896–1978), Chairman of the Economic Commission, and President Charles de Gaulle's chief economic advisor. Each one was a professional economist who had received his training during the pre-Keynesian era of economics. Each was directly or indirectly influenced by the Viennese (Austrian) school of economics (most notably by Ludwig von Mises). As outspoken critics of the doctrines of inflationism and socialized investment even after the arrival of the new era of economics, they reduced or halted inflation, lowered or eliminated existing currency controls, and established the *Lira*, the *Deutschmark*, and the *Franc* as hard monies. They lifted or relaxed import tariffs and quotas in order to open their countries to world competition, and they eliminated or reduced price controls, removed or lowered barriers to free entry, and cut tax rates and government spending so as to promote production, competition, and private-sector growth.

While these policies created an economic miracle in post-World War II Western European, and transformed Italy, France, and Germany into modern, industrialized societies with expanding labor forces and steadily rising per capita incomes,[10] the liberal ideas that had inspired them did not hold sway for long. After the successful reduction in the size of the West European governments, the natural inclination of all governments and their representatives toward higher tax revenues, higher expenditures, and increased economic control immediately resumed, and by the mid-1960s to mid-1970s the direction of economic policy had once again changed. Constrained by democratic, multi-party elections, the governments of Western Europe set out on a steady course of trading increased taxation and paper money creation for increased interest-group legislation, and Western Europe thus returned to the policies of increased (rather than decreased) governmental interference in private property, private ownership rights, and free-market exchange that had damaged it so severely between the wars.[11]

[10]By the early 1970s, agricultural employment had declined to 15 percent in Italy, 13 percent in France, and seven percent in West Germany; and per capita incomes, until the late 1960s, had increased by an average of about five percent per year.

[11]In Italy, total government expenditures as a percentage of GNP was 35 percent in 1938, and about 40 percent in 1947. From this level, it continuously declined until the late 1950s, to below 30 percent. It then began to increase again, reaching its pre-World War II level by the late 1960s, and exceeding 50 percent by the mid-1970s. In Germany, it stood close to 40 percent in 1938, and at less than 30 percent in 1950. By the mid-1960s, it had grown back to its pre-World War II level, and by the late 1970s, it had reached 50 percent. In France, it was 30 percent in 1938, 38 percent in 1947, and above 40 percent in 1956. It then fell slightly, did not again exceed its 1956 level until the late 1970s, and reached the 50 percent mark in the early 1980s. One might compare this to the United Kingdom, one of Western Europe's less-successful post-war economies: 29 percent in 1938, 36 percent in 1948, a

In exchange for the socialist–egalitarian vote, governments expanded steadily expenditures on their welfare and labor-protection programs. In exchange for the conservative vote, trade regulations and business-protection laws proliferated. In conjunction with these measures, beginning with the Rome Treaty of 1957, the policy of West European economic integration and the establishment of the European Community (E.C.) was used by the member states—originally six and presently twelve—to coordinate and harmonize their tax, regulation, and welfare structures at an ever-higher level, so as to eliminate all *economic* reasons for intra-Western European population and capital movements (while at the same time lifting all *physical* restrictions on such movements, such as border controls).

As a result, by the 1980s, total government expenditures had typically increased to around 50 percent of GNP (from around 30), rather than falling as during the early post-World War II period. Facilitated by the abolishment of the last remnants of the international gold-exchange standard in 1971, Western European inflation rates during the 1970s and 1980s were typically more than double those characteristic of the 1950s and 1960s. As long as it was unanticipated, the rise in the rate of inflation had generated a few phases of illusory prosperity. Yet these booms, built on nothing but paper money, inevitably ended in liquidation crises—recessions. Once the higher inflation rates became expected, they merely produced stagflation. Annual growth rates fell from an average of around five percent during the 1950s and 1960s to about half of this level during the 1970s, while the 1980s were characterized by either stagnation or negative growth rates. Unemployment rates, which had either been extremely low or falling during both the 1950s and 1960s, steadily increased during the 1970s, and reached a seemingly permanent higher plateau, averaging close to 10 percent, during the 1980s.

Rather than increasing as it had early on, total employment stagnated or even fell. Intra-West European migration—generally from South to North—which had continually increased during the previous two decades, came to a halt in the 1970s; and during the 1980s, the number of southern European *Gastarbeiter* declined. Simultaneously the social time-preference rate—the degree by which present consumption is preferred to future consumption

---

low point of 32 percent in 1955, and then a continuous increase, reaching 40 percent by the mid-1960s, and 50 percent a decade later. On the other hand, Switzerland, Europe's most successful country, showed 24 percent in 1938, 25 percent in 1948, 20 percent in 1950, a low point of 17 percent in 1956, 20 percent again by the mid-1960s, and not until the mid-1970s did it return to its pre-war level.

and saving—significantly increased. Despite its initially low standards of living (but *rising* incomes), Western European, and in particular the Italian, German, and French, saving ratios were exceptionally high (often reaching or exceeding 20 percent of personal disposable income, lower only than Japan's). From 1970–90, although standards of living were by then much higher (but with now stagnating real incomes), saving ratios all across Western Europe (with the sole exception of Switzerland) experienced a significant decline.

VI

With a recalcitrant unemployment problem and stagnating economies, the rising tide of East European immigrants presented and still presents a serious threat to the stability of the Western European welfare democracies—and immigration restrictions appear to be the only safe way out.

To allow free immigration (i.e., to permit entry and grant all foreign residents the same legal status and protection as natives have, except, perhaps, the right to vote and be elected) would be *economically* impossible as long as the current economic policies remained in effect. Free entry into the labor market is prevented by downward inflexible wage rates (as the result of collective bargaining and labor union legislation). And, as a result of business protection laws, free entry into the employer market is hampered by increasingly high levels of business accreditation costs (corporate taxes, licensing requirements, and fees). As such, free immigration would immediately raise the number of unemployed and would generate a sharp increase in the demand for government welfare handouts. To finance these, either taxes or the rate of inflation would have to be increased. However, with an even-heavier burden imposed on private producers, the already listless economies of Western Europe would collapse.[12]

Nor would it be a viable solution to let the immigrants enter and then deny them a work permit or exclude them from the standard welfare entitlements, since this would result in a sharp increase in black-market activities. On the one hand, this would lead to a deterioration of the relative competitiveness of the *official* economy and would give rise to expanding welfare expenditures. On the other hand, it would be *politically* impossible, as

[12]This collapse would come even sooner if East European immigrants were given the right to vote, as most of them, having spent a lifetime under full-blown socialism, are economically illiterate, with welfare statist notions deeply ingrained in their mental make-up.

it would create a society of legally distinct classes—or castes—of residents, and thus provide a hot-bed for nationalist and racial sentiments which could easily get out of government control.

For somewhat different reasons, it is also impossible, or at least quite dangerous, to do what is economically (as well as ethically) sensible: to offer refuge, but at the same time to systematically reverse the course of economic policy and de-statize (or re-privatize) economic life, and dismantle the welfare state. Such a change in policy would assure the integration of the East European immigrants, lead to higher overall standards of living, and possibly even produce a higher total tax revenue (if private producers were to react "elastic" to cuts in tax or regulation rates). However, any West European government that put such a policy into effect would quickly encounter severe problems, for the certain beneficial consequences of these policies would not take effect immediately. Temporarily, the very same policies would inevitably cause substantial disturbances (such as rising unemployment and business failures). Whether or not they turn out successfully (from the government's point of view) depends on the public's time-preference rate, and on the degree to which government tenure is subject to majority control. As regards both determining factors, the prospects of success appear dim.

All West European governments are subject to recurring elections (on local, state, and federal levels), and, hence, democratic politicians typically have relatively short planning horizons, and, thus, place disproportionate weight on the short-run consequences of their actions. Moreover, the general public, which votes the politicians in or out of power, has become increasingly short-term oriented, i.e., its time-preference rate has risen as the expansion of compulsory welfare schemes has steadily relieved it—as much as disabled it—from taking private provisionary action. On account of their own former policies, then, governments are now afraid that the public will no longer wait until the success of a policy of liberalizing private property becomes obvious to everyone, but will vote them out of power.

From the point of view of government, then, the potentially least-destabilizing solution to the problem is to leave everything as it is internally and instead raise the immigration restrictions. By resorting to this measure, the bankruptcy of the Western welfare states as universal models of social organization is revealed, too. Not only is it an economically counterproductive measure which lowers the standards of living for foreigners and inlanders alike, but it is also unethical, because it prohibits inlanders and foreigners from striking certain types of mutually beneficial bargains concerning their own properties. In forcing potential immigrants to stay where they are, it implies support for the communist or semi-communist regimes of Eastern Europe. Yet similar counter-productive measures and unethical, if legal, expropriations of private property owners have characterized the agenda of governments for quite some time without much public protest. With foreigners apparently the sole victims, increased immigration controls are considered downright popular, and are depended upon to assure public forgiveness of the support that is thereby given to communist regimes. If any protests against immigration restrictions are voiced at all, they come from classical-liberal quarters. Yet, while there are a few isolated liberal spokesmen, nowhere in Western Europe does a popular ideological movement dedicated to old liberalism exist.

VII

In fact, classical liberalism, as a political movement, has been all but dead for a long time, and the post-World War II liberalization phase in Western Europe, in particular in Italy, West Germany, and France, must be considered merely a passing aberration—the result more of happy circumstances than of systemic reasons—in a lengthy process of decline.[13]

Old liberalism's decline had begun before World War I—not least because of a strategic error of its own. Classical liberalism had centered around the notion of private property as the prerequisite of human liberty and prosperity, and accordingly had opposed any interference with private property rights, governmental or otherwise. Governments, if necessary at all, were supposed to be of minimal size, entrusted exclusively with the task

---

[13]The Italian and German reforms came in the face of military defeat and occupation, and were carried out largely contrary to, and shielded from, prevailing, left-leaning, public opinion. Luigi Einaudi's temporary influence was not due to the strength of his political party basis, but rather to the fact that he represented a clean break with fascism as much as a return to pre-fascist bourgeois (commercial, Northern) Italy. Already prominent as an economic writer and politician, Einaudi had resigned from public life after the fascist takeover, and had spent the last few years of the fascist era in Swiss exile. Ludwig Erhard, untainted by association with the national socialists, yet with no name or political power base to speak of, was actually appointed to his position as economic Czar by the occupying military forces, and implemented his initial reform package by administrative fiat, uncontrolled and unconstrained by any democratic procedure whatsoever. Similarly, Jacques Rueff's influence lacked a party base, but was due to his personal connection with de Gaulle and the enhanced powers that de Gaulle had created for his presidency under the constitution of the Fifth Republic.

of safeguarding their citizen's private property rights—a night-watchman state. The nineteenth-century liberal movement committed the error of believing it possible to promote this goal by supporting republican (as opposed to monarchic) and democratic (as opposed to aristocratic) causes. Yet, republicanism only promoted nationalism, and allied to it, an originally universal and internationalist liberalism gradually turned nationalist. Democratization—the gradual extension of the franchise from the propertied to the propertyless, which took place during the nineteenth century in Western Europe, and which liberalism, if somewhat reluctantly, had supported—only furthered the growth of socialist-egalitarian and conservative-protectionist parties, simultaneously draining an essentially aristocratic liberal movement of its support.

The outbreak of World War I accelerated liberalism's perversion into a nationalist creed, and in the wake of the war's outcome—the downfall of the Romanovs, Hohenzollerns, and Habsburgs, in defeated Russia, Germany, and Austria-Hungary, respectively, and the Bolshevik takeover in Russia—West European liberalism literally disappeared as a political movement. The threat of the Soviet revolution and the "dictatorship of the proletariat" spreading westward, represented by a strong and radicalized movement of socialist and communist parties, produced as its "bourgeois" response an equally radical movement of national socialist and fascist parties. In the increasingly violent power struggle between these competing socialist forces, which typically ended with the latter's almost complete victory, the liberal movement was pulverized.

As a result of World War II—and the military defeat of national socialism and fascism—Western Europe came under almost total control of the United States and its political system of democratic republicanism. President Woodrow Wilson's foreign policy of "making the world safe for democracy" and his militant anti-monarchism which had been imposed on Europe for the first time after World War I and which had just failed dramatically, was restored and expanded (Serbia-Yugoslavia and Italy abolished their monarchies).

In the countries of Eastern Europe, conceded to Soviet domination by the Roosevelt and Truman administrations, a "dictatorship of the proletariat" was established, and whatever was left of classical liberalism was stamped out in its course. In Western Europe, the pre-fascist and pre-nazi political party system reemerged—but this time without explicitly fascist or national socialist parties, which had been outlawed by the Allied Armed Forces, and without a significant representation of monarchistic parties.

Encouraged initially by the triumph of socialism in the Eastern European peoples' republics, orthodox socialist and communist parties re-established themselves as major forces on the political scene (drawing heavily on former fascist or national-socialist voters). Greece and Italy stood on the verge of communist takeovers in the aftermath of World War II. In France, the communists emerged as the strongest political party, and all socialist parties together consistently gathered a majority of votes until the late 1950s. In Great Britain, the Labour Party rose to government power. The Scandinavian countries were firmly in the grip of the social democrats.[14]

A second major political force in post-World War II Western Europe, a bloc of bourgeois, anti-communist parties of nationalist, social-conservative, and Christian-social orientation emerged. Nominally liberal parties—by then almost unrecognizable from their classic beginnings—were but a small part of this bourgeois camp and hailed a national-social (and anti-clerical) liberalism. Switzerland had been and remained firmly under such bourgeois control; likewise, bourgeois parties gained the upper hand in West Germany and Italy; and Christian-social or social-conservative parties emerged as the strongest single political force in Austria, Belgium, and the Netherlands.

Yet, this time, the rivalry between the proletarian and the bourgeois party bloc did not lead to continuously increased and sharpened political conflict and the paralysis or abolition of the multi-party democratic system, as it had during the period between the wars. Instead, throughout Western Europe, it led to a gradual ideological homogenization, and liberalism in particular, rather than being stamped out, gave up its identity voluntarily to become submerged in a grand and uniform—conservative-liberal-socialist—welfare-statist consensus.

Two interrelated factors contributed to this development. For one thing, to every neutral Western observer it became quickly obvious that the repetition of the socialization experiment in the countries of Eastern Europe produced the very same grim results that it had produced in Russia before, thus disproving once and for all the myth that the Soviet economic mess was only due to a special "Asian mentality" of the Russian people. Second, the

---

[14]Socialist parties were least popular, and have remained so ever since, in Switzerland, with a typical voter turnout of around 25 percent.

above-mentioned liberal reforms, which were simultaneously put into effect across Western Europe, in particular in West Germany and Italy (largely against, and shielded from, an overwhelmingly statist-socialist public opinion[15]), unexpectedly but quickly produced an economic miracle, and sharply widened the welfare gap between West and East.

In light of this public experience—and in search of a popular majority—all Western parties made programmatic adjustments. In particular, the orthodox socialist-communist parties had to undergo a transformation and abandon their central idea of a socialized economy. It was this "embourgeoization" of the left that provided the catalyst for the trend toward ideological uniformity.

Typical of this trend were the developments in West Germany. Of all major countries, the contact with Soviet-style socialism was most direct here, and millions of people had ample opportunity to see with their own eyes the mischief that it inflicted on the people in East Germany. Here, Ludwig Erhard's 1948 reforms had produced Western Europe's first and most dramatic economic recovery, and here the process of ideological uniformation was actually most profound. Support for the Communist Party fell from a low of five percent to insignificance within a few years. The conservative Christian Democratic Union, under Konrad Adenauer's leadership, abandoned all former plans for a nationalization of "vital" industries as early as 1949, and embraced instead the concept of a "social market economy." Most decisively, a decade later, in 1959, the West German Social Democrats, compelled by eroding voter support, adopted a new party program in which all obvious traces of a Marxist past were conspicuously absent, and which talked about socialization only as a measure of last resort, emphasizing instead the importance of social policies in "correcting the failures" of markets. Consequently, in 1966, for the first time the Social Democratic Party gained entrance into the Federal government as the junior partner in a *grand* coalition with the Christian Democratic Union. From 1969 to 1982, a *small* coalition between the Social Democrats, now as senior partners, and the liberal Free Democratic Party followed. And since 1982, the Free Democrats have been junior partners of the Christian Democratic Union again, as they were from 1949 to

---

[15]Indicative of the dominant statist-socialist public opinion is the fact that even West Germany's newly founded conservative Christian Democratic Union, in its Ahlen program of 1947, stated that "the capitalist economic system has not done justice to the vital interests of the German people in state and society" and accordingly demanded large-scale socialization policies.

1957 and from 1961 to 1966. The process of ideological homogenization had thus gone full circle: conservatism, liberalism, and socialism had been homogenized, and the liberals had actually presided over and participated in the final destruction of their own ideological heritage.

In countries farther removed from the Iron Curtain, such as France, Italy, and Great Britain, and also after the fall of the autocratic Salazar and Franco regimes in Portugal and Spain respectively, the process of ideological homogenization was less pronounced or took somewhat longer, but ultimately, all across Western Europe the same pattern emerged,[16] and by the 1980s, the ideological uniformation of Western Europe was nearly complete. "Western European," as defined across all party lines, had come to mean multi-party democracy and social market economy: a private-property-based market economy, regulated and "corrected" by a democratic government according to its definition of "socially desirable" (or "undesirable"). And the socially desirable outcome typically included not only the nationalization, and government monopoly, of external and internal defense and of law and law administration (army, police, and courts), it also included the nationalization of all or most of education and culture (schools, universities, libraries, theaters, operas, museums), of traffic and communication (roads, rivers, coasts, railroads, airports, airlines and airways, mail, telephone, radio, television, and airwaves), and of money and banking (a national fiat currency, a central bank, and a fractional-reserve banking cartel). It meant the nationalization of most natural resources (oil, gas, minerals), and the monopolization or cartelization of most public utilities (water, electricity, gas, disposal services), and of much of insurance (retirement provisions, health insurance, and unemployment benefits). It meant that government systematically took care of, and subsidized, agriculture and housing; that it accorded special protection against market competition to a myriad of "vital" industries (such as mining, coal, steel, cars, airplanes,

---

[16]The best indicator for the ideological uniformation all across Western Europe is the decline of the communist parties and the simultaneous rise of socialist and social democratic parties. As in West Germany, after a relatively strong showing in the immediate aftermath of World War II, the communist parties in Austria, Switzerland, Belgium, the Netherlands, and the Scandinavian countries were quickly reduced to insignificance. The results in post-autocratic Portugal and Spain were similar. In France, the systematic decline of the communist party began in the late 1950s; in Italy it began during the 1970s; and the 1980s saw the de-marxification of the British Labour Party. All the while the popularity of the reformed, social-democratic wing of the socialist movement grew steadily; and during the 1970s and 1980s, social democratic parties reached the pinnacle of power for the first time not only in Germany but also in Austria, Spain, Portugal, Greece, and France.

computers, and textiles); and that in performing all these tasks, government would become a country's largest employer, real-estate owner, and capitalist, and its expenditures would typically absorb about half of a country's national product.

VIII

In this ideological climate of Western Europe, the old liberal idea of freedom of migration has become increasingly alien. At the same time, the classical-liberal idea of removing the very cause of the migration problem has disappeared from public discussion. In fact, just as the Western governments are unwilling to allow free immigration, they cannot afford to allow Eastern Europe to follow the classical-liberal prescriptions of radical privatization, minimal tax, minimal regulation, and free trade, since these policies would bring westward migration to a halt, or even reverse the direction of the flow.[17]

If such policies were put into effect, all future production in Eastern Europe would immediately be less costly than production in the highly taxed and regulated economies of the West, and accordingly, capital would begin to flow from the West to the East. The flight of capital would aggravate the economic stagnation of Western Europe, and would compel the Western governments to enact the very same desocialization policies which they currently are trying to avoid. Hence, in conjunction with their anti-immigration policies, the Western European governments, individually and in a concerted effort by the European Community, are now trying to explain the Eastern misery—falsely[18]—as the result of a lack of democracy rather than of private property, and are promoting the idea of Eastern Europe replacing socialism with the Western model of a social market economy, rather than with the classical liberal one of a private-property economy.

IX

Ominously, these Western interests coincide nearly perfectly with those of Eastern Europe's post-communist governments.

Notwithstanding the dramatic convulsions that have occurred since 1989, the size of East European governments in terms of personnel and resource ownership is still overwhelming, even by the already high Western standards. Furthermore, government

[17]See also note 5 above.
[18]See note 2 above.

personnel at local, provincial, and federal levels still largely consists of the same individuals as before 1989, and many of the post-communist political leaders of Eastern Europe were already prominent, and had risen to eminent positions, under communist rule. To most of them, classical-liberal ideas are simply unthinkable, while they are all-too-familiar with welfare-statist notions.

Moreover, if the liberal prescriptions of instant and complete privatization of all collective property, and of minimal government dedicated exclusively to the defense of private-property rights were put into effect, most government jobs would disappear immediately. Current government employees would be left to the vagaries of the market and forced to find new, productive occupations. Alternatively, if the familiar Western European welfare-state model is accepted as exemplary, and if the Eastern bureaucracies take charge of the irreversible trend toward desocialization, and thereby control and regulate the privatization of non-vital parts of their massive resource holdings (down to—but not below—Western levels), most bureaucratic jobs not only may be secured,[19] but government revenue and the salaries of bureaucrats may actually increase.

In addition, because of Western governments' interests in an orderly transition from socialism to welfare statism, Eastern bureaucracies and leaders adopting such a reform course can expect that at least part of the risks associated with it will be assumed, or financed, by their Western counterparts.

There is a risk that even if the welfare-statist transformation were complete, the westward migration might be reduced, but it cannot be stopped. Here, the West has already assumed the risk by not permitting immigration. And there is the problem that a gradual, government-controlled process of partial privatization, while ultimately bringing about partial improvement, will in the short run lead to increased economic hardship and social tension. In this respect, welfare-statist reformers can now count on Western assistance, too.

During the former communist era, cooperation between East and West was extremely limited. As a result of the inefficiencies of socialist production, Eastern Europe was incapable of selling anything to the West except for raw materials and basic consumer goods, and Western transactions with the East bloc typically

[19]For comparison, total government employment in Western Europe typically amounts to five to ten percent of the population. In Eastern Europe, communist party membership was typically around 15 percent.

accounted for less than five percent of foreign trade. Foreign ownership in Eastern Europe was essentially outlawed. Not a single Eastern currency was freely convertible to Western currencies, and accordingly, even political contacts were comparatively rare. However, since the collapse of communism, the Eastern European governments have something to offer.

West–East trade is still low, and has even fallen in the wake of the revolutionary upheavals across Eastern Europe. But absent the dogma that social means the collective ownership of factors of production, some of the nationalized wealth of Eastern Europe has suddenly come up for grabs; and with the Eastern governments in control of the denationalization process, Western political leaders—and government-connected bankers and big businessmen—immediately increased the contact with their Eastern counterparts. In exchange for Western aid during the transition phase, Eastern governments now have real assets to sell. In addition, the East can assure eager Western buyers that from the outset, the tax-and-regulation structure of the newly emerging economies of Eastern Europe will be harmonized with European Community standards. Most importantly, Eastern governments can sell the assurance that Eastern Europe's new banking system will be set up along familiar Western lines, with a governmentally controlled central bank, a fractional-reserve banking cartel of privately owned commercial banks, and a convertible fiat money backed by reserves of Western fiat currencies, thereby allowing the Western banking system to initiate an internationally coordinated credit expansion, and thus, to establish monetary and financial hegemony over the newly emerging Eastern European economies.

X

The Eastern European governments, in particular in East Germany, Poland, The Czech Republic, Slovakia, Hungary, and the Baltic states, are well on the way toward Western welfare-statism. Although the transition problems of falling production and mass unemployment have taken on dramatic proportions everywhere, and the governmental welfare transfer from West to East has put an additional burden on the already stagnating Western economies, the chances of governments in the East and West of successfully reaching their goals must be evaluated positively. Due to the partial privatization and the elimination of most of the price controls, Eastern Europe's economic performance must eventually begin to improve beyond its desperate showing. This recovery, in turn, must also bring its Western payoff in the form of increased economic integration: a widening of markets, an extensification and intensification of the division of labor, and, hence, an expanding volume of mutually beneficial international trade.

Nonetheless, two fundamental problems remain. First, even if the presently pursued welfare-statist reform strategy is successfully completed, it cannot fulfill the popular demand for quick and steady economic improvement. Due to the gradual approach and the limited extent of privatization, the Eastern recovery process will be much slower and more painful than need be. Moreover, because the average size of government in the newly emerging united Europe will be larger than is presently the case in Western Europe alone, the stimulus given to the Western economies will only be a temporary one, and economic recovery and expansionism will soon be replaced by stagnation in the West and—on a permanently lower level—East alike.

Second, the entire reform process might still be derailed, and the "cunning of reason" may produce a rebirth of classical liberalism. For, as the unintended consequence of the Western immigration halt and the welfare-statist reform path chosen by Eastern governments, the likelihood of secession has increased. If migration is prevented, and if there is little or no hope for domestic reforms leading to quick improvements, or if these reforms and economic improvements lag too far behind popular expectations, the only other escape from economic deprivation is through secession.

Indeed, with the collapse of communism and the beginning of Eastern Europe's welfare-statist transformation, all across Eastern Europe secessionist movements have come to the fore. Yugoslavia has already fallen apart into its various national components. The Soviet Union no longer exists. Demands for national independence, even for independence from newly independent nations, are gaining steam everywhere. For the first time in many centuries of European history, the seemingly irreversible trend toward larger territories and a smaller number of independent governments appears on the verge of systematic reversal.

To be sure, on Europe's southeastern flank there was the progressive disintegration of the Ottoman Empire from the height of its power in the sixteenth century until after World War I with the establishment of modern Turkey. In central Europe, the discontiguous Habsburg Empire was gradually dismembered from the time of its greatest expansion under Charles V in the sixteenth century until it disappeared in 1918 with the founding of modern Austria. But the overriding trend in Europe has been in the opposite direction. Until very recently, Europe consisted of about thirty countries. Yet, at the beginning of this millennium, it consisted of many hundreds or even thousands of independent territories. And for most of the time in between, one of Europe's dominating themes was that of territorial expansion and increased concentration of governments. Innumerous small, independent territories and governments were eliminated, for instance, before France emerged in its modern size and shape at the end of the sixteenth century, and England during the second half of the seventeenth. The development in Russia was similar, where the present extension was reached only during the first half of the nineteenth century. In Italy and Germany, where the political anarchy of decentralized powers was particularly pronounced, the centralization process came to an end only a little over a hundred years ago.[20]

It is natural then, that the secessionist movements in Eastern Europe and the reversal of the trend toward centralization appear as deadly threats to all central governments. But it is another testimony of the eclipse of classical liberalism—while at the same time it attests to the fact that history is typically written by its victors, and to their powers of ideological control— that the secessionist movement is perceived as atavistic by large parts of the general public and the overwhelming majority of intellectuals in West and East; and that even among the movements' supporters, many accept it only out of expediency, as politically inevitable, rather than out of principle. Is not secession contrary to economic integration? Was not the territorial consolidation created through the concentration of governmental power a decisive cause for the rise of the capitalist West in general and the Industrial Revolution in particular? And is not secession a step backwards from the goal of economic advancement?

As classical liberalism recognized, from the point of view of economic theory, each question must be categorically denied. In particular, the interpretation of history as implied in the second question must be rejected as self-serving statist propaganda, incompatible with both theory and history. Secession, i.e., political disintegration, is always compatible with economic integration. However, territorial expansion of government power—political integration—may or may not further economic development. Moreover, under the given circumstances, secession must be

---

[20]For example, Germany, during the second half of the seventeenth century, consisted of 234 independent countries, 51 free cities, and about 1500 independent knightly manors. By the beginning of the nineteenth century, the number of independent territories had fallen to below 50.

considered the only remaining means of advancing economic integration and prosperity well beyond the meager results that can be expected from the current reform course.

XI

When the Slovenes seceded from Yugoslavia, and the Baltic states left the Soviet Union, this initially implied nothing more than a shifting of control over the nationalized wealth from the larger, central governments to smaller, regional ones. Whether or not this will lead to more or less economic integration depends in large part on the new, regional governments' policies. However, the sole fact of secession has already had a positive impact on production, for one of the most important reasons for secession is characteristically the belief on the part of the secessionists that they and their territory are being exploited by others. The Slovenes felt, and rightly so, that they were systematically being robbed by the Serbs and the Serbian-dominated central Yugoslavian government. The Balts resented the fact that they had to pay tribute to the Russians and the Russian-dominated government of the Soviet Union. By virtue of the act of secession, hegemonic domestic relations were replaced by contractual, mutually beneficial foreign relations. Rather than being subordinate to the Serbs or to the Russians, the governments of the Baltic states and Slovenia have become their former rulers' independent equals.

All further effects on economic integration depend on the new governments' policies concerning domestic and foreign exchange. First, ignoring domestic policies for a moment and assuming that the same course of moderate desocialization is followed that the central government would have chosen (or is choosing for the remaining territories), the new governments face but one alternative: free trade or protectionism, partial or total. Insofar as they follow a free-trade policy, allowing an unhindered flow of goods in and out of their territory, economic integration will be advanced. Even the smallest territory will be fully integrated into the world market, and can partake of all advantages of the division of labor, if it adopts an uncompromising policy of free trade.[21] On the other hand, insofar as the secessionist governments resort to foreign trade restrictions and outlaw or hamper the importation or exportation of goods, they will spread economic disintegration. For interference with foreign trade, regardless of the motive involved—whether it is to protect specific domestic jobs, firms,

[21]Although not entirely without sin concerning their free-trade policies, Switzerland and even-smaller Liechtenstein provide excellent examples of this.

industries, or products—forcibly limits the range of mutually be-neficial inter-territorial exchanges, and thus leads to a relative impoverishment, at home as well as abroad.

The size of the territory and the number of its inhabitants are systematically unrelated to the question of inter-regional economic integration, and have only an indirect, albeit impor-tant, bearing upon it. The larger the size of a territory and of in-ternal markets, the more widely the positive or negative wealth effects from either free trade or protectionism will be diffused. Likewise, the smaller the territory and the internal market, the more concentrated will be the positive and negative effects. For instance, a country the size and population of Russia could prob-ably attain a comparatively high average standard of living even if it were to renounce all foreign trade, provided it possessed an unrestricted internal capital and consumer goods market. On the other hand, if predominantly Serbian cities or counties seced-ed from surrounding Croatia, and if they pursued the very same policy of complete self-sufficiency, this would likely spell eco-nomic disaster. Accordingly, other things being equal, the small-er the territory and its internal market, the more likely it will opt for free trade, otherwise the price per person in terms of loss-es of wealth will be higher.[22]

Secondly, as regards domestic policies, the secessionist gov-ernments likewise face one fundamental question: how much of the nationalized wealth should be privatized, and what should be the degree of taxation and internal regulations imposed on the domestic economy? The larger the extent of privatization, the lower the degree of taxation, and the fewer internal regulations, the greater the contribution to economic integration and economic growth.

The collapse of socialism was due precisely to the fact that no real estate and capital goods market, no capitalists, no entre-preneurs, and no cost accounting existed. By outlawing these insti-tutions and functions, socialism had, in fact, abolished all but a small remainder of the division of labor and domestic markets, and it had essentially reverted to the stage of a single, self-suf-ficient household economy, in which the division of labor, and

[22]Consider a single landowner as the conceivably smallest independent territory. By engaging in free trade, there is nothing to prevent this owner from becoming the wealthiest person on earth. The existence of any wealthy individual anywhere is living proof of this elementary truth. On the other hand, if the same owner on the same territory decided—voluntarily, since he is the only person involved—that he would want to forego all inter-territorial trade, abject poverty would result. The fact that hermits are practically nonexistent illustrates the fact that the costs of protectionism becomes ever-more prohibitive, the smaller the internal market.

hence of markets, is restricted to intra-household partitionings and exchanges. Any privatization of real estate or capital goods, then, represents an extensification and an intensification of the inter-household and inter-territorial division of labor. Accordingly, domestic economic integration would reach its optimum no sooner than, and the absolute and comparative advantages of the division of labor could be reaped to the fullest only if, literally all real estate and capital goods are privatized, i.e., if no production factors are compulsorily, that is, through legal prohibitions against their sale, withheld from the market.

Further, given the size of the private-property economy, the higher the taxes that are imposed on income derived from a private-property owner's participation in the social division of labor and his integration into domestic markets, the higher the incentive to withdraw from integration and to revert to self-sufficiency or non-production (leisure consumption). Accordingly, economic integration and domestic economic output would reach an optimum if all coercive levies on productive agents were abolished.

Finally, with the extent of private-property ownership and taxation given, the more extensive the regulations regarding domestic production and trade, the more disintegration will occur. Domestic economic integration and the value of productive output would reach their optimum if a single principle ruled all domestic activities: every owner may employ his property in any way he sees fit, so long as in so doing he does not uninvitedly impair the physical integrity of another person's body or property. In particular, he may engage in trade with any other property owner that is deemed mutually beneficial. Only when each property owner's rights concerning his possessions and its physical integrity are absolute will each undertake the greatest possible value-productive efforts—efforts to increase, or prevent from decreasing, the value of his physical possessions—and will the social stock of material goods and the value embodied in it reach their optimum.

As in the case of foreign trade, the size of a territory and its inhabitants is also systematically unrelated to the question of how much domestic economic integration there is. Yet again a highly important indirect relationship between both variables exists. The relationship is dialectic in nature (and the opposite of what orthodoxy holds it to be).

On the one hand, the larger a government-controlled territory and the smaller the number of independent territories, the more likely is domestic disintegration. A world government that

rules a single all-encompassing domestic market—the order promoted by many politicians and most intellectuals—would, in
fact, provide the least-favorable conditions for domestic integration, because a producer could no longer vote with his feet against
a government's tax-and-regulation structure and migrate to somewhere else, since the situation would be the same everywhere.
By eliminating economically motivated migration, however, a
systematic limitation on governmental power is gone as well, and
the likelihood that governments will raise taxes, expand regulations, and increase public ownership so as to maximize their
own income is increased to the utmost. At the other extreme, with
as many independent territories as there are private households,
the opportunities for economically motivated migration are max-
imized—the number and the variety of immigration possibilities
is as large as it can possibly be—and governmental power over a
domestic economy tends to be lowest. In fact, for a single-person
household, taxation, regulation, or confiscation are inconceiv-
able, since no one can impose anything but voluntary restrictions
upon himself and his possessions. But in the case of a village, or
even a multi-member household, the chances of the village government or the household head successfully imposing anything
but the smallest amount of income and property taxation or regulation are extremely slim. Because their power does not reach
beyond the household or village, and because other independent
households or villages exist, migration will quickly ensue.[23]

On the other hand, no central government ruling over large-
scale territories and millions of citizens could come into existence
ab ovo. Rather, insofar as institutions possessed of the power to
tax, regulate, and confiscate private property can come into being
at all, they must begin small. Historically, it took centuries for

---

[23]It is obviously possible—witness the countries of Western Europe—for the central
governments of large-scale territories with millions of citizens to impose taxes upon
their economies which amount to half or more of the domestic product. Obviously,
it was also possible for central governments to go as far as expropriating almost all
private property (witness the communist past of Eastern Europe). In contrast, it is
difficult to imagine how a father could tax his son or a mayor the village population to the same extent without causing a rebellion or emigration. Indeed, due to
the limited size of the territories involved and the existence of a multitude of other, independent households or villages, even regimes of personal slavery tended to
be less taxing on their subjects than the large-scale central government slave ownership characteristic of the former Soviet Union. The killing of personal slaves—the
ultimate form of economic disintegration—was rare under systems of personal
slavery. In the Soviet Union, it took place on a massive scale, with several million
casualties. Similarly, the life-expectancy of personal slaves increased, along with
the general trend. In the Soviet Union, it fell in recent decades (even excluding
the millions of casualties).

the present, highly centralized state of affairs emerged from its very modest beginnings. Yet, in order for a government to gradually expand its power from initially very small territories to increasingly larger ones and successively eliminate its competitors in a process of territorial concentration, it is of decisive importance that such a government provide for a comparatively high degree of domestic economic integration. Other things being equal, the lower the tax-and-regulation burden imposed by a government on its domestic economy, the larger its population tends to grow—for internal reasons as well as due to migration gains—and the larger the amount of the domestically produced wealth on which a government can—parasitically—draw upon in its attempt to eliminate its neighboring competitors through war and military domination. It is for this reason that the process of political integration was frequently—although not without exceptions, as other things are not always equal—correlated with increased economic integration. However, the further the process of relatively more liberal (in the classical sense) governments militarily outstripping less liberal ones proceeds—the larger the territories, the fewer and more distant the remaining competitors, and the more costly inter-territorial migration—the lesser a government's need to continue in its domestic liberalism.[24]

XII

The secessionist movements across Eastern Europe are the best possible institutional device for advancing the popular goal of a quick economic recovery. Regardless of the generally welfare

---

[24]In light of these considerations regarding the dialectic relationship between political and economic integration, much of modern European history falls into place. First, that political disintegration and economic integration are not only compatible but positively correlated is illustrated by the fact that the first flourishing of capitalism occurred under conditions of highly decentralized political power: in northern Italy and southern Germany. Second, that the process of political integration (territorial expansion) does not necessarily hamper economic integration, but in fact may further it insofar as it involves the territorial conquest of less-liberal by more-liberal rulers is illustrated by the fact that the modern Industrial Revolution occurred in centralized England and France. And third, that political integration will lead to economic disintegration the closer the process of territorial concentration comes to its conclusion is illustrated by the fact that a formerly dominant liberalism has been gradually replaced by a rising welfare statism since the last third of the nineteenth century. The process of intra-European concentration came to a halt with the political unification of Italy and Germany—and even more so since the end of World War I and particularly since World War II— since the United States established itself as the militarily dominant, hegemonical power over Western Europe (and much of the rest of the world) and made it its foreign policy objective to safeguard the territorial status quo.

statist political predilections or intentions of a secessionist government, secession has a liberating dynamic of its own: it eliminates with one stroke the oppressive and exploitative relations between various ethnic, cultural, religious or linguistic communities which to this day characterize Eastern Europe, and in particular the Soviet Union and Yugoslavia. By virtue of the simple fact that secession involves the breaking away of a smaller from a larger number of people, it is a vote against the principle of democracy (majority rule) in favor of private (decentralized)—rather than majoritarian—property and ownership. The smaller a country, the more pressure a government is under to opt for free trade. It is, technically, easier to desocialize smaller holdings than larger ones. By increasing the number of competing governments and territories and the opportunities for inter-territorial migration, a secessionist government is under increased pressure to adopt more liberal domestic policies, i.e., a larger private sector, and lower taxes and regulations. And throughout, for all of government policies, it holds that the smaller the size of the seceded territory, the quicker any mistake will be recognized, and possibly repaired.

In addition, although classical-liberal thought is spread extremely thin throughout Eastern Europe, due to decades of ruthless oppression and censorship, the liberal ideas of a society based on private property and contractualism are not distributed equally sparsely everywhere. Egalitarian propaganda notwithstanding, enormous differences with respect to the degree of cultural advancement (Westernization) exist in Yugoslavia, for instance, between Slovenes, Croats, Serbs, Macedonians, Montenegrins, and Albanians, as well as between Catholics, Orthodox, and Muslims; or in the Soviet Union between Germans, Poles, Ukrainians, Russians, Georgians, Rumanians, Armenians, Aszerbaijanis, Turkmenis, Kazaks, and so on. In the past, these people had been subject to forced integration by their central governments. Catholic–Croatian communities, for example, were compelled to not "discriminate" against orthodox Serbs, and to accept them into their midst. Likewise, Lithuanians were forced to associate with Russians, even if the Lithuanians would have preferred separation.

But compulsory integration did not lead to the emergence of a new, universal, and presumably higher culture, or to inter-ethnic harmony, as is now painfully clear. On the contrary, as could have been expected, it intensified ethnic strife and hostility and de-civilized all the cultures and people involved. By means of secession, the forced integration of the past is replaced with the voluntary physical segregation of distinct cultures and their competition as separate-but-equal and independent people.

The first result of such a separation is that the variety of government forms and culturally distinct policies will increase. Some of them may turn out worse (from the point of view of economic integration and prosperity) than those that would have prevailed if the central government had remained in power. Some others will be better, with the outcome depending largely on the segregated culture's degree of Westernization as compared to the dominant, central government's culture. It may well be worse for Aszerbaijanis, for instance, to be ruled by a native government than by one made up of Russians; or for Kosovo-Albanians to fall into the hands of some of their own rather than those of a Serbian government. At the same time, the economic reforms in Lithuania, Estonia, and Latvia will likely be better than what a Russian government would have had in store. Clearly, Croatians will prosper more under Croatian rule than under Serbian rule.

More importantly, because the failure to achieve the popular goal of quick economic recovery and sustained growth can no longer be attributed to foreign cultural domination, but must be accepted as homegrown, the public at large as well as the government involved will have to accept a greater responsibility for their own actions. Under forced integration, any mistake could be blamed on a foreign culture, and all success claimed as one's own, and hence there was little or no reason for any culture to learn from any other. Under a regime of "separate but equal," people must face up to the reality not only of cultural diversity but in particular also of visibly distinct ranks of cultural advancement. If a people now wants to improve or maintain its relative position *vis-à-vis* a competing culture, nothing will help but discriminating learning. It must imitate, assimilate, and if possible, improve upon the skills, traits, practices, and rules characteristic of more advanced cultures, and it must avoid those characteristic of lesser-advanced societies. Rather than promoting a downward leveling of cultures as under forced integration, secession stimulates a competitive process of cultural selection and advancement.

XIII

Whether the liberating dynamic set in motion by the secessions will be strong enough to change the scenario from a welfare-statist transformation of Eastern Europe into a self-accelerating, liberal, laissez-faire capitalist revolution, depends directly on the strength of the opposing central and centralizing government forces.

Despite a number of significant defeats, these forces remain powerful to this day. Poland, Rumania, and Bulgaria are still territorially intact—despite secessionist tendencies among Germans in Poland, Hungarians and Germans in Rumania, and Turks and Macedonians in Bulgaria. The unification of West and East Germany is an instance of centralization. The Czechs and the Slovaks have separated, but the Slovaks show no inclination of letting their Hungarian minority go. Yugoslavia has fallen irreparably apart, if only after a bloody and destructive war by the central government against the secessionists.[25] But newly independent Croatia still prevents predominantly Serbian districts from likewise seceding from Croatia, and the Serbian government is still holding on to most of former Greater Serbia and its various ethnic minorities, and is even trying to round out its territory at the expense of Croatia. The situation in the former Soviet Union is similar. The central union government has disappeared, but it has been replaced by only a dozen or so of the fifteen former union republics which are now independent states, while there actually exist hundreds of ethnically distinct populations within the former union.

Almost all further-reaching secessionist attempts, including those by the former Volga Germans to separate from Russia, or by the Ossetians to become independent from Georgia, have been successfully suppressed by their new central governments, or they are violently opposed, as in the case of Aszerbaijan and the Armenian Nagorno-Karabakh province. With the formation of a new Commonwealth of Independent States under the leadership of Russia, and with most of the former union republics as members, *re*centralizing tendencies have even appeared.

Indeed, the tendencies in Eastern Europe toward decentralization may represent a temporary disruption in an ongoing process in the opposite direction. They may turn out to be no more than a regional distraction from the fact that, as seen from a global perspective, the process of political concentration is much

---

[25]The Yugoslavian central government had been encouraged to engage in these rather drastic measures by the anti-secessionist proclamations sounded by the governments of the European Community and the United States. The acceptance of acts of secession as legitimate by Western governments, in Yugoslavia in the case of Slovenia and Croatia as well as in that of the Baltic states in the Soviet Union, has invariably come only after the facts, unpleasant as they might be, could no longer be ignored.

closer than ever before to its ultimate conclusion of a one-world government. Strong indications for this exist. Even before the dissolution of the Soviet Union, the United States had attained hegemonical status over Western Europe (most notably over West Germany) and the Pacific rim countries (most notably over Japan) as indicated by the presence of U.S. troops and military bases, the NATO and SEATO pacts, the U.S. Federal Reserve System as the lender or liquidity provider of last resort to the entire Western banking system, the role of the U.S. dollar as the ultimate international reserve currency, and by institutions such as the International Monetary Fund (IMF) and the World Bank.

Likewise, under U.S. hegemony, the political integration of Western Europe was advanced: the European Community was set for completion before the turn of the century with the establishment of a European Central Bank and a European Currency Unit (ECU) money—a goal whose likelihood of fulfillment is now in serious doubt.

In the absence of the Soviet Empire and the Soviet military threat, the United States has emerged as the world's sole and undisputed military superpower. Thus, it is only natural that the U.S. government and its European junior partners are now trying to use their superior military and financial resources to expand their power and incorporate Eastern Europe—on a lower rank in the hierarchy of power—into the existing Western government-and-central-banking cartel. Of course, secessionist events would be disturbing and complicating factors in these Western endeavors. However, as the example of Western Europe shows, national independence and international political integration, i.e., the coordination and harmonization of the tax-and-regulation structures of various countries are quite compatible. Further, despite an increasing number of European states, the fall of the Soviet Empire may actually be the beginning of the political integration of all of Europe, and it might ring in the era of a U.S.-led "new world order."

Ultimately, the relative strength of the centralizing versus decentralizing forces depends on public opinion, and it might be that the decentralizing forces cannot be brought under control. If the reality of the economic recovery of Eastern Europe falls far short of popular expectations, secessionist sentiments are likely to intensify. If these sentiments should become grounded in and supported by the recognition that—contrary to orthodox, statist propaganda myths—political disintegration and economic integration are fully compatible, thus rendering secession economically rational, the secessionist forces may grow strong enough to successfully break through the still-held statist taboos that: (a) each independent territory must be contiguous (there can be no 'islands' within a territory); and, (b) each must be defined by either ethnic or linguistic criteria (no secession can occur within an ethnically or linguistically homogeneous territory, and there can be no territory that includes people of different ethnicity or language and that defines its identity in terms of purely cultural criteria).

If this happens and the former Soviet empire should disintegrate into a patchwork of hundreds of independent territories, regions, and cities, the odds become overwhelming that the liberating dynamic of secessions will gain enough momentum to set a genuine capitalist revolution in motion, and will spare Eastern Europe the economic disappointments of welfare-statism and the humiliating exactions of Western hegemony.

If the disintegration of the Soviet empire proceeds in this fashion, such developments will also have direct and immediate repercussions for Western domestic policies. The emergence of a handful of Eastern European "Hong Kongs" or "Singapores," and the imitation of their success by neighboring territories would quickly attract substantial amounts of Western capital and entrepreneurial talent. This movement of capital and talent would aggravate the stagnation of the Western welfare states. Confronted with growing economic and fiscal crises, Western governments would be forced to begin de-socializing, de-taxing and de-regulating their own economies. In addition, encouraged by the Eastern developments, and in order to free themselves from the economic oppression and exploitation by their own central governments, secessionist forces in Western Europe would be strengthened—among them the Irish, the Scots, and the Welsh in Great Britain, the Flemish in Belgium, the Basques and the Catalonians in Spain, and the South Tyrolians in Italy, to name a few.

Rather than indirectly contributing to the formation of a politically integrated Europe—the ideal of the great West European welfare-state consensus—the disintegration of the socialist Soviet Empire may become the first decisive step in the direction of the fundamentally opposed, almost completely forgotten, classical-liberal ideal of a unified Europe: a Europe of hundreds of distinct countries, regions, and cantons, and of thousands of independent free cities (such as the present-day oddities of Monaco, St. Marino, and Andorra); a Europe with greatly increased opportunities for economically motivated migration, and of small, liberal governments; and a Europe which is integrated through free trade and an international commodity money such as gold.

XIV

There seems little hope today that Eastern European socialism will be replaced by anything but Western welfare statism and a hierarchically structured, Western-dominated government cartel of managed migration, trade, and fiat money. Nonetheless, the proponent of classical liberalism has a better chance today than ever of changing all this, if only he complements his free-trade and free-immigration stance with an unequivocal advocacy of the right to secede.

This may not do much to enliven liberalism in the West—although it would certainly help its popularity if it were pointed out that the much feared "right-to-free-immigration" always finds its natural limitation in other people's right to secede and in each segregated territory's right to set its own admission standards. In Eastern Europe, where secession is in the air, where governmental legitimacy is low and the fear of renewed foreign hegemony high, the proponent of classical liberalism, by providing people with an ethical and economic rationale for their largely unarticulated secessionist desires and by advocating the liberal vision of a unified Europe, can easily place himself in the forefront of post-communist politics, and thus help bring about the renaissance of a popular classical–liberal movement.

10
A SECESSIONIST VIEW OF QUEBEC'S OPTIONS

Pierre Desrochers and Eric Duhaime

The purpose of this article is to provide a classical-liberal perspective on behalf of the secession of Quebec from Canada. Our main argument is that, by its very nature, Canada cannot avoid a number of economic and political pitfalls, but that Quebec secession offers a way out. To understand how this came to be, we will briefly examine Canada's and Quebec's social, economic, and political history. The current effects of this historical process on Canadian federalism will then be analyzed. It will be argued that secession, mostly by getting rid of futile attempts to build a country against economic and geographic common sense, is likely to result in more good than harm.

HISTORICAL PERSPECTIVE

Early History (1534–1867)

Quebec's–Canada's history[1] began in 1534 when Jacques Cartier set foot on the Gaspe Peninsula. French rulers, however, did not show any interest in the new territory for almost a century. In 1604, Samuel de Champlain founded and settled Port-Royal, in what is now Nova Scotia, followed four years later by Quebec City along the St. Lawrence River. The French colony, in time stretching from the St. Lawrence River to New Orleans, eventually became a thriving center for the fur trade. However, because of its harsh climate, the quasi-exclusion of Huguenot immigration, and the mercantilist policies that forbade most local industries in the new territories, the French colony had only a population of 60,000[2] when it fell under British rule in 1760.

---

[1]To write a Canadian history from a *Québécois* point of view for a foreign audience, is no simple task. First, people of French lineage in this corner of North America have changed names five times in nine generations. We were first known as French, and subsequently as Canadians, French-Canadians, Québécois, and more recently as *Québécois pure-laine* (pure wool). It should also be noted that most Québécois are really troubled by English–Canadian claims that the history of French-speaking people in North America before the English conquest is part of our common cultural background.

[2]This figure is the most commonly cited one, although it represents only the population living in the St. Lawrence Valley, between Quebec City and Montreal. It is impossible to know exactly how many Frenchmen were still alive in the rest of the colony after the end of the Seven Years War. The most cited number of deaths and departures is 10,000. See J. Lacoursière, J. Provencher, and D. Vaugeois, *Canada*

After their defeat, French people living in the colony had the choice of either staying and becoming British citizens or returning to Europe. Most of the French elite—army officers, colonial administrators and prominent merchants—left while the small farmers, hunters, and trappers had to stay and live under the conquerors' rule.[3]

For the first years following the conquest, French-speaking citizens were not allowed to bear arms,[4] and Catholics were kept out of government jobs and discriminated against by many British colonists. Yet, by most standards, the occupier's rule was benevolent. In 1792, the predominantly French-speaking British colony was given the right to have its own Parliament, which had the mandate to solve the local daily problems. Following this institutional reform, two conflicting views of the fate of the French-speaking population gradually emerged. Some thought that this would be the first step toward the establishment of a separate country, while others saw Britain as a benevolent power protecting the French-speaking identity against cultural assimilation if that territory were annexed to the U.S.[5] Most, if not all, historians of Quebec point out that this benevolence was the result of the presence of a powerful and, at that time, hostile political entity south of the border.

For almost a century after the thirteen U.S. colonies broke away, British North America was a diverse collection of colonies and privately-owned territories. There were few troubles except in 1837, when the issue of responsible government led to a small revolt against colonial authorities in both the French-speaking colony of Lower Canada and the English-speaking colony of Upper Canada.[6] The ruling power crushed resistance, and killed its leaders or forced them into exile. As a result, the Colonial power's will to assimilate the French-speaking population became more explicit while the views of the most conservative and pro-British elements of the French-speaking population became dominant. The most direct consequence of this episode was the fusion of Lower and Upper Canada into a joint government in

---

Quebec: Synthèse historique (Montreal: Édition du renouveau pedagogique, 1970), p. 193.

[3]Lacoursière, et al., *Canada-Québec: Synthèse historique*, p. 193.

[4]Owing to the lack of soldiers under the French regime, every able man was a *de facto* militiaman.

[5]For a brief introduction to the topic, see Maurice Seguin, *L'idée d'indépendance au Québec. Genèse et historique*, (Trois-Rivières, Quebec: Boréal Express, 1986).

[6]Lower Canada is in what is now southern Quebec, and Upper Canada is in what is now southern Ontario.

1840.[7] This forced union proved politically unworkable, and did not last more than a generation. Nonetheless, there were many positive achievements in the following years, most notably the abolition of feudal rights in L.C., and general economic prosperity in the wake of free-trade with the United States between 1854 and 1864.

The British North America Act (1867)

In 1867, things changed drastically with the signature of the British North America Act and the sale of Rupert's Territory[8] to the new legislature. With a new central administration and more than 2,500,000 square miles of new territory, modern-day Canada was born. There were many reasons behind the Act, but from our view none of them expressed a unanimous collective will to build a country or any move toward economic efficiency. Administrative and political decisions guided the whole process. It was obvious from the beginning that such a geographical and social aberration would not be viable without strong government intervention.

Historians usually provide many reasons for the creation of Canada, although they do not always agree on their relative significance. There was the U.S. threat to the small British Colonies in the wake of British support of the rebellious south in previous years, then the end of free trade between British North America and the U.S., and the purchase of Alaska by the U.S. from Russia in 1867. There was also a lack of interest in the British Colonial Office for the defense of British North America and the perceived need for a strong central government that would put an end to perennial internal disputes and ensure the successful completion of a transcontinental railway.

An Unnatural Binding of Canada (1867–1914)

In economic terms, the first years of the new Dominion were hard, partly because of alleged American protectionist practices.

[7]The two governments also joined their debts: U.C.'s was 1,200,000 pounds, while L.C.'s was only 95,000 pounds. See Mason Wade, *Les canadiens francais de 1760 à nos jours*, 2nd ed. (Montreal: Le Cercle du Livre de France, 1966), p. 249. This episode is a landmark in the history of Quebec nationalism. It was also the first time that the French-speaking population became a minority within its own country, with 45 percent of the total population.

[8]Rupert's Territory belonged to the Hudson Bay Company, and included what are now the three Prairie provinces (Alberta, Saskatchewan, and Manitoba), northern Ontario, northern Quebec, the Yukon, and the Northwest Territories. The Hudson Bay Company reportedly wanted to sell its property to the United States, but the British Crown prevented this sale.

Quebecers started to migrate south to the textile and industrial towns of New England in search of work in the mills. In two decades, half of the French–Canadian population had left for better opportunities brought by industrialization. The French-speaking population was almost totally assimilated and integrated into the American melting pot. Back home, Canadians began advocating protectionist and immigration policies patterned after the American model. In 1879, the Conservative Party was voted in, establishing a "National Policy" of high tariffs, government control of natural resources, and railway and ship channel-building programs. The main idea was, of course, to build a wall that would not let the sirens' songs of Boston, New York, Buffalo, Detroit, Chicago, and other places reach Canadian ears. The real consequences of this policy are still debated, but it is not far fetched to say that English–Canadian historians and intellectuals view it as a much more successful experiment than do their counterparts in Quebec.[9] From then on, Canadian policy makers pursued a policy of promoting ties with the United Kingdom as a counter to the overwhelming influence of the United States.[10]

Trade policy and nation-building remained top priorities on the Canadian political agenda for many decades. In 1911, Prime Minister Sir Wilfrid Laurier was voted out of office mainly because of his support of a free-trade offer by U.S. President Taft. History almost repeated itself in 1947–48, when secret negotiations for free-trade agreements were undertaken with Washington, but then Prime Minister McKenzie King backed off, fearing a negative outcome in the following election.

Thus, Canada was built on protectionism, as well as on a railway system that did not make economic sense.[11] Theoretically at least, this system ensured that trade would go east-west, instead

[9]For the English–Canadian view, see Craig Brown, *Histoire générale du Canada* (Montreal: Boreal, 1990); see also Michael Bliss, *The Evolution of Industrial Policies in Canada: An Historical Survey* (Ottawa: Conseil économique du Canada, 1982). For the French–Canadian view, see P.-A. Linteau, R. Durocher, J.-C. Robert, *Histoire du Québec contemporain. De la Confédération à la crise* (Montreal: Boreal, 1979); also P. Fréchette and J.-P. Vézina, *L'économie du Québec*, 4th ed. (Montreal: Editions Etudes Vivantes, 1990).

[10]Historically, the Conservative Party was the stronghold of stronger ties with the U.K., while the Liberals were pro-American until 1968, when the Watkins Report recommended stronger governmental intervention to prevent the economic takeover of Canada. In the last two decades, things have changed drastically, and now the Liberals are the representatives of Anglo-Canadian nationalism.

[11]On this issue, see Pierre Berton, *Le grand défi, le chemin de fer canadien* (Montreal: Editions du Jour, 1975). Cf. Lacoursière, et al., *Canada-Quebec: Synthèse historique*, p. 373, who also argued that the huge public debt incurred to build the transcontinental railway was the main reason behind the raising of customs duties.

of north-south. As early as 1891, this practice was denounced by Goldwin Smith in *Canada and the Canadian Question*.[12] However, the lesson was not learned and this Canadian way of doing things was applied to new activities in the following decades.[13] Periodically, however, geographic common sense and U.S. investments were stronger than English–Canadian nationalism and lobbying by the protectionist industries, but political activism always stepped in.

The Inevitable Continentalisation of the Canadian Economy (1914–1995)

The American economic presence started to become dominant in Canada at the outbreak of World War I. Protectionist policies, cheap labor, huge hydro-electric power potential, and abundant natural resources close to home caused American money to begin flooding Quebec and Canada. The amounts exceeded the value of U.K. investments, which had hitherto been the dominant foreign investments.

With the end of World War II, Canada's federal government became the dominant player in the national economy. Although established as a temporary measure, the idea of a planned economy and industrial reliance on government contracts and subsidies culminated in 1945, with the adoption of a strongly interventionist economic agenda.[14] From 1945 to 1957, the Federal Government economic policy had three main components: a Keynesian management of demand, the building of a welfare state, and the liberalization of trade and growth of international cooperation.[15]

Meanwhile, another wave of American investments began in the 1950s. This time, however, it was directed toward conglomerate building and was known as *The Big Take Over*. This episode would eventually bring various responses from the federal government: when commercial airlines were established in the U.S., the Canadian government followed suit and created *Trans Canada Airlines*; when commercial broadcasting became viable, the *Canadian Broadcasting Corporation* was founded; when the

---

[12]Linteau, et al., *Histoire du Québec contemporain*, p. 85.

[13]In the British North America Act of 1867, it is explicitly written that all new activities should be under federal jurisdiction. However, this did not prevent provinces from meddling in them, too. For example, provincial intervention in television and immigration were justified under education considerations, which were, indeed, a provincial field of intervention.

[14]See the 1945 Federal Government White Paper on Employment and Revenue.

[15]Bliss, *The Evolution of Industrial Policies in Canada*, p. iii.

privately-owned oil industries did not show enough Canadian nationalism, *Petro-Canada* was born, and so on.

Fiscal policies and subsidies were the favorite mode of intervention. They began in the early 1960s and abated somewhat with the coming into power of the Progressive Conservative Party in 1984. Their goal was mainly to direct investments toward targeted industries and designated regions. That administration ended in a fiscal and bureaucratic nightmare that provided no effective results to the poorest parts of the country. If anything, studies show that regional discrepancies are higher in Canada than in the United States.[16]

Other tools to preserve Canada's identity were also put into place: most notably the Foreign Investment Review Agency, a national law on bank ownership, and a national regulatory agency to enforce "Canadian content" quotas on the airwaves. One of the most damaging enactments to Quebec, though, was the federal policy toward the petro-chemical industry. Back in the days when oil was cheap and Western Canada's crude barrels were uncompetitive, federal legislators decided to draw a line along the Ottawa River. Petroleum products that were bought cheaply on the international market and refined in Montreal were not allowed to cross that line, killing the oil refining industry of Montreal to benefit uncompetitive oil producers Western Canada and Ontario.

In short, Canadian economic policy left Quebec with an economy dominated by foreign branch-plants, large and bureaucratized public utilities corporations, an expanding federal bureaucracy, and taxpayers subsidizing all kinds of uncompetitive producers. Despite Canada's efforts at economic nationalism, more than 80 percent of its external trade is still conducted with the United States. The recent ratification of the North American Free Trade Agreement (NAFTA) should only enhance these commercial links.

Quebec's Attempts at Policy Planning (1960–1995)

In Quebec, other cultural differences notwithstanding, the economic culture had long been the same as that of English Canada. For many years, the future was thought to lie in exploiting our natural resources and attracting foreign owned companies. Here too, economic activism for the sake of nation-building took its toll, but it was long in the making.

[16]Mario Polese, *Économie urbaine et régionale* (Paris: Economica, 1994).

In 1959, the death of long-time premier Maurice Duplessis resulted in changes in practices of government and in the subsequent coming into power of an *avant-garde* group of young technocrats holding diplomas from the most prestigious universities. This marked the beginning of what has since been known as Quebec's Quiet Revolution. Enlightened by so-called "scientific planning" and fashionable economic theories, they embarked on grandiose schemes to close the gap between Quebec and the rest of the industrialised world. Hydroelectric power companies were nationalized, followed by steel, mining and logging companies, airlines, and many others. The education and the health systems became public monopolies. Cultural barriers and regional development schemes of all sorts were set up. Numerous ministries and agencies were created and provided jobs and subsidies to almost anyone who asked for them.

For many Quebec nationalists, there was a close link between taking care of their own business and the intervention of the Government of Quebec. The French population in Quebec was poorer than its English–Canadian counterpart. Many Francophones believed that the only way to catch up with their rivals was through the strong intervention of their government—the one dominated by French speakers in America.

Beginning in the 1960s, many political parties, activists, and terrorist groups were founded to promote Quebec's sovereignty. All those secessionist forces—with the exception of the radical terrorist groups[17]—would eventually merge with the Parti Québécois which, in 1976, won the provincial campaign in Quebec with just 40 percent of the popular vote. The Parti Québécois had, at the time, a social-democratic platform. The main objective was secession but other realizations included language regulation, subsidies to small French-owned businesses, asbestos nationalization, rural land zoning, etc.

A long-awaited referendum on sovereignty was held in May 1980. Nearly 60 percent of Quebecers voted No while more than 40 percent voted Yes. It was mostly a campaign of fear. Federalist politicians scared older people by leading them to believe that they would lose their pensions, and the general population by claiming that there would be no trade between Quebec and the rest of Canada, if the referendum were to pass. On the other hand, billions of dollars of public investments would pour into the province if it remained within the Canadian federation.

---

[17]Although Quebec's terrorist movement was usually referred to as the *Front de Libération du Québec*, there were many factions, each carrying its own agenda.

The following decade was marked by endless constitutional battles, the most notable being the repatriation of the Canadian constitution from Great Britain in 1982. Almost all Quebec politicians, separatists and federalists, voted against it in Quebec's National Assembly. Quebec was the only province that did not sign the repatriation law, mainly because it gave more power to the central government to intervene in provincial matters.

Most Quebec technocrats became infatuated with dirigism because they were convinced that they held the right recipe for economic growth. But more often than not, their motivation was nationalist in essence. Ottawa could not be allowed to outdo Quebec City in its own backyard. Jacques Parizeau, Quebec's former premier and one of the leading technocrats of that time, became a separatist on a journey aboard the transcontinental railway when he realized that there could not be two centralist states governing Quebec.[18] Thus, following the famous "Vive le Québec libre!"[19] of General Charles de Gaulle, there were countless flag wars carried on both in the various regions of Quebec and abroad in some instances.

Canadian and Quebecois Contemporary Nationalisms

Throughout Canada's history, two conflicting loyalties have developed: one toward Canada, the other toward Quebec. These loyalties are now at odds on major points.

French–Canadian nationalism emerged in the second half of the nineteenth century. It was a conservative movement concerned mainly with the "survival of the race." It promoted a high birth rate and close-knit Catholic society.[20] This brand of nationalism, however, died with the coming of the Quiet Revolution. Most Quebec nationalists now pride themselves on being progressive, cosmopolitan, and tolerant,[21] although they support government intervention, especially concerning language laws. Yet, according to the late sovereignist leader René Levesque, one

[18]In Parizeau's official biography, Laurence Richard describes in detail how Parizeau became a sovereignist in three days. See Laurence Richard, *Jacques Parizeau, Un bâtisseur* (Montreal: Les Editions de l'homme, 1992).

[19]"Long Live Free Quebec!"

[20]In the nineteenth century, French–Canadian classical liberalism centered around *L'Institut Canadien*. (Remember, at that time, the *Canadians* were the French-speakers.) It clashed with, and was defeated by, the Catholic Church.

[21]For arguments advocating Quebec's secession, and building on the classical-liberal and non-nationalist tradition, see Martin Masse, *Identites collectives et civilisation* (Montreal: VLB Editeur, 1994).

of the reasons he wanted political sovereignty is "precisely so that we will not have to legislate on questions which should be as clear as the air we breathe."[22] Quebecers are the only Canadians who overwhelmingly supported the recent free trade agreements.[23] In other words, all sovereignists—with the exception of secessionist union leaders[24]—are now strongly supportive of these trade deals and of the idea of free trade generally, which would allow expansion of the North–South economic flow and bring greater prosperity.

Meanwhile, English-Canadians also went through an identity crisis with the fall of the British Empire upon which the sun had never set. Some politicians and intellectuals have, thus, been trying for the last three decades to build a distinct Canadian identity, and for most of them, their Canada includes Quebec. However, their vision of Canada is a highly planned economy, where the central government aims at a uniform and "just society" and where federal–provincial transfer payments and other economic aid hold the country together.

For example, Philip Resnick, a political scientist at the University of British Columbia, said that he was

> as much touched by English–Canadian nationalism and our (sic) own struggle for a distinct identity as any Quebec nationalist may be touched by that of Quebec.

He went on to say that considers us as *semblables* (counterparts) and *frères* (brothers) but felt betrayed by the Quebecois overwhelming support of free trade in the 1988 federal election. He explained why he was, "from the depths of his soul," opposed to the liberalization of commerce:

> In truth, the deal was much less about trade than about the model of society we wish for ourselves in the 1990s and beyond. Canadian identity in the postwar era has become more caught up with communitarian values of the liberal-left. Medicare, the Canada Pension Plan, and regional equalization programs were some of its symbols, along with the CBC, the Canada Council, and Petro-Canada. Supporters of all of these have been disproportionately drawn from the center

[22]Jane Jacobs, *The Question of Separatism: Quebec and the Struggle over Sovereignty* (New York: Random House, 1980), p. 111.

[23]As of this writing, NAFTA is supported by 58 percent of the population in Quebec, 45 percent in Ontario, 41 percent in British Columbia, and 39 percent in the Atlantic Provinces. See Presse Canadienne, "Les Québécois sont les plus endettés," *Le Journal de Montreal* (8 April 1994).

[24]The three main unions in Quebec (Fédération des travailleurs du Québec, Centrale de l'enseignement du Québec, and Confédération des syndicats nationaux) are actively supporting Quebec's secession.

and left of the political spectrum, and therefore from social forces other than big business.[25]

Most English-Canadians have, so far, found nothing else to build their national identity upon other than their national programs. Things are, however, beginning to change as Ottawa is going bankrupt and regional sentiments are, once again, on the rise.

CURRENT DILEMMA

The Current Economic Situation

Canadians are now saddled with countless agencies on the federal and provincial levels, and nowhere is this more apparent than in Quebec. As a rule, the provincial agency is always trying to outdo its federal counterpart and *vice versa*.[26] It is estimated that if the duplicate functions carried out by Ottawa and Quebec City were eliminated, the savings could be in the order of $3 billion annually. A huge sum, but not sufficient to rally people toward secession.

The most stunning result of all the federal and provincial interventions, however, is that Canada is now being proclaimed "an honorary member of the Third World in the unmanageability of its debt problem" by the *Wall Street Journal*.[27] Canada also has the second-highest debt-to-G.D.P. ratio of any industrialized country. The deficit is equivalent to 5.4 percent of Canada's G.D.P., compared to about 2.6 percent in the United States.[28] According to Statistics Canada, on 31 March 1994 the net debt *per capita* in Canada was $23,065, while Quebecers were the most indebted of all Canadians, at $25,118.[29] Even worse, 44 percent of the Canadian debt is held by foreigners, and 35 percent of all federal revenues now go to service the debt. When the provincial and federal debts are added, the sum total is as large as the economy itself.

In 1991, total government expenditures in Canada amounted to 51.1 percent of the G.D.P. Since 1979, real public expenditure *per capita* went up by 52 percent and according to economist Pierre

---

[25]Philip Resnick, *Letters to a Quebecois Friend* (Kingston: McGill-Queen's University Press, 1990), p. 55.

[26]Victor Boldt, "The Canada I Want to See," *The Humanist in Canada* (October 1992), p. 14.

[27]Editorial, "Bankrupt Canada?" *Wall Street Journal* (12 January 1995).

[28]Anne Swardson, "Up North, Dollar Crisis is Brewing," *Washington Post* (11 January 1995).

[29]Presse Canadienne, "Les Québécois sont les plus endettés."

Lemieux, during this period "regulations have probably grown more rapidly than expenditures."[30] He adds that taxes in Canada are high and that the federal government levies close to half of them, which amounts to 33 percent more than all provincial governments combined and that this is the first reason why Ottawa is responsible for the high level of Canadian taxes.[31] Elimination of the central government would thus be a major step toward a downsizing of political–bureaucratic activism. In the Canadian context, secession provides the only serious opportunity to get rid of the many coercive and costly institutions suffocating individual prosperity and liberty. In view of the current political system and national culture, there are simply no other alternatives.

Canada's International and Internal Trade

One might think that the expended Canadian market has had some positive results; however, these are not clear. Consider, for example, some statistics about the movement of goods and services in the country.

A recent study on *Canada's Interprovincial Trade Flows of Goods, 1984–88* noted that "the provinces and territories trade extensively with each other (about one-quarter of production)."[32] In odd contrast is the fact that in fiscal year 1989 (the latest year available), the provinces traded $146 billion worth of goods and services with each other, while Canadians traded $160 billion with the rest of the world.[33] Although one might assume that this is proof of Canada's integration with the world economy, remember that more than 80 percent of this trade is directed toward the United States. This does not show Canada's openness but rather its geographical absurdity. As Mihlar pointed out, since the implementation of the Free Trade Agreement in 1989, trade between the world's two largest trading partners, Canada and the U.S., has increased by 75 percent, as compared with a ten percent increase in Canada's trade with the rest of the world.[34]

---

[30]See Pierre Lemieux, "Government Growth in Canada: From 5% to 51% of GDP," *Research Memo*, no. 7 (14 November 1994).

[31]Pierre Lemieux, "Taxes in Canada are High, Thanks Mainly to the Feds," *Research Memo*, no. 4 (24 October 1994).

[32]Hans Messinger, "Canada's Interprovincial Trade Flows of Goods, 1984–88," *Canadian Economic Observer* (Ottawa: Statistics Canada, 1993), Cat. No. 11-010.

[33]*Provincial Trade Wars: Why the Blockade Must End*, Filip Palda, ed. (Vancouver: Fraser Institute, 1994).

[34]Fazil Mihlar, "FTA/NAFTA: A Win-Win-Win Situation," *Fraser Forum* (April 1995): 22–23.

The more detailed examination of the Canadian trade data also clearly points toward the importance of transportation costs and the importance of regional economies. The authors of the Statistics Canada study thus admit that "due to Canada's geographic vastness, trade tended to be concentrated among neighboring provinces."[35] Ontario and Quebec are each other's largest trading partners, with about 60 percent of Quebec's export making up nearly the same proportion of Ontario's imports, and just over 40 percent of Ontario's export sales, accounting for three-quarters of Quebec imports. These proportions, however, represented about the same dollar value (approximately $15.5 billion and $14 billion respectively in 1988). This trade flow accounts for two-thirds of the total value of interprovincial trade. According to the study, strong trade ties also existed between Nova Scotia and New Brunswick, Saskatchewan and Alberta, and British Columbia and Alberta.

Further, the study noted that "only minimal trade occured between Atlantic and western Canada," that "only Ontario and Quebec had substantial export links to both eastern and western Canada," and that "Ontario and Quebec showed only minimal dependence on the Atlantic and western provinces, except for purchase of mineral fuel from Alberta."[36] Clearly, more than 125 years of nation-building have not achieved much. If secession was to occur and trade liberalization to follow, it is a sure bet that trade between, for example, the Pacific Northwest and Vancouver, Montreal and New England, and Toronto and the Midwest would be much greater and benefit all parties.

Quebec's International Trade

Quebec's economy is one of the most open in the world. Today its exports make up about 43 percent of its GDP, higher than most industrialized countries. It follows that Quebec's standard of living depends on its access to foreign markets. However, this openness to the outside, like that of Canada, is not very diversified: almost 90 percent of those exports go either to the rest of Canada (48 percent) or to the United States (41 percent). So the fact that Quebec favors the greatest possible access to both Canadian and American markets should come as no surprise.

However, it can be noted that Quebec's dependency and vulnerability are largely counterbalanced by its own importance as a

---

[35]Messinger, "Canada's Interprovincial Trade Flows of Goods, 1984–88."

[36]Once more, one must recall that this situation is entirely the result of a protectionist policy favoring Ontario's refining industry and Alberta's oil producers. Ibid.

market for its main neighbors. The Quebec market is the second largest export market for the rest of Canada, and is the eighth-largest trading partner of the United States, far ahead of any other country in the hemisphere, excepting only Canada and Mexico.[37]

Inter-provincial Barriers

One might argue that Canadians have enjoyed the benefits of a truly integrated national market, which they might not have had if British North America had remained a grouping of many smaller constituencies. The truth, however, is that Canada remains, to this day, a much less integrated economic unit than Western Europe, and that there are probably greater obstacles to trade between the provinces than there are to trade between Canada and the rest of the world.[38] An estimated 500 trade barriers among Canadian provinces still exist at a time when trade between Canada, the U.S., Mexico, and Europe is becoming even freer.[39] The cost of these barriers is conservatively estimated to be at least $6.5 billion a year.[40]

Many provinces or public utilities have policies similar to *buy state* practices. Ontario even has an *Ontario Union Made* policy. A few years ago, a Quebec-based firm, *Laval Spirotube*, faced this harsh reality. It was the only maker of a particular type of ventilation system in Canada, and it won a contract in Ottawa (Ontario). However, the workers who had been hired to install the system would not do it because of the "foreign origin" of the product, even though they were members of the same union as the workers of *Laval Spirotube*.[41] As one observer put it, "Canada's situation is unique in the Western World. Its internal protectionism has now become one of its main obstacles to economic growth."[42] Last year, Canada had yet another inter-provincial conference on this issue where officials again agreed to disagree.

More than 125 years of living together has brought only slight gains on this issue, and most of these gains were achieved in recent years under the Canada–U.S. free-trade agreement. There is no doubt that an independent Quebec would soon find its

[37]*Business America* (April 1994).

[38]S. Loizides and M. Grant, "Barriers to Interprovincial Trade: Implications for Business," *Conference Board of Canada Report 93–92* (1992), p. 6.

[39]Boldt, "The Canada I Want to See."

[40]*Provincial Trade Wars: Why the Blockade Must End*, Filip Palda, ed.

[41]Bernard Landry, *Commerce sans frontieres* (Montreal: Editions du Jour, 1987), p. 58.

[42]Jean-Benoit Nadeau, "Les dix solitudes," *Revuew Commerce* (1992).

place in the world, and that it would still trade mostly with the rest of Canada and the United States and, to a lesser extent, with Mexico, Europe, and other dynamic countries of the globe.

Sovereignist Agenda

As with hockey, our national sport, Quebec politicians say that the sovereignist agenda has three periods. After the failure of the referendum on the Charlottetown Agreement (an attempt to bring Quebec back into the 1982 Canadian constitution, turned down by 57 percent of Quebecers in 1992), separatists had to win the Quebec constituencies in the Federal elections in 1993, then the provincial elections in 1994, and finally the referendum on secession. Sovereignists succeeded at the federal level when the Bloc Quebecois won 54 seats out of 75 in Quebec with 50 percent of the votes in October 1993.

But along with the Bloc Quebecois, another regional party, the Reform Party, has sprung up in Western Canada, mainly as a reaction against the centralization this country has witnessed in the past decades. Actually, the results of this election are a good indication of where this country is going. Ontario and its "two dependencies" (the Atlantic provinces and Manitoba) voted clearly for stronger central government intervention by electing almost exclusively Liberal Members of Parliament; Quebec, with the exception of the English-speaking districts of Montreal and federal bureaucrats in constituencies of Quebec bordering the Canadian capital, voted in a huge majority for the Bloc Quebecois, Alberta and British Columbia gave a strong majority to the Reform Party and Saskatchewan was split evenly between the socialist New Democratic Party and the Reform Party.

Quebecois secessionists also succeeded at the September 1994 provincial election by electing 77 Members of the National Assembly out of 125, but this time with only 45 percent of the popular support. Many theories have been proposed to explain that drop in popular support. On the one hand, another soft-sovereignist party (Action démocratique du Québec) ran for the first time and obtained 6.5 percent of the votes. On the other hand, the then-leader of the Bloc Quebecois and leader of the Official Opposition of Canada, Lucien Bouchard, is more popular than the former leader of the Parti Quebecois and Premier of Quebec, Jacques Parizeau. There is also another relevant explanation: the support for the Bloc was an easy protest vote with no big repercussion. The election of a separatist government in Quebec was much more serious and could not be interpreted as a protest vote.

Nevertheless, as promised, Quebec's separatist government tabled a draft bill on the sovereignty of Quebec in December 1994. Sovereignty was defined by the National Assembly as

> the accession of Quebec to a position of exclusive jurisdiction, through its democratic institutions, to make laws and levy taxes in its territory and to act on the international scene for the making of agreements and participating in various international organisations.[43]

The process proposed by the Government of Quebec included six steps:

1. Publication of the draft bill (December 1994);

2. An information and participation process in every region of Quebec (February–March 1995);

3. A debate on the bill and its passage by the National Assembly (Spring or Fall 1995);

4. Approval of the Act by more than 50 percent of the population of Quebec (Spring or Fall 1995);

5. A period of discussion on transitional measures with Canada, particularly the holdings and debts, and the drafting of a new Quebec constitution (Winter 1995–1996 and Spring 1996);

6. Accession of Quebec to sovereignty and recognition by the international community (24 June 1996).

If we wish to compare this process to a hockey game, the Quebec secessionists (or "separatists," as their opponents say) almost won the third period with 49.5 percent of the popular vote on 30 October 1995. In that tie game, secessionists claim that the momentum is on their side, and that the game is about to go into overtime. Another "neverendum" (as Canadian nationalists call this process) on Quebec's secession is planned before the year 2000. In between, Quebec government spokespersons claim they will put Quebec's public finances in order. Meanwhile, Canadian nationalists have resorted to scare tactics. Quebec's partition is their weapon of choice, along with the argument that the Canadian government won't recognize the results of the next referendum if the question is unclear and if the winning margin is too narrow. Meanwhile, the federal government of Canada asked the Supreme Court to declare Quebec's secession unconstitutional.

---

[43]Government du Québec, *Avant-projet de loi sur la souveraineté du Québec* (Québec: Éditeuri officiel du Québec, 1994), p. 2.

Economic Viability of an Independent Quebec

To most people, secession is alarming because, in their opinion, getting smaller inexorably means deterioration. However, it should be noted that there does not seem to be any optimal country size. Hong Kong, Singapore, and Switzerland are all fairly prosperous economies while many large countries have miserable economies. On the other hand, many small countries have been economic fiascos, while Japan and the United States are undeniably hotbeds of economic activity. The smaller economic size of Quebec would thus not be a major factor as to its economic well-being. It should however be noted that its G.D.P., the value of which is close to U.S. $160 billion, would put it in 16th place among industrialized countries, far ahead of most Latin American countries.

Ultimately, Quebec's success will rest on its entrepreneurial spirit, its population and businesses' capacity to adapt to changing technologies and markets and to compete with its neighbors. Secession by itself won't solve all of Quebec's problems, but it might just get rid of the many illnesses "built into" Canada that we have been describing. This is becoming clear even to some English–Canadians fed up with big government. As one of them, Gordon Gibson, put it:

> In any case, the political culture that would be likely to emerge in the more homogeneous Canadian state [following Quebec's secession] would offer less support for minority language rights, official multiculturalism, and aboriginal peoples, due to a new focus in ROC (Rest of Canada) on individualism, in opposition to the kinds of collective rights that have been notionally validated by the Quebec fact.[44]

CONCLUSION

Some ideas are deeply ingrained in all of us simply because we have grown up with things being the way they are. However, in economic terms, being bigger has probably meant more harm than good for Canada. A strong case can be made that Canada does not make sense economically or geographically, and that its very existence is conditional upon futile attempts at maintaining nation-building and ruinous economic policies that have not only not solved anything, but have even worsened regional resentments. Putting an end to this is the main reason that we support Quebec secession. As Nobel laureate Gary Becker pointed out,

---

[44]Gordon Gibson, *Plan B: The Future of the Rest of Canada* (Vancouver: Fraser Institute, 1994), pp. 96–97.

separation could also help the economies of English-speaking Canada because it would reduce cultural battles and eliminate the confrontations with Quebec over the allocation of tax revenues and government expenditures.[45]

Our argument is echoed by many scholars or popular writers that have put nation-states under intense scrutiny in recent years. One of them, Kenichi Ohmae, the influential Japanese economist who coined the term "The Triad Economy," has argued that national governments are now more than ever before gradually becoming irrelevant in the economic realm as globalization takes over. They are being superseded at one end by multi-national corporations and a body of supra-national regulations and at the other end by toiling entrepreneurs and by demanding consumers who show little respect for government edict.[46] In short, globalization and local Renaissance go hand in hand.

Looking at Canada's economic situation, even *The Globe and Mail*'s editorial writers wrote during the course of the 1993 federal elections that

> As the Bloc [Quebecois] appears to consolidate its position in Quebec, and Reform gains momentum in Alberta and British Columbia, an exhilarating sense of the possible emerges in many streets. Why should Canada be less exposed to sharp and unpredictable shifts in its political arrangements than Europe, the Middle East, Japan or the rest of the world? The era of post-modern politics is defined by such sudden leaps from the status quo to new ground. Looking back, we can see their logic, built up over time under a cloak of conventional wisdom and linear thought.

Quebecois and Canadians live in a country admired by the entire world for its pacifism, tolerance, and open-mindedness. Our new challenge is now to make sure that our political rupture also sets the standards for all countries dealing with nationalist tensions.

---

[45]Gary S. Becker, "Why so Many Mice are Roaring," *Business Week* (7 November 1994): 20.
[46]Kenichi Ohmae, *The Borderless World* (New York: Harper Business, 1990).

11

HOW TO SECEDE IN BUSINESS WITHOUT REALLY LEAVING: EVIDENCE OF THE SUBSTITUTION OF ARBITRATION FOR LITIGATION

Bruce L. Benson

T he term secession is generally taken to imply a territorial division from one existing government into two or more new governments. Yet, it is possible to consider secession to be a much more limited issue, dealing not with a territorial removal from a government, but simply with withdrawal from particular governmental activities. In such a context, we can recognize many activities as being secessionist in nature. For example, parents who home-school their children, or send them to private schools, have seceded from the government school system. People who charter their businesses in foreign countries are seceding from the American bureaucratic regulatory agencies, and firms that locate plants in Kansas or other right-to-work states do so to avoid politically imposed requirements to allow unionization. Cash markets and barter trade are common ways to secede from state monitoring of retail markets in order to collect taxes. Increasing numbers of Canadian citizens travel to the U.S. for rapid delivery of complex medical treatment, seceding from the Canadian system of socialized medicine.

In much of the legal literature, arbitration is seen as a procedural choice, but the contention here is that it also can be a jurisdictional choice. That is, the substitution of arbitration for litigation often is, in essence, a secession from the jurisdiction of the state courts in order to have the dispute settled in light of the terms of the contract, business practice, and tradition (customary commercial law), rather than government by statute or precedent law. Thus, this discussion of arbitration is intended to illustrate that our secession need not be a complete one or a territorial one; if we believe that a government may be legitimate (or simply that it is better than the existing alternatives) in some of what it does, we can still choose to opt out of a particular governmental activity.

Taken in this light, private arbitration appears to be an attractive substitute for litigation in a wide variety of commercial disputes,[1] because (1) arbitration can be accomplished faster, less formally, and with less expense than litigation; (2) arbitration is less adversarial than litigation, so it is more likely to allow for a continuation of mutually beneficial business relationships; (3) arbitrators can be selected on the basis of their expertise in matters pertinent to specific disputes, while public judges need have no such expertise; (4) privacy can be maintained through arbitration; and (5) businessmen may wish to avoid the application of statutory law by agreeing to something in a contract that would be overturned in a public court, while an arbitrator looks to the contract, rather than to statutes or common-law precedent, in deciding a case.[2] It is frequently contended, however, that arbitration clauses in contracts are effective, and that arbitration rulings are accepted, primarily *because* the public courts, backed by the coercive power of the state, enforce such contracts and rulings. That is, arbitration requires complementary inputs from the state to be effective. This contention is typically based on the belief that without the threat of litigation, there is no effective sanction against someone who refuses an arbitration settlement,

[1]No accurate estimate of the proportion of business disputes being resolved by arbitration within the United States is available. The American Arbitration Association has sufficient records to provide a picture of their commercial dispute-resolution activity, but a substantial majority of the arbitration in the United States is carried out by other arbitration forums. In particular, many trade associations have their own arbitration tribunals. Jerold S. Auerbach, *Justice Without Law?* (New York: Oxford University Press, 1983), p. 113, suggests that by the 1950s, almost 75 percent of all commercial disputes were being arbitrated, but the accuracy of such an estimate is unclear. Similarly, estimates from surveys in the early 1960s indicate that the use of commercial arbitration was increasing at about 10 percent per year. On this, see Steven Lazarus, John J. Bray, Jr., Larry L. Carter, Kent H. Collins, Bruce A. Giedt, Robert V. Holton, Jr., Phillip D. Matthews, and Gordon C. Willard, *Resolving Business Disputes: The Potential for Commercial Arbitration* (New York: American Management Association, 1965), p. 20. The issue is a little clearer when it comes to international business disputes. According to Harold J. Berman and Felix J. Dasser, "The 'New' Law Merchant and the 'Old': Sources, Content, and Legitimacy," in *Lex Mercatoria and Arbitration: A Discussion of the New Law Merchant*, Thomas E. Carbonneau, ed. (Dobbs Ferry, N.Y.: Transnational Juris Publications, 1990), p. 33, almost all international-trade contracts expressly refer any dispute to arbitration.

[2]Berman and Dasser, "The New Law Merchant and the Old"; Lazarus, et al., *Resolving Business Disputes*; Bruce L. Benson, "The Spontaneous Evolution of Commercial Law," *Southern Economic Journal* 55 (January 1989): 644–61; idem, *The Enterprise of Law: Justice Without the State* (San Francisco: Pacific Research Institute, 1990); idem, "Customary Law as a Social Contract: International Commercial Law," *Constitutional Political Economy* 2 (Winter 1992): 1–27; Soia Mentschikoff, "Commercial Arbitration," *Columbia Law Review* 61 (May 1961): 846–69; Leon E. Trakman, *The Law Merchant: The Evolution of Commercial Law* (Littleton, Colo.: Fred B. Rothman, 1983); and Oliver E. Williamson, "Transaction-Cost Economics: The Governance of Contractual Relations," *Journal of Law and Economics* 22 (October 1979): 233–61.

or who breaches a contract to arbitrate.[3] The contention is backed by evidence that the passage of modern arbitration statutes, commanding the common-law courts to enforce arbitration agreements and rulings, beginning with New York's in 1920, provided the major stimulus for the growth of commercial arbitration.[4]

The primary purposes of the following presentation are (1) to reject the hypothesis that the threat of state-enforced litigation is a necessary complement to arbitration; and (2) to support the alternative hypothesis that arbitration is a substitute for litigation, and indeed, that arbitration is a way for businesses to escape the control of the state, at least on some dimensions. When the state's courts or legislatures propagate rules of business behavior that businessmen prefer not to follow, the businessmen can

[3]For instance, William F. Willoughby, *Principles of Judicial Administration* (Washington, D.C.: Brookings Institute, 1929), p. 56; Lazarus, et al., *Resolving Business Disputes*, pp. 31 and 125; William M. Landes and Richard A. Posner, "Adjudication as a Private Good," *Journal of Legal Studies* 8 (March 1979): 247; American Arbitration Association, *Lawyers' Arbitration Letters, 1970–1979* (New York: Free Press, 1981), p. 34; Martin Domke, *Domke on Commercial Arbitration*, rev. ed. by Gabriel M. Wiker (Willmette, Ill.: Gallaghen, 1984), p. 27; and John S. Murray, Alan Scott Rau, and Edward F. Sherman, *Processes of Dispute Resolution: The Role of Lawyers* (Westbury, N.Y.: Foundation Press, 1989), p. 435. This assumption often arises explicitly in the context of an explanation for the passage of modern arbitration statutes, in which it is generally combined with a presumption, as in Murray, et al., *Processes of Dispute Resolution*, p. 435, that "the traditional attitude of judges toward arbitration has been one of considerable hostility." Agreements to arbitrate were supposedly not considered binding under common law, and presumably hostile judges felt free to overturn arbitration decisions if one of the parties chose to litigate. See Lazarus, et al., *Resolving Business Disputes*, p. 18; Morton Horwitz, *The Transformation of American Law, 1780–1860* (Cambridge, Mass.: Harvard University Press, 1977); Murray, et al., *Processes of Dispute Resolution*, p. 435; and John R. Allison, "The Context, Properties, and Constitutionality of Nonconsensual Arbitration: A Study of Four Systems," *Journal of Dispute Resolution* 1 (1990): 11. However, this argument apparently is not valid either. See, e.g., Ian R. MacNeil, *American Arbitration Law* (New York: Oxford University Press, 1992); Jacob T. Levy, "The Transformation of Arbitration Law, 1835–1870: The Lessening of Judicial Hostility Towards Private Dispute Resolution" (Brown University, May 1993, photocopy); also Bruce L. Benson, "An Exploration of the Impact of Modern Arbitration Statutes on the Development of Arbitration in the United States," *Journal of Law, Economics and Organization* 11 (October 1985): 479–501. The second assumption often arises in this same context.

[4]For example, Willoughby, *Principles of Judicial Administration*, p. 56, and Malcolm M. Lucas, "The Future of Arbitration," *Arbitration Journal* 42 (June 1987): 55. Statutes regarding arbitration were in effect in most states prior to 1920. However, beginning in 1920, these statutes have largely been replaced by what the literature describes as "modern" arbitration statutes. The key factor distinguishing modern from pre-modern statutes is that modern statutes make executory agreements to arbitrate disputes, and particularly future disputes, irrevocable and fully enforceable. See MacNeil, *American Arbitration Law*, p. 15.

make their own rules through contract, and in the event of a dispute, clarify those rules through arbitration. That is, arbitration of contract disputes is a way for businesses to partially secede from the control of the state without actually leaving. These purposes are accomplished, in part, by illustrating that the assumption and evidence listed above, which underlie the belief that court backing is required for arbitration, are contradicted by historical evidence, and that this historical evidence is more consistent with the alternative.[5]

The first section, "Recognition of Legal Authority in the Absence of State Coercion," offers a brief discussion of the potential theoretical sources of authority for arbitration in the absence of state coercive power. Essentially, this section emphasizes that there are two different potential sources of cooperation.[6] Coercive command produced by the state is one, but it is not the only potential motivation for cooperation in the form of accepting an arbitrator's ruling. "Contractual coordination" based on symmetrical expectations of longer-term gains can be a source of "peace and conciliatory settlement of disputes."[7] The history of commercial arbitration in the United States is examined in "Commercial Arbitration in the United States" to demonstrate that arbitration was well established, and indeed flourishing, long before modern arbitration statutes were passed, thus rejecting the evidence supposedly supporting the claim that court backing is a prerequisite for arbitration.

Historical evidence is also offered in support of the hypothesis that arbitration is a substitute for litigation. The discussion

---

[5]These assumptions have already been challenged in the context of related issues, such as the development of the medieval "Law Merchant." On this, see Harold J. Berman, *Law and Revolution: The Formation of Western Legal Tradition* (Cambridge, Mass.: Harvard University Press, 1983); Trakman, *The Law Merchant*; Benson, "The Spontaneous Evolution of Commercial Law"; idem, *The Evolution of Law*; and Paul R. Milgrom, Douglas C. North, and Barry R. Weingast, "The Role of Institutions in the Revival of Trade: The Law Merchant, Private Judges, and the Champagne Fairs," *Economics and Politics* 2 (March 1990): 1–23. On the issue of modern arbitration of international commercial disputes, see Trakman, *The Law Merchant*; Berman and Dasser, "The New Law Merchant and the Old"; Benson, *The Enterprise of Law*; and idem, "Customary Law as a Social Contract." Similarly, William Wooldridge, *Uncle Sam, The Monopoly Man* (New Rochelle, N.Y.: Arlington House, 1970), Auerbach, *Justice Without Law?*, and Benson, *The Evolution of Law*, question the assumptions with regard to domestic arbitration, but without the theoretical analysis or historical detail that follows (although much of what follows draws from Benson, "An Exploration of the Impact of Modern Arbitration Statutes," and others have more carefully examined various aspects of the historical record,).

[6]Ludwig von Mises, *Human Action: A Treatise on Economics*, 3rd rev. ed. (Chicago: Contemporary Books, 1949), p. 195.

[7]Ibid., p. 197.

in "Commercial Arbitration in the United States" of widespread use of arbitration in the United States prior to the development of modern arbitration statutes clearly provides some support for this view, but there is additional evidence as well. Specifically, "Political Demands for Modern Arbitration Statutes" explains that, in contrast to the conventional wisdom,[8] the enactments of modern state and federal arbitration statutes, beginning in 1920, were largely because of the lobbying efforts by state and national Bar Associations, rather than by the business community. It is contended that certain members of the legal profession served as the leading advocates for passage of state and federal arbitration statutes because they perceived the growing trend toward substitution of arbitration without lawyers for litigation as a threat to their livelihood, and through the implementation of the modern arbitration statutes, many lawyers were able to become involved in arbitration as well as litigation. Some consequences of these statutes are also discussed in order to illustrate that these consequences are more easily explained in light of this alternative hypothesis than under the widely accepted view that the statutes were necessary prerequisites for arbitration to develop, and, therefore, demanded by business groups.

RECOGNITION OF LEGAL AUTHORITY IN THE ABSENCE OF STATE COERCION

Mises quite convincingly argues that, *given* the existence of the long-run objectives instilled by private-property rights, cooperation in the form of division of labor and trade emerge naturally, and therefore, under these circumstances, "there is no need to enforce cooperation by special orders or prohibitions."[9] His explanation is clear: when private-property rights are defined and enforced, the

> reason why the market economy can operate without government orders telling everybody precisely what he should do and how he should do it is that it does not ask anybody to deviate from those lines of conduct which best serve his own interests. What integrates the individual's actions into the whole of the social system of production is the pursuit of his own purposes. In indulging in his acquisitiveness, each actor

[8]For instance, some publications by various Bar Associations claim that such statutes were "prompted by business" in recognition of the need for court backing before arbitration could become effective. For example, see The Florida Bar, *Arbitration in Florida* (Tallahassee: The Florida Bar Continuing Legal Education Publications, 1979), p. 4.

[9]Mises, *Human Action*, p. 725.

contributes his share to the best possible arrangement of production activities.[10]

But the theoretical rationale offered by Mises as to why this is
the case also explains incentives for cooperation in establishing,
recognizing, and enforcing private-property rights.[11] Given long-
run goals rather than short-run concerns, individuals have incentives to enter cooperative arrangements that reduce their costs of
defending possession claims, and to enhance the property's value
by increasing the potential for mutually beneficial interaction,
including division of labor and market exchanges.

Of course, property rights are never fully delineated, so new
circumstances can lead to disputes over what the rights are.[12] One
potential function of adjudication, therefore, is the clarification
of property rights. Likewise, the incentives to cooperate in the
establishment and enforcement of property rights also apply to
adjudication of disputes.[13] After all, there is a probability that a
businessman will face some sort of misunderstanding or disagreement at some point with some other party. This is particularly
likely in a rapidly developing and changing economy, where new
property rights and contractual arrangements must develop to account for new products and technologies. Of course, disputes can be
solved with violence, broadly defined to include both explicit
and implicit force.[14] Indeed, under some circumstances, such violence may be necessary in order to obtain what appears to be a
non-violent resolution to a dispute. For instance, if each contact
between businessmen involves a discrete, simultaneous, one-shot
game, then voluntary acceptance of a non-violent dispute-resolution process and compliance with the decision generated by that
process are not likely to occur in the absence of a threat to use coercive force, such as that which backs litigation in public courts.
After all, uncertainty about the behavior of the other individual
in a resulting one-shot prisoners-dilemma situation induces non-
cooperative behavior. Essentially, this is the view of business
activity that underlies the assumption that government backing
is a prerequisite for arbitration.

[10]Ibid., pp. 725–26.

[11]Bruce L. Benson, "The Impetus for Recognizing Private Property and Adopting
Ethical Behavior in a Market Economy: Natural Law, Government Law, or Self-
Interest," *Review of Austrian Economics* 6 (1993): 43–80.

[12]Bruce L. Benson, "Emerging From the Hobbesian Jungle: Might Takes and Makes
Rights," *Constitutional Political Economy* 5 (Spring–Summer 1994): 129–58.

[13]Benson, "The Impetus for Recognizing Private Property."

[14]John Umbeck, "Might Makes Rights: A Theory of the Formation and Initial Distribution of Property Rights," *Economic Inquiry* 19 (January 1981): 38–59; also Benson,
"Emerging from the Hobbesian Jungle."

The fact is, however, that the prisoners-dilemma analogy does not characterize most kinds of commercial interactions. Cooperation in a market process, as Mises explains, generally arises out of long-term incentives, as markets generate long-run benefits for everyone involved.[15] Thus, most businessmen expect to be active for a long time, and perhaps to be involved in interactions with a group of other businessmen over and over (the same is true of members of families, primitive kinship groups, stable neighborhoods, religious organizations, and many entities contracting to jointly produce some good or service[16]).

It might be argued that a more appropriate characterization of business interaction is a multi-contact or repeated game, as the same individuals interact (e.g., contract, trade, solve disagreements) with one another many times. In a repeated-game setting with a finite uncertain horizon, cooperation becomes possible.[17] Specifically, such cooperation can lead to the development and acceptance of a commonly recognized set of rules of behavior, such as rules that establish a dispute-resolution procedure. Indeed, without recognizing the game-theoretic underpinnings of his arguments, legal theorist Lon Fuller suggests that a mutually recognized obligation becomes clear and voluntarily acceptable to the individuals affected if: (1) "the relationship of reciprocity out of which the duty arises must result from a voluntary agreement between the parties immediately affected; they themselves create the duty"; (2) the reciprocal performance of duty must be equitable in the sense that both parties must expect to gain from such performance, that is, the exchange cannot be one-sided so that one person gains and another loses; and (3) the parties must expect to interact on a fairly regular basis because "the relationship of duty must in theory and in practice be reversible."[18]

[15]Ludwig von Mises, *Theory and History: An Interpretation of Social and Economic Evolution* (Auburn, Ala.: Ludwig von Mises Institute, 1985), p. 236.

[16]For a few examples of legal arrangements similar to those described below, but outside of commercial law, see Bruce L. Benson, "An Evolutionary Contractarian View of Primitive Law: The Institutions and Incentives Arising Under Customary Indian Law," *Review of Austrian Economics* 5 (1991): 65–89; idem, "Are Public Goods Really Common Pools: Considerations of the Evolution of Policing and Highways in England," *Economic Inquiry* 32 (April 1994): 249–71; idem, *The Evolution of Law*; Robert C. Ellickson, *Order Without Law: How Neighbors Settle Disputes* (Cambridge, Mass.: Harvard University Press, 1991); and David Friedman, "Private Creation and Enforcement of Law: A Historical Case," *Journal of Legal Studies* 8 (March 1979): 399–415. Many others exist or have existed.

[17]Drew Fudenberg and Eric Maskin, "The Folk Theorem in Repeated Games with Discounting or with Incomplete Information," *Econometrica* 54 (1986): 533–54.

[18]Lon L. Fuller, *The Morality of Law* (New Haven, Conn.: Yale University Press, 1964), pp. 23–24.

Fuller notes that the kind of society in which his three conditions—which make a mutually recognized duty under customary law, such as voluntary acceptance of a non-violent dispute-
resolution process and its decisions, clear and acceptable to those
affected—are most likely to be met is

> in a society of economic traders. By definition the members of
> such a society enter direct and voluntary relationships of
> exchange. . . . It is only with the aid of something like a free
> market that it is possible to develop anything like an exact
> measure for the value of disparate goods. . . . Finally, econom-
> ic traders frequently change roles, now selling now buying.
> The duties that arise out of their exchanges are therefore re-
> versible, not only in theory but in practice.[19]

Fuller suggests that this result might be surprising. However, it
is not surprising when it is recognized that, for the most part, businessmen have long-run goals rather than short-run objectives. Indeed, Fuller's first two conditions reflect fundamental economic
tenets.

First, as Mises explains,

> In a hypothetical world in which the division of labor
> would not increase productivity, there would not be any so-
> ciety. There would not be any sentiments of benevolence and
> good will.[20]

Furthermore:

> Man gives to other men in order to receive from them. Mutu-
> ality emerges. Man serves in order to be served.
>
> The exchange relation is the fundamental social rela-
> tion. Interpersonal exchange of goods and services weaves
> the bonds which unite man into society.[21]

Thus, underlying all incentives to cooperate is the fact that the
division of labor and reciprocal exchange can enhance the well-
being of all parties involved.

Fuller's last condition implies that a repeated-game situation will facilitate voluntary acceptance of an obligation to use
non-violent dispute-resolution procedures. Under these circumstances, each individual may recognize that the long-term benefits of remaining on good terms with the other party, by behaving as expected even when a dispute arises, are likely to be greater than the immediate benefits of not cooperating (i.e., refusing

[19]Ibid., p. 24.
[20]Mises, *Human Action*, p. 144.
[21]Ibid., p. 194.

to accept an adjudication process or ruling). Thus, in a dispute with individual B, individual A may agree, explicitly or implicitly, to accept a dispute-resolution forum—a forum which may rule against A—in exchange for B's similar cooperation, either simultaneously or in future relationships with A.

Even the repeated-game situation that Fuller implicitly envisions involves weaker incentives for businessmen to cooperate in this fashion than those which exist in many groups,[22] including many subsets of the business community.[23] In particular, each individual enters into several different games each with different players. Thus, violent dispute resolution (including a threatened use of "transaction-rupturing"[24] public courts backed by the government's coercive power), fraud, or other forms of refusal to recognize widely held rules of conduct within one game can affect a person's reputation, thus limiting his ability to enter into other games to the extent that reputation travels from one game to another. When there are players who value ongoing relationships with several other reliable players more than they value the potential benefits associated with refusing to follow accepted conduct in any one single game, then the potential for cooperation is even greater than in simple repeated games.[25] The incentives to cooperate that arise from repeated games are effectively reinforced, because anyone who chooses a non-cooperative strategy in one game will have difficulty finding a partner in future games.[26] Therefore, in order to maintain a reputation for dealing under recognized rules of behavior (i.e., for fair and ethical dealings or high moral standards, including amicable acceptance of fair and non-violent dispute resolution), each player's dominant strategy is to behave as expected throughout each game that he plays, whether it is a repeated or a one-shot game. Thus, if the rules of conduct do not clearly apply to some situation, and a disagreement thereby arises, each reputable player has incentives to accept what others in the relevant community will consider to be a fair resolution of the dispute. In essence, reputation is the transaction-specific investment that motivates trilateral governance via arbitration.[27]

---

[22]Benson, "The Impetus for Recognizing Private Property."

[23]Gordon Tullock, "Adam Smith and the Prisoners' Dilemma," *Quarterly Journal of Economics* 100 (1985): 1073–81; Benson, "Customary Law as a Social Contract."

[24]Williamson, "Transaction-Cost Economics," p. 250.

[25]David Schmidtz, *The Limits of Government: An Essay on the Public Goods Argument* (Boulder, Colo.: Westview Press, 1991), p. 102.

[26]Tullock, "Adam Smith and the Prisoners' Dilemma," pp. 1075–76.

[27]Williamson, "Transaction-Cost Economics."

Under such circumstances, a mutually acceptable arbitrator might be chosen from the business community or from a recognized pool of arbitration specialists to consider a dispute. Since the arbitrator must be acceptable to both parties in the dispute, fairness becomes embodied in the adjudication process. As Buchanan emphasizes, "Players would not consciously accept the appointment of a referee who was known to be unfair in his enforcement of the rules of the game or at least they would not agree to the same referee in such cases."[28] If one of the businessmen in a dispute is unwilling to arbitrate, or is unwilling to accept a ruling from an agreed-upon arbitrator, simply because the resolution in question is expected to be costly to him, then he will incur long-run costs in the form of a reduction in the value of his investment in building a reputation: other businessmen who hear of his behavior may be unwilling to deal with him.

Repeated games and reputation effects are likely to be sufficient to induce cooperation in dispute resolution in many business relationships. In some situations, however, there may be a problem that also must be overcome for efficient interaction to develop prior to the potential for a dispute arising at all. But the institutions developed to alleviate this problem can also impact the dispute-resolution process, perhaps making it more effective.[29] An individual may want to deal with others, for instance, but because of frictions in the communications process that leave uncertainty about the reputation of a potential player (i.e., some relatively new entrant into a trade, or someone from some distant state or country with whom the businessman has not previously traded), he may be reluctant without some sort of assurance that the other party is not actually looking for short-term gains rather than being concerned with longer-term consequences (e.g., reputation). Each party's commitments to accept commonly expected rules of behavior must be credible. Thus, in many instances, individuals with mutual interests in long-term interaction (e.g., business dealings) have strong incentives to form contractual groups or associations (such as trade associations, mercantile exchanges, or chambers of commerce) as a solution to the assurance problem. As Mises said:

> social cooperation becomes, for almost every man, the great
> means for attainment of all ends. An eminently human common
> interest, the preservation and intensification of social

---

[28]James M. Buchanan, *The Limits of Liberty* (Chicago: University of Chicago Press, 1975), p. 68.

[29]Benson, "Customary Law as a Social Contract."

bonds, is substituted for pitiless biological competition. . . .
Man becomes a social being. . . . Other people become his fel-
lows. . . . For man, until the optimum size of population is
reached, it means rather an improvement than a deterioration
in his quest for material well-being.[30]

Thus, group membership can create a credible signal of reputable
behavior (e.g., a bond).

These groups can facilitate the performance of another function as well: they can serve as the basis for mutual support for arbitration and enforcement of legal matters.[31] Indeed, there often
is a simultaneous development of cooperation in law enforcement
and in other forms of interaction, since most interactions require
some degree of certainty about legal obligations.[32] That is to say,
the rules which facilitate cooperation, and the institutions for
enforcement of such rules, are endogenously determined by the
same forces that produce incentives to cooperate. Thus, when assurance groups form, institutions tend to evolve whereby group
members are generally obligated to: (1) act as or provide access to
third parties to arbitrate (or mediate) any dispute between members; (2) assess the judgments of an arbitrator to make sure that it
is just and consistent with the group's customs and practices; and,
if necessary, (3) help enforce the adjudicated ruling.[33]

The formation of such mutual support groups is not a necessary requirement for cooperative dispute resolution. Nonetheless,
these groups tend to enhance and reinforce both reciprocities and
reputation effects. In a sense, they make explicit what would
otherwise be an implicit threat to a businessman's reputation,
and they provide a formal mechanism to overcome any frictions
in communication, ensuring that information about an individual's non-cooperative behavior will be transmitted to others in
the relevant business community. Given that the arbitrator has
convinced individuals in the affected group that his judgment
should be accepted, the ruling can then be backed by an explicit
threat of ostracism by the members of the entire group: refusal to
cooperate (e.g., to conduct business and dispute resolution according to the accepted rules of conduct) can be punished by exclusion
from some—or even all—future interaction with other members

---

[30]Mises, *Theory and History*, p. 56.

[31]Buchanan, *The Limits of Liberty*, p. 66.

[32]Benson, "The Spontaneous Evolution of Commercial Law."

[33]Benson, *The Enterprise of Law*, and Milgrom, et al., "The Role of Institutions in the
Revival of Trade." Umbeck, in "Might Makes Rights," also suggests that groups will
form in order to lower the cost of establishing and enforcing property rights, because individual reliance on violence can be a costly means of doing so.

of the group.[34] Similar results can clearly arise without a formal organized group, but the formal group may reduce the transactions costs of ostracism, thereby making the threat to reputation more obvious and more credible.

Fear of a boycott sanction reinforces the self-interest motives associated with the maintenance of reputation and reciprocal arrangements. In other words, because each individual has made an investment in establishing himself as part of the community (in establishing a reputation), that investment can be "held hostage" by the business group in order to insure that the commitment to cooperate is credible.[35] Indeed, a valuable reputation is an ideal hostage. After all, a good hostage is something that the hostage-giver values highly and that the hostage-taker values little, so the giver has strong incentives to live up to promises, and the receiver has no incentives to appropriate the hostage.

Indeed, in an arrangement between two reputable parties, both have something of value to lose by breaking a promise, but little to gain. In addition, there appears to be lower transactions costs (e.g., storage, security precautions) when reputation serves as the hostage rather than some tangible asset (or person). In general, however, the threat of ostracism is not likely to be necessary. The process of arbitration and its decision are generally accepted by businessmen not because of the power of some strong individual or institution to destroy a reputation but because each self-interested individual recognizes the benefits of behaving in accordance with the expectations held by the other individuals within the group of businesses that frequently interacts (whether that group is a formal contractual association or not).

Self-interest motives to make arbitration attractive and viable, so violence in the form of a threat of state-backed coercive force created by statutory mandates of court backing are not necessary. If reciprocity and reputation effects are not sufficiently strong, groups can formalize these effects and make them explicit. Thus, it should not be surprising to find that arbitration developed prior to the passage of such statutes. As Rothbard contends,

> no State or similar agency contrary to the market is needed to define or allocate property rights. This can and will be done

[34]Benson, "The Spontaneous Evolution of Commercial Law"; idem, *The Enterprise of Law*; idem, "An Evolutionary Contractarian View of Primitive Law"; and idem, "Customary Law as a Social Contract"; also Trakman, *The Law Merchant*; and Milgrom, et al., "The Role of Institutions in the Revival of Trade."
[35]Oliver E. Williamson, "Credible Commitments: Using Hostages to Support Exchange," *American Economic Review* 83 (September 1983): 519–40.

by the use of reason and through market processes themselves; any other allocation or definition would be completely arbitrary and contrary to the principles of the free society.[36]

Indeed, throughout history, commercial law primarily consisted
of customary laws in the form of accepted business practices and
contracts.[37] During some relatively recent periods, nation-states
have been active in the adjudication and enforcement of commercial law, but at other times, adjudication and enforcement has
been left entirely up to the commercial community.[38]

COMMERCIAL ARBITRATION IN THE UNITED STATES[39]

A relative lack of litigation regarding arbitration issues appears to be the evidence that many have looked to in contending
that arbitration was not in widespread use prior to 1920. A large
increase in litigation over arbitration rulings and procedures followed passage of the first "modern" arbitration statutes by New
York (1920), New Jersey (1923), the federal government (1925),
Oregon (1925), Massachusetts (1925), Pennsylvania (1927), and
California (1927),[40] suggesting to many that the use of arbitration
itself was stimulated by these statutes. Public court records do not
provide a clear picture of the historic level of arbitration activity, however, in part because the vast majority of arbitration decisions are not appealed to these courts, and in part because the
incentives to appeal became stronger with passage of these statutes, as is explained below. Thus, for instance, William C. Jones
uses newspapers, merchant letters, and the records of the New
York Chamber of Commerce, as well as legal records, and finds
that arbitration was in constant and widespread use throughout
both the Dutch colonial period (1624 to 1664), and the British

[36]Murray N. Rothbard, *Power and Market: Government and the Economy* (Kansas
City, Mo.: Sheed Andrews and McMeel, 1970), p. 3.

[37]Benson, "The Spontaneous Evolution of Commercial Law," and Trakman, *The
Law Merchant*. On the particular manner in which these practices developed, see
Benson, "The Impetus for Recognizing Private Property."

[38]William C. Jones, "Three Centuries of Commercial Arbitration in New York: A
Brief Survey," *Washington University Law Quarterly* 1956 (February 1956): 193–221;
Benson, "The Spontaneous Evolution of Commercial Law"; Trakman, *The Law
Merchant*; Milgrom, et al., "The Role of Institutions in the Revival of Trade"; and
Berman, *Law and Revolution*.

[39]This section and the next draw upon Benson, "An Exploration of the Impact of
Modern Arbitration Statutes."

[40]See Wesley A. Sturges, *A Treatise on Commercial Arbitrations and Awards* (Kansas
City, Mo.: Vernon Law Book Company, 1930).

colonial period (1664 to 1783) in New York.[41] As Aiken explains in his examination of the Dutch period in New York, for example: "Arbitration in New Netherlands in the 17th century . . . was frequent, swift, and relatively simple compared to the English common law."[42] Indeed, there is substantial evidence demonstrating that merchants established their own system of law and dispute resolution in each of the American colonies.[43] Furthermore, commercial arbitration was also used to settle disputes between businessmen from different colonies; New York and Philadelphia business communities were arbitrating disputes in the seventeenth century, for instance.[44]

Perhaps the most complete record of an arbitration tribunal is that of the New York Chamber of Commerce. One of this organization's actions taken at its first meeting, on 5 April 1768, was to make provisions for arbitration, and the Chamber's first arbitration committee was appointed that year on 7 June.[45] There is also evidence of considerable demand for the Chamber's arbitration services, as committees were appointed regularly until 1775, when the Chamber temporarily suspended meetings because of the war.[46] On 7 September 1779, a committee was again appointed, and arbitration continued throughout the revolutionary period. In fact, during the British occupation of New York, the arbitration committee was the only court for civil cases—disputes were even referred to the Chamber by the British.[47]

After the revolution, the New York Chamber of Commerce continued to provide arbitration to its members,[48] and there is also substantial evidence of arbitration in the other states.[49] The fact is that government courts of the period did not apply the

---

[41]Jones, "Three Centuries of Commercial Arbitration in New York," p. 209.

[42]John R. Aiken, "New Netherlands Arbitration in the Seventeenth Century," *Arbitration Journal* 29 (June 1974): 145–60.

[43]Ibid.; Jones, "Three Centuries of Commercial Arbitration in New York;" George S. Odiorne, "Arbitration Under Early New Jersey Law," *Arbitration Journal* 8 (1953): 117–25; George S. Odiorne, "Arbitration and Mediation Among the Early Quakers," *Arbitration Journal* 9 (1954): 161–69; and Joseph H. Smith, *Colonial Justice in Western Massachusetts* (Cambridge, Mass.: Harvard University Press, 1961), pp. 180 and 188.

[44]Aiken, "New Netherlands Arbitration," and Jones, "Three Centuries of Commercial Arbitration in New York."

[45]Ibid., p. 207.

[46]Ibid., p. 207.

[47]Ibid., p. 209.

[48]Ibid., p. 211.

[49]Ibid., p. 219; Smith, *Colonial Justice in Western Massachusetts*, pp. 180 and 188; Odiorne, "Arbitration Under Early New Jersey Law"; Odiorne, "Arbitration and Mediation Among the Early Quakers"; and Auerbach, *Justice Without Law?*

commercial law in what the merchant community considered to be a just and expeditious fashion: "Not only did courts, according to one New York merchant, dispense 'expensive endless law'; they were slow to develop legal doctrine that facilitated commercial development."[50] Indeed, in the early part of the nineteenth century, the common-law courts in America were generally hostile toward arbitration.[51] Therefore, businessmen who chose to use arbitration were doing so, in large part, to escape the hostile legal environment of the state courts. They were seceding from their states' legal systems and establishing their own.

The use of commercial arbitration developed during the colonial and post-revolutionary periods despite the fact that the relevant body of precedent law for the American courts, first in the English colonies and then in the newly formed country, was English common law, and a 1609 common-law ruling had presumably undermined the use of arbitration in common-law jurisdictions. The dictum pronounced by Lord Edward Coke in *Vynior's Case*, in reviewing a case previously judged under private arbitration, was

> that though one may be bound to stand to the arbitrament yet he may countermand the arbitrator . . . as a man cannot by his own act make such an authority power or warrant not countermandable which by law and its own . . . nature is countermandable.[52]

This ruling meant that the decisions of arbitrators could be reversed by the common-law courts, because an arbitrator's purpose was, according to Coke, to find a suitable compromise, while a judge's purpose was to rule on the merits of the case. Furthermore, contracts to submit to arbitration were declared to be revokable. This precedent was viewed to be binding for the next two to three centuries in both England and the United States. Indeed, while this ruling occurred before the common-law doctrine of binding contracts was fully formed, as common-law courts began enforcing all contracts to which parties intended to bind themselves, they continued to treat arbitration clauses as revokable. In fact, the *Vynior's Case* doctrine of revocability was later justified—and even reinforced—in *Kill v Hollister*, when it was declared that contracts to arbitrate are revokable because they "oust courts of their jurisdiction."[53] Thus, the first defenders of the revocability

[50]Auerbach, *Justice Without Law?* p. 33.
[51]Horwitz, *The Transformation of American Law*, and Levy, "The Transformation of Arbitration Law, 1835–1870."
[52]4 Eng Rep 302 (1609).
[53]1 Wilson 129 (1746).

doctrine spoke of the interests of the courts, rather than the interests of parties contracting to use arbitration, suggesting that the common-law courts of England saw arbitration as a threat to their control of dispute resolution, that is, as a possible substitute for their services. The same view generally characterizes the American courts during the early part of the nineteenth century, where an increasing willingness to overturn arbitrators' decisions for issues relating to either law or fact is evident.[54]

Of course, no legal system ever completely deters undesirable actions, such as the use of violence to resolve disputes, and this is equally true of the business community's arrangements to promote arbitration and deter the use of litigation. Thus, as arbitration became more widespread, some of the arbitration rulings were challenged in common-law courts, and these courts' attitudes toward arbitration can be examined.[55] The Pennsylvania Supreme Court's decision in *Gross v Zorger* typifies this view; the court declared that an arbitration award could be reversed for "a clear, plain, evident mistake in law or fact, which affects the justice and honesty of the case."[56] The United States Supreme Court, in *Williams v Paschall*, reached a similar decision.[57] The U.S. Supreme Court was also willing to overturn arbitration decisions due to procedural matters, as were state courts, even if there was no evidence of fraud.[58] In Massachusetts, for instance, the state Supreme Court overturned arbitration decisions for a wide variety of minor procedural issues,[59] despite a state statute presumably protecting arbitration. The U.S. Supreme Court used the argument underlying the English common-law doctrine of revocability, the concern over "ousting the jurisdiction of the courts," in ruling that an agreement to arbitrate which had not yet been fulfilled could

[54]Levy, "The Transformation of Arbitration Law, 1835–1870."

[55]The discussion of court decisions draws from ibid.; also see Benson, "An Exploration of the Impact of Modern Arbitration Statutes."

[56]3 Yates 521 (1803). Note that this is in contrast to the way that arbitration awards were treated by English Courts as constrained by the Arbitration Act of 1698, which stated that once an arbitration award is made, the common-law courts should not overturn the award, either for an error in law or an error of fact. Thus, the English courts were directed to let arbitration awards stand unless they were made under fraudulent or otherwise unfair procedures. The doctrine of revocability was not overturned by the statute, however, and more significantly, the common-law courts of post-revolutionary America were not constrained by this English Statute.

[57]4 U.S. 284 (1803).

[58]*Maybin v Coulon*, 4 U.S. 298 (1804).

[59]*Mansfield v Doughty*, 3 Mass. 398 (1807); *Monoseit v Post*, 4 Mass. 832 (1808).

not be used to prevent civil action.[60] Thus, an agreement to arbitrate was not binding in the eyes of U.S. courts. In fact, a dispute that had already been settled by an arbitrator could be appealed to an American common-law court, and, for all intents and purposes, be treated as a dispute that had never been investigated.[61]

Given such precedents, private arbitration in the American colonies and early states clearly did not take its authority from the common-law courts, and indeed, according to the relevant precedent law, arbitration decisions had no legal authority. They actually did, however: authority arose from reciprocal arrangements developed within the business community, and from individual recognition of potential reputation effects associated with refusing to accept an arbitration decision. "These penalties were far more fearsome than the cost of the award with which he disagreed. Voluntary and private adjudications were voluntarily and privately adhered to if not out of honor, out of self interest."[62] Thus, even though the attitude of the courts toward arbitration might even be described as one of increasing hostility throughout the period of 1775 to 1835,[63] "there was no time during the period when arbitration was not known and used by a significant number of people."[64] In fact, new sources of arbitration emerged to supplement or replace other arrangements. For example, in New York, as the economy grew and diversified, the Chamber of Commerce gradually became less important as a provider of arbitration services, as more narrowly focused, specialized groups and associations developed internal arbitration procedures.[65] For instance, the New York Stock Exchange, founded in 1792, formally provided for arbitration in its 1817 constitution, and it "has been working successfully ever since," primarily to rectify disputes between New York Stock Exchange members and their customers.[66]

As arbitration continued to develop, the trend of increasing hostility by common-law courts toward arbitration began to be reversed in the 1830s in some states.[67] However, arbitration was

---

[60]*The Hope*, 35 U.S. 138 (1836).

[61]Horwitz, *The Transformation of American Law*, p. 153.

[62]Wooldridge, *Uncle Sam, the Monopoly Man*, pp. 100–1.

[63]Levy, "The Transformation of Arbitration Law, 1835–1870."

[64]Jones, "Three Centuries of Commercial Arbitration in New York," p. 213.

[65]Ibid., p. 212.

[66]Lazarus, et al., *Resolving Business Disputes*, p. 27.

[67]Levy, "The Transformation of Arbitration Law, 1835–1870." An examination of records from appellate courts, including state supreme courts, suggests that the first evidence of a changing attitude toward arbitration awards appears in Virginia

firmly in place before this gradual reversal in court attitude began; furthermore, arbitration developed in states whose courts were relatively slow to change, such as New York, as well as in states whose courts changed more rapidly.[68] For instance, there is

---

(Levy, "The Transformation of Arbitration Law, 1835–1870"), where the state's Supreme Court argued that common-law precedent allowed courts to overrule arbitrators only when there was an "error of fact or of law *apparent on its face*" (emphasis added), and not whenever a court might be able to discover one (*Doolittle v Malcolm*, 8 Leigh 608 [Virginia 1837]). The court found that the claim that arbitrators in a case had not considered all of the evidence presented and had used personal knowledge of the facts in reaching a decision to be insufficient grounds for setting aside the award, even if the claims were true. Thus, Virginia courts were no longer to treat a previously arbitrated dispute as if it had never been tried before. Other state appellate courts adopted similar views toward arbitration over the next several decades. For instance, in *Ebert v Ebert* (5 Md. 353 [1854]), the Maryland Supreme Court stated that "every reasonable intendment is now made in favor of [arbitration] awards . . . and that all matters have been decided by them, unless the contrary shall appear on the face of the award." The United States Supreme Court also signalled the end of the period of strict judicial scrutiny of and hostility toward arbitration by federal courts as early as 1842. In *Hobson v McArthur* (41 U.S. 182), the court considered a procedural issue: the court ruled that courts should construe arbitration contracts according to the intent of the participants, and that despite the fact that the participants had not specified the voting rule in the contract for the three-person arbitration tribunal, the arbitration ruling should stand. That is, courts should not construe arbitration agreements in the narrow way that they had been, searching for reasons to overturn settlements on procedural grounds. Then, in *Burchell v Marsh* (58 U.S. 344 [1854]), the Court stated that

> Arbitrators are judges chosen by the parties to decide the matters submitted to them, finally and without appeal. As a method of settling disputes it should receive every encouragement for courts of equity. If the award is within the submission, and contains the honest decisions of the arbitrators, after a full and fair hearing of the parties, a court of equity will not set aside for error, either in law or in fact. A contrary course . . . would make the award the commencement, not the end, of litigation.

Williams v Paschall was not explicitly overturned, but the language of *Burchell v Marsh* implicitly did so. Thus, the assumption of court hostility toward arbitration in the late nineteenth century is clearly rejected for some courts, and probably for most, according to MacNeil, *American Arbitration Law*, p. 19. Indeed, on p. 35, MacNeil finds even earlier evidence of common-law judges' support for arbitration than suggested here, citing *Underhill v Cortland*, 2 Johns. Ch. 339, 361 (1817), and suggests that the "prevailing spirit" at that time was one of support. However, he does not provide evidence that this support was widespread or accepted upon appeal, and the cases cited above suggest that it was not.

[68]The doctrine of revocability of arbitration contracts was also being reconsidered by many common-law courts during the same period, for instance, although New York's courts did not do so. English courts began pulling back from the doctrine of revocability in *Scott v Avery* (5 H.L. Cas. 811 [1855]), holding that contracts to arbitrate specific future disputes were binding but contracts to arbitrate "any disagreement arising under the terms of the contract" were revocable. Furthermore, in Scotland the doctrine was explicitly rejected, after being characterized as "irrational" and "absurd" (*Drew v Drew*, 2 Macqueen's Cases on Appeal [1855]).

evidence of arbitration for members of the New York Commercial Exchange at least as early as 1861, and perhaps earlier.[69] As merchants organized into various associations and exchanges, provisions were *always* made for the arbitration of disputes among members. Thus, there is considerable evidence of widespread use of arbitration provisions in contracts, despite the common-law doctrine of revocability,[70] as well as evidence of arbitration performed under the auspices of trade associations and mercantile exchanges. The volume of evidence is particularly heavy for the last four decades of the nineteenth century,[71] well in advance of the passage of modern arbitration statutes.[72]

As new arbitration arrangements were being created, some older arbitration forums were less in demand. This is true of the

---

Similarly, Pennsylvania's Supreme Court rejected the doctrine entirely in 1857 in *Snodgrass v Gavit*, 28 Pa. 221, concluding that "Where parties stipulate that disputes, whether actual or prospective, shall be submitted to the arbitrament of a particular individual or tribunal, they are bound by their contract, and may not seek redress elsewhere." The Virginia Court of Appeals reached a similar decision in *Condon v Southside R.R. Company* (14 Grat. 320 [Virginia, 1858]). The court held that "The ancient principle, that agreements for the final settlement of disputes by arbitration were against the policy of the law and void because tending to oust the courts of their jurisdiction, is against the spirit of modern times, and courts are now very liberally inclined toward submission of matters to arbitration, and place as liberal a construction upon the submission as the intentions of the parties justify. The intention of the parties is the guiding star in construing the submission." No other state appellate courts besides those in Pennsylvania and Virginia completely rejected revocability during this era (1835–1870), and some, like New York, continued to apply the doctrine. Nonetheless, the general movement, particularly after 1870, was in the direction of holding contracts to arbitrate specific future disputes to be binding while general contracts to arbitrate any disagreement under the contract were revocable, the standard that applied in England after *Scott v Avery*. Indeed, while New York judges maintained the doctrine of revocability until the state's 1920 arbitration statute commanded its demise, it is clear that some New York judges were becoming increasingly less hostile toward arbitration, and might even have overturned the doctrine had the statute not passed. For instance, in *D & H Canal Co. v Pa. Coal Co.*, (50 N.Y. 250 [1872]), despite upholding the doctrine, the court stated that "it is not easy to assign at this day any good reason why the contract should not stand, and the parties made to abide by it, and the judgment of the tribunal of their choice." Similarly, in *Fudickar v Guardian Mutual Life Insurance Co.* (62 N.Y. 392 [1875]), when revocability was again upheld, the court still felt that "the jealousy with which, at one time, courts regarded the withdrawal of controversies from their jurisdiction by the agreement of parties, has yielded to a more sensible view, and arbitrations are now encouraged as an easy, expeditious, and inexpensive method of settling disputes, and as tending to prevent litigation."

[69]Jones, "Three Centuries of Commercial Arbitration in New York," p. 217.

[70]Ibid.

[71]Jones, "Three Centuries of Commercial Arbitration in New York," pp. 214–15.

[72]Also see Wooldridge, *Uncle Sam, the Monopoly Man*; Auerbach, *Justice Without Law?*; and MacNeil, *American Arbitration Law*.

New York Chamber of Commerce in particular, and its declining importance as a source of arbitration services is of particular interest in the context of the following discussion of the political impetus for modern arbitration statutes. The Chamber continued to offer its members arbitration services, "at least in a desultory fashion, throughout the nineteenth century,"[73] but use of the Chamber's services gradually declined through the first half of the century, and ultimately disappeared altogether. As its dominant position in New York commercial arbitration was lost, the Chamber "began to seek support from the State in its efforts to provide adjudicatory facilities for its members."[74] Its state charter was amended in 1861 to explicitly provide for an arbitration committee, and to provide that awards of the committee could be entered as judgments of courts of record if the parties desired such court enforcement. Despite this legislatively mandated court backing, however, the Chamber continued to lose ground to other arbitration arrangements. Thus, an 1874 legislative amendment to the charter was obtained which provided for appointment by the state governor of "an arbitrator of the Chamber of Commerce of the State of New York" to be paid by the chamber; in addition, members could be *summoned* to arbitrate their disputes, although they could escape the Chamber's jurisdiction by filing an objection with the arbitrator.[75] An 1874 act was added which specified that members of the Chamber of Commerce "could be required by requisition to bring their cases before this [the Chamber's arbitration] court whose judge was to be paid by the state."[76]

Why was such legislation sought by the New York Chamber? The Chamber's arbitration tribunal had lost sight of some of the factors that make arbitration attractive. It had a permanently sitting judge, rather than allowing parties the ability to choose an arbitrator with particular expertise. The judge was even to be paid by the state, so those businessmen who might prefer to escape the government's influence might have been wary of the Chamber's arbitrator. Beyond that, this arbitration tribunal began to lose many of the low-cost characteristics of arbitration: indeed, Chamber arbitration decisions were "arrived at with increasing formality and even reached the dignity of a court of justice."[77] Thus, once these three things happened—a judge was appointed, Chamber members were required by statute to take their

[73]Jones, "Three Centuries of Commercial Arbitration in New York," p. 215.
[74]Ibid.
[75]Ibid., p. 216.
[76]Ibid.
[77]G. Gwynne, "The Oldest American Tribunal," *Arbitration Journal* 1 (1937): 117–25.

disputes to this judge, and a Chamber arbitration ruling took on the force of court rulings if the parties agreed—the Chamber attracted virtually no new arbitration business. Instead, businessmen turned to their smaller formal and informal groups to arbitrate their disputes, even though the decisions of such groups did not enjoy the same state support or recognition that Chamber-arbitrated dispute resolutions did. Consequently, the Chamber's arbitration judge was only paid by the state for the first two years after his appointment. As Jones points out, "It would appear thus that the Chamber constantly tried to provide arbitration facilities for its members, but it never devised a completely satisfactory system."[78] This discussion illustrates an important point that arises again below: competition for commercial dispute-resolution business was a key factor in shaping statute law, as attempts were made to either lower transactions costs of using their forum, or raise transactions costs of using an alternative.

Some observers have argued that the decline—and ultimate disappearance—of Chamber arbitration reflected a general decline and disappearance of all commercial arbitration during the nineteenth century, with business disputes shifting into the state courts.[79] However, the fact is that commercial arbitration was in constant use throughout the century under the auspices of informal business groups, formal trade associations, and organized mercantile exchanges.

The late part of the nineteenth century saw an even more rapid development of arbitration relative to litigation. One factor explaining the increasing use of arbitration relative to litigation, including New York Chamber of Commerce arbitration, was the growing problem of public-court congestion and trial delay. As Cheung explains, wealth is dissipated under non-price rationing processes, and therefore individuals

> seek to minimize the dissipation subject to constraints. This will be done either through seeking alternatives in using or producing the good [or service] . . . or through forming alternative contractual arrangements to govern the use or production of the good [or service] with the least rise in transactions costs, or through the least costly combination of the two.[80]

When litigation is rationed by waiting, even some of those who, in the absence of the time costs, might prefer litigation, will look

[78]Jones, "Three Centuries of Commercial Arbitration in New York," p. 216.
[79]For example, Auerbach, *Justice Without Law?*
[80]Steven N. S. Cheung, "A Theory of Price Control," *Journal of Law and Economics* 17 (April 1974): 61.

for substitutes (arbitration) and establish contractual arrangements (e.g., develop rules of arbitration through trade associations) to govern dispute resolution.

The cost of using litigation may have been rising in other ways as well. Uncertainty regarding the credibility of the commitment of the public courts to support business contracts was apparently also increasing as "the growth of the regulatory state unsettled advocates of commercial autonomy who turned to arbitration as a shield against government intrusion."[81] Thus, as costs rose in terms of both waiting time and uncertainty regarding the way a business dispute might be settled, more and more businessmen looked to arbitration as a substitute for litigation in order to secede from the control of evolving state legal systems.

By the end of World War I, arbitration had clearly made "the courts secondary recourse in many areas and completely superfluous in others."[82] Indeed, the rapid expansion in arbitration created incentives for the New York Chamber of Commerce's efforts to supply arbitration arrangements to reemerge around the turn of the century. In fact, the Chamber apparently enjoyed an increasing role as a supplier of arbitration services.[83] In all likelihood, to the degree that the Chamber was successful in attracting arbitration business, it probably also began to emulate the practices and procedures of its competitors in formal and informal commercial organizations in order to attract such business. In addition, however, not all business firms were members of such organizations, so as the use of the public courts became more costly, they faced a choice: bear the cost of organizing such a group, use the increasingly costly public courts, or use the Chamber's services. Some apparently found the relative price of Chamber arbitration to be the lowest.

Clearly, arbitration in the U.S. "did not suddenly come into being [in 1920] . . . because of the passage of a statute making agreements to arbitrate future disputes enforceable. Rather it has existed with and without the benefit of statutes" for several centuries.[84] So why were these statutes passed?

[81] Auerbach, *Justice Without Law?* p. 101. Note that commercial arbitration also rapidly expanded in England during the 1860s, due to the public courts' congestion and inability to deal with the rapidly developing complexities in business dealings. See Wooldridge, *Uncle Sam, the Monopoly Man*, p. 99; Willoughby, *Principles of Judicial Administration*, pp. 58–64.

[82] Wooldridge, *Uncle Sam, the Monopoly Man*, p. 101.

[83] Auerbach, *Justice Without Law?*

[84] Jones, "Three Centuries of Commercial Arbitration in New York," p. 218. Actually, this statement by Jones is not quite accurate. Indeed, as MacNeil explains in

POLITICAL DEMANDS FOR
MODERN ARBITRATION STATUTES

During the second decade of the twentieth century, political pressure began to build for some state legislatures to pass arbitration statutes that would officially sanction the judgments of private arbitration courts. Surprisingly, some of the early support for these measures came from the legal profession.[85] After all, trial lawyers dominated litigation in the public courts, and arbitration was clearly an increasingly important alternative to the use of those courts for commercial disputes. Furthermore, this alternative, as it was developing, not only avoided the use of lawyers, but was hostile toward the legal profession. In fact, forty years later, approximately 40 percent of the trade associations were still explicitly discouraging or forbidding attorney representation in arbitration, and attorney involvement in the other 60 percent of the arbitration processes of trade associations was "highly unlikely."[86] The feelings that many trade associations had regarding lawyer involvement in their arbitration processes is probably represented by an officer of the Silk Association, who suggested that businessmen can settle their disputes better than lawyers because a lawyer "is going to dominate the situation and bind the thing up with technicalities and precedents" rather than yield to business expertise and an "ordinary understanding of what is right and what is wrong."[87] Why would lawyers support statutes that are generally claimed to have been "aimed at making the arbitration more efficient by giving it legislative sanction,"[88] when arbitration was so hostile to lawyers?

First, it must be noted that many, and perhaps most, lawyers may not have recognized a direct self-interest stake in the arbitration issue, since the bulk of the lawyers did very little litigation. Of course, some lawyers, especially those who specialized

---

American Arbitration Law, pp. 15–19, both common law and statute law regarding arbitration were evolving throughout the nineteenth century, so that "contrary to modern folklore . . . , the pre-modern statutory law of arbitration was largely supportive of that institution, as was the common law." The statement should say that arbitration existed without the support of modern arbitration statutes (see note 4 in this regard), although some states, such as Illinois, had arbitration statutes which were in many ways similar to those passed beginning in 1920, and others, like Virginia and Pennsylvania, had established something very much like the modern treatment of arbitration through precedent, rather than statute.

[85]Auerbach, *Justice Without Law?* p. 103.

[86]Mentschikoff, "Commercial Arbitration," p. 857.

[87]Auerbach, *Justice Without Law?* p. 108.

[88]Domke, *Domke on Commercial Arbitration*, p. 27.

in business disputes in the public courts, or who wished to develop such a specialization, were obviously threatened by arbitration. Beyond that, the fact that most lawyers are probably never involved in litigation does not mean that arbitration did not pose at least some indirect threat to many of them. For instance, consider commercial and corporate lawyers who specialize in writing agreements in an effort to avoid disputes. The demand for the services of contract-drafting lawyers is, in theory, a function of the cost of disputes: carefully drafted contracts and dispute-resolution procedures are substitutes, at least to a degree. If the cross elasticity is of any consequence, commercial lawyers who draft contracts might perceive arbitration as a threat, just as trial lawyers specializing in business disputes would. After all, as noted above, trade associations demonstrated considerable animosity toward lawyers,[89] and the availability of their internal arbitration arrangements (along with standardized contracts, etc.) may have allowed members to avoid some expenses for contract-drafting lawyers as well as for trial lawyers.

Furthermore, the demand for those lawyers who specialize in drafting contracts increases as the prospect of state-imposed sanctions increases. When such sanctions are available, the demands placed on formal contract writing are increased. When reputation or ostracism sanctions alone apply, less formality in contracting may be required, because the parties are intimately familiar with business practice and custom in their particular area of transactions, so they understand what a general statement in a contract means, *and* they can choose an arbitrator with similar intimate understanding. However, a judge is much less likely to have such an understanding, so a contract that may face judicial scrutiny will have to be much more specific and formal in order to avoid a high probability of judicial error.[90] Thus, the growth of arbitration was probably a threat to contract-writing lawyers as well as to trial lawyers. Creating a potential state-imposed sanction for arbitration agreements also increased the requirements for formal, specific contracts that required the expertise of contract-writing lawyers.

Whether all lawyers recognized self-interest concerns about the threat that arbitration posed, or whether a vocal minority within various Bar Associations was responsible for their lobbying efforts, cannot be determined from the records of the period, but it is clear that some Bar Association members were concerned

[89]Mentschikoff, "Commercial Arbitration," p. 857.
[90]David Charny, "Nonlegal Sanctions in Commercial Relationships," *Harvard Law Review* 104 (December 1990): 385, 388, and 403–5.

about arbitration, and that following their urging, the Bar Associations took the lead in advocating statutory changes. Indeed, it was apparently not difficult to secure a fairly general consensus among (or at least acquiescence by) bar association members, despite their general dislike for arbitration,[91] because virtually all lawyers recognized that respect for the legal profession and the courts in general was on the decline during the early twentieth century. Furthermore, they recognized that court congestion was becoming a relatively significant problem, and was contributing to the general decline in respect for their profession.[92] For instance, New York had 26,000 cases pending in 1923, up from 18,000 six years earlier,[93] and the New York Court of Appeals had delays of two years or longer between 1896 and 1921.[94] Thus, trial lawyers and judges in particular, but to a degree, members of the legal professionals in general, were on the defensive.[95] They were searching for a means to reduce court congestion as part of an overall effort to increase the standing of judges and lawyers. However, if an alternative forum to the public courts was to be used, trial lawyers wanted a forum that they might be able to influence, and perhaps even dominate. Arbitration had already developed as an alternative forum, and those lawyers directly impacted clearly recognized the competitive threat that commercial arbitration posed to the lawyer-dominated, court-based, adversarial dispute-resolution process.

Public support of arbitration was seen by at least some influential Bar Association members as a way to improve the profession's public image without losing clients,[96] assuming they could also establish a significant role for themselves in the arbitration process; in this way they hoped to regain control over business dispute resolution.[97] For example, before the 1914 meeting of the

[91]Lazarus, et al., *Resolving Business Disputes*, pp. 98–124, conducted a survey of 170 law firms, and found a "somewhat negative attitude toward arbitration" (p. 119) among the lawyers surveyed. They concluded: "Lawyers *generally* . . . are strongly opposed to the so-called general arbitration clause" (p. 118, emphasis added).

[92]On this, see Willoughby, *Principles of Judicial Administration*, pp. 7–26; Lazarus, et al., *Resolving Business Disputes*, p. 128; Auerbach, *Justice Without Law?* p. 103.

[93]Lazarus, et al., *Resolving Business Disputes*, p. 128.

[94]Stephen L. Wasby, Thomas B. Marvell, and Alexander B. Aikman, *Volume and Delay in State Appellate Courts: Problems and Responses* (Williamsburg, Va.: National Center for State Courts, 1979), p. 39.

[95]Auerbach, *Justice Without Law?* p. 103.

[96]Ibid., p. 104.

[97]Interestingly, trial-lawyers' incentives in the twentieth century were similar to the kings' and judges' incentives in the sixteenth and seventeenth centuries when Coke's ruling was handed down. Kings obtained revenues through the business of

Missouri Bar Association, a St. Louis attorney argued that some private disputes should be diverted to arbitration, where a *lawyer* chosen by the disputants would serve as the arbitrator. This, he suggested, would increase respect for the judiciary as court delay should diminish, and given that only attorneys with "character and learning" would serve as arbitrators, "suspicion and reproach" of the bar would also recede. Furthermore, by publicly supporting arbitration as an alternative to the courts, the Bar could claim that it was actively pursuing the "public interest."[98]

In that same year, the New York State Bar Association established a Committee on the Prevention of Unnecessary Litigation.[99] In 1916, that committee adopted a set of "Rules for the Prevention of Unnecessary Litigation" which included:

> Where differences cannot be adjusted between the parties or their attorneys and the intervention of a third party becomes necessary, there are several forms which arbitration may take. The arbitration may be (1) informal, (2) under the Code, (3) under the auspices of a commercial body, or (4) under the auspices of a bar association.[100]

The second and fourth points stand out here, since neither were yet relevant as arbitration was developing at the time. The 1918 national Conference of Bar Association Delegates adopted a similar resolution encouraging use of arbitration.

The New York Bar Association *initiated* a 1920 lobbying effort to establish a statutory backing of commercial arbitration

---

dispensing justice (Benson, *The Enterprise of Law*, chap. 3; Bruce Lyon, *A Constitutional and Legal History of Medieval England*, 2nd ed. [New York: W. W. Norton, 1980], pp. 163 and 190), and royal judges' income came largely from court fees (Landes and Posner, "Adjudication as a Private Good," p. 258; and J. H. Baker, *An Introduction to English Legal History* [London: Buttersworth, 1971], p. 31), so their incentives were to absorb other legal systems into royal law. State judges are not paid out of litigation fees, and government no longer sees justice as a source of revenue, but many lawyers' incomes clearly depend, to a great degree, on their involvement in dispute resolution (or its substitute, the writing of dispute-avoiding contracts). They dominated the public courts, but they had virtually no role in arbitration as it was evolving. Trial lawyers would benefit if the incentives to use arbitration were reduced so that commercial disputes were shifted back to the public courts, just as English kings and judges had benefitted centuries earlier. However, if they could establish a lucrative role for themselves in arbitration, then absorption by the public courts was not as necessary for them as it had been for kings and royal judges centuries earlier.

[98]Percy Werner, "Voluntary Tribunals," *Missouri Bar Association Proceedings* 32 (1914), p. 146.

[99]Julius H. Cohen, "The Law of Commercial Arbitration and the New York Statute," *Yale Law Journal* 31 (December 1921): 147.

[100]Ibid., p. 148.

decisions.[101] Three committees of the Association combined with the Committee on Arbitration of the New York Chamber of Commerce to draft what became the Arbitration Law of the State of New York in 1920.[102] This statute made arbitration agreements binding and enforceable in New York courts.

The legal profession's interest in arbitration statutes was not homogeneous and universal. At least some Bar Association members preferred to discourage arbitration, while others probably hoped to benefit from involvement in it. For instance, while the New York statute (and some of the other statutes discussed below) recognizes clauses inserted into contracts providing that all disputes arising under the contracts will be settled by arbitration, many lawyers found this aspect of the statute to be very undesirable.[103] The 1919 meeting of the New York Bar Association involved a vigorous debate over this issue, with lawyers arguing that such clauses should be illegal because they required businessmen to sign away their right to a fair trial. The fear that arbitration clauses would significantly reduce legal business was explicitly stated by many Association members and "echoed throughout the arbitration debate."[104] But Charles Bernheimer, a spokesman for the Chamber of Commerce, addressed a conference of Bar Association delegates and reminded them of their profession's low public image. He suggested that a united effort by the Chamber and the Bar to reduce litigation and court crowding through arbitration could restore respect for the legal profession.[105] The price of Chamber support for the Bar Association's statute was clearly a willingness on the part of the Bar to compromise.[106] The members of the Bar naturally wanted Chamber

[101]Frances Kellor, *American Arbitration: Its History, Functions, and Achievements* (Port Washington, N.Y.: Kennikat Press, 1948), p. 10; and Robert MacCrate, "The Legal Community's Responsibilities for Dispute Resolution," *Arbitration Journal* 43 (September 1988): 15.

[102]Cohen, "The Law of Commercial Arbitration," p. 148.

[103]This is the key factor that the literature on arbitration statutes generally sites to distinguish the "modern" statutes from the pre-modern statutes (see note 4).

[104]Auerbach, *Justice Without Law?* pp. 105–6. Lawyers continued to be strongly opposed to general arbitration clauses into the 1960s (see note 106).

[105]Ibid., p. 106.

[106]But conflicts were far from over, as differences quickly came into focus after passage of the New York statute. As the Chamber and the Bar "struggled for control over commercial arbitration, the arbitration movement, dedicated to dispute settlement, suddenly found itself dispute-ridden" (ibid., p. 108). In particular, lawyers did not give up on the issue of arbitration clauses (also see the discussion of the formation of the American Arbitration Association below). In 1925, the Commission on Uniform State Laws, which functioned under the auspices of the American Bar Association, drafted a proposed uniform arbitration law, including a

support because they wanted to appear to be championing a beneficial alternative to the public courts (opposition, whether passive or active, by a group which might appear to represent the users of the alternative, may not have defeated their efforts but it would have been cause for doubting their sincerity, and the Chamber apparently was the only "business" group willing to support such legislation), and because they clearly had to work with at least some segments of the business community if they were to establish a dominant role for lawyers in the arbitration process.

The New York Bar Association was able to win the support of the Chamber of Commerce in the lobbying effort that the Association had initiated.[107] The Chamber even assisted in drafting the statute. Thus, this statute does not solely reflect Bar Association interests. Some writers view the support of the Chamber of Commerce as evidence that the primary demand for this statute came from "commercial interests using arbitration."[108] However, the Chamber clearly did not represent most business interests when it came to arbitration issues, as explained above, and there does not appear to be any evidence that other business organizations, such as trade associations and commercial exchanges, who were relying on their own arbitration arrangements, took an active part in the lobbying process regarding the arbitration statutes, probably in reflection of their recognition that the statutes were not needed as backing for their arbitration arrangements.

Arbitration Statutes Outside of New York

A substantial portion of the nation's commercial disputes occurred in New York in the 1920s, because it was the commercial center of the country. Very significant amounts of arbitration occurred elsewhere as well, however, so the American Bar Association "took the lead" in securing enactment of the Federal Arbitration Act of 1925, which was drafted by the Association.[109] As Willoughby states,

---

provision that arbitration laws should not cover future disputes arising under a contract: they should only apply to disputes as they arise. The American Bar Association adopted this position and endorsed the proposed legislation (Willoughby, *Principles of Judicial Administration*, p. 70). Some states adopted the proposed statute—see additional discussion on this matter below.

[107]Kellor, *American Arbitration*, p. 10.

[108]MacNeil, *American Arbitration Law*, p. 26; Auerbach, *Justice Without Law?*

[109]Willoughby, *Principles of Judicial Administration*, pp. 66 and 70; MacCrate, "The Legal Community's Responsibilities for Dispute Resolution," p. 15.

> The Association had this bill introduced in Congress, and, through the presentation of testimony and the submission of briefs and memoranda at hearings on the bill, it brought to bear the necessary pressure to secure favorable consideration.[110]

Lobbying support also came from the Arbitration Society of America (ASA), an organization created by some members of the American and New York Bar Associations (discussed below), and from the Chamber of Commerce of the United States. This law was patterned after the New York statutes, but applied to disputes arising in interstate commerce. Lobbying efforts instigated by Bar Associations, the ASA, and the Chamber also led to passage of similar laws in New Jersey (1923), Oregon (1925), and Massachusetts (1925).[111]

The American Arbitration Association (AAA), the successor to the lawyer-dominated ASA, also became an important participant in the political process. For instance, in 1927, both Pennsylvania and California adopted arbitration statutes which followed the "Draft State Arbitration Act" written and recommended by the AAA.[112] The Bar Associations and Chambers of Commerce were also instrumental lobbying forces for passage of these statutes.[113] Wyoming, North Carolina, and Nevada adopted arbitration statutes before the end of the 1920s as well, but they were not modern arbitration statutes: they were based on the Uniform Arbitration Act, which was recommended by the Commission on Uniform State Laws.[114] The Commission on Uniform

---

[110]Willoughby, *Principles of Judicial Administration*, p. 66.

[111]Ibid., pp. 65–66; MacNeil, *American Arbitration Law*, pp. 42–46.

[112]American Arbitration Association, *The Practice of Commercial Arbitration* (New York: Oxford University Press, 1928), pp. 117 and 182.

[113]Willoughby, *Principles of Judicial Administration*, p. 66.

[114]American Arbitration Association, *The Practice of Commercial Arbitration*, pp. 162, 173, and 203. Several hypotheses are suggested with regard to the passage of these statutes. For instance, given the argument that arbitration is a substitute for courts, it would be appropriate to ask about the impact of various components of the full price of using public courts. In particular, did arbitration develop first in the states with the greatest court congestion or with the greatest level of government interference with business, and did the resulting statutes vary in reflection of such factors? Unfortunately, data are simply not available to explore such questions. For example, while many state and local court systems publish annual reports during the period discussed here, including performance data, there are no standard counting methods to reflect court delays or backlogs. No systematic effort to compile such data even existed prior to the mid-1950s, and cross-state comparisons were still not appropriate because of the lack of standard reporting criteria (Thomas W. Church, Jr., Jo-Lynne Q. Lee, Teresa Tan, Alan Carlson, and Virginia McConnell, *Pre-trial Delay: A Review and Bibliography* [Williamsburg, Va.: National Center for State Courts, 1978], p. 7; and Wasby, et al., *Volume and Delay in State Appellate*

State Laws functioned under the auspices of the American Bar Association, however, which endorsed and promoted the proposed legislation.[115] Other states followed over the next several

---

Courts, p. 12). It is clear, however, that court delay was substantial before and during the 1920s in several of the states which passed arbitration statutes in that decade. For example, in the span of ten years, the Oregon Supreme Court's delay increased from seven months (just before 1920) to more than two years (Wasby, et al., *Volume and Delay in State Appellate Courts*, p. 39). Relative levels of state intrusion into business matters cannot be determined either.

The six states noted above which enacted modern arbitration statutes in the early to mid-1920s involve several of the nation's leading commercial and urban centers, including several international trade centers and ports. Thus, urbanization and levels of commercial activity may help explain the passage of the statutes. However, these states also include five of the ten with the largest numbers of lawyers in 1920: New York ranked first with 18,473 judges and lawyers, Pennsylvania was third with 6,784 [Illinois was second and the Illinois arbitration statute passed in 1873 actually was very similar to the statutes passed in these states in the 1920s (MacNeil, *American Arbitration Law*, pp. 17–18)], California was fourth with 6,745, Massachusetts was seventh with 4,954, and New Jersey was ninth with 3,918 (Department of Commerce, Bureau of the Census, *Fourteenth Census of the United States in the Year 1920*, vol. 4, *Population 1920, Occupations* [Washington, D.C.: Government Printing Office, 1923], Table 15). Of course, two of the three states with the smallest numbers of lawyers (Nevada was 47th with 230 lawyers and judges while Wyoming was 46th with 268) passed new statutes during the same period which appear to be relatively more preferred by many lawyers, but these two states actually have large numbers of lawyers per capita. Nevada had more lawyers per capita than any other state in 1920 with 3.594, followed by California with 2.349, Oregon with 2.228, and New York with 2.198; Wyoming was 11th with 1.775, ahead of states like Massachusetts (1.594) and Pennsylvania (1.002). Thus, the Bar Associations in these states might have been relatively powerful lobbying groups.

[115]Willoughby, *Principles of Judicial Administration*, p. 70. There were some relatively minor differences between these statutes (e.g., California, Nevada, New Jersey, North Carolina, and Wyoming required a party to apply to the court for enforcement of an award within three months, while Massachusetts, New York, and Pennsylvania allowed up to a year, and Oregon required that an exception be filed within twenty days or the award automatically had the force of the court behind it), but the major difference had to do with provisions recognizing the validity of agreements to arbitrate future disputes. Wyoming, Nevada, and North Carolina had no such provisions. Note that these were the three most-rural and least-commercial states in the group at the time. This suggests that a political counterweight, such as the one provided by the Chamber of Commerce in New York, that would lead the Bar to compromise and include provisions to recognize the validity of arbitration clauses in contracts, may not have been strong enough in these less-commercialized states. This possibility is reinforced by the fact that over time, as commercial activity spread through the country, most states' arbitration statutes included or were amended to add provisions for the recognition of agreements to arbitrate future disputes. The three states discussed above that had no such provisions ultimately adopted them, for instance, and by the end of the 1970s, only eleven states remained without such provisions: Alabama, Iowa, Kentucky, Mississippi, Missouri, Montana, Nebraska, North Dakota, Tennessee, Vermont, and West Virginia (David M. Cohen, "Sales Transactions," in *Arbitration: Commercial Disputes, Insurance, and Tort Claims*, Alan I. Widiss, ed. [New York: Practicing Law Institute,

decades. By 1965, 22 states had modern arbitration statutes modeled after the New York statute, the AAA Draft statute, or the Federal Statute—the states which contained the largest shares of commercial activity in the U.S. and where the greatest volume of litigation is conducted. Since then, arbitration statutes have gradually spread to virtually all of the other states.[116]

Impacts of Modern Arbitration Statutes

Shortly after the New York arbitration act's passage in 1920, Cohen observed that it

> establishes legal machinery for protecting, safeguarding and *supervising* commercial arbitration. Instead of narrowing the jurisdiction of the Supreme Court it broadens it. . . . Instead of being ousted of jurisdiction over arbitration, the courts are given jurisdiction over them, and . . . the party aggrieved has his ready recourse to the courts.[117]

Before passage of the statute, arbitrated commercial law in New York arising from general arbitration clauses took its authority from reciprocity and reputation incentives, including threats of ostracism. Upon passage, the state essentially asserted that it was the source of authority over such legal issues. Before the statute, New York courts had no mandated role in or jurisdiction over the legal issues that businessmen settled through arbitration clauses. After its passage, an enormous number of court cases were filed as businessmen tried to determine what characteristics of arbitration would be considered to be legal by the public courts.[118] Cases involved such issues as the appropriate way to select arbitrators, whether lawyers had to be present (indeed, many lawyers became active in arbitration because of these statutes, just as they had presumably intended when they advocated their passage), whether stenographic notes of the proceedings

---

1979], p. 18). Other explanations are obviously possible, of course. For example, several of the states discussed above that adopted such provisions early contained relatively important international trade businesses and important ports. Even lawyers who might object to arbitration clauses in contracts between domestic firms tend to consider them to be desirable in international contracts (Lazarus, et al., *Resolving Business Disputes*, p. 123), so both lawyers and businessmen might tend to be more familiar with and favorably disposed toward such clauses in important international trade centers, and such an appreciation may develop as international trade becomes important to a state. At any rate, relatively rural, relatively non-commercialized states resisted this movement for the longest time.

[116]Ibid., p. 126. Note that the Texas statute was passed in 1965, after publication of this reference.

[117]Cohen, "The Law of Commercial Arbitration," p. 150, emphasis added.

[118]See Sturges, *A Treatise on Commercial Arbitrations and Awards.*

should be taken, and so on. As similar statutes were passed in other states, arbitration litigation mounted. One case ultimately involved courts in two states, led to two appeals before a circuit court of appeals, produced five court opinions—three on jurisdictional issues—and took more than five years to resolve.[119] Businessmen, forced to pay attention to the prospect of judicial review, had to make their arbitration processes compatible with statute and precedent law, including public-court procedure. In order to do so, they had to consult and involve lawyers in the arbitration. A Harvard business law professor observing the period immediately following passage of the 1920s statutes, wrote

> There is irony in the fate of one who takes precautions to avoid litigation by submitting to arbitration, and who, as a reward for his pain, finds himself in court fighting not on the merits of his case but on the merits of arbitration. . . . [This] monumental tragicomedy . . . [demonstrates the success of the government legal process at] thwarting legitimate efforts to escape its tortuous procedure.[120]

Indeed, following the passage of the New York statute,

> a series of extremely narrow interpretive decisions, often referred to as the Draft Act rules, were handed down . . . which severely interpreted arbitrators' jurisdiction, as defined in specific [contract] clauses.[121]

It might be suggested that the wave of litigation following the passage of the earliest modern statutes was simply a response that often follows new legislation as individuals attempt to define the new legal margins. If this were true, however, the level of litigation should have diminished over time as precedent was established. But, as Ashe observes, the early 1980s were still witnessing a "growing number of court challenges to arbitration awards."[122] He also contends that this reflects the increasing use of lawyers in arbitration, suggesting that there is a stronger tendency for a losing attorney to circumvent the arbitrator's decision than there is for the losing party (when lawyers are not involved), who tends to have greater "allegiance to the

---

[119] Auerbach, *Justice Without Law?* p. 110.

[120] Nathan Isaacs, "Review of Wesley Sturges, *Treatise on Commercial Arbitration and Awards*," *Yale Law Journal* 40 (1930): 149–51.

[121] Lazarus, et al., *Resolving Business Disputes*, p. 119. It is interesting to note that litigation and the resulting limits on arbitration's jurisdiction under specific contract clauses actually "prompted adoption and promotion of the general clause."

[122] Bernard F. Ashe, "Arbitration Finality: Myth or Reality?" *Arbitration Journal* 38 (December 1983): 42.

system of arbitration itself."[123] In as much as such an attorney can influence a businessman's decisions, perhaps due to asymmetries in information about legal matters, appeal becomes more likely.

The possibility of appeal to the public courts implies that arbitrated commercial law became less decisive law than it had been. Indeed, Ashe maintains that the growing number of appeals is "threatening to undermine the finality of the process."[124] Parties in a dispute have weaker incentives to abide by arbitrated settlements when they are subject to potential appeal, and indeed, weaker incentives to use arbitration in the first place rather than public courts.[125] Thus, as Willoughby notes, even though an arbitration statute ostensibly establishes judicial backing for properly made arbitration awards, such statutes have not had that effect,

> because the awards were not deemed to be final but were subject to revision by the courts; and because inadequate provision was made for arbitrators securing from the courts rulings upon points of law.[126]

In addition to undermining the legal authority of private arbitration, some of the most attractive aspects of the arbitration alternative were substantially reduced as a direct result of the statutory legalization of the process: while procedure still remained quite simple relative to public courts, arbitration had to take on a more complex legalistic character. While still relatively expeditious, arbitration was less of a summary proceeding than it had been. While business practice and custom remained very important for arbitrated dispute resolution, concern for government-imposed laws became more significant. While litigation was still generally more expensive than arbitration, arbitration became costlier. Indeed, arbitration is less expensive than litigation *only* if

> parties do not take advantage of certain states' statutes allowing them to resort to court prior to arbitration or to demand review of the arbitrators' award through appeal.[127]

Thus, arbitration statutes undermine the expectation of low-cost dispute resolution by creating an expectation of a possible appeal particularly as growing numbers of appeals are observed.

[123]Ibid.

[124]Ibid.

[125]Charny, "Nonlegal Sanctions in Commercial Relationships," p. 427.

[126]Willoughby, *Principles of Judicial Administration*, p. 64.

[127]Lazarus, et al., *Resolving Business Disputes*, p. 106; Charny, "Nonlegal Sanctions in Commercial Relationships," p. 427.

One reason for and consequence of all of these changes, particularly outside the trade associations, is that arbitration was becoming less likely to be performed by and between businessmen, and more likely to be performed by and between lawyers. Business practice and custom were becoming relatively less important in such judgments because disputants who wished to avoid the public courts had to be relatively more concerned with the way those courts would react to the arbitration judgment; thus, they increasingly had to turn to lawyers with their expertise in common law and statute law, rather than to businessmen with expertise in commerce. For example, lawyer participation as counsel in arbitration conducted by the American Arbitration Association rose from 36 percent in 1927 to 70 percent in 1938, 84 percent in 1942, and 91 percent in 1947.[128]

Lawyers and the American Arbitration Association

The Arbitration Society of America (ASA) was formed in 1922 by a number of the leaders of the New York and National Bar Associations. The ASA's active leader, Moses H. Grossman, was a former municipal court judge. While he was very concerned about court delay, and eager to encourage cooperation between lawyers and businessmen, he considered dispute resolution without lawyer involvement to be "absolutely ridiculous."[129] The ASA actively began seeking arbitration statutes in other states, as mentioned above. Furthermore, ASA members sought a *single*, integrated, centralized, organized, structured, national system of arbitration with standardized rules and procedures.[130] They had hoped that this system would replace all the dispute-resolution arrangements which had been established by various independent business groups. On the other hand, most commercial interests wanted to have arbitration performed by decentralized trade associations and other business groups using relatively informal and flexible procedures; that is, they wanted to "continue commercial arbitration as it had come down through the ages."[131] Indeed, even the Chamber of Commerce saw the ASA's efforts as a potential threat to the Chamber's efforts to become a more important and influential source of arbitration. In order to support this more diversified "business" view of arbitration, several of its proponents formed the American Arbitration Foundation (AF)

---

[128]Auerbach, *Justice Without Law?* p. 111; Kellor, *American Arbitration*, p. 26.

[129]Auerbach, *Justice Without Law?* pp. 106–7.

[130]Kellor, *American Arbitration*, pp. 22–28.

[131]Ibid., p. 16.

in 1925 with Chamber spokesman Charles Bernheimer as president. They did so, in large part, to counter the ASA.

The AF and ASA recognized that neither would get its way if open political conflict persisted, so, fittingly, they agreed to arbitrate their own differences. After a year of negotiation, they reached a merger agreement, and the AAA was formed, a development that was applauded by the American Bar Association.[132] This is not surprising since, as Auerbach contends, "consolidation was an indisputable victory for the bench and the bar."[133] In support of Auerbach's contention, it is clearly the case that judges and lawyers have had a significant presence in the AAA both as members of the Board of Directors and of various committees. Furthermore, they joined the organization in strength, and have had a substantial influence over AAA policies and procedures.[134] Thus, the AAA "opened to lawyers a general practice that is lucrative to them,"[135] and a result was the increasing level of lawyer representation before AAA arbitration tribunals documented above. However, Auerbach may put too much emphasis on the success lawyers have had in influencing the AAA as evidence of what he believes has been a virtually complete "legalization" of commercial arbitration. There is no doubt that the AAA is an important source of commercial arbitration, but it is not the only source. In fact, a study conducted in the mid-1950s concluded that the AAA provided only 27 percent of all commercial arbitration.[136] It is not clear how accurate this estimate was, or how it relates to current conditions, but a substantial portion of commercial arbitration definitely does not involve the AAA. The trade associations and exchanges did not join this organization, and most now have their own arbitration procedures.

Trade association animosity toward lawyers has already been noted. Statistical information as to the extent of arbitration today by non-AAA affiliates is simply not available,[137] however, nor is information regarding the level of lawyer involvement in trade-association dispute resolution. Nonetheless, it appears

[132]MacCrate, "The Legal Community's Responsibilities for Dispute Resolution," p. 15.

[133]Auerbach, *Justice Without Law?* p. 108.

[134]Kellor, *American Arbitration*, p. 18.

[135]Ibid., p. 69.

[136]Mentschikoff, "Commercial Arbitration," p. 857.

[137]Landes and Posner, "Adjudication as a Private Good," p. 250. Nonetheless, it is clear that commercial arbitration continues to grow. See note 1 in this regard. The advantages of commercial arbitration are simply too significant relative to congested public courts.

that the trade associations still tend to rely more on business custom with relatively informal, flexible procedures less encumber-
ed by lawyers, although they too must pay attention to the prospect of judicial review (their ostracism threats may be quite effective at discouraging appeals, however, thus alleviating this
concern somewhat).

It is in the AAA, with no particular set of business practices
for a guide, that the goals which stimulated lawyers' demands
for arbitration statutes have been most completely achieved. In
fact, the AAA "openly encourages lawyer participation at all
steps of the arbitration procedure, from the drafting of arbitration clauses in contracts to the hearing itself,"[138] contending that
lawyers are essential to the process.[139] However, Soia Mentschikoff's seminal research on arbitration by the AAA casts a very
different light on the consequences of lawyer involvement with
arbitration than that projected by the AAA. Using AAA records
as well as personal observations, she concludes that

> in the great majority of cases . . . lawyer participation not on-
> ly failed to facilitate decision, but was so inadequate as to
> materially lengthen and complicate the presentation of the
> cases.[140]

Mentschikoff finds that lawyers did not understand the business
usages and practices that typically were relevant to business disputes. Likewise, lawyers tended to make the proceedings unduly
technical and to create unnecessary delays. Similarly, Lazarus,
et al. conclude, on the basis of an arbitrator questionnaire, that
lawyers tended to be less than adequately prepared to represent
clients in arbitration hearings, and that they were "reluctant to
abandon practices condoned and valued in the courtroom."[141] Furthermore, arbitration's "strongest points lie in those areas where
it most widely differs from courts," but arbitration proceedings by
the AAA have "been altered to accommodate lawyers" making
them more like court proceedings as a result.[142] Ashe similarly
argues that with more and more lawyers used in AAA arbitration,

> as arbitration becomes more like a court proceeding, the ben-
> efit to the participants for whom it was designed diminishes.

[138]Lazarus, et al., *Resolving Business Disputes*, p. 92.

[139]American Arbitration Association, *The Lawyer and Arbitration* (AAA Pamphlet,
1964), pp. 6–7.

[140]Mentschikoff, "Commercial Arbitration," p. 14.

[141]Lazarus, et al., *Resolving Business Disputes*, p. 95.

[142]Ibid., p. 102.

> Such a development is destructive of the process, not only be-
> cause of the increased time and cost that accompanies it, but
> because it encourages the process to be viewed by the courts
> as only one more step in the already lengthy litigation pro-
> cess.[143]

Thus, the strong resistance by trade associations to lawyers in arbitration may be very reasonable.

If Ashe, Mentschikoff, and Lazarus, et al. are correct,[144] one
might ask why the AAA gets any arbitration business at all? But
it must be recognized that everything is relative. There appears
to be some gain from specialization in arbitration, but there are
also significant transactions costs in setting up acceptable arbitration arrangements. The large trade associations have already
overcome the cost of organizing a natural reciprocal support arrangement, so it has been relatively easy for them to establish
their own specialized arbitration systems. Other businessmen,
who may not have ready access to such established procedures,
perhaps because the group they interact with is more diversified
and less organized than those industries with formal trade associations, can still attempt to avoid the slow and costly public
courts by using the arbitration specialists provided by the AAA
(e.g., by including arbitration clauses in contracts, or by agreeing
to arbitrate after the fact). Thus, the AAA has been able to attract a good deal of arbitration because it provides arbitration
specialists for individuals and groups who may not be able to establish their own arbitration system at comparable costs.[145]

In fact, it is inappropriate to speak of the "business community" as an aggregation with some common set of objectives. There
are many different business communities, some of which are
highly organized with formal arbitration tribunals, while others are organized much more informally, if at all. The differences
in benefits and transactions costs of organizing mean that some
businessmen are only bilaterally organized through contract, and
in those cases, the AAA's standard arbitration clause may be the
only substitute for the public courts that they are aware of. Thus,

[143]Ashe, "Arbitration Finality," p. 42.

[144]Also see Willoughby, *Principles of Judicial Administration*, p. 58; and Auerbach, *Justice Without Law?* p. 108.

[145]This does not mean that the AAA would be the low-cost provider for such dispute resolutions in the absence of arbitration statutes and the resulting need for
lawyers' expertise when a trade association's standardized practices and customs
are not available as a guide; an alternative, even less-costly forum with little or no
lawyer involvement might have developed in the absence of the statutes. Indeed,
alternatives appear to be developing as a private for-profit court industry is now
being established. See Benson, *The Enterprise of Law*.

the choice among existing alternatives involves relative prices (or relative transactions costs), and given a heterogeneous business community, it is not surprising to see a variety of alternatives arise in the face of relatively high-cost litigation. Indeed, many businessmen are never in a dispute that they cannot resolve through direct negotiation or exit (i.e., their low-cost solution may be to simply concede, absorb the costs, and get on with business), so they may not be familiar with the arbitration option.

A lack of knowledge regarding the institution of arbitration, as well as uncertainty about the process, may lead such people to a lawyer and to the relatively more-familiar public courts if an unsolvable dispute should arise. So the existence of heterogeneity in the business world suggests that some may find the public courts still to be the low-cost means of dispute resolution.[146]

However, as Charny explains, the existence of legal sanctions may stifle the development of trust relationships from which nonlegal sanctioning mechanisms often spring, because the honoring of any commitment may often be perceived to arise primarily because of the deterrent effect of legal sanctions.[147] The

---

[146]This provides a partial answer to the related question: if the business community can enforce its law through reciprocities and reputation effects without state backing, why is it not able to induce its members not to use lawyers and not to appeal to government courts through the same threat to reputation? Some business communities actually can. Others cannot, but there are no sanctions established by any legal authority which completely eliminate the sanctioned behavior, of course, so some businessmen choose to use lawyers or to appeal to the courts even when they know about arbitration. Indeed, they may do so by appealing an arbitration ruling. For instance, a businessman verging on bankruptcy may not be very concerned with long-run reputation effects, and such a businessman who expects to lose may use the public-court congestion and resulting delay to his advantage. Indeed, for such a businessman, the public courts may be a low-cost substitute for the relatively rapid arbitration alternative. This does not disprove the existence or effectiveness of reciprocity and reputation effects in most circumstances (a related issue is discussed in note 145). Individuals have the ability to commit murder, and some of them do so, despite the existence of strong legal sanctions. Similarly, arbitration statutes gave businessmen the ability to appeal an arbitration ruling despite significant threats to reputation. The fact that it happens does not mean that the relevant business community is ineffective at enforcing its own rules. In fact, it may be relatively effective, compared to the criminal justice system, for example: indeed, it is difficult to tell how many lawyers are used and what portion of arbitration rulings are appealed for the vast majority of arbitrated business disputes carried out within business groups rather than by the AAA. Lazarus, et al., *Resolving Business Disputes*, p. 92, surveyed 1,673 trade associations in the spring of 1965, for example, and asked if representation by counsel in arbitration was (1) forbidden, (2) permitted given notice of intent to the association, (3) permitted with no limitations, or (4) encouraged. All respondents indicated that legal representation was "not encouraged."

[147]Charny, "Nonlegal Sanctions in Commercial Relationships," p. 428.

point is that the incentives to develop nonlegal sanctions may be undermined by these statutes. Indeed, as Charny notes, the prospect of having courts intervene to enforce commitments that parties would prefer to have enforced by reputation sanctions may "chill" commitment-making. An expectation that the costs of legal enforcement may not be avoided can mean that some otherwise feasible commitments to arbitrate simply are not made at all.[148] Thus, it does not follow that in the absence of modern arbitration statutes, the level of arbitration would be dramatically less than it is today. Lawyers would be less prevalent, and there would be fewer appeals, but because stronger incentives would exist to develop mechanisms for the imposition of reputation sanctions, arbitration would still be flourishing, even outside existing associations and exchanges.

CONCLUSIONS

The question addressed here can be summarized very simply: is commercial arbitration a substitute for public-court litigation of business disputes, or are these two dispute-resolution forums complements? The widely held belief that arbitration clauses in contracts are effective, or that arbitration rulings are accepted, primarily *because* arbitration statutes force the public courts to enforce such contracts and rulings, suggests that the threat of litigation in the public courts is a necessary complement to arbitration. However, the assumptions upon which this belief is based are rejected above. First, it is demonstrated that many business communities can develop effective sanctions against someone who breaches a contract to arbitrate, or who refuses an arbitration settlement, so public-court backing is not necessary. Second, an exploration of the history of commercial arbitration in the United States illustrates that the so-called modern arbitration statutes, which command courts to recognize arbitration settlements and arbitration clauses in contracts, were not the major stimulus for the growth of commercial arbitration that they are often assumed to have been: arbitration was well established and growing rapidly long before the statutes were passed. Since the assumptions underlying the view that arbitration statutes were necessary in order to force judges to accept arbitration are rejected, the presumption that commercial groups demanded this state legislation is also questioned and rejected. An examination of the political demands for the enactment of the state and federal arbitration statutes reveals that their passage was largely due to

[148]Ibid.

the initiative of lobbying efforts by state and national Bar Associations.

None of this proves that public-court backing of arbitration settlements does not make arbitration more attractive (i.e., that supportive courts are not complements to arbitration), of course. Rather, it demonstrates that the arbitration statutes themselves probably had little impact, if any, in stimulating court support for arbitration. This is not a particularly startling conclusion by itself. Politically motivated statutes often are endogenous consequences of the same forces they are intended to address, rather than being exogenous factors that exert significant influences on those forces.[149] Theoretically, one good or service (e.g., arbitration) can be a gross substitute for a second good or service (e.g., public courts), while the second (courts) is a gross complement to the first (arbitration). As the full price of using courts has risen for businessmen (e.g., for instance, with regard to time cost arising from court delays), it does appear that arbitration is being substituted for court-based dispute resolution.

The question is this: does the increasing acceptance of arbitration by common-law judges imply a decrease or an increase in the full price of arbitration? If, as the traditional view contends, it represents a decrease because it provides a *significantly* stronger threatened sanction, then the increased level of appeals of arbitration rulings to common-law courts suggests that the courts are complements to arbitration. But if, as suggested above, acceptance of arbitration by judges has raised the full price of arbitration, in part by inducing an increased involvement of lawyers, then the increased level of appeals implies that the courts are not complements for arbitration, but rather, in these cases, courts

---

[149]Indeed, it might reasonably be suggested that the arbitration statutes did little more than codify emerging common law, an argument consistent with the increasingly supportive views that courts were adopting throughout the mid- to late-1800s. But perhaps more significantly, the fact that courts were increasingly supportive of arbitration *before* the statutes were enacted might imply that the emerging common-law support, rather than the statutes themselves, was the impetus for the emergence of arbitration, thereby resurrecting the contention that court backing is a necessary complement to arbitration. However, arbitration was in place and developing in the colonies and then the states even during the period of court hostility. In addition, international commercial arbitration is widely practiced without the uniform backing of national courts (Trakman, *The Law Merchant*; Berman and Dasser, "The New Law Merchant and the Old"; and Benson, "Customary Law as a Social Contract"), and the medieval law merchant, with its participatory courts of arbitration, clearly emerged without the support of national courts (Berman, *Law and Revolution*; Trakman, *The Law Merchant*; Benson, *The Enterprise of Law*; and idem, "The Spontaneous Evolution of Commercial Law").

are being substituted for arbitration.[150] If the courts are complements to arbitration, then a more benign public-interest story
about the motivation of lawyers who led the Bar Associations to
lobby for arbitration statutes might explain the historical process as well as or better than the special-interest story provided
here. If they are substitutes, then self-interest considerations explain arbitration statutes.

Consideration of the evidence and arguments provided here,
in conjunction with recent literature on the medieval Law Merchant[151] and on modern international arbitration,[152] suggests that
arbitration is more likely to be a substitute for litigation that can
and does develop without the complementary backing of the public courts. In fact, in the absence of public-court litigation before
judges who are reasonably responsive to business demands for fair
contract dispute resolution, arbitration would probably be relatively *more widespread* rather than less, since the incentives to
establish some form of third-party dispute resolution mechanism
could be even stronger.[153]

Furthermore, while this discussion focuses on the more tangible aspects of arbitrated commercial law (arbitration as a substitute for litigation), the use of arbitration also reflects the potential for greater reliance on customary law in commerce as opposed to statute, public court precedent, or administrative law.[154]
That is, arbitration is also a substitute for legislation.[155] Indeed,
the combination of contracts and arbitration allows businessmen
to effectively repeal state-made law, thereby seceding from certain aspects of state control without actually leaving. If a rule

[150]The fact that both arbitration and court appeals increased simultaneously does
not prove that they are complements, because the *ceteris paribus* assumption does
not hold. The full price of using both has been changing simultaneously.

[151]Berman, *Law and Revolution*; Trakman, *The Law Merchant*; Benson, *The Enterprise
of Law*; idem, "The Spontaneous Evolution of Commercial Law"; and Milgrom, et
al., "The Role of Institutions in the Revival of Trade."

[152]Berman and Dasser, "The New Law Merchant and the Old"; and Benson,
"Customary Law as a Social Contract."

[153]For instance, consider the merchant courts of the markets and fairs under the
medieval Law Merchant. See Berman, *Law and Revolution*; Trakman, *The Law Merchant*; Benson, *The Enterprise of Law*; idem, "The Spontaneous Evolution of Commercial Law"; see also Milgrom, et al., "The Role of Institutions in the Revival of
Trade."

[154]Since state-made law provides all lawyers with their legal frame of reference,
the use of arbitration to avoid such law provides yet another reason for lawyers to
want to either limit or gain control of arbitration.

[155]Benson, *The Enterprise of Law*; idem, "The Spontaneous Evolution of Commercial
Law"; idem, "Customary Law as a Social Contract"; and Wooldridge, *Uncle Sam, the
Monopoly Man*, p. 101.

made by a state inhibits potentially mutually beneficial interaction, businessmen can develop a contract clause which expressly rejects that rule in favor of some other mutually acceptable behavioral rule. Thus, they create their own law. Of course, if a dispute arises under such a contract, the state courts will enforce the state's law and label the clause illegal, so businessmen who have chosen to repeal the state's law through contract will also include an arbitration clause in the contract. An arbitrator looks to the contract in resolving a dispute.

Some people argue that the common law evolves in a fashion that produces efficient rules.[156] While the assumptions underlying these conclusions can be questioned, there may be some truth to the argument for commercial law. To the degree that businessmen can contract around inefficient court-made rules, and can use arbitration to avoid court enforcement of those rules, the business community can ignore inefficient common-law rules. Thus, the common-law rules for commercial contracts that are likely to become relevant for the business community are those that enhance efficiency. Furthermore, if the common-law courts want to attract business disputes, they have to contend with the fact that arbitration offers a very competitive substitute for their services. In order to compete with arbitration, the common-law courts will have to attempt to establish and enforce the same kinds of rules that arbitrators do. Competitive pressures could lead to adoption of efficient rules.

Unfortunately, the playing field is not a fair one. Because the state courts are backed by coercive powers, they can alter their law in ways that undermine the use of arbitration. For instance, courts can attempt to erect barriers to business efforts to encourage arbitration and apply ostracism threats, thereby raising the full price of arbitration, and creating incentives to seek alternatives such as public-court backing. Indeed, in *Paramount Lasky Corporation v United States*,[157] an explicit agreement to boycott, designed to back an arbitration system, was struck down. A group of motion-picture producers had agreed to place an arbitration clause in all contracts with motion picture exhibitors, *and to boycott any exhibitor who refused arbitration or refused to accept an arbitration ruling. This boycott agreement was held to be illegal despite the fact that there was no evidence that the purpose of the agreement was anything other than to make arbitration effective (e.g., it was not an attempt to police a cartel).

---

[156]Landes and Posner, "Adjudication as a Private Good."

[157]*Paramount Lasky Corporation v United States*, 282 U.S. 30 (1930).

What may appear to be a liberalization of the Paramount–Lasky ruling was rendered in the *Silver v New York Stock Exchange*.[158] Enforcement of stock-exchange rules by boycott was not held to be in violation of the antitrust laws, given that adequate procedural safeguards existed in the exchange's procedures. "Yet before *Silver* it was generally assumed that the antitrust laws had no application to the private self-government scheme of the regulated exchanges."[159] The courts were granted authority to supervise arbitration by statute. They clearly maintain the power to make rulings which could undercut an effort to supplant their authority, at least to a degree. How successful such an effort would be depends on the transactions costs of enforcing limits on nonlegal sanctions, and on the relative benefits of arbitration, given such efforts. Arbitration developed in the United States when courts were quite hostile, however, and given the high cost of using public courts today, even an outright ban on arbitration might not raise the price of arbitration enough to bring all business disputes into the courts.

A more significant threat to arbitration is an indirect one: limiting the scope of contracting. For instance, under the common law, product-liability issues were contract issues until 1916. Manufacturers owed a duty of care only to those who contracted directly with the manufacturer. If the courts made inefficiently large or small damage awards, the liability for potential harms arising from use of a product could be addressed in a contract. If some unanticipated harm arose, the resulting dispute could be arbitrated. However, in *MacPherson v Buick Motor Co.*,[160] this duty was expanded to include those who purchase from others in the distribution chain (e.g., retailers), so that the direct contractual linkages were no longer relevant. Then, in *Henningsen v Bloomfield Motors, Inc.*,[161] the New Jersey Supreme Court extended the manufacturer's duty beyond the purchasers of the product to include members of the purchaser's family and any other people who were likely to use or be exposed to the product, an extension that has been adopted by several other states as well. The result of these changes is that there is no longer any way to contract around inefficient court-made rulings regarding product liability. Since 1960, product-liability tort litigation has exploded, court-made rules have changed dramatically. As a result, there are

[158]*Silver v New York Stock Exchange*, 373 U.S. 341 (1963).

[159]Landes and Posner, "Adjudication as a Private Good," p. 257.

[160]*MacPherson v Buick Motor Co.*, 217 N.Y. 382, 111 N.E. 1050 (1916).

[161]*Henningsen v Bloomfield Motors, Inc.*, 32 N.J. 358, 161 A.2d 69 (1960).

entire domestic industries threatened with extinction. The results clearly cannot be described as enhancing efficiency.

Therefore, while contracting and arbitration can provide an
avenue for partial secession as businessmen escape the laws imposed by the state's legal apparatus, the state's coercive powers
also suggest that this partial escape route may be precarious. If
they want to escape the inefficiencies of government law, businessmen may ultimately actually have to leave .

APPENDIX A:
THE DECLARATION OF INDEPENDENCE

IN CONGRESS, JULY 4, 1776

THE UNANIMOUS DECLARATION OF
THE THIRTEEN UNITED STATES OF AMERICA

When in the Course of human events, it becomes necessary for one people to dissolve the political bands which have connected them with another, and to assume among the powers of the earth, the separate and equal station to which the Laws of Nature and of Nature's God entitle them, a decent respect to the opinions of mankind requires that they should declare the causes which impel them to the separation.

— We hold these truths to be self-evident, that all men are created equal, that they are endowed by their Creator with certain unalienable Rights, that among these are Life, Liberty and the pursuit of Happiness.

— That to secure these rights, Governments are instituted among Men, deriving their just powers from the consent of the governed.

— That whenever any Form of Government becomes destructive of these ends, it is the Right of the People to alter or to abolish it, and to institute new Government, laying its foundation on such principles and organizing its powers in such form, as to them shall seem most likely to effect their Safety and Happiness. Prudence, indeed, will dictate that Governments long established should not be changed for light and transient causes; and accordingly all experience hath shewn, that mankind are more disposed to suffer, while evils are sufferable, than to right themselves by abolishing the forms to which they are accustomed. But when a long train of abuses and usurpations, pursuing invariably the same Object evinces a design to reduce them under absolute Despotism, it is their right, it is their duty, to throw off such Government, and to provide new Guards for their future security.

— Such has been the patient sufferance of these Colonies; and such is now the necessity which constrains them to alter their former Systems of Government. The history of the present King of Great Britain is a history of repeated injuries and usurpations, all having in direct object the establishment of an absolute Tyranny over these States. To prove this, let Facts be submitted to a candid world.

— He has refused his Assent to Laws, the most wholesome and necessary for the public good.

— He has forbidden his Governors to pass Laws of immediate and pressing importance, unless suspended in their operation till his Assent should be obtained; and when so suspended, he has utterly neglected to attend to them.

— He has refused to pass other Laws for the accommodation of large districts of people, unless those people would relinquish the right of Representation in the Legislature, a right inestimable to them and formidable to tyrants only.

— He has called together legislative bodies at places unusual, uncomfortable, and distant from the depository of their public Records, for the sole purpose of fatiguing them into compliance with his measures.

— He has dissolved Representative Houses repeatedly, for opposing with manly firmness his invasions on the rights of the people.

— He has refused for a long time, after such dissolutions, to cause others to be elected; whereby the Legislative powers, incapable of Annihilation, have returned to the People at large for their exercise; the State remaining in the mean time exposed to all the dangers of invasion from without, and convulsions within.

— He has endeavoured to prevent the population of these States; for that purpose obstructing the Laws for Naturalization of Foreigners; refusing to pass others to encourage their migrations hither, and raising the conditions of new Appropriations of Lands.

— He has obstructed the Administration of Justice, by refusing his Assent to Laws for establishing Judiciary powers.

— He has made Judges dependent on his Will alone, for the tenure of their offices, and the amount and payment of their salaries.

— He has erected a multitude of New Offices, and sent hither swarms of Officers to harrass our people, and eat out their substance.

— He has kept among us, in times of peace, Standing Armies without the Consent of our legislatures.

— He has affected to render the Military independent of and superior to the Civil power.

— He has combined with others to subject us to a jurisdiction foreign to our constitution, and unacknowledged by our laws; giving his Assent to their Acts of pretended Legislation:

— For quartering large bodies of armed troops among us;

— For protecting them, by a mock Trial, from punishment for any Murders which they should commit on the Inhabitants of these States;

— For cutting off our Trade with all parts of the world;

— For imposing Taxes on us without our Consent;

— For depriving us in many cases, of the benefits of Trial by Jury;

— For transporting us beyond Seas to be tried for pretended offences;

— For abolishing the free System of English Laws in a neighbouring Province, establishing therein an Arbitrary government, and enlarging its Boundaries so as to render it at once an example and fit instrument for introducing the same absolute rule into these Colonies;

— For taking away our Charters, abolishing our most valuable Laws, and altering fundamentally the Forms of our Governments;

— For suspending our own Legislatures, and declaring themselves invested with power to legislate for us in all cases whatsoever.

— He has abdicated Government here, by declaring us out of his Protection and waging War against us.

— He has plundered our seas, ravaged our Coasts, burnt our towns, and destroyed the lives of our people.

— He is at this time transporting large Armies of foreign Mercenaries to compleat the works of death, desolation and tyranny, already begun with circumstances of Cruelty & perfidy scarcely paralleled in the most barbarous ages, and totally unworthy the Head of a civilized nation.

— He has constrained our fellow Citizens taken Captive on the high Seas to bear Arms against their Country, to become the executioners of their friends and Brethren, or to fall themselves by their Hands.

— He has excited domestic insurrections amongst us, and has endeavoured to bring on the inhabitants of our frontiers, the merciless Indian Savages, whose known rule of warfare, is an undistinguished destruction of all ages, sexes and conditions.

— In every stage of these Oppressions We have Petitioned for Redress in the most humble terms: Our repeated Petitions have been answered only by repeated injury. A Prince, whose character is thus marked by every act which may define a Tyrant, is unfit to be the ruler of a free people.

— Nor have We been wanting in attentions to our British brethren. We have warned them from time to time of attempts by their legislature to extend an unwarrantable jurisdiction over us. We have reminded them of the circumstances of our emigration and settlement here. We have appealed to their native justice and magnanimity, and we have conjured them by the ties of our common kindred to disavow these usurpations, which, would inevitably interrupt our connections and correspondence. They too have been deaf to the voice of justice and of consanguinity. We must, therefore, acquiesce in the necessity, which denounces our Separation, and hold them, as we hold the rest of mankind, Enemies in War, in Peace Friends.

— We, therefore, the Representatives of the United States of America, in General Congress, Assembled, appealing to the Supreme Judge of the world for the rectitude of our intentions, do, in the Name, and by Authority of the good People of these Colonies, solemnly publish and declare, That these United Colonies are, and of Right ought to be Free and Independent States; that they are Absolved from all Allegiance to the British Crown, and that all political connection between them and the State of Great Britain, is and ought to be totally dissolved; and that as Free and Independent States, they have full Power to levy War, conclude Peace, contract Alliances, establish Commerce, and to do all other Acts and Things which Independent States may of right do.

— And for the support of this Declaration, with a firm reliance on the protection of divine Providence, we mutually pledge to each other our Lives, our Fortunes, and our sacred Honor.

JOHN HANCOCK[1]

---

[1]Also signed by: Button Gwinnett, Lyman Hall, Geo. Walton, Wm. Hooper, Joseph Hewes, John Penn, Edward Rutledge, Thos. Heyward, Jr., Thomas Lynch, Jr., Arthur Middleton, Samuel Chase, Wm. Paca, Thos. Stone, Charles Carroll of Carrollton, George Wyethe, Richard Henry Lee, Thos. Jefferson, Benj. Harrison, Thos. Nelson, Jr., Francis Lightfoot Lee, Carter Braxton, Robt. Morris, Benjamin Rush, Benjamin Franklin, John Morton, Geo. Clymer, Jas. Smith, Geo. Taylor, James Wilson, Geo. Ross, Caesar Rodney, Geo. Reed, Thos. M. Kean, Wm. Floyd, Phil. Livingston, Francis Lewis, Lewis Morris, Richard Stockton, John Witherspoon, Francis Hopkinson, Jonh Hart, Abra Clark, Josiah Bartlett, Wm. Whipple, Samuel Adams, John Adams, Robt. Treat Payne, Elbridge Gerry, Stephen Hopkins, William Ellery, Roger Sherman, Samuel Huntington, Wm. Williams, Oliver Wolcott, Matthew Thornton.

APPENDIX B:
THE ARTICLES OF CONFEDERATION
AND PERPETUAL UNION

BETWEEN THE STATES OF NEW HAMPSHIRE, MASSACHUSETTS BAY, RHODE ISLAND AND PROVIDENCE PLANTATIONS, CONNECTICUT, NEW YORK, NEW JERSEY, PENNSYLVANIA, DELAWARE, MARYLAND, VIRGINIA, NORTH CAROLINA, SOUTH CAROLINA, GEORGIA

ARTICLE 1. The style of this confederacy shall be "The United States of America."

ART. 2. Each State retains its sovereignty, freedom and independence, and every power, jurisdiction, and right, which is not by this confederation expressly delegated to the United States, in Congress assembled.

ART. 3. The said states hereby severally enter into a firm league of friendship with each other for their common defence, the security of their liberties and their mutual and general welfare; binding themselves to assist each other against all force offered to, or attacks made upon them, or any of them, on account of religion, sovereignty, trade, or any other pretence whatever.

ART. 4. The better to secure and perpetuate mutual friendship and intercourse among the people of the different states in this union, the free inhabitants of each of these states, paupers, vagabonds, and fugitives from justice excepted, shall be entitled to all privileges and immunities of free citizens in the several states; and the people of each State shall have free ingress and regress to and from any other State, and shall enjoy therein all the privileges of trade and commerce, subject to the same duties, impositions, and restrictions, as the inhabitants thereof respectively; provided, that such restrictions shall not extend so far as to prevent the removal of property, imported into any State, to any other State of which the owner is an inhabitant; provided also, that no imposition, duties, or restriction, shall be laid by any State on the property of the United States, or either of them.

If any person guilty of, or charged with treason, felony, or other high misdemeanor in any State, shall flee from justice and be found in any of the United States, he shall, upon demand of the governor or executive power of the State from which he fled, be delivered up and removed to the State having jurisdiction of his offence.

Full faith and credit shall be given in each of these states to the records, acts, and judicial proceedings of the courts and magistrates of every other State.

ART. 5. For the more convenient management of the general interests of the United States, delegates shall be annually appointed, in such manner as the legislature of each State shall direct, to meet in Congress, on the 1st Monday in November in every year, with a power reserved to each State to recall its delegates, or any of them, at any time within the year, and to send others in their stead for the remainder of the year.

No State shall be represented in Congress by less than two, nor by more than seven members; and no person shall be capable of being a delegate for more than three years in any term of six years; nor shall any person, being a delegate, be capable of holding any office under the United States, for which he, or any other for his benefit, receives any salary, fees, or emolument of any kind.

Each State shall maintain its own delegates in a meeting of the states, and while they act as members of the committee of the states.

In determining questions in the United States, in Congress assembled, each State shall have one vote.

Freedom of speech and debate in Congress shall not be impeached or questioned in any court or place out of Congress: and the members of Congress shall be protected in their persons from arrests and imprisonments, during the time of their going to and from, and attendance on Congress, except for treason, felony, or breach of the peace.

ART. 6. No State, without the consent of the United States, in Congress assembled, shall send any embassy to, or receive any embassy from, or enter into any conference, agreement, alliance, or treaty with any king, prince, or state, nor shall any person, holding any office of profit or trust under the United States, or any of them, accept of any present, emolument, office or title, of any kind whatever, from any king, prince, or foreign state; nor shall the United States, in Congress assembled, or any of them, grant any title of nobility.

No two or more states shall enter into any treaty, confederation, or alliance, whatever, between them, without the consent of the United States, in Congress assembled, specifying accurately the purposes for which the same is to be entered into, and how long it shall continue.

No state shall lay any imposts or duties which may interfere with any stipulations in treaties entered into by the United States, in Congress assembled, with any king, prince, or state, in pursuance of any treaties already proposed by Congress to the courts of France and Spain.

No vessels of war shall be kept up in time of peace by any State, except such number only as shall be deemed necessary by the United States, in Congress assembled, for the defence of such State or its trade; nor shall any body of forces be kept up by any State, in time of peace, except such number only as, in the judgment of the United States, in Congress assembled, shall be deemed requisite to garrison the forts necessary for the defence of such State; but every State shall always keep up a well regulated and disciplined militia, sufficiently armed and accoutred, and shall provide, and consistently have ready for use, in public stores, a due number of field pieces and tents, and a proper quantity of arms, ammunition and camp equipage.

No State shall engage in any war without the consent of the United States, in Congress assembled, unless such State be actually invaded by enemies, or shall have received certain advice of a resolution being formed by some nation of Indians to invade such State, and the danger is so imminent as not to admit of a delay till the United States, in Congress assembled, can be consulted; nor shall any State grant commissions to any ships or vessels of war, nor letters or marque or reprisal, except it be after a declaration of war by the United States in Congress assembled, and then only against the kingdom or state, and the subjects thereof, against which war has been so declared, and under such regulations as shall be established by the United States, in Congress assembled, unless such State be infested by pirates, in which case vessels of war may be fitted out for that occasion, and kept so long as the danger shall continue, or until the United States, in Congress assembled, shall determine otherwise.

ART. 7. When land forces are raised by any State for the common defence, all officers of or under the rank of colonel, shall be appointed by the legislature of each State respectively, by whom such forces shall be raised, or in such manner as such State shall direct; and all vacancies shall be filled up by the State which first made the appointment.

ART. 8. All charges of war and all other expences, that shall be incurred for the common defence or general welfare, and allowed by the United States, in Congress assembled, shall be defrayed out of a common treasury, which shall be supplied by the several states, in proportion to the value of all land within each State, granted to or surveyed for any person, as such land and the buildings and improvements thereon shall be estimated according to such mode as the United States, in Congress assembled, shall, from time to time, direct and appoint.

The taxes for paying that proportion shall be laid and levied by the authority and direction of the legislatures of the several states, within the time agreed upon by the United States, in Congress Assembled.

ART. 9. The United States, in Congress assembled, shall have the sole and exclusive right and power of determining on peace and war, except in the cases mentioned in the 6th article; of sending and receiving ambassadors; entering into treaties and alliances, provided that no treaty of commerce shall be made, whereby the legislative power of the respective states shall be restrained from imposing such imposts and duties on foreigners as their own people are subjected to, or from prohibiting the exportation or importation of any species of goods or commodities whatsoever; of establishing rules for deciding, in all cases, what captures on land or water shall be legal, and in what manner prizes, taken by the land of naval forces in the service of the United States, shall be divided or appropriated; of granting letters of marque and reprisal in times of peace; appointing courts for the trial of piracies and felonies committed on the high seas, and establishing courts for receiving and determining, finally, appeals in all cases of captures; provided that no members of Congress shall be appointed a judge of any of the said courts.

The United States, in Congress assembled, shall also be the last resort on appeal in all disputes and differences now subsisting, or that hereafter may arise between two or more states concerning boundary, jurisdiction or any other cause whatever; which authority shall always be exercised in the manner following: whenever the legislative or executive authority, or lawful agent of any State, in controversy with another, shall present a petition to Congress, stating the matter in question, and praying for a hearing, notice thereof shall be given, by order of Congress, to the legislative or executive authority of the other State in controversy, and a day assigned for the appearance of the parties by their lawful agents, who shall then be directed to appoint, by joint consent, commissioners or judges to constitute a court for hearing and determining the matter in question; but, if they cannot agree, Congress shall name three persons out of each of the United States, and from the list of such persons each party shall alternatively strike out one, the petitioners beginning, until the number shall be reduced to thirteen; and from that number not less than seven, nor more than nine names, as Congress shall direct, shall, in the presence of Congress, be drawn out by lot; and the persons whose names shall be so drawn, or any five of them, shall be commissioners or judges to hear and finally determine the controversy, so always as a major part of the judges who shall hear the cause shall agree in the determination; and if either party shall neglect to attend at the day appointing, without shewing reasons which Congress shall judge sufficient, or, being present, shall refuse to strike, the Congress shall proceed to nominate three persons out of each State, and the secretary of Congress shall strike in behalf of such party absent or refusing; and the judgment and sentence of the court to be appointed, in the manner before prescribed, shall be final and conclusive; and if any of the parties shall refuse to submit to the authority of such court, or to appear or defend their claim or cause, the court shall nevertheless proceed to pronounce sentence or judgment, which shall, in like manner, be final and decisive, the judgment or sentence and other proceedings being, in either case, transmitted to Congress, and lodged among the acts of Congress for the security of the parties concerned: provided, that every commissioner, before he sits in judgment, shall take an oath, to be administered by one of the judges of the supreme or superior court of the State where the cause shall be tried, "well and truly to hear and determine the matter in question, according to the best of his judgment, without favour, affection, or hope of reward:" provided, also, that no State shall be deprived of territory for the benefit of the United States.

All controversies concerning the private right of soil, claimed under different grants of two or more states, whose jurisdictions, as they may respect such lands and the states which passed such grants, are adjusted, the said grants, or either of them, being at the same time claimed to have originated antecedent to such settlement of jurisdiction, shall, on the petition of either party to the Congress of the United States, be finally determined, as near as may be, in the same manner as is before prescribed for deciding disputes respecting territorial jurisdiction between different states.

The United States, in Congress assembled, shall also have the sole and exclusive right and power of regulating the alloy and value of coin struck by their own authority, or by that of the respective states; fixing the standard of weights and measures through the United States; regulating the trade and managing all affairs with the Indians not members of any of the states; provided that the legislative right of any State within its own limits be not infringed or violated; establishing and regulating post offices from one State to another throughout all the United States, and exacting such postage on the papers passing through the same as may be requisite to defray the expences of the said office; appointing all officers of the land forces in the service of the United States, excepting regimental officers; appointing all the officers of the naval forces, and commissioning all officers whatever in the service of the United States, making rules for the government and regulation of the said land and naval forces, and directing their operations.

The United States, in Congress assembled, shall have authority to appoint a committee to sit in the recess of Congress, to be denominated "a Committee of the States," and to consist of one delegate from each State, and to appoint such other committees and civil officers as may be necessary for managing the general affairs of the United States, under their direction; to appoint one of their number to preside; provided that no person be allowed to serve in the office of president more than one year in any term of three years; to ascertain the necessary sums of money to be raised for the service of the United States, and to appropriate and apply the same for defraying the public expences; to borrow money or emit bills on the credit of the United States, transmitting, every half year, to the respective states, an account of the sums of money so borrowed or emitted; to build and equip a navy; to agree upon the number of land forces, and to make requisitions from each State for its quota, in proportion to the number of white inhabitants in such State; which requisitions shall be binding; and, thereupon, in the legislature of each State shall appoint the regimental officers, raise the men, and cloathe, arm, and equip them in a soldier-like manner, at the expence of the United States; and the officers and men so cloathed, armed, and equipped, shall march to the place appointed and within the time agreed on by the United States, in Congress Assembled; but if the United States, in Congress assembled, shall, on consideration of circumstance, judge properly that any State should not raise men, or should raise a smaller number than its quota, and that any other State should raise a greater number of men than the quota thereof, such extra number shall be raised, officered, cloathed, armed, and equipped in the same manner as the quota of such State, unless the legislature of such State shall judge that such extra number cannot be safely spared out of the same, in which case they shall raise, officer, cloathe, arm, and equip as many of such extra number as they judge can be safely spared. And the officers and men so cloathed, armed, and equipped, shall march to the place appointed and within the time agreed on by the United States, in Congress assembled.

The United States, in Congress assembled, shall never engage in a war, nor grant letters of marque and reprisal in time of peace, nor enter into any treaties or alliances, nor coin money, nor regulate the value thereof, nor ascertain the sums and expences necessary for the defence and welfare of the United States, or any of them: nor emit bills, nor borrow money on the credit of the United States, nor appropriate money, nor agree upon the number of vessels of war to be built or purchased, or the number of land or sea forces to be raised, nor appoint a commander in chief of the army or navy, unless nine states assent to the same; nor shall a question on any other point, except for adjourning from day to day, be determined, unless by the votes of a majority of the United States, in Congress assembled.

The Congress of the United States shall have power to adjourn to any time within the year, and to any place within the United States, so that no period of adjournment be for a longer duration than the space of six months, and shall publish the journal of their proceedings monthly, except such parts thereof, relating to treaties, alliances or military operations, as, in their judgment, require secrecy; and the yeas and nays of the delegates of each State on any question shall be entered on the journal, when it is desired by any delegate; and the delegates of a State, or any of them, at his, or their request, shall be furnished with a transcript of the said journal, except such parts as are above excepted, to lay before the legislatures of the several states.

ART. 10. The committee of the states, or any nine of them, shall be authorized to execute, in the recess of Congress, such of the powers of Congress as the United States, in Congress assembled, by the consent of nine states, shall, from time to time, think expedient to vest them with; provided, that no power be delegated to the said committee, for the exercise of which, by the articles of confederation, the voice of nine states, in the Congress of the United States assembled, is requisite.

ART. 11. Canada acceding to this confederation, and joining in the measures of the United States, shall be admitted into and entitled to all the advantages of this union; but no other colony shall be admitted into the same, unless such admission be agreed to by nine states.

ART. 12. All bills of credit emitted, monies borrowed and debts contracted by, or under the authority of Congress before the assembling of the United States, in pursuance of the present confederation, shall be deemed and considered as a charge against the United States, for payment and satisfaction whereof the said United States and the public faith are hereby solemnly pledged.

ART. 13. Every State shall abide by the determinations of the United States, in Congress assembled, on all questions which, by this confederation, are submitted to them, and the articles of this confederation shall be inviolably observed by every State, and the union shall be perpetual; nor shall any alteration at any time hereafter be made in any of them, unless such alteration be agreed to in a Congress of the United States, and be afterwards confirmed by the legislatures of every State.

These articles shall be proposed to the legislatures of all the United States, to be considered, and if approved of by them, they are advised to authorize their delegates to ratify the same in the Congress of the United States; which being done, the same shall become conclusive.

APPENDIX C:
THE CONSTITUTION OF THE UNITED STATES

WE THE PEOPLE of the United States, in Order to form a more perfect Union, establish Justice, insure domestic Tranquility, provide for the common defence, promote the general Welfare, and secure the Blessings of Liberty to ourselves and our Posterity, do ordain and establish this Constitution for the United States of America.

ARTICLE I

Section 1. All legislative Powers herein granted shall be vested in a Congress of the United States, which shall consist of a Senate and House of Representatives.

Section 2. The House of Representatives shall be composed of Members chosen every second Year by the People of the several States, and the Electors in each State shall have the Qualifications requisite for Electors of the most numerous Branch of the State Legislature. No Person shall be a Representative who shall not have attained to the Age of twenty five Years, and been seven Years a Citizen of the United States, and who shall not, when elected, be an Inhabitant of that State in which he shall be chosen. Representatives and direct Taxes shall be apportioned among the several States which may be included within this Union, according to their respective Numbers, which shall be determined by adding to the whole Number of free Persons, including those bound to Service for a Term of Years, and excluding Indians not taxed, three fifths of all other Persons. The actual Enumeration shall be made within three Years after the first Meeting of the Congress of the United States, and within every subsequent Term of ten Years, in such Manner as they shall by Law direct. The Number of Representatives shall not exceed one for every thirty Thousand, but each State shall have at Least one Representative; and until such enumeration shall be made, the State of New Hampshire shall be entitled to choose three, Massachusetts eight, Rhode Island and Providence Plantations one, Connecticut five, New York six, New Jersey four, Pennsylvania eight, Delaware one, Maryland six, Virginia ten, North Carolina five, South Carolina five and Georgia three. When vacancies happen in the Representation from any State, the Executive Authority thereof shall issue Writs of Election to fill such Vacancies. The House of Representatives shall choose their Speaker and other Officers; and shall have the sole Power of Impeachment.

Section 3. The Senate of the United States shall be composed of two Senators from each State, chosen by the Legislature thereof, for six Years; and each Senator shall have one Vote. Immediately after they shall be assembled in Consequence of the first Election, they shall be divided as equally as may be into three Classes. The Seats of the Senators of the first

Class shall be vacated at the Expiration of the second Year, of the second Class at the Expiration of the fourth Year, and of the third Class at the Expiration of the sixth Year, so that one third may be chosen every second Year; and if Vacancies happen by Resignation, or otherwise, during the Recess of the Legislature of any State, the Executive thereof may make temporary Appointments until the next Meeting of the Legislature, which shall then fill such Vacancies. No Person shall be a Senator who shall not have attained to the Age of thirty Years, and been nine Years a Citizen of the United States, and who shall not, when elected, be an Inhabitant of that State for which he shall be chosen. The Vice-President of the United States shall be President of the Senate, but shall have no Vote, unless they be equally divided. The Senate shall choose their other Officers, and also a President pro tempore, in the Absence of the Vice-President, or when he shall exercise the Office of President of the United States. The Senate shall have the sole Power to try all Impeachments. When sitting for that Purpose, they shall be on Oath or Affirmation. When the President of the United States is tried, the Chief Justice shall preside: And no Person shall be convicted without the Concurrence of two thirds of the Members present. Judgment in Cases of Impeachment shall not extend further than to removal from Office, and disqualification to hold and enjoy any Office of honor, Trust or Profit under the United States: but the Party convicted shall nevertheless be liable and subject to Indictment, Trial, Judgment and Punishment, according to Law.

Section 4. The Times, Places and Manner of holding Elections for Senators and Representatives, shall be prescribed in each State by the Legislature thereof; but the Congress may at any time by Law make or alter such Regulations, except as to the Places of choosing Senators. The Congress shall assemble at least once in every Year, and such Meeting shall be on the first Monday in December, unless they shall by Law appoint a different Day.

Section 5. Each House shall be the Judge of the Elections, Returns and Qualifications of its own Members, and a Majority of each shall constitute a Quorum to do Business; but a smaller Number may adjourn from day to day, and may be authorized to compel the Attendance of absent Members, in such Manner, and under such Penalties as each House may provide. Each House may determine the Rules of its Proceedings, punish its Members for disorderly Behavior, and, with the Concurrence of two-thirds, expel a Member. Each House shall keep a Journal of its Proceedings, and from time to time publish the same, excepting such Parts as may in their Judgment require Secrecy; and the Yeas and Nays of the Members of either House on any question shall, at the Desire of one fifth of those Present, be entered on the Journal. Neither House, during the Session of Congress, shall, without the Consent of the other, adjourn for more than three days, nor to any other Place than that in which the two Houses shall be sitting.

Section 6. The Senators and Representatives shall receive a Compensation for their Services, to be ascertained by Law, and paid out of the Treasury of the United States. They shall in all Cases, except Treason,

Felony and Breach of the Peace, be privileged from Arrest during their Attendance at the Session of their respective Houses, and in going to and returning from the same; and for any Speech or Debate in either House, they shall not be questioned in any other Place. No Senator or Representative shall, during the Time for which he was elected, be appointed to any civil Office under the Authority of the United States, which shall have been created, or the Emoluments whereof shall have been increased during such time; and no Person holding any Office under the United States, shall be a Member of either House during his Continuance in Office.

Section 7. All Bills for raising Revenue shall originate in the House of Representatives; but the Senate may propose or concur with Amendments as on other Bills. Every Bill which shall have passed the House of Representatives and the Senate, shall, before it become a Law, be presented to the President of the United States; If he approve he shall sign it, but if not he shall return it, with his Objections to that House in which it shall have originated, who shall enter the Objections at large on their Journal, and proceed to reconsider it. If after such Reconsideration two thirds of that House shall agree to pass the Bill, it shall be sent, together with the Objections, to the other House, by which it shall likewise be reconsidered, and if approved by two thirds of that House, it shall become a Law. But in all such Cases the Votes of both Houses shall be determined by yeas and Nays, and the Names of the Persons voting for and against the Bill shall be entered on the Journal of each House respectively. If any Bill shall not be returned by the President within ten Days (Sundays excepted) after it shall have been presented to him, the Same shall be a Law, in like Manner as if he had signed it, unless the Congress by their Adjournment prevent its Return, in which Case it shall not be a Law. Every Order, Resolution, or Vote to which the Concurrence of the Senate and House of Representatives may be necessary (except on a question of Adjournment) shall be presented to the President of the United States; and before the Same shall take Effect, shall be approved by him, or being disapproved by him, shall be repassed by two thirds of the Senate and House of Representatives, according to the Rules and Limitations prescribed in the Case of a Bill.

Section 8. The Congress shall have Power to lay and collect Taxes, Duties, Imposts and Excises, to pay the Debts and provide for the common Defence and general Welfare of the United States; but all Duties, Imposts and Excises shall be uniform throughout the United States; To borrow Money on the credit of the United States; To regulate Commerce with foreign Nations, and among the several States, and with the Indian Tribes; To establish a uniform Rule of Naturalization, and uniform Laws on the subject of Bankruptcies throughout the United States; To coin Money, regulate the Value thereof, and of foreign Coin, and fix the Standard of Weights and Measures; To provide for the Punishment of counterfeiting the Securities and current Coin of the United States; To establish Post Offices and Post Roads; To promote the Progress of Science and useful Arts, by securing for limited Times to Authors and Inventors the exclusive Right to their respective Writings and Discoveries; To constitute Tribunals inferior to the Supreme Court; To define and punish Piracies and Felonies committed on the

high Seas, and Offences against the Law of Nations; To declare War, grant
Letters of Marque and Reprisal, and make Rules concerning Captures on
Land and Water; To raise and support Armies, but no Appropriation of
Money to that Use shall be for a longer Term than two Years; To provide
and maintain a Navy; To make Rules for the Government and Regulation of
the land and naval Forces; To provide for calling forth the Militia to execute the Laws of the Union, suppress Insurrections and repel Invasions; To
provide for organizing, arming, and disciplining, the Militia, and for governing such Part of them as may be employed in the Service of the United
States, reserving to the States respectively, the Appointment of the Officers,
and the Authority of training the Militia according to the discipline prescribed by Congress; To exercise exclusive Legislation in all Cases whatsoever, over such District (not exceeding ten Miles square) as may, by Cession of particular States, and the Acceptance of Congress, become the Seat
of the Government of the United States, and to exercise like Authority over
all Places purchased by the Consent of the Legislature of the State in which
the Same shall be, for the Erection of Forts, Magazines, Arsenals, dock-
Yards, and other needful Buildings;—And To make all Laws which shall
be necessary and proper for carrying into Execution the foregoing Powers,
and all other Powers vested by this Constitution in the Government of the
United States, or in any Department or Officer thereof.

Section 9. The Migration or Importation of such Persons as any of the
States now existing shall think proper to admit, shall not be prohibited by
the Congress prior to the Year one thousand eight hundred and eight, but a
Tax or duty may be imposed on such Importation, not exceeding ten dollars
for each Person. The Privilege of the Writ of Habeas Corpus shall not be
suspended, unless when in Cases of Rebellion or Invasion the public Safety
may Require it. No Bill of Attainder or ex post facto Law shall be passed.
No Capitation, or other direct, Tax shall be laid, unless in Proportion to
the Census or Enumeration herein before directed to be taken. No Tax or
Duty shall be laid on Articles exported from any State. No Preference shall
be given by any Regulation of Commerce or Revenue to the Ports of one
State over those of another: nor shall Vessels bound to, or from, one State,
be obliged to enter, clear, or pay Duties in another. No Money shall be
drawn from the Treasury, but in Consequence of Appropriations made by
Law; and a regular Statement and Account of the Receipts and Expenditures of all public Money shall be published from time to time. No Title of
Nobility shall be granted by the United States; And no Person holding any
Office of Profit or Trust under them, shall, without the Consent of the Congress, accept of any present, Emolument, Office, or Title, of any kind whatever, from any King, Prince, or foreign State.

Section 10. No State shall enter into any Treaty, Alliance, or Confederation; grant Letters of Marque and Reprisal; coin Money; emit Bills of
Credit; make any Thing but gold and silver Coin a Tender in Payment of
Debts; pass any Bill of Attainder, ex post facto Law, or Law impairing the
Obligation of Contracts, or grant any Title of Nobility. No State shall,
without the Consent of the Congress, lay any Imposts or Duties on Imports
or Exports, except what may be absolutely necessary for executing its

inspection Laws: and the net Produce of all Duties and Imposts, laid by any State on Imports or Exports, shall be for the Use of the Treasury of the United States; and all such Laws shall be subject to the Revision and Controul of the Congress. No State shall, without the Consent of Congress, lay any Duty of Tonnage, keep Troops, or Ships of War in time of Peace, enter into any Agreement or Compact with another State, or with a foreign Power, or engage in War, unless actually invaded, or in such imminent Danger as will not admit of delay.

ARTICLE II

Section 1. The executive Power shall be vested in a President of the United States of America. He shall hold his Office during the Term of four Years, and, together with the Vice-President, chosen for the same Term, be elected, as follows: Each State shall appoint, in such Manner as the Legislature thereof may direct, a Number of Electors, equal to the whole Number of Senators and Representatives to which the State may be entitled in the Congress: but no Senator or Representative, or Person holding an Office of Trust or Profit under the United States, shall be appointed an Elector. The Electors shall meet in their respective States, and vote by Ballot for two Persons, of whom one at least shall not be an Inhabitant of the same State with themselves. And they shall make a List of all the Persons voted for, and of the Number of Votes for each; which List they shall sign and certify, and transmit sealed to the Seat of the Government of the United States, directed to the President of the Senate. The President of the Senate shall, in the Presence of the Senate and House of Representatives, open all the Certificates, and the Votes shall then be counted. The Person having the greatest Number of Votes shall be the President, if such Number be a Majority of the whole Number of Electors appointed; and if there be more than one who have such Majority, and have an equal Number of Votes, then the House of Representatives shall immediately choose by Ballot one of them for President; and if no person have a Majority, then from the five highest on the List the said House shall in like Manner choose the President. But in choosing the President, the Votes shall be taken by States, the Representation from each State having one Vote; A quorum for this Purpose shall consist of a Member or Members from two thirds of the States, and a Majority of all the States shall be necessary to a Choice. In every Case, after the Choice of the President, the Person having the greatest Number of Votes of the Electors shall be the Vice-President. But if there should remain two or more who have equal Votes, the Senate shall choose from them by Ballot the Vice-President. The Congress may determine the Time of choosing the Electors, and the Day on which they shall give their Votes; which Day shall be the same throughout the United States. No Person except a natural born Citizen, or a Citizen of the United States, at the time of the Adoption of this Constitution, shall be eligible to the Office of President; neither shall any Person be eligible to that Office who shall not have attained to the Age of thirty five Years, and been fourteen Years a Resident within the United States. In Case of the Removal of the President from Office, or of his Death, Resignation, or Inability to discharge the Powers and Duties of the said Office, the Same shall devolve on the Vice-President, and the Congress may by Law provide for the Case of Removal, Death, Resignation or Inability, both of the President and Vice-President, declaring what Officer shall then act as President, and such Officer shall act accordingly, until the Disability be removed, or a President shall be elected. The President shall, at stated Times, receive for his Services, a Compensation, which shall neither be increased nor diminished during the Period for which he shall have been elected, and he shall not receive within that Period any other Emolument from the United States, or any of them. Before he enter on the Execution of his Office, he shall take the following Oath or Affirmation: "I do solemnly swear (or affirm) that I will faithfully execute the Office of President of the United States, and will to the best of my Ability, preserve, protect and defend the Constitution of the United States."

Section 2. The President shall be Commander-in-Chief of the Army and Navy of the United States, and of the Militia of the several States, when called into the actual Service of the United States; he may require the Opinion, in writing, of the principal Officer in each of the executive Departments, upon any Subject relating to the Duties of their respective Offices, and he shall have Power to grant Reprieves and Pardons for Offenses against the United States, except in Cases of Impeachment. He shall have Power, by and with the Advice and Consent of the Senate, to make Treaties, provided two thirds of the Senators present concur; and he shall nominate, and by and with the Advice and Consent of the Senate, shall appoint Ambassadors, other public Ministers and Consuls, Judges of the supreme Court, and all other Officers of the United States, whose Appointments are not herein otherwise provided for, and which shall be established by Law: but the Congress may by Law vest the Appointment of such inferior Officers, as they think proper, in the President alone, in the Courts of Law, or in the Heads of Departments. The President shall have Power to fill up all Vacancies that may happen during the Recess of the Senate, by granting Commissions which shall expire at the End of their next Session.

Section 3. He shall from time to time give to the Congress Information of the State of the Union, and recommend to their Consideration such Measures as he shall judge necessary and expedient; he may, on extraordinary Occasions, convene both Houses, or either of them, and in Case of Disagreement between them, with Respect to the Time of Adjournment, he may adjourn them to such Time as he shall think proper; he shall receive Ambassadors and other public Ministers; he shall take Care that the Laws be faithfully executed, and shall Commission all the Officers of the United States.

Section 4. The President, Vice-President and all civil Officers of the United States, shall be removed from Office on Impeachment for, and Conviction of, Treason, Bribery, or other high Crimes and Misdemeanors.

ARTICLE III

Section 1. The judicial Power of the United States, shall be vested in one supreme Court, and in such inferior Courts as the Congress may from time to time ordain and establish. The Judges, both of the supreme and inferior Courts, shall hold their Offices during good Behaviour, and shall, at stated Times, receive for their Services, a Compensation, which shall not be diminished during their Continuance in Office.

Section 2. The judicial Power shall extend to all Cases, in Law and Equity, arising under this Constitution, the Laws of the United States, and Treaties made, or which shall be made, under their Authority; to all Cases affecting Ambassadors, other public Ministers and Consuls; to all Cases of admiralty and maritime Jurisdiction; to Controversies to which the United States shall be a Party; to Controversies between two or more States; between a State and Citizens of another State; between Citizens of different States; between Citizens of the same State claiming Lands under Grants of different States, and between a State, or the Citizens thereof, and foreign States, Citizens or Subjects. In all Cases affecting Ambassadors, other public Ministers and Consuls, and those in which a State shall be Party, the supreme Court shall have original Jurisdiction. In all the other Cases before mentioned, the supreme Court shall have appellate Jurisdiction, both as to Law and Fact, with such Exceptions, and under such Regulations as the Congress shall make. The trial of all Crimes, except in Cases of Impeachment, shall be by Jury; and such Trial shall be held in the State where the said Crimes shall have been committed; but when not committed within any State, the Trial shall be at such Place or Places as the Congress may by Law have directed.

Section 3. Treason against the United States, shall consist only in levying War against them, or in adhering to their Enemies, giving them Aid and Comfort. No Person shall be convicted of Treason unless on the Testimony of two Witnesses to the same overt Act, or on Confession in open Court. The Congress shall have Power to declare the Punishment of Treason, but no Attainder of Treason shall work Corruption of Blood, or Forfeiture except during the Life of the Person attainted.

ARTICLE IV

Section 1. Full Faith and Credit shall be given in each State to the public Acts, Records, and judicial Proceedings of every other State. And the Congress may by general Laws prescribe the Manner in which such Acts, Records and Proceedings shall be proved, and the Effect thereof.

Section 2. The Citizens of each State shall be entitled to all Privileges and Immunities of Citizens in the several States. A Person charged in any State with Treason, Felony, or other Crime, who shall flee from Justice, and be found in another State, shall on Demand of the executive Authority of the State from which he fled, be delivered up, to be removed to the State having Jurisdiction of the Crime. No Person held to Service or Labour in one State, under the Laws thereof, escaping into another, shall, in Consequence of any Law or Regulation therein, be discharged from such Service or Labour, but shall be delivered up on Claim of the Party to whom such Service or Labour may be due.

Section 3. New States may be admitted by the Congress into this Union; but no new States shall be formed or erected within the Jurisdiction of any other State; nor any State be formed by the Junction of two or more States, or Parts of States, without the Consent of the Legislatures of the States concerned as well as of the Congress. The Congress shall have Power to dispose of and make all needful Rules and Regulations respecting the Territory or other Property belonging to the United States; and nothing in this Constitution shall be so construed as to Prejudice any Claims of the United States, or of any particular State.

Section 4. The United States shall guarantee to every State in this Union a Republican Form of Government, and shall protect each of them against Invasion; and on Application of the Legislature, or of the Executive (when the Legislature cannot be convened) against domestic Violence.

ARTICLE V

The Congress, whenever two thirds of both Houses shall deem it necessary, shall propose Amendments to this Constitution, or, on the Application of the Legislatures of two thirds of the several States, shall call a Convention for proposing Amendments, which, in either Case, shall be valid to all Intents and Purposes, as Part of this Constitution, when ratified by the Legislatures of three fourths of the several States, or by Conventions in three fourths thereof, as the one or the other Mode of Ratification may be proposed by the Congress; Provided that no Amendment which may be made prior to the Year One thousand eight hundred and eight shall in any Manner affect the first and fourth Clauses in the Ninth Section of the first Article; and that no State, without its Consent, shall be deprived of its equal Suffrage in the Senate.

ARTICLE VI

All Debts contracted and Engagements entered into, before the Adoption of this Constitution, shall be as valid against the United States under this Constitution, as under the Confederation. This Constitution, and the Laws of the United States which shall be made in Pursuance thereof; and all Treaties made, or which shall be made, under the Authority of the United States, shall be the supreme Law of the Land; and the Judges in every State shall be bound thereby, any Thing in the Constitution or Laws of any State to the Contrary notwithstanding. The Senators and Representatives before mentioned, and the Members of the several State Legislatures, and all executive and judicial Officers, both of the United States and of the several States, shall be bound by Oath or Affirmation, to support this Constitution; but no religious Test shall ever be required as a Qualification to any Office or public Trust under the United States.

ARTICLE VII

The Ratification of the Conventions of nine States, shall be sufficient for the Establishment of this Constitution between the States so ratifying the Same.

Done in Convention by the Unanimous Consent of the States present the Seventeenth Day of September in the Year of our Lord one thousand seven hundred and Eighty seven and of the Independence of the United States of America the Twelfth, In Witness whereof We have hereunto subscribed our Names,

GO. WASHINGTON—
President and deputy from Virginia[1]

AMENDMENTS
ARTICLE I[2]

Congress shall make no law respecting an establishment of religion, or prohibiting the free exercise thereof; or abridging the freedom of speech, or of the press; or the right of the people peaceably to assemble, and to petition the Government for a redress of grievances.

ARTICLE II

A well regulated Militia, being necessary to the security of a free State, the right of the people to keep and bear Arms, shall not be infringed.

ARTICLE III

No Soldier shall, in time of peace be quartered in any house, without the consent of the Owner, nor in time of war, but in a manner to be prescribed by law.

ARTICLE IV

The right of the people to be secure in their persons, houses, papers, and effects, against unreasonable searches and seizures, shall not be violated, and no Warrants shall issue, but upon probable cause, supported by Oath or affirmation, and particularly describing the place to be searched, and the persons or things to be seized.

[1]Also signed by: John Langdon, Nicholas Gilman (New Hampshire); Nathaniel Gorman, Rufus King (Massachusetts); Wm. Saml. Johnson, Roger Sherman (Connecticut); Alexander Hamilton (New York); Wil. Livingston, David Brearley, Wm. Paterson, Jona. Dayton (New Jersey); B. Franklin, Robt. Morris, Thos. FitzSimmons, James Wilson, Thomas Mifflin, Geo. Clymer, Jared Ingersoll, Gouv. Morris (Pennsylvania); Geo. Read, John Dickinson, Jaco. Broom, Gunning Bedford Jun, Richard Bassett (Delaware); James McHenry, Danl. Carroll, Dan of St. Thos. Jenifer (Maryland); John Blair, James Madison Jr. (Virginia); Wm. Blount, Hu Williamson, Rich'd. Dobbs Spaight (North Carolina); J. Rutledge, Charles Pinckney, Charles Cotesworth Pinckney, Pierce Butler (South Carolina); William Few, Abr. Baldwin (Georgia); Attest: William Jackson, Secretary.

[2]Articles I through X were ratified 15 December 1791.

ARTICLE V

No person shall be held to answer for a capital, or otherwise infamous crime, unless on a presentment or indictment of a Grand Jury, except in cases arising in the land or naval forces, or in the Militia, when in actual service in time of War or public danger; nor shall any person be subject for the same offence to be twice put in jeopardy of life or limb; nor shall be compelled in any criminal case to be a witness against himself, nor be deprived of life, liberty, or property, without due process of law; nor shall private property be taken for public use without just compensation.

ARTICLE VI

In all criminal prosecutions, the accused shall enjoy the right to a speedy and public trial, by an impartial jury of the State and district wherein the crime shall have been committed, which district shall have been previously ascertained by law, and to be informed of the nature and cause of the accusation; to be confronted with the witnesses against him; to have compulsory process for obtaining witnesses in his favor, and to have the assistance of counsel for his defence.

ARTICLE VII

In Suits at common law, where the value in controversy shall exceed twenty dollars, the right of trial by jury shall be preserved, and no fact tried by a jury, shall be otherwise re-examined in any Court of the United States, than according to the rules of the common law.

ARTICLE VIII

Excessive bail shall not be required, nor excessive fines imposed, nor cruel and unusual punishments inflicted.

ARTICLE IX

The enumeration in the Constitution, of certain rights, shall not be construed to deny or disparage others retained by the people.

ARTICLE X

The powers not delegated to the United States by the Constitution, nor prohibited by it to the States, are reserved to the States respectively, or to the people.

ARTICLE XI[3]

The Judicial power of the United States shall not be construed to extend to any suit in law or equity, commenced or prosecuted against one of the United States by Citizens of another State, or by Citizens or Subjects of any foreign State.

[3]Sent to the states 5 March 1794, ratified 7 February 1795.

ARTICLE XII[4]

The Electors shall meet in their respective States, and vote by ballot for President and Vice-President, one of whom, at least, shall not be an inhabitant of the same state with themselves; they shall name in their ballots the person voted for as President, and in distinct ballots the person voted for as Vice-President, and they shall make distinct lists of all persons voted for as President, and of all persons voted for as Vice-President, and of the number of votes for each, which lists they shall sign and certify, and transmit sealed to the seat of the government of the United States, directed to the President of the Senate; The President of the Senate shall, in the presence of the Senate and House of Representatives, open all the certificates and the votes shall then be counted; the person having the greatest number of votes for President, shall be the President, if such number be a majority of the whole number of Electors appointed; and if no person have such majority, then from the persons having the highest numbers not exceeding three on the list of those voted for as President, the House of Representatives shall choose immediately, by ballot, the President. But in choosing the President, the votes shall be taken by states, the representation from each state having one vote; a quorum for this purpose shall consist of a member or members from two-thirds of the states, and a majority of all the states shall be necessary to a choice. And if the House of Representatives shall not choose a President whenever the right of choice shall devolve upon them, before the fourth day of March next following, then the Vice-President shall act as President, as in the case of the death or other constitutional disability of the President. The person having the greatest number of votes as Vice-President, shall be the Vice-President, if such number be a majority of the whole number of Electors appointed, and if no person have a majority, then from the two highest numbers on the list, the Senate shall choose the Vice-President; a quorum for the purpose shall consist of two-thirds of the whole number of Senators, and a majority of the whole number shall be necessary to a choice. But no person constitutionally ineligible to the office of President shall be eligible to that of Vice-President of the United States.

ARTICLE XIII[5]

Section 1. Neither slavery nor involuntary servitude, except as a punishment for crime whereof the party shall have been duly convicted, shall exist within the United States, or any place subject to their jurisdiction.

Section 2. Congress shall have power to enforce this article by appropriate legislation.

ARTICLE XIV[6]

Section 1. All persons born or naturalized in the United States, and subject to the jurisdiction thereof, are citizens of the United States and of

[4]Sent to the states 12 December 1803, ratified 25 September 1804.
[5]Sent to the states 1 February 1865, ratified 6 December 1865.
[6]Sent to the states 16 June 1866, ratified 9 July 1868.

the State wherein they reside. No State shall make or enforce any law which shall abridge the privileges or immunities of citizens of the United States; nor shall any State deprive any person of life, liberty, or property, without due process of law; nor deny to any person within its jurisdiction the equal protection of the laws.

Section 2. Representatives shall be apportioned among the several States according to their respective numbers, counting the whole number of persons in each State, excluding Indians not taxed. But when the right to vote at any election for the choice of Electors for President and Vice-President of the United States, Representatives in Congress, the Executive and Judicial officers of a State, or the members of the Legislature thereof, is denied to any of the male inhabitants of such State, being twenty-one years of age, and citizens of the United States, or in any way abridged, except for participation in rebellion, or other crime, the basis of representation therein shall be reduced in the proportion which the number of such male citizens shall bear to the whole number of male citizens twenty-one years of age in such State.

Section 3. No person shall be a Senator or Representative in Congress, or elector of President and Vice-President, or hold any office, civil or military, under the United States, or under any State, who, having previously taken an oath, as a member of Congress, or as an officer of the United States, or as a member of any State legislature, or as an executive or judicial officer of any State, to support the Constitution of the United States, shall have engaged in insurrection or rebellion against the same, or given aid or comfort to the enemies thereof. But Congress may by a vote of two-thirds of each House, remove such disability.

Section 4. The validity of the public debt of the United States, authorized by law, including debts incurred for payment of pensions and bounties for services in suppressing insurrection or rebellion, shall not be questioned. But neither the United States nor any State shall assume or pay any debt or obligation incurred in aid of insurrection or rebellion against the United States, or any claim for the loss or emancipation of any slave; but all such debts, obligations and claims shall be held illegal and void.

Section 5. The Congress shall have power to enforce, by appropriate legislation, the provisions of this article.

ARTICLE XV[7]

Section 1. The right of citizens of the United States to vote shall not be denied or abridged by the United States or by any State on account of race, color, or previous condition of servitude.

Section 2. The Congress shall have power to enforce this article by appropriate legislation.

[7]Sent to the states 27 February 1869, ratified 3 February 1870.

ARTICLE XVI[8]

The Congress shall have power to lay and collect taxes on incomes, from whatever source derived, without apportionment among the several States and without regard to any census or enumeration.

ARTICLE XVII[9]

The Senate of the United States shall be composed of two senators from each State, elected by the people thereof, for six years; and each Senator shall have one vote. The electors in each State shall have the qualifications requisite for electors of the most numerous branch of the State legislature. When vacancies happen in the representation of any State in the Senate, the executive authority of such State shall issue writs of election to fill such vacancies: Provided, That the legislature of any State may empower the executive thereof to make temporary appointments until the people fill the vacancies by election as the legislature may direct. This amendment shall not be so construed as to affect the election or term of any Senator chosen before it becomes valid as part of the Constitution.

ARTICLE XVIII[10]

Section 1. After one year from the ratification of this article, the manufacture, sale, or transportation of intoxicating liquors within, the importation thereof into, or the exportation thereof from the United States and all territory subject to the jurisdiction thereof for beverage purposes is hereby prohibited.

Section 2. The Congress and the several States shall have concurrent power to enforce this article by appropriate legislation.

Section 3. This article shall be inoperative unless it shall have been ratified as an amendment to the Constitution by the legislatures of the several States, as provided in the Constitution, within seven years from the date of the submission hereof to the States by the Congress.

ARTICLE XIX[11]

The right of citizens of the United States to vote shall not be denied or abridged by the United States or by any States on account of sex.

Congress shall have power to enforce this article by appropriate legislation.

[8]Sent to the states 12 July 1909, ratified 3 February 1913.
[9]Sent to the states 16 May 1912, ratified 8 April 1913.
[10]Sent to the states 18 December 1917, ratified 16 January 1919, became effective 16 January 1920.
[11]Sent to the states 4 June 1919, ratified 18 August 1920.

ARTICLE XX[12]

Section 1. The terms of the President and Vice-President shall end at noon on the 20th day of January, and the terms of Senators and Representatives at noon on the third day of January, of the years in which such terms would have ended if this article had not been ratified; and the terms of their successors shall then begin.

Section 2. The Congress shall assemble at least once in every year, and such meeting shall begin at noon on the third day of January, unless they shall by law appoint a different day.

Section 3. If, at the time fixed for the beginning of the term of the President, the President-elect shall have died, the Vice-President-elect shall become President. If a President shall not have been chosen before the time fixed for the beginning of his term, or if the President-elect shall have failed to qualify, then the Vice-President-elect shall act as President until a President shall have qualified; and the Congress may by law provide for the case wherein neither a President-elect nor a Vice-President-elect shall have qualified, declaring who shall then act as President, or the manner in which one who is to act shall be selected, and such person shall act accordingly until a President or Vice-President shall have qualified.

Section 4. The Congress may by law provide for the case of the death of any of the persons from whom the House of Representatives may choose a President whenever the right of choice shall have devolved upon them, and for the case of the death of any of the persons from whom the Senate may choose a Vice-President whenever the right of choice shall have devolved upon them.

Section 5. Sections 1 and 2 shall take effect on the 15th day of October following the ratification of this article.

Section 6. This article shall be inoperative unless it shall have been ratified as an amendment to the Constitution by the legislatures of three-fourths of the several States within seven years from the date of its submission.

ARTICLE XXI[13]

Section 1. The eighteenth article of amendment to the Constitution of the United States is hereby repealed.

Section 2. The transportation or importation into any State, Territory, or possession of the United States for delivery or use therein of intoxicating liquors, in violation of the laws thereof, is hereby prohibited.

Section 3. This article shall be inoperative unless it shall have been ratified as an amendment to the Constitution by conventions in the several

---

[12]Sent to the states 3 March 1932, ratified 23 January 1933, became effective 15 October 1933.

[13]Sent to the states 20 February 1933, ratified 5 December 1933.

States, as provided in the Constitution, within seven years from the date of the submission hereof to the States by the Congress.

ARTICLE XXII[14]

Section 1. No person shall be elected to the office of the President more than twice, and no person who has held the office of President, or acted as President, for more than two years of a term to which some other person was elected President shall be elected to the office of the President more than once. But this Article shall not apply to any person holding the office of President when this Article was proposed by the Congress, and shall not prevent any person who may be holding the office of President, or acting as President, during the term within which this Article becomes operative from holding the office of President or acting as President during the remainder of such term.

Section 2. This article shall be inoperative unless it shall have been ratified as an amendment to the Constitution by the legislatures of three-fourths of the several States within seven years from the date of its submission to the States by the Congress.

ARTICLE XXIII[15]

Section 1. The District constituting the seat of Government of the United States shall appoint in such manner as the Congress may direct: A number of electors of President and Vice-President equal to the whole number of Senators and Representatives in Congress to which the District would be entitled if it were a State, but in no event more than the least populous State; they shall be in addition to those appointed by the States, but they shall be considered, for the purposes of the election of President and Vice-President, to be electors appointed by a State; and they shall meet in the District and perform such duties as provided by the twelfth article of amendment.

Section 2. The Congress shall have power to enforce this article by appropriate legislation.

ARTICLE XXIV[16]

Section 1. The right of citizens of the United States to vote in any primary or other election for President or Vice-President, for electors for President or Vice-President, or for Senator or Representative in Congress, shall not be denied or abridged by the United States or any State by reason of failure to pay any poll tax or other tax.

---

[14]Sent to the states 21 March 1947, ratified 27 February 1951.
[15]Sent to the states 16 June 1960, ratified 29 March 1961.
[16]Sent to the states 27 August 1962, ratified 23 January 1964.

Section 2. The Congress shall have power to enforce this article by appropriate legislation.

ARTICLE XXV[17]

Section 1. In case of the removal of the President from office or of his death or resignation, the Vice-President shall become President.

Section 2. Whenever there is a vacancy in the office of the Vice-President, the President shall nominate a Vice-President who shall take office upon confirmation by a majority vote of both Houses of Congress.

Section 3. Whenever the President transmits to the President pro tempore of the Senate and the Speaker of the House of Representatives his written declaration that he is unable to discharge the powers and duties of his office, and until he transmits to them a written declaration to the contrary, such powers and duties shall be discharged by the Vice-President as Acting President.

Section 4. Whenever the Vice-President and a majority of either the principal officers of the executive departments or of such other body as Congress may by law provide, transmit to the President pro tempore of the Senate and the Speaker of the House of Representatives their written declaration that the President is unable to discharge the powers and duties of his office, the Vice-President shall immediately assume the powers and duties of the office as Acting President. Thereafter, when the President transmits to the President pro tempore of the Senate and the Speaker of the House of Representatives his written declaration that no inability exists, he shall resume the powers and duties of his office unless the Vice-President and a majority of either the principal officers of the executive department or of such other body as Congress may by law provide, transmit within four days to the President pro tempore of the Senate and the Speaker of the House of Representatives their written declaration that the President is unable to discharge the powers and duties of his office. Thereupon Congress shall decide the issue, assembling within forty-eight hours for that purpose if not in session. If the Congress, within twenty-one days after receipt of the latter written declaration, or, if Congress is not in session, within twenty-one days after Congress is required to assemble, determines by two-thirds vote of both Houses that the President is unable to discharge the powers and duties of his office, the Vice-President shall continue to discharge the same as Acting President; otherwise, the President shall resume the powers and duties of his office.

ARTICLE XXVI[18]

Section 1. The right of citizens of the United States, who are eighteen years of age or older, to vote shall not be denied or abridged by the United States or by any State on account of age.

---

[17]Sent to the states 10 July 1965, ratified 10 February 1967.
[18]Sent to the states 23 March 1971, ratified 1 July 1971.

Section 2. The Congress shall have power to enforce this article by appropriate legislation.

ARTICLE XXVII[19]

No law, varying the compensation for the services of the Senators and Representatives, shall take effect, until an election of representatives shall have intervened.

[19]Originally proposed 25 September 1789, ratified 7 May 1992.

APPENDIX D:
THE CONSTITUTION OF
THE CONFEDERATE STATES OF AMERICA

We, the people of the Confederate States, each State acting in its sovereign and independent character, in order to form a permanent federal government, establish justice, insure domestic tranquility, and secure the blessings of liberty to ourselves and our posterity—invoking the favor and guidance of Almighty God—do ordain and establish this Constitution for the Confederate States of America.

ARTICLE I

Section 1

All legislative powers herein delegated shall be vested in a Congress of the Confederate States, which shall consist of a Senate and House of Representatives.

Section 2

1. The House of Representatives shall be composed of members chosen every second year by the people of the several States; and the electors in each State shall be citizens of the Confederate States, and have the qualifications requisite for electors of the most numerous branch of the State Legislature; but no person of foreign birth, not a citizen of the Confederate States, shall be allowed to vote for any officer, civil or political, State or Federal.

2. No person shall be a Representative who shall not have attained the age of twenty-five years, and be a citizen of the Confederate States, and who shall not when elected, be an inhabitant of that State in which he shall be chosen.

3. Representatives and direct taxes shall be apportioned among the several States, which may be included within this Confederacy, according to their respective numbers, which shall be determined by adding to the whole number of free persons, including those bound to service for a term of years, and excluding Indians not taxed, three-fifths of all slaves. The actual enumeration shall be made within three years after the first meeting of the Congress of the Confederate States, and within every subsequent term of ten years, in such manner as they shall by law direct. The number of Representatives shall not exceed one for every fifty thousand, but each State shall have at least one Representative; and until such enumeration shall be made, the State of South Carolina shall be entitled to choose six; the State of Georgia ten; the State of Alabama nine; the State of Florida two; the State of Mississippi seven; the State of Louisiana six; and the State of Texas six.

4. When vacancies happen in the representation from any State the executive authority thereof shall issue writs of election to fill such vacancies.

5. The House of Representatives shall choose their Speaker and other officers; and shall have the sole power of impeachment; except that any judicial or other Federal officer, resident and acting solely within the limits of any State, may be impeached by a vote of two-thirds of both branches of the Legislature thereof.

Section 3

1. The Senate of the Confederate States shall be composed of two Senators from each State, chosen for six years by the Legislature thereof, at the regular session next immediately preceding the commencement of the term of service; and each Senator shall have one vote.

2. Immediately after they shall be assembled, in consequence of the first election, they shall be divided as equally as may be into three classes. The seats of the Senators of the first class shall be vacated at the expiration of the second year; of the second class at the expiration of the fourth year; and of the third class at the expiration of the sixth year; so that one-third may be chosen every second year; and if vacancies happen by resignation, or other wise, during the recess of the Legislature of any State, the Executive thereof may make temporary appointments until the next meeting of the Legislature, which shall then fill such vacancies.

3. No person shall be a Senator who shall not have attained the age of thirty years, and be a citizen of the Confederate States; and who shall not, then elected, be an inhabitant of the State for which he shall be chosen.

4. The Vice President of the Confederate States shall be president of the Senate, but shall have no vote unless they be equally divided.

5. The Senate shall choose their other officers; and also a president pro tempore in the absence of the Vice President, or when he shall exercise the office of President of the Confederate States.

6. The Senate shall have the sole power to try all impeachments. When sitting for that purpose, they shall be on oath or affirmation. When the President of the Confederate States is tried, the Chief Justice shall preside; and no person shall be convicted without the concurrence of two-thirds of the members present.

7. Judgment in cases of impeachment shall not extend further than to removal from office, and disqualification to hold any office of honor, trust, or profit under the Confederate States; but the party convicted shall, nevertheless, be liable and subject to indictment, trial, judgment, and punishment according to law.

Section 4

1. The times, places, and manner of holding elections for Senators and Representatives shall be prescribed in each State by the Legislature thereof, subject to the provisions of this Constitution; but the Congress may, at

any time, by law, make or alter such regulations, except as to the times and places of choosing Senators.

2. The Congress shall assemble at least once in every year; and such meeting shall be on the first Monday in December, unless they shall, by law, appoint a different day.

Section 5

1. Each House shall be the judge of the elections, returns, and qualifications of its own members, and a majority of each shall constitute a quorum to do business; but a smaller number may adjourn from day to day, and may be authorized to compel the attendance of absent members, in such manner and under such penalties as each House may provide.

2. Each House may determine the rules of its proceedings, punish its members for disorderly behavior, and, with the concurrence of two-thirds of the whole number, expel a member.

3. Each House shall keep a journal of its proceedings, and from time to time publish the same, excepting such parts as may in their judgment require secrecy; and the yeas and nays of the members of either House, on any question, shall, at the desire of one-fifth of those present, be entered on the journal.

4. Neither House, during the session of Congress, shall, without the consent of the other, adjourn for more than three days, nor to any other place than that in which the two Houses shall be sitting.

Section 6

1. The Senators and Representatives shall receive a compensation for their services, to be ascertained by law, and paid out of the Treasury of the Confederate States. They shall, in all cases, except treason, felony, and breach of the peace, be privileged from arrest during their attendance at the session of their respective Houses, and in going to and returning from the same; and for any speech or debate in either House, they shall not be questioned in any other place.

2. No Senator or Representative shall, during the time for which he was elected, be appointed to any civil office under the authority of the Confederate States, which shall have been created, or the emoluments whereof shall have been increased during such time; and no person holding any office under the Confederate States shall be a member of either House during his continuance in office. But Congress may, by law, grant to the principal officer in each of the Executive Departments a seat upon the floor of either House, with the privilege of discussing any measures appertaining to his department.

Section 7

1. All bills for raising revenue shall originate in the House of Representatives; but the Senate may propose or concur with amendments, as on other bills.

2. Every bill which shall have passed both Houses, shall, before it becomes a law, be presented to the President of the Confederate States; if he approve, he shall sign it; but if not, he shall return it, with his objections, to that House in which it shall have originated, who shall enter the objections at large on their journal, and proceed to reconsider it. If, after such reconsideration, two-thirds of that House shall agree to pass the bill, it shall be sent, together with the objections, to the other House, by which it shall likewise be reconsidered, and if approved by two-thirds of that House, it shall become a law. But in all such cases, the votes of both Houses shall be determined by yeas and nays, and the names of the persons voting for and against the bill shall be entered on the journal of each House respectively. If any bill shall not be returned by the President within ten days (Sundays excepted) after it shall have been presented to him, the same shall be a law, in like manner as if he had signed it, unless the Congress, by their adjournment, prevent its return; in which case it shall not be a law. The President may approve any appropriation and disapprove any other appropriation in the same bill. In such case he shall, in signing the bill, designate the appropriations disapproved; and shall return a copy of such appropriations, with his objections, to the House in which the bill shall have originated; and the same proceedings shall then be had as in case of other bills disapproved by the President.

3. Every order, resolution, or vote, to which the concurrence of both Houses may be necessary (except on a question of adjournment) shall be presented to the President of the Confederate States; and before the same shall take effect, shall be approved by him; or, being disapproved by him, shall be repassed by two-thirds of both Houses, according to the rules and limitations prescribed in case of a bill.

Section 8

The Congress shall have power–

1. To lay and collect taxes, duties, imposts, and excises for revenue, necessary to pay the debts, provide for the common defense, and carry on the Government of the Confederate States; but no bounties shall be granted from the Treasury; nor shall any duties or taxes on importations from foreign nations be laid to promote or foster any branch of industry; and all duties, imposts, and excises shall be uniform throughout the Confederate States.

2. To borrow money on the credit of the Confederate States.

3. To regulate commerce with foreign nations, and among the several States, and with the Indian tribes; but neither this, nor any other clause contained in the Constitution, shall ever be construed to delegate the power to Congress to appropriate money for any internal improvement intended to facilitate commerce; except for the purpose of furnishing lights, beacons, and buoys, and other aids to navigation upon the coasts, and the improvement of harbors and the removing of obstructions in river navigation; in all which cases such duties shall be laid on the navigation facilitated thereby as may be necessary to pay the costs and expenses thereof.

4. To establish uniform laws of naturalization, and uniform laws on the subject of bankruptcies, throughout the Confederate States; but no law of Congress shall discharge any debt contracted before the passage of the same.

5. To coin money, regulate the value thereof, and of foreign coin, and fix the standard of weights and measures.

6. To provide for the punishment of counterfeiting the securities and current coin of the Confederate States.

7. To establish post offices and post routes; but the expenses of the Post Office Department, after the 1st day of March in the year of our Lord eighteen hundred and sixty-three, shall be paid out of its own revenues.

8. To promote the progress of science and useful arts, by securing for limited times to authors and inventors the exclusive right to their respective writings and discoveries.

9. To constitute tribunals inferior to the Supreme Court.

10. To define and punish piracies and felonies committed on the high seas, and offenses against the law of nations.

11. To declare war, grant letters of marque and reprisal, and make rules concerning captures on land and water.

12. To raise and support armies; but no appropriation of money to that use shall be for a longer term than two years.

13. To provide and maintain a navy.

14. To make rules for the government and regulation of the land and naval forces.

15. To provide for calling forth the militia to execute the laws of the Confederate States, suppress insurrections, and repel invasions.

16. To provide for organizing, arming, and disciplining the militia, and for governing such part of them as may be employed in the service of the Confederate States; reserving to the States, respectively, the appointment of the officers, and the authority of training the militia according to the discipline prescribed by Congress.

17. To exercise exclusive legislation, in all cases whatsoever, over such district (not exceeding ten miles square) as may, by cession of one or more States and the acceptance of Congress, become the seat of the Government of the Confederate States; and to exercise like authority over all places purchased by the consent of the Legislature of the State in which the same shall be, for the erection of forts, magazines, arsenals, dockyards, and other needful buildings; and

18. To make all laws which shall be necessary and proper for carrying into execution the foregoing powers, and all other powers vested by this Constitution in the Government of the Confederate States, or in any department or officer thereof.

Section 9

1. The importation of negroes of the African race from any foreign country other than the slaveholding States or Territories of the United

States of America, is hereby forbidden; and Congress is required to pass such laws as shall effectually prevent the same.

2. Congress shall also have power to prohibit the introduction of slaves from any State not a member of, or Territory not belonging to, this Confederacy.

3. The privilege of the writ of habeas corpus shall not be suspended, unless when in cases of rebellion or invasion the public safety may require it.

4. No bill of attainder, ex post facto law, or law denying or impairing the right of property in negro slaves shall be passed.

5. No capitation or other direct tax shall be laid, unless in proportion to the census or enumeration herein before directed to be taken.

6. No tax or duty shall be laid on articles exported from any State, except by a vote of two-thirds of both Houses.

7. No preference shall be given by any regulation of commerce or revenue to the ports of one State over those of another.

8. No money shall be drawn from the Treasury, but in consequence of appropriations made by law; and a regular statement and account of the receipts and expenditures of all public money shall be published from time to time.

9. Congress shall appropriate no money from the Treasury except by a vote of two-thirds of both Houses, taken by yeas and nays, unless it be asked and estimated for by some one of the heads of departments and submitted to Congress by the President; or for the purpose of paying its own expenses and contingencies; or for the payment of claims against the Confederate States, the justice of which shall have been judicially declared by a tribunal for the investigation of claims against the Government, which it is hereby made the duty of Congress to establish.

10. All bills appropriating money shall specify in Federal currency the exact amount of each appropriation and the purposes for which it is made; and Congress shall grant no extra compensation to any public contractor, officer, agent, or servant, after such contract shall have been made or such service rendered.

11. No title of nobility shall be granted by the Confederate States; and no person holding any office of profit or trust under them shall, without the consent of the Congress, accept of any present, emolument, office, or title of any kind whatever, from any king, prince, or foreign state.

12. Congress shall make no law respecting an establishment of religion, or prohibiting the free exercise thereof; or abridging the freedom of speech, or of the press; or the right of the people peaceably to assemble and petition the Government for a redress of grievances.

13. A well-regulated militia being necessary to the security of a free State, the right of the people to keep and bear arms shall not be infringed.

14. No soldier shall, in time of peace, be quartered in any house without the consent of the owner; nor in time of war, but in a manner to be prescribed by law.

15. The right of the people to be secure in their persons, houses, papers, and effects, against unreasonable searches and seizures, shall not be violated; and no warrants shall issue but upon probable cause, supported by oath or affirmation, and particularly describing the place to be searched and the persons or things to be seized.

16. No person shall be held to answer for a capital or otherwise infamous crime, unless on a presentment or indictment of a grand jury, except in cases arising in the land or naval forces, or in the militia, when in actual service in time of war or public danger; nor shall any person be subject for the same offense to be twice put in jeopardy of life or limb; nor be compelled, in any criminal case, to be a witness against himself; nor be deprived of life, liberty, or property without due process of law; nor shall private property be taken for public use, without just compensation.

17. In all criminal prosecutions the accused shall enjoy the right to a speedy and public trial, by an impartial jury of the State and district wherein the crime shall have been committed, which district shall have been previously ascertained by law, and to be informed of the nature and cause of the accusation; to be confronted with the witnesses against him; to have compulsory process for obtaining witnesses in his favor; and to have the assistance of counsel for his defense.

18. In suits at common law, where the value in controversy shall exceed twenty dollars, the right of trial by jury shall be preserved; and no fact so tried by a jury shall be otherwise reexamined in any court of the Confederacy, than according to the rules of common law.

19. Excessive bail shall not be required, nor excessive fines imposed, nor cruel and unusual punishments inflicted.

20. Every law, or resolution having the force of law, shall relate to but one subject, and that shall be expressed in the title.

Section 10

1. No State shall enter into any treaty, alliance, or confederation; grant letters of marque and reprisal; coin money; make anything but gold and silver coin a tender in payment of debts; pass any bill of attainder, or ex post facto law, or law impairing the obligation of contracts; or grant any title of nobility.

2. No State shall, without the consent of the Congress, lay any imposts or duties on imports or exports, except what may be absolutely necessary for executing its inspection laws; and the net produce of all duties and imposts, laid by any State on imports, or exports, shall be for the use of the Treasury of the Confederate States; and all such laws shall be subject to the revision and control of Congress.

3. No State shall, without the consent of Congress, lay any duty on tonnage, except on seagoing vessels, for the improvement of its rivers and harbors navigated by the said vessels; but such duties shall not conflict with any treaties of the Confederate States with foreign nations; and any surplus revenue thus derived shall, after making such improvement, be paid into the common treasury. Nor shall any State keep troops or ships of war

in time of peace, enter into any agreement or compact with another State, or with a foreign power, or engage in war, unless actually invaded, or in such imminent danger as will not admit of delay. But when any river divides or flows through two or more States they may enter into compacts with each other to improve the navigation thereof.

ARTICLE II

Section 1

1. The executive power shall be vested in a President of the Confederate States of America. He and the Vice President shall hold their offices for the term of six years; but the President shall not be reeligible. The President and Vice President shall be elected as follows:

2. Each State shall appoint, in such manner as the Legislature thereof may direct, a number of electors equal to the whole number of Senators and Representatives to which the State may be entitled in the Congress; but no Senator or Representative or person holding an office of trust or profit under the Confederate States shall be appointed an elector.

3. The electors shall meet in their respective States and vote by ballot for President and Vice President, one of whom, at least, shall not be an inhabitant of the same State with themselves; they shall name in their ballots the person voted for as President, and in distinct ballots the person voted for as Vice President, and they shall make distinct lists of all persons voted for as President, and of all persons voted for as Vice President, and of the number of votes for each, which lists they shall sign and certify, and transmit, sealed, to the seat of the Government of the Confederate States, directed to the President of the Senate; the President of the Senate shall, in the presence of the Senate and House of Representatives, open all the certificates, and the votes shall then be counted; the person having the greatest number of votes for President shall be the President, if such number be a majority of the whole number of electors appointed; and if no person have such majority, then from the persons having the highest numbers, not exceeding three, on the list of those voted for as President, the House of Representatives shall choose immediately, by ballot, the President. But in choosing the President the votes shall be taken by States—the representation from each State having one vote; a quorum for this purpose shall consist of a member or members from two-thirds of the States, and a majority of all the States shall be necessary to a choice. And if the House of Representatives shall not choose a President, whenever the right of choice shall devolve upon them, before the 4th day of March next following, then the Vice President shall act as President, as in case of the death, or other constitutional disability of the President.

4. The person having the greatest number of votes as Vice President shall be the Vice President, if such number be a majority of the whole number of electors appointed; and if no person have a majority, then, from the two highest numbers on the list, the Senate shall choose the Vice President; a quorum for the purpose shall consist of two-thirds of the whole number of Senators, and a majority of the whole number shall be necessary to a choice.

5. But no person constitutionally ineligible to the office of President shall be eligible to that of Vice President of the Confederate States.

6. The Congress may determine the time of choosing the electors, and the day on which they shall give their votes; which day shall be the same throughout the Confederate States.

7. No person except a natural-born citizen of the Confederate States, or a citizen thereof at the time of the adoption of this Constitution, or a citizen thereof born in the United States prior to the 20th of December, 1860, shall be eligible to the office of President; neither shall any person be eligible to that office who shall not have attained the age of thirty-five years, and been fourteen years a resident within the limits of the Confederate States, as they may exist at the time of his election.

8. In case of the removal of the President from office, or of his death, resignation, or inability to discharge the powers and duties of said office, the same shall devolve on the Vice President; and the Congress may, by law, provide for the case of removal, death, resignation, or inability, both of the President and Vice President, declaring what officer shall then act as President; and such officer shall act accordingly until the disability be removed or a President shall be elected.

9. The President shall, at stated times, receive for his services a compensation, which shall neither be increased nor diminished during the period for which he shall have been elected; and he shall not receive within that period any other emolument from the Confederate States, or any of them.

10. Before he enters on the execution of his office he shall take the following oath or affirmation: "I do solemnly swear (or affirm) that I will faithfully execute the office of President of the Confederate States, and will, to the best of my ability, preserve, protect, and defend the Constitution thereof."

Section 2

1. The President shall be Commander-in-Chief of the Army and Navy of the Confederate States, and of the militia of the several States, when called into the actual service of the Confederate States; he may require the opinion, in writing, of the principal officer in each of the Executive Departments, upon any subject relating to the duties of their respective offices; and he shall have power to grant reprieves and pardons for offenses against the Confederate States, except in cases of impeachment.

2. He shall have power, by and with the advice and consent of the Senate, to make treaties; provided two-thirds of the Senators present concur; and he shall nominate, and by and with the advice and consent of the Senate shall appoint, ambassadors, other public ministers and consuls, judges of the Supreme Court, and all other officers of the Confederate States whose appointments are not herein otherwise provided for, and which shall be established by law; but the Congress may, by law, vest the appointment of such inferior officers, as they think proper, in the President alone, in the courts of law, or in the heads of departments.

3. The principal officer in each of the Executive Departments, and all persons connected with the diplomatic service, may be removed from office at the pleasure of the President. All other civil officers of the Executive Departments may be removed at any time by the President, or other appointing power, when their services are unnecessary, or for dishonesty, incapacity, inefficiency, misconduct, or neglect of duty; and when so removed, the removal shall be reported to the Senate, together with the reasons therefor.

4. The President shall have power to fill all vacancies that may happen during the recess of the Senate, by granting commissions which shall expire at the end of their next session; but no person rejected by the Senate shall be reappointed to the same office during their ensuing recess.

Section 3

1. The President shall, from time to time, give to the Congress information of the state of the Confederacy, and recommend to their consideration such measures as he shall judge necessary and expedient; he may, on extraordinary occasions, convene both Houses, or either of them; and in case of disagreement between them, with respect to the time of adjournment, he may adjourn them to such time as he shall think proper; he shall receive ambassadors and other public ministers; he shall take care that the laws be faithfully executed, and shall commission all the officers of the Confederate States.

Section 4

1. The President, Vice President, and all civil officers of the Confederate States, shall be removed from office on impeachment for and conviction of treason, bribery, or other high crimes and misdemeanors.

ARTICLE III

Section 1

1. The judicial power of the Confederate States shall be vested in one Supreme Court, and in such inferior courts as the Congress may, from time to time, ordain and establish. The judges, both of the Supreme and inferior courts, shall hold their offices during good behavior, and shall, at stated times, receive for their services a compensation which shall not be diminished during their continuance in office.

Section 2

1. The judicial power shall extend to all cases arising under this Constitution, the laws of the Confederate States, and treaties made, or which shall be made, under their authority; to all cases affecting ambassadors, other public ministers and consuls; to all cases of admiralty and maritime jurisdiction; to controversies to which the Confederate States shall be a party; to controversies between two or more States; between a State and citizens of another State, where the State is plaintiff; between citizens claiming lands under grants of different States; and between a State or the

citizens thereof, and foreign states, citizens, or subjects; but no State shall be sued by a citizen or subject of any foreign state.

2. In all cases affecting ambassadors, other public ministers and consuls, and those in which a State shall be a party, the Supreme Court shall have original jurisdiction. In all the other cases before mentioned, the Supreme Court shall have appellate jurisdiction both as to law and fact, with such exceptions and under such regulations as the Congress shall make.

3. The trial of all crimes, except in cases of impeachment, shall be by jury, and such trial shall be held in the State where the said crimes shall have been committed; but when not committed within any State, the trial shall be at such place or places as the Congress may by law have directed.

Section 3

1. Treason against the Confederate States shall consist only in levying war against them, or in adhering to their enemies, giving them aid and comfort. No person shall be convicted of treason unless on the testimony of two witnesses to the same overt act, or on confession in open court.

2. The Congress shall have power to declare the punishment of treason; but no attainder of treason shall work corruption of blood, or forfeiture, except during the life of the person attainted.

ARTICLE IV

Section 1

1. Full faith and credit shall be given in each State to the public acts, records, and judicial proceedings of every other State; and the Congress may, by general laws, prescribe the manner in which such acts, records, and proceedings shall be proved, and the effect thereof.

Section 2

1. The citizens of each State shall be entitled to all the privileges and immunities of citizens in the several States; and shall have the right of transit and sojourn in any State of this Confederacy, with their slaves and other property; and the right of property in said slaves shall not be thereby impaired.

2. A person charged in any State with treason, felony, or other crime against the laws of such State, who shall flee from justice, and be found in another State, shall, on demand of the executive authority of the State from which he fled, be delivered up, to be removed to the State having jurisdiction of the crime.

3. No slave or other person held to service or labor in any State or Territory of the Confederate States, under the laws thereof, escaping or lawfully carried into another, shall, in consequence of any law or regulation therein, be discharged from such service or labor; but shall be delivered up on claim of the party to whom such slave belongs, or to whom such service or labor may be due.

Section 3

1. Other States may be admitted into this Confederacy by a vote of two-thirds of the whole House of Representatives and two-thirds of the Senate, the Senate voting by States; but no new State shall be formed or erected within the jurisdiction of any other State, nor any State be formed by the junction of two or more States, or parts of States, without the consent of the Legislatures of the States concerned, as well as of the Congress.

2. The Congress shall have power to dispose of and make all needful rules and regulations concerning the property of the Confederate States, including the lands thereof.

3. The Confederate States may acquire new territory; and Congress shall have power to legislate and provide governments for the inhabitants of all territory belonging to the Confederate States, lying without the limits of the several States; and may permit them, at such times, and in such manner as it may by law provide, to form States to be admitted into the Confederacy. In all such territory the institution of negro slavery, as it now exists in the Confederate States, shall be recognized and protected by Congress and by the Territorial government; and the inhabitants of the several Confederate States and Territories shall have the right to take to such Territory any slaves lawfully held by them in any of the States or Territories of the Confederate States.

4. The Confederate States shall guarantee to every State that now is, or hereafter may become, a member of this Confederacy, a republican form of government; and shall protect each of them against invasion; and on application of the Legislature, or of the Executive when the Legislature is not in session, against domestic violence.

ARTICLE V

Section 1

1. Upon the demand of any three States, legally assembled in their several conventions, the Congress shall summon a convention of all the States, to take into consideration such amendments to the Constitution as the said States shall concur in suggesting at the time when the said demand is made; and should any of the proposed amendments to the Constitution be agreed on by the said convention—voting by States—and the same be ratified by the Legislatures of two-thirds of the several States, or by conventions in two-thirds thereof—as the one or the other mode of ratification may be proposed by the general convention—they shall thenceforward form a part of this Constitution. But no State shall, without its consent, be deprived of its equal representation in the Senate.

ARTICLE VI

Section 1

1. The Government established by this Constitution is the successor of the Provisional Government of the Confederate States of America, and all the laws passed by the latter shall continue in force until the same shall be repealed or modified; and all the officers appointed by the same shall

remain in office until their successors are appointed and qualified, or the offices abolished.

2. All debts contracted and engagements entered into before the adoption of this Constitution shall be as valid against the Confederate States under this Constitution, as under the Provisional Government.

3. This Constitution, and the laws of the Confederate States made in pursuance thereof, and all treaties made, or which shall be made, under the authority of the Confederate States, shall be the supreme law of the land; and the judges in every State shall be bound thereby, anything in the constitution or laws of any State to the contrary notwithstanding.

4. The Senators and Representatives before mentioned, and the members of the several State Legislatures, and all executive and judicial officers, both of the Confederate States and of the several States, shall be bound by oath or affirmation to support this Constitution; but no religious test shall ever be required as a qualification to any office or public trust under the Confederate States.

5. The enumeration, in the Constitution, of certain rights shall not be construed to deny or disparage others retained by the people of the several States.

6. The powers not delegated to the Confederate States by the Constitution, nor prohibited by it to the States, are reserved to the States, respectively, or to the people thereof.

ARTICLE VII

Section 1

1. The ratification of the conventions of five States shall be sufficient for the establishment of this Constitution between the States so ratifying the same.

2. When five States shall have ratified this Constitution, in the manner before specified, the Congress under the Provisional Constitution shall prescribe the time for holding the election of President and Vice President; and for the meeting of the Electoral College; and for counting the votes, and inaugurating the President. They shall, also, prescribe the time for holding the first election of members of Congress under this Constitution, and the time for assembling the same. Until the assembling of such Congress, the Congress under the Provisional Constitution shall continue to exercise the legislative powers granted them; not extending beyond the time limited by the Constitution of the Provisional Government. Adopted unanimously by the Congress of the Confederate States of South Carolina, Georgia, Florida, Alabama, Mississippi, Louisiana, and Texas, sitting in convention at the capitol, in the city of Montgomery, Alabama, on the eleventh day of March, in the year Eighteen Hundred and Sixty-One.

HOWELL COBB, President of the Congress.[1]

---

[1]Also signed by South Carolina: R. Barnwell Rhett, C.G. Memminger, Wm. Porcher Miles, James Chesnut, Jr., R.W. Barnwell, William W. Boyce, Lawrence M. Keitt,

T.J. Withers;

Georgia: Francis S. Bartow, Martin J. Crawford, Benjamin H. Hill, Thos. R.R. Cobb;

Florida: Jackson Morton, J. Patton Anderson, Jas. B. Owens;

Alabama: Richard W. Walker, Robt. H. Smith, Colin J. McRae, William P. Chilton, Stephen F. Hale, David P. Lewis, Tho. Fearn, Jno. Gill Shorter, J.L.M. Curry;

Mississippi: Alex. M. Clayton, James T. Harrison, William S. Barry, W.S. Wilson, Walker Brooke, W.P. Harris, J.A.P. Campbell;

Louisiana: Alex. de Clouet, C.M. Conrad, Duncan F. Kenner, Henry Marshall;

Texas: John Hemphill, Thomas N. Waul, John H. Reagan, Williamson S. Oldham, Louis T. Wigfall, John Gregg, William Beck Ochiltree.

ABOUT THE CONTRIBUTORS

Bruce Benson is Distinguished Research Professor of Economics at Florida State University.

Scott Boykin is Adjunct Professor of Political Science at the University of Alabama at Birmingham.

Thomas DiLorenzo is Professor of Economics at Loyola College and an adjunct scholar of the Ludwig von Mises Institute.

Pierre Desrochers is completing his Ph.D. in geography at the University of Montreal.

Eric Duhaime received his MPA from the National School of Public Administration and is employed by the Leader of the Bloc Québecois in Ottawa.

David Gordon is a Senior Fellow of the Ludwig von Mises Institute, edits *The Mises Review*, and co-edits the *Journal of Libertarian Studies*.

Hans-Hermann Hoppe is Professor of Economics at the University of Nevada, Las Vegas, co-editor of *The Review of Austrian Economics*, co-editor of the *Journal of Libertarian Studies*, and a Senior Fellow of the Ludwig von Mises Institute.

Donald W. Livingston is Professor of Philosophy at Emory University.

James Ostrowski is a practicing attorney in New York, and an adjunct scholar of the Ludwig von Mises Institute.

Murray N. Rothbard (1926–1995) was S.J. Hall Distinguished Professor of Economics at the University of Nevada, Las Vegas, and academic vice president at the Ludwig von Mises Institute.

Historian Joseph R. Stromberg is an adjunct scholar of the Center for Libertarian Studies.

Clyde N. Wilson is Professor of History at the University of South Carolina, editor of *The Papers of John C. Calhoun*, and an adjunct scholar of the Ludwig von Mises Institute.

Steven Yates is an independent scholar of philosophy.

INDEX

egalitarianism and, 108–9
in the North, 128–29
in the South, 128–33
individualism and, 106–8
mercantilism and, 107–8
secession and, 110
Resnick, Philip, 233, 234
Responsibility, 46
Revolution, Three Concepts of, 3–5
Rhett, Robert Barnwell, 114, 131
Richard, Laurence, 232
Riemer, Neal, 102
Rights, xi
  government interference, 42
  group, 51, 69
  inalienable, 188
  individual, 52
  law and, 41
  limited, x
  natural, ix, 40, 43, 123
  positive and negative, 46
  private property, 247, 254
  to abolish government, 49
  unenumerated, 166
Risjord, Norman K., 108
Ritchie, Thomas, 107
Roane, Spencer, 121
Robbins, Caroline, 101
Robert, J.-C., 228
Roche, George, 44
Romanovs, 204
Rome Treaty of 1957, 200
Roosevelt, Franklin, 204
Rossiter, Clinton, 102
Rothbard, Murray N., ix, xv, 40, 44, 45, 104, 118, 120, 181, 184, 188, 254
Rousseau, Jean-Jacques, 3, 53, 96
Rueff, Jacques, 198, 203
Rupert's Territory, 227
Russia, 212

Salazar, Antonio de Oliviera, 207
Samuel, B., 175, 185
Samuelson, Paul, 193
Say, Jean-Baptiste, 106
Scanlon, T.M., 68
Schachner, Nathan, 113
Schengen Accord, 195, 196
Schmidtz, David, 251
Scots, 22, 80
Scott v Avery, 260
Scott, Winfield, 143
Secession
  abolitionists and, 14

accession and, 57
American Revolution and, 114–19
American tradition of, 1–33
arbitration as, xvi
Articles of Confederation and, 25, 35, 162
as a modern political act, 2
as alteration, ix
as an aggregate right, 3
as jurisdictional choice, 243
as political divorce, 35
borders and, 83–86
by border states, 29–30
capitalism and, 222
central states' attempt at, 13
collective action and, 69
Constitution and, 20, 110, 123, 157, 163, 189
contractualism and, 68–69
contrasted with expulsion, 184
contrasted with revolution, 3–5
contrasted with treason, 18
denotation of, 1, 8
developments since 1861, 185–89
economic integration and, 217
economic viability and, 73
ethics of, 65–78
financial consequences, 168
government compensation and, 74–75
group rights and, 69–72
in Eastern Europe, 213, 214, 217–21
in the Soviet Union, 10, 80
in Western Europe, 222
judging alternatives to, 77–78
majoritarianism and, 181
morality and, 66–69
New England attempts at, 11, 27, 105–6, 114, 135–50
New York City attempts at, 14
non–territorial 243–45
normative individualism and, 66–68
northern newspapers on, 150–53
party politics and, 131
privatization and, 84–86
procedural versus rectificatory, 77
Quebec attempts at, 225–41
republican theory and, 110–23
Roxbury, Mass. attempts at, 181
second wave of, 63
self-determination and, 1, 8–9, 71

CPSIA information can be obtained at www.ICGtesting.com
Printed in the USA
LVOW11s2023281214

420689LV00001B/19/P